THE SUNDAY LECTURES, VOL. I

THE SUNDAY LECTURES

VOL. I

By Peter Deunov

Translated by Demitri Emanuel

EAGLE ROCK
PUBLISHING

Originally published as "Сила и Живот" [Strength and Life] by Царска Придворна Печатница [Royal Court Press], in two parts, in the years 1915 and 1917, respectively. These lectures are now in the public domain.

THE SUNDAY LECTURES, VOL. I. Copyright © 2020 by Eagle Rock Publishing, LLC. Published in the United States of America. The text of the Sunday Lectures, Vol. I may be quoted or reprinted without prior written permission with the following qualifications: (1) up to and including 100 sentences may be quoted in printed form or displayed digitally, as long as the sentences make up less than 10% of the total work in which they are quoted; (2) The Sunday Lectures, Vol. I quotations must conform accurately to the text. Any use of the text must include a proper acknowledgement as follows:

The Sunday Lectures, Vol. I. Copyright © 2020 by Eagle Publishing, LLC. Translated by Demitri Emanuel. Used by permission. All rights reserved.

For quotation requests not covered by the above guidelines, write to Eagle Rock Publishing, LLC, Attention: Text Rights and Permissions, 2355 Westwood Blvd. #173, Los Angeles, CA, 90064.

All Rights Reserved.

eaglerockpublishing@gmail.com

ISBN: 978-1-952996-01-6

First Edition, **PAPERBACK**.

CONTENTS

	Editor's Note	vii
1.	Behold the Man	1
2.	The Grain of Wheat	13
3.	The Four Main Elements	27
4.	Know Truth and the Truth Will Set You Free	31
5.	The Manifestation of the Spirit	35
6.	The Talents	50
7.	Love	61
8.	Joseph's Dreams	76
9.	The Law of Service	89
10.	The Importance of Small Things	101
11.	Peace Be with You	109
12.	The Need to Know God	118
13.	How much higher man stands from sheep!	133
14.	Pharisee and Tax Collector	146
15.	The Conditions of Eternal Life	165

16.	Fear	184
17.	In the Beginning was the Word	197
18.	The Spirit and the Flesh: Ebb and Flow in Life	215
19.	The Milk of the Word	233
20.	The Teachers	242
21.	If you Love Me	263
22.	Eight Thousand Years	268
23.	Easter	271
24.	The Valuable Pearl	284
25.	The New Foundation	301
26.	Divine Providence	320
27.	Temptation	327
28.	The Prodigal Son	335
29.	Prayer	347
30.	The Good Samaritan	358
31.	Old and New Wineskins	367
32.	Freedom of the Spirit	378

EDITOR'S NOTE

Without a doubt, the best way to read Peter Deunov's lectures is in the original Bulgarian language. However, the hardest thing I found wasn't the translation from Bulgarian to English, but simply wrapping my head around a 19th century mindset that caused so many scholars to furnish their lectures and treatises with incredibly long sentences. For that, we have Søren Kierkegaard to thank, for providing us a sentence of more than 300 words!

For the most part, sentences could be translated directly as seen, that is, verbatim. The problem arises first in the length of the sentences: Deunov may speak on a topic quite extensively, which would, by English standards, be referred to as a run-on sentence. Since they were spoken words in a different language, I took the liberty in breaking down long sentences where punctuation seemed to fit best, where there seemed to be a natural pause or a turning away from one topic to another.

Like many translators, my primary objective is to maintain authenticity, but I always asked myself how far I was willing to go with this. I could potentially translate everything word for word, but hardly any of it would be rendered sensible to the common reader. I maintain the Bible as my standard: there, one can find long run-on sentences, not to mention the countless lines of text beginning with "and," or, "but," yet these don't obstruct the reading in any way. They are deemed allowable, and as such, I translated as much as I could that would be considered permissible by the average person, where standards of grammar could be temporarily suspended.

The other issue deals with word choice: the English language has many more words at its disposal, whereas Bulgarian may be limited to less, but they are very powerful in their context. Being a Slavic language, Bulgarian has a way of expressing itself that is very direct and unchangeable. This is in direct contrast to English, which can easily morph from one meaning to another. I will give an example: In the lecture, The Blessed, Deunov refers to the Old Christians as being "persecuted," and then makes a reference to the horses that need to be chased around in order to till the fields. The Bulgarian word for persecute is "гонитба," [gonitba] but it can also mean to "chase." In English, however, one must use "persecute" in reference to tracking someone down, a criminal for instance, like the way the Christians were sought out. But the same word cannot be used when referring to horses. One cannot say "I am persecuting my horses," and mean the same thing. Yet the same word is used in Bulgarian, and the analogy is much clearer.

In relation to the Biblical verses that appear at the start of each lecture, I used several translations, namely the New King James Version (NKJV), the King James Version (KJV), the New International Version (NIV), and the World English Bible (WEB). The purpose for this has to do with Deunov's use of Biblical citations: I simply used the translation that most closely resembles his cited verse in Bulgarian. A lot of times this reduces to a particular word, like "persecution," or "servant," that Deunov then uses throughout his lecture. And it is on the basis of these words that I make the choice as to which translation best fits the narrative of the lecture.

For those who have the luxury of knowing Bulgarian, or even another Slavic language, there is nothing better than reading these lectures in the original. I can only hope that the work presented here will leave the reader as hallowed as any Bulgarian reader.

I wish all readers blessings of Wisdom and light in their Divine development!

—*Demitri Emanuel*
June 2020, Los Angeles

BEHOLD THE MAN

"Then came forth Jesus, wearing the crown of thorns, and the purple robe. And Pilate saith unto them, Behold the man!"—John 19:5 (KJV)

In the word chovek [man] or chelovek [the man] in Bulgarian is understood as a being who lives a whole century. But in the original language, the language that gave expression to this phrase, chovek has a different meaning. It means Jesus, the Man, who came to earth, the brother of those who suffer. What must we understand in these words? When we go out into the world, will they speak of us, "behold the man?" To honor man with this name it is necessary to contain four things within oneself: to be wealthy, to be strong, to have knowledge, to have virtues. But you will all say, "what does wealth seek?" Wealth is the soil, the condition in which man may develop; it is the condition where strength develops. But the latter brings warmth and light, which affect growth and development. When we reach knowledge, it's the method by which it is necessary to understand and regulate our lives. Virtue, however, is the target to which we must aspire. Frequently people ask the question, "what should we do?" Sow a single grain of wheat and it will show what you should do. You'll ask, "how?" Add moisture and the sun's rays will show where the grain grows—in one direction—towards the sun, the wellspring of life. We too must be like the grain of wheat; we must strive towards God. But someone might ask, "when the grain grows, does it reach the sun? I too want to find God." You don't need to know where God is, but just to strive towards Him. The grain has understood what the sun is, and it accepts what it desires. The same law applies to us, and we must produce the same result—we must be planted. Our lives will surely have sufferings that make up these small but necessary obstacles, like the grain of wheat—some pressure is needed, and then the process of growth and knowledge will come, and when we produce fruit, this is now virtue. We must therefore be planted—some soil must cover us so there can be a little pressure; afterwards we must grow upwards and acquire knowledge, and this knowledge (once [it has] grown to some extent) must immediately become a grain of wheat. Afterwards the Master will be sent to reap the wheat, and He will separate the necessary from the useless—the wheat from the chaff. We are born, which means we emerge from the soil; we grow, we develop, we die, and we're buried in the grave: this is trampling, threshing. From the threshing floor the Lord will gather what He needs. This corresponds to the barn and the granary; the chaff is deposited in the barn while the grains go in the granary.

I read to you the 19th chapter of John's Gospel to see the four things Christ was carrying on the cross—four things we also need to learn by putting the virtue of the head that was not nailed on the left; from the right—the power, and from the bottom—the wealth, and we will then have the crucified man. Essentially, by nailing wealth, strength, and knowledge, their *essence* will rise to the head, to virtue. When the Lord wants to make someone good, He keeps him on the cross—nailing his riches, strength, knowledge. He is saying, "when I work, you will be calm." And because one does not want to stand still, the Lord says, "nail him down, so I can be calm and work…" And when we are nailed on this cross, we should not weep because the Lord is then working for us. Unhappy is the one who isn't nailed to the cross. Whoever wants the Lord to help him must go through this process of development. I speak to you allegorically.

Before this process of development there must definitely be faith—unwavering faith in the common Divine plan which takes into account all of God's creation. We mustn't doubt God, for He is perfect, all-powerful. Even Jesus at one point says, "what is impossible for man is possible for God." The Divine paths are uncharted. The thought that these paths can be distorted and obstructed should not enter our minds; it's impossible.

And when we are invited and set in the Divine way, we must have that simple faith that children have, and avoid deficiencies such as those outlined in the following narrative: In England, a great artist wanted to make a painting that portrays extreme poverty. For days and months he wandered around London to find a subject to portray this idea. He finally finds a child with torn clothes that speaks to his heart and he says to himself, "this is the face that will suit the painting." He approaches him, gives his business card and tells him, "come in four days. I have something to discuss with you." Seeing how the man is dressed, the child says to himself, "how can I go to him in this condition, all torn up," and goes to see some acquaintances to dress up a little, to present himself the way people present themselves to kings. He finds clothes, dresses himself, and goes to the painter. "Who are you?" asks the painter. "I'm so-and-so."—"Why don't you go your way! If I wanted one dressed like this I can find them by the thousands. I needed you the way I saw you then." When the Heavens invite us to work we too want to dress up. But the power is neither in our clothes, hats, gloves and shoes, nor in our collars, neckties and watches—they do not comprise anything important. The power is in our minds, our hearts, in the noble aspirations and eagerness to do good. When we have these things the others will come of their own accord at their appointed time. When we go to Heaven we don't have to bring our clothes from here, do we? When the Lord calls us up to Heaven, He undresses us here. He doesn't want our rags but says, "bring him as he is." When someone dies, every one of us is disgusted by him, even those who loved him. They say, "get him out sooner!" Where, then, is their love? But God is not disgusted and says, "bring him to me. I need him the way he is." And when they put us in the grave and leave us, what does the Lord do? He begins to talk to us, not as some think, that the dead are released. He asks us: "Well, did you understand life? Did you understand the meaning of the life I gave you?" In this very conversation the Lord paints His great picture. Then the process begins: After sending him away, the people begin to cry and list all his good qualities—they see the Holy picture portrayed in these qualities.

We must endure the sufferings that come to us and draw lessons from them. With His earthly sufferings, Jesus wanted to give us an example that we should obey this Divine process. At one point He says, "don't I have authority to ask my Father to send thousands of angels to deliver me? But if I do not do what I came to do, how will the people evolve?" He Himself wanted to rise to a higher level. You are on the Earth but one day you too will find yourselves in storms, sufferings, and perhaps the same fate. But when the time comes don't think of it as misfortune, not even in the least regard, because where there is no suffering there is no wealth; where there are sorrows there are joys; where there is death, there is also a resurrection. And the one who doesn't want to participate in the suffering of mankind won't gain anything. And what is suffering? The consequences of mistakes caused by us from misunderstanding. These very mistakes are corrected through the process of suffering. This process is a way of adapting and reaching those higher, ascending vibrations that await us in Heaven. There must be 100 sorrows [in order] to endure a single *Divine* joy. That's how we'll appreciate that joy and *keep* it. And that's why the Lord begins with sufferings—to toughen us, as the ironsmith tempers steel to make it fit for work, to endure the joy that will come later.

Every one of us is necessary and very much required by the Lord. You may not represent anything in the world and be a zero, but to God you are an important unit. Only the Lord who sent you to earth appreciates our sufferings and therefore you must not worry about what the world thinks of you. Whoever sent you, He thinks of you and appreciates you. It's important for you to have the approval of God. If the Lord is with you, you will be beautiful, and the world loves beauty; if He is with you, you'll be rich, strong, good—and goodness is always honored.

I will now speak to you of God, not as an abstract being, as the philosophers say, scattered throughout space, Whom you know not where He is, but I preach of the Lord who thinks of us, Who observes our actions, Who makes our paths straight, corrects us, punishes, dresses, undresses, tells us when to be born and when to die. What is death? The Lord is performing surgery; seeing that you'll lose a lot, He shortens the process of your life: "So that he doesn't accumulate more debt, take the capital I gave him. The time is not favorable now; leave him for another time. Bring him to Me." And in this process we think the world has forgotten us. But if the world has forgotten us, the Lord thinks of us. And the world must surely forget us. An unmarried girl can never marry if she loves all the young men; she must choose one and say, "this is my world." This fact is also true in life; you must have only one God. There are many gods in the world who will want to take you in, but you must find your God, with Whom you can live, grow, become rich.

The Scripture says, "God is not only in Heaven; He lives in the hearts of the humble ones." Therefore, the first quality that you must acquire in order for Him to live in you is humility. But this humility is not like the humility of sheep—when they beat you or break your legs, you say, "there's nothing to do!" There's no humility when you take all the riches and say, "we have humbled ourselves." Humility is when you have all the riches, strength, knowledge, goodness, and to consciously say, "Lord! You have everything I have." Now everyone does the following: they all preach the Gospel and always try to fix the world, but as soon as the Lord comes near their overfilled money pouches they say, "oh, you can't touch that! We can give half, you see, but not all." When it comes to strength they say, "you can't have all my strength." Yet when we are in need, we want Him and plead with Him to guide and help us. This outlook and understanding of life has prevailed in all philosophies for thousands of years. And our misfortunes stem exactly from this point of view. And with

His life, Jesus wants to show us the way. Many Christians believe that by becoming Christian they have to give up earthly things. You may give up your houses, riches, wives, children, and still think of them. You can go to a secluded monastery and still think, "whatever happened to my wife and kids? How is my house?" This means you haven't given up on them, that you aren't free. Letting go of things doesn't mean forgetting them, but giving people freedom—letting the woman act as she knows, allowing the son to do what he thinks is best. To give up on the world means to leave it, not hinder it—let it go its own way. Can we stop the flow of the river? We have to let it go along its way. We can only do one thing—*use* it. So we can't stop life, but just use what is given to us. And Jesus clearly and positively tells us, "if you love Me"—and we must love Him—He doesn't say at all, "woe to you if you don't love Me!" No! The Lord never wants forced sacrifices from us.

People say, "if the Lord is omnipotent why doesn't He fix the world?" How should He fix it? "Whoever lies, let his tongue wither; whoever steals, let his hand wither." Well, then, we would have a world full of only dumb and crippled people. What do you think? Would we enjoy a world full of only defective people? The Lord, however, gives a diametrically opposing maxim which is the reverse of this process: He says that whoever wants to be a *master* must be a *servant*. This process can be seen in the following [example]: Strong people usually want all rivers to flow into their river, but in good [people], the process is just the opposite—the Lord spills into small rivers, and instead of managing them, He lets them manage themselves. You can attempt a small experiment at home: get rid of the idea that you're in command. Instead, set your mind to become a servant—to become a servant for the sake of the Lord; then you'll know what it's like to be in His place. You seek the Lord in Heaven, but He isn't there; when you groan and suffer, He *is* in you. And what people call growth or progress—God takes part in this process. He's the best worker. Some complain: "Doesn't God see our sufferings?"

but He says, "I have no time. I'm so busy with your work. I'm busy with your much more important issues. When there's time, I'll deal with your external petty misunderstandings." This isn't an allegory, but reality. There is a verse in the Sacred Scriptures in which the Lord says, "I was in Israel as a loaded cart in which people continually put everything." The sufferings we are experiencing here are the sufferings of the Lord. He suffers and weeps in you. You say, "I weep, my soul is grieved," but when we say, "Lord! forgive—I have caused you so much suffering with unclean thoughts and actions," then you'll come to that *real* path that will deliver you from the present evil. Ultimately, we must let our Lord come and attach Himself to us. We have bound Him with ropes, and we have nailed Him. We have to lay Him down and leave Him calmly in the grave, and He will then resurrect and deliver us. And be certain of one thing: those who obstruct His way—it's us, the people; the devils don't hinder the way of the Lord. Because He established the law of freedom, He cannot, and does not, want to change this law. Until we make a conscious decision to voluntarily obey, He will not deliver us. A deep awareness of *being* like Him must penetrate us. Then we may use our wealth, power, and virtues to rise higher, and lift our brothers, our fellow men. Each of you should seek and value the *souls* of your brethren, and not just their bodies. And I can tell you that Jesus, having come here, hasn't left the earth; He lives among men, works among them, and must rise again in us. We must have faith, but not that faith and fear that the Jews had: "We have no king but Caesar," and when Caesar destroyed Jerusalem after a few years and then their temple, they gave up. Now someone might say, "Caesar is my king," but the consequences will be the same.

Let me return: We must live in this world and prepare. We can't live in Heaven because there the heat and light are too bright. Like a gardener, when he uproots pines taken from a higher elevation, he makes various transplants until he acclimates them. In the same way, the Heavenly Father cannot take us here and plant us directly in the Garden of Eden. Even our school system is organized this way: first we have to go to primary school, then secondary, after that—the classes, university, and finally we go out into the world. These are all methods of our culture: whoever wants to advance must adapt to them. A Christian, in my view, shouldn't be a stupid person and say, "whatever God gives." When you plow your fields, you sow wheat, because if you don't sow grain what will the Lord give? Weeds and thorns. Till the vineyard, plant it, and it'll give you fruit. And whatever vine you plant, that's the fruit it will yield. If you plant low quality sticks, they'll yield crabapples. The Lord has given your child a good mind, but what did *you* plant in his mind—is it those seeds that will yield good fruit? We want to be virtuous, strong, rich. We can have virtue, strength, and wealth, and they are necessary for us. The conditions in which they thrive and develop are the Divine *seed*, Divine *Law*, and Divine *balance*. Balance—this is virtue; the law—this is knowledge; the conditions—they are power; the seed—this is wealth. But you'll ask me, "how will we find the Lord?" It's a very easy thing. Someone wanted to play a joke and annoy another one who said to him, "we are in a garden where there are lots of great apples."—"But I don't see anything," the other replied. When he closed his eyes his friend gave him a slap, and he looked again and saw. In the same way, the Lord sometimes gives us a slap, and we see. Those of you whose eyes are shut should open your eyes. The modern world argues and says, "where is the Lord?" He is in the trees, in the stones, and in the earth. But when misery comes, everyone turns upwards and sees that He is there, and calls out, "Lord!" This is why there is misfortune—it's the slap the Lord gives us, telling us, "I created you to see, not to stand with your eyes closed." And we, in order to ascend, must cultivate the condition of children—to seek and be open-minded.

    Now I'll tell you something else: What is our method for work? From now on, we must always be connected through mind and heart with everyone on earth, because salvation is in our common prayers—"unity makes strength."[1] And when the minds and hearts of the people unite then the Kingdom of God will come to earth. If we truly love a friend we shouldn't look at his shortcomings; like ourselves, he may have them. Shortcomings are the outer garment with which a man is dressed, but the human soul is pure; it can't spoil, it can't be destroyed. No one may taint your Divine soul. It may get dirty on the outside, but not on the inside, because God dwells there. And it's impossible to destroy something safeguarded by God. We may submit to the world, as Jesus answered Pilate when the latter said, "I have the power to crucify you."—"I obey the One who has given you this authority, but my soul is free." We must submit to the temporary sufferings. We can't understand them, but when we die and rise, we'll understand why they came. Everybody suffers from fear and trembling in life. But this is not life. Life is when a person is filled with noble feelings. Fortunate is the one who is joyful to have done a good deed unselfishly. Someone offends you, you don't tip your hat to him, you don't shake his hand. You can even shake hands, but it doesn't mean it's a real handshake. You can tip your hat to him, but it doesn't mean respect. And we usually tip our hats to those well-off, but with this [act] we are somehow telling him, "can you bring me up to a higher position?" There's a *wicked fish*[2] in the sea, and whoever it meets along the way, it greets him. And someone grabs another by the hand—why? These wicked fingers say a lot. For instance, the pinky says, "can you give me money? I need to start a business; I have a lot of losses; I was robbed—can you help me out?" The *nameless* finger[3]—"I seek artistic glory and knowledge." The middle finger—"I want rights

---

1   The national motto of Bulgaria

2   The term "wicked fish" or "devil fish" may be a Bulgarian expression of a bad habit from antiquity. In this case, Deunov refers to an old habit that people do without awareness.

3   In Bulgaria, and most Slavic cultures, it is called the nameless finger. However, in the United States and other Western European countries it is referred to as the ring finger, or fourth finger.

and privileges." The index finger—"I need respect and honor." The greeter, if he can and wants to, will give these to him. And two, then three, go along in society to form a clique, but they don't find what they're looking for. And finally Jesus comes and says, "what you are looking for—wealth, strength, knowledge, goodness—I can give these to you. There are none of you who have left father and mother for Me and have not accepted a hundredfold in the future life." Behold the man who can shake hands with us, who can give us riches, and strength, and knowledge, and goodness. But the people said, "get him away, crucify Him!" to which Pilate remarked, "you are losing Him." Jesus stands before you even today, and I tell you, "behold the Man whom you are seeking; the Man, who can only bring peace to your hearts; who can give you a sound mind; who can give you health, social status; who can lift you, who can show you the way, to bring clarity to your minds." But in your doubts you say, "show Him to us, so we can see Him."—I'll give you an analogy: A man with a small candle is seen from afar. I say, "behold the man who brings you light." You however see the candle but don't see the man. You'll see him. When? When the sun rises. Seek the light yourselves, which is carried by the Man—it'll help you find the path on which you're walking. That's how you must understand the matter. I'll give you another more clear analogy: Suppose I bring you into a rich but dark reception room, and I say to you, "this is a room with marvelous ornaments, with tremendous riches. There in that corner is this, and in the other—such and such."—"Maybe, but who knows, I cannot see anything," you object. I bring a small candle, then the nearby objects begin to emerge. I bring one more, the objects are more clearly outlined. By increasing the candles the room gradually becomes more and more illuminated. When the electric lamp lights up, the objects become clear, and when the daylight comes everything is visible. The world is like this room, and each of us must be a light-bearer—to carry a candle. And when we all go in with our candles, and put them together, we magnify the light; we'll see a lot. Your brains—these are candles. I don't like people who carry extinguished candles, but only those who carry candles like on Good Friday. Each of us must have a lit candle. A faithful, loving, good person is a lit candle. And it's a big mistake for a person to be an extinguished candle. You ask, "what should we do?" You need to pray for each other, to send good thoughts to your friends, to pray for them, to wish a blessing upon them, and when the Lord blesses them, He will bless you too. But why should we pray? In the summer season of 1899 in Novopazarsko there was a great drought. From 39 surrounding villages the Turks gathered to pray for rain, and it rained. The Bulgarians said to themselves, "since God sends them rain, He'll send us some too." But no rain fell on their villages and their cattle died of starvation. When people pray, you also [should] pray, and you have to make your petition. The Lord will not hold a particular opinion of you if you don't pray. Prayer has great power and modern people must be people of prayer: with prayer we'll prepare our minds and our hearts. And we shouldn't pray just for ourselves—that's selfishness. I don't want to deal with the minds of the people; my desire is to deal with their hearts, because all evil is in the heart. The Lord Himself says, "my son, give your heart." We have to start a cleanup now, like for Easter—to open the windows and wash the floor. We all groan under a burden; everywhere there is general disharmony; men and women cannot agree—they divide the house, they divide the money; the woman is not satisfied that the man holds the money. Whether the man or the woman holds them is indifferent. Make an agreement on who should be treasurer. They argue who will hold first position at home—whether the hen or cock should sing. Why bother with hens and cocks? It doesn't make any difference in life. I said that something else is important.

Jesus came and worked, and when the light comes, it comes gradually, quietly, without noise. He won't come as thunder, as some expect Him. That can also happen, but Jesus isn't there. When Elijah the prophet went into the wilderness and gave himself unto fasting and prayer, a storm and fire came, and Elijah covered his eyes. God was not in the storm and the fire, but in the quiet voice that spoke. The Lord is not in your sufferings, in your power, in your knowledge. Where is He? In the love. If you love, He is in you. If you don't love, He isn't there. You too must love—that's the decree. We don't love but wait for people to love us! It means to sit in front of a fire stove and to wait for someone else to bring wood so we can warm ourselves. We—we ourselves must have this fuel that can be used by others. We who follow Jesus, who gave us enough strength, must at long last allow Him to enter us. Now, I leave you this Man: will you accept or crucify Him? Will you let him near or will you say, "we don't want Him." This is the question you have to decide. If you say, "let Him be, He is our Lord," you have resolved the matter, and the blessing will come. Then the words of the Scripture will be fulfilled: "My Father and I will come and make our dwelling in you." Then the light will be in us, and we'll all be reconciled.

Lecture held on 16 March 1914

THE GRAIN OF WHEAT

"Very truly I tell you, unless a kernel of wheat falls to the ground and dies, it remains only a single seed. But if it dies, it produces many seeds."—John 12:24 (NIV)

The grain of wheat is a symbol of the human soul. It represents a great history in the development of nature. If you could unfurl the leaves of the grain and trace its history, you would fully understand the history of the human soul. Just as the grain of wheat falls to earth and dies, then grows and gives seed, the same happens with the human soul. Perhaps the grain to you is something very small, something of hardly any value—a sixteenth-thousandth part of a kilogram: how low would you price it, when one kilogram is worth a penny? But the grain of wheat has power, possibility—the spirit of self-denial, by which it feeds itself and others. And when you sit at the table you don't think about the grain at all; you don't know how much joy it brings you, the thoughts it carries. You don't know its origin. People don't appreciate it, neither do the chickens—nobody appreciates it. But it is a great mystery in the world.

Now, what's in this grain of wheat? It's a symbol of life. And if we take the Bulgarian letter "Ж,"[1] with which the word starts, it fully corresponds to the grain of wheat—two feet at the bottom, two branches at the top. When we sow it, it shows where we should strive for. The grain of wheat tells us that we must strive for the One from whom we have come—towards God—that in order to strive for God we should branch out, grow twigs, bloom, and give

---

1 "Жито," the Bulgarian word for grain.

food to the world; that is, "to help and sacrifice yourselves for your fellow-man as I do." This is why in another part Jesus says, "I am the living bread Who comes from Heaven." And what is bread made of? From grain. Modern-day people say their lives are miserable; they are all dissatisfied—both kings and princes, from the lowest to the highest. They constantly want something and when they get it they're still unsatisfied and want again. If you ask them why they're unhappy, they're looking for something more. But let us turn to the history of the grain of wheat: When it gets sown into the ground, what would you say if you were in its place? You'll say, "we are done, our life is gone, it's rotting away!" But the grain of wheat has more faith than you. When it is buried in the soil it rots and decays, but it immediately understands the language of the sun. When the first rays appear it says to itself, "I won't die, but I'll rise and give fruit to others," and an energy arises within it to strive for the sun: It springs up and blooms. But the people don't leave it alone: they take the sickle and cut it.

But the sufferings of the grain don't end there: After reaping, they tighten it in bundles, then stab it with forks and throw it in the cart. They take it to the threshing floor and stack it up, one on top of the other in mounds like mountains. After that, they pull horses and threshing-boards over it. What would you think if you were in its place? Human life also goes through the same process. You'll ask, "why should we go through this whole process?" Man must learn something from this example with the grain of wheat. They pass the threshing-board and horse's hooves over the grain, remove it and put it in the barn. But its sorrows don't end here: They sift it, leaving the bad grains beneath and the good ones above. They throw it into sacks and take it to the mill, under those two heavy stones to rub and crush it completely. If you were in the grain's place what would you say? "Is this life, and is this the world God created?" But the grain of wheat has great patience; it says, "you have yet to see my full tale." They take it from the mill, now as flour, bring it home and still don't leave it alone. Now the woman prepares her sieve, sifting it, removing one, leaving another and pouring it on the other side; she adds the leaven and kneads bread. If you were in the grain's place you would say, "our sufferings are over now." No! When it rises, into the oven it goes, and when they pull it out we see those nice loaves. If you were in the grain's place you would say, "at last our suffering is over!" But when some time passes, they start to break those nice loaves and eat. In this way the grain of wheat enters the stomach, where gastric juices form and enter our minds. Now what happens? Great thoughts form in our minds; in our hearts—new desires. The grain of wheat wears the garment that *clothes* our feelings; it pours into the quills of writers and poets; it pours into the bow of the violinist. This is what the grain gives. And if this grain didn't spend the process in this development, we would never have seen those good things in nature. Why? Because the grain of wheat gives us the power to look and see. This is why Christ says, "I am the living bread." And in order for a person to be alive, he must be in communion with his environment, to go into it to offer and receive help. Just as the grain has passed through this process, we too have to sacrifice in the same way. And the sacrifice isn't so severe.

Now let's turn to the story of Christ's life, the history of the Jewish people. How can you explain this contradiction: A nation waits for thousands of years for their Redeemer, their King to come and give them freedom, and at that time, when He appears, the Hebrew high priests and princes complain against Him? You would say that if Christ comes in our time, you would do better. I doubt it. And I will relate to you one fact: See how a man acts towards his wife and vice versa, and you will know how you would act towards Christ. When Truth is revealed in the world, She will not wear a festive dress, but the most modest garment, and therefore Christ also appeared among the Jewish people in this simple form. This is the reason why people cannot comprehend Truth. Such are the laws of this world.

But there is another law in the world that manifests itself in the sunlight. When the sun begins to shine on all organisms and beings on earth, this light, which in man produces delight and joy, produces hatred and malice in others. The light that brings a good disposition to some makes others ferocious! The light and warmth that fall on a wolf make him think where he might find sheep to eat. When the latter falls on a thief, he starts thinking how to steal your money. Should they fall on a person who wishes to do good, he will think of finding a poor person, to help him. Give a grain to the chicken and she'll grow nice feathers; give it to swine and it'll grow nice bristles; give it to the wolf and it'll grow nice teeth and claws; give it to the fish and it'll grow nice scales. Physiologists cannot explain this process. Every creature accommodates food, heat, and light according to its development and understanding. You can understand this law when you try these two opposing worlds. No one can explain why evil resides in people, why they prefer hatred over love, deceit over truth; we can't explain this. Many questions asking "why" will remain unanswered. The Bulgarian word "защо" [why] is a question that implies "аз искам" [I want]. Why should we want? There is a law that says we should strive for progress.

Christ says if the grain of wheat that falls on the earth doesn't die it remains only in this world. What is loneliness in life? Loneliness is the most painful suffering that a person can experience. To multiply is the meaning of life. All the suffering in the world stems from the fact that people want to live for themselves. Evil is always born of this desire to be alone and to become the center of the world. But according to the Divine laws this is unthinkable. Our thoughts and desires collapse because we build them on sand. In the world we can be happy only when we live for the Lord. And we must live for Him. The explanation for this is found in nature herself: When the sun rises in the morning, it rises for everyone because it loves everyone; it is attentive to all beings, from the lowest to the highest, and so they all turn their eyes to it. That's where this energy comes from, which resurrects and elevates you. But, does the sun say that we have to go into it? It tells us to take advantage of the goods it gives us, and just as it illuminates the world, we too must spread light, enlightening those around us. In our minds there are some false concepts that arise from our individual lives. For instance, if you enter a house with only one window, but have 20-30 guests, you would say, "you have no right, I just want to watch," and when you watch the sun everyone else would be deprived of its light. But you must expose it to them so they too can see it, to show them the way outside the house so they can see the light. That's why it's not good for a person to hold a lot of people close to himself, because they can't all enjoy and make use of the sunlight and warmth. We must tell them to go outside. That's why Jesus says, "He that loveth himself ought to go forth," and elsewhere, "He who loves his father and his mother more than Me is not worthy of Me." So if a being approaches the window too closely, it would obstruct the whole horizon for the others. Keep 20-30 paces away. This is the physical environment. By this, Jesus wants to say that life is not contained in material goods; they are just a simple training aid, just as textbooks, slates,[2] and pens are a tool for students. Don't think the Lord prepared for you only these small things; He prepared greater things for you. Ask a frog what her beliefs are about life, she'll say, "above the swamp where I live, I want more bugs to fly, and to be closer so I can catch them." And when you see her sometimes, it's as if she's staring philosophically in silence. She's observing the flies: When they come close to her she can snatch them. This is her understanding of life. As we walk up this ladder, don't think we're already at the peak of our development; upon this ladder of development there is still a long way to go. The distance between humans and angels is so vast; it's almost the same relationship that exists between a tadpole, from which the frog

---

    2   A slate is also known as a chalkboard or blackboard. Students used to practice writing with chalk on slates in classrooms.

develops, and man. From the angels' point of view we are still little frogs. Some say, "aren't people created in God's image and likeness?" But we still haven't acquired this image and likeness. You see what we're doing. To say, "we are created in God's image and likeness," we must have God's traits. And what are his traits? They are Virtue, Love, Wisdom, and Truth. Virtue excludes evil; Love—hatred; Wisdom—thoughtlessness; Truth—lying. Are these things excluded in us? If they are excluded in us we have God's likeness; if they are not excluded, we are still little frogs. I have nothing against this frog; she needs to eat flies. And why does she eat flies? I'll tell you: Because as it flies, this fly lives in a better condition. Now the frog, who has this same aspiration to fly in the air, wants to receive the vibrations of the fly, to develop them and take off. Why does the wolf eat sheep? He must eat sheep to become gentle, because as we eat good things, we become good. Actors have made an attempt: When they want to play a role of ideal love they eat sheep's meat for a long time, because that meat predisposes them to such feelings. Therefore, the wolf has the right to eat sheep if he wants to be gentle. And it will surely happen because the wolf is now much humbler than ever before. And when people eat sheep and chickens, I tell you that they eat sheep because they want to become good; they eat chickens because they want to develop wings like the angels. And you have the right to eat these. The evil is not in eating. When they forbid the consumption of some food it is out of consideration not to cause suffering for the creature used for food. I say you can eat. Go to the henhouse and when you grab the chicken, if it doesn't cluck, you can kill it and eat it. If it clucks, leave it. The same with the sheep—if it bleats, leave it; it wants to live. So you have to ask them. Ask which sheep and chicken want to live inside you. Christ says, "I am the bread of life and whoever eats from Me will have eternal life."

To understand Christ's words we need to be purified; to purify our sight, to also purify our mind. The mind is a wonderful tool when we know how to use it, but it is also a very dangerous weapon when we don't understand how to utilize it. When you plow an open field with the intent of sowing it, it is your right; you are doing something natural. But when you plow a sowed field, this is nonsense. Some people say, "we must think and criticize," because science cannot exist without criticism. But how to criticize? Criticism, like surgery, is like cutting a diseased part of the human body. I understand; it's useful. But to cut into a healthy part—I don't understand. To be such a surgeon is not that difficult; anyone can do it—take a saw and rub it over someone's legs. Every one of you has this ability, but few know how to do their surgery properly. To learn, we must surely obsess over the laws of Virtue and Love. When I speak of Love, do not think that I preach a doctrine of peace and tranquility. A person who wants to love has to experience the greatest suffering in the world. Whoever did not suffer cannot experience this Divine principle of Love. To love God we must be willing to sacrifice as God sacrifices for us. To know Him, you say, "Lord! Give us what we need."—"Give, give, give!"—this is the call that gets carried from one end of the world to the other. And money has never been as cheap as today. Every one of us today takes, perhaps, a salary 3-4 times bigger than people have ever taken, and we still don't have enough. Money is devalued because there is nothing to match it. We should have asked for wheat, corn, pears, apples. You say, "Lord! I want to be beautiful, I want to be rich." You want to usurp many things but do you know that it's a misfortune for you? Because once you become rich everyone will think to do you harm, and in order to protect yourself, you'll need people, the way rich Americans take 3-4 bodyguards to protect them, because every step they take someone is looking to blackmail them. We need not riches, but the basic things that make life good. We have abandoned the development of our hearts and therefore we have to return to this basic principle—to develop and ennoble our hearts. Evil doesn't breed in the mind, but in the heart. Each of us should ask his heart what it wants. Our heart is corrupt and it's our fault; we've done it many times, like maids—to lie, to think evil, and so on. The Lord says in the Scripture, "my son, give me your heart." He knows and sees the mistakes of men and wants nothing else but to open our hearts to Him so He may enter. You would say, "how?" Just as we open the window to get light into our room. It is said, "a room where light enters, a doctor doesn't enter, illness doesn't reign," or, "where the light doesn't enter, then a doctor doesn't leave," also, in that human heart in which the Lord enters, the devil doesn't enter. The Lord is the doctor in this sense. When the doctor comes in he says, "you have to eat more, you have to drink more, you have to do this-and-that," and we tolerate; we tolerate until finally our spine breaks. We frequently appear like that camel driver who traveled across the desert with a camel that could barely carry the load. When he found a fox fur along the way he tossed it on top of the camel but the camel's spine broke and the cargo remained in the desert. The back of the camel can only carry a certain amount of weight. The camel—this is us: we're traveling, and if we put more cargo on our back than we can carry, one day we'll stumble in our development. I don't recommend poverty with this; I recommend a tripartite direction: not just physical, not just mental, but also spiritual. Heaven wants ones who have these riches, because they can be generous. And when Christ says, "gather treasures," He means such treasures. Put your surplus in Heaven so the Lord may use your interest to feed the poor on earth. The angels are not the ones who bring our salvation; we ourselves must do this. And we have all the conditions to do it. The law is not to be equally educated; everyone needs to know as much as he needs. Someone says, "my brain is small." I answer: If you can't look after a small horse, how can you take care of a bigger one? If you have a small heart and don't know how to manage it, how will you manage a larger heart that has greater desires?

What should we do? We shouldn't think about the future, but use all the prosperity given to us on this day for good. It carries all future prosperity. The law is such that God, who gives the proper conditions for this day, will give it for other days too. We need not think what will happen in the future, but must be calm. There are some laws that regulate people's relations. The fact that someone can do [something] mischievous is not at all arbitrary; it'll take place according to the law itself. Any misfortune, however, will bring you a blessing; every difficulty will reveal to you a new outlook. You can always examine this yourselves, so don't worry about the misfortunes that may happen to you. Some people ask me about Bulgaria's political circumstances: "What will happen?" How strange! Well, what happened [up until] now? Bulgaria is getting a little *massage*—that's all. They've taken down some of her burden and given her a new experience and task to solve. We don't sit down to think wisely over the laws that regulate life, but are looking for the guilty ones. Who is to blame? You won't find the guilty ones now. The individual life of man is guilty. When someone wants to rule the people as king—he's guilty. And the one who wants to take down a king—he's guilty too. It's indifferent to us who is king—one or the other, the third or the fourth; everybody walks along the same path. I'm not saying that man must not wish to become king or queen. But over whom? Over himself, over his mind, over his heart, his will. How are your subjects—your thoughts, feelings, and desires? Are they subject to you? Have you established organization and order within yourselves? You must be the first to give a model to the world. What kind of preacher would I be if I turn to the people and say, "be generous," but I myself am a miser? Or if I say, "do not steal," but I myself steal; "do not lie," but I myself lie? A teacher who teaches people should be a model—to lead by example. And Jesus, when He came to teach the people, was first to provide a model. And if we absorb His teaching, the world will change immediately. There is a dynamic power hidden in us that we cannot use because we don't know how to work. A thorn bush once grew upon a road and blocked the people's way. Passengers passed by, hitting it with their canes, but the more they hit it the more it grew, until the wagons started tipping over. The people found themselves in a quandary, but then someone came with a pick axe and said, "I too will reveal my talent," and he started digging the roots from far away. The thorn started to laugh at first, saying to itself, "so many people couldn't do anything, and now are you threatening me?" But the pick axe dug deeper and the thorn then said, "I think this son of a woman found my weak spot." Until you take a pick axe to work within yourselves the thorn will always laugh at you and say, "I will grow bigger." This is an allegory you need to grasp. What is this pick axe? Think and you will find. We should always be like a judge. For instance, during the American Civil War, they brought two criminals: one of them was blind, the other—without legs. Their crime was the following: they went to steal apples. The gardener caught them and brought them to the court, but the blind one said, "I'm blind. I didn't steal apples but I extended my arms and took some from the ground." And the other, the one without legs, said, "I have no legs and cannot go and steal." After considering, the judge said, "put the maimed one on the blind one's back," and added: "The one who has eyes found the apple tree, but the one without legs has arms; he picked the apples." And indeed, that's how they caught them. Man is also like this: everyone consists of two beings; one—blind; the other—without legs. When the Lord catches them at the crime scene, each one of them says, "I didn't steal, I didn't touch, I didn't set foot," but God says, "put one on top of the other," and so judges them. Who is the one without eyes? The human instinct. The one without legs? The human mind. They both say, "let's steal!" They get up and start stealing apples, and when they're caught, one says, "why are you beating me?" and the other says, "why are you beating me?" but they're both guilty.

We need to evolve: Even greater blessings await us, but we have to become quite smart, quite good, to *grow up*[3] so we can be entrusted with this inheritance. These three things I listed—Virtue,

---

3   Deunov uses the term "да възмъжеем," which means "to become men," or to enter manhood.

Righteousness, Wisdom—are great riches, and when you have them you'll be healthy and happy.

But you'll say, "how can we apply this teaching in the world?" It's not required of us to fix the world; the world is fixed. There are no anomalies in the world: Everything goes in a certain order; the current affairs, natural or political—we know why they come. We need not turn over this current. But one thing is necessary—to uplift the *individual personality* in the world, whether male or female. When the *personality* rectifies, her children will be rectified—sons and daughters, and when they're rectified, their close [relatives] will too, and the entire world itself. As the leaven is, so will the fermented dough be. This is the principle laid down by Christ, and Christ acts to realize it. And as a cocoon progresses and forms later on, so will the world progress and change for the better. There's great anxiety in the world because all those who cannot wrap a cocoon are afraid; they don't know how they'll prepare for the approaching winter. The transformation must therefore take place in the mind, in the heart, in the will, and when this transformation takes place we will feel there is some *inner* power in us. Then we'll come in contact with those higher beings who are advanced, whom we call saints. As we make contact with them, our minds will be enlightened as disciples become enlightened among their teachers. The saints are teachers of humanity, and we all have to receive guidance from them—they teach the world how to live. But you'll say, "where are these teachers? Where is their abode? We see their images in church." Everything has its shadow, and through it we can find the object. Your wishes in the world are a shadow, your aspirations too. You want to understand the essence; you have to follow the law—from the heart, up to your mind, to think of God. How should we imagine God? We can imagine Him as the kindest, most perfect Man, in Whom there is no malice, no hatred; Who loves people as a true father loves his children—such is the attitude of God toward us. What do you think? Is He listening to us now, or not? He hears and works in our minds. The disposition we have every day is owed to Him. Just as the sun gives us a good disposition every day when it rises, so the happy moments in life are due to this *inner* sun that shines on us. And in the spiritual life there is a rising and setting. In mature age the sun is rising—you are at noontime; in old age you are setting, so you can rise again. The Lord will rise in the hearts and minds of many but there are also many for whom He will not rise. Those in whom the Lord shines will feel happiness and joy, but those for whom He does not rise will say, "for us life is misery, sorrow, suffering." They have to wait—why? Because they lack the proper conditions for rising; because if He rises prematurely it'll be a misfortune for them. It's better for them to rest now. I'm not saying they'll die, not in the least. I'm just citing a law.

When talking about setting, everyone thinks of dying. What is death? It's an assumption. Every one of you must have died to be able to explain death, but now you only imagine it. This is what Tolstoy says in one of his accounts: He meets an 85-year-old Russian monk with a white beard and asks, "what were the reasons that prompted you to become a monk?" And the monk gave a summary of his story: "I am from a princely family. When I was between 21-25 years old my father and mother wanted to marry me off to a princess. At that time, I fell into a lethargic sleep. Doctors came, they took my pulse—'The heart stopped, he's dead,' they noticed and said to bury me. I said to myself, 'is this death?' I couldn't give a sign that I was alive. The fiancée and her father came, and I hear him telling her to cry a little—'So the people can say you loved him.'—'I never loved him, but I love his wealth,' she answered. And I said to myself, 'If the Lord returns me in the world, I will take up a different life.' How hard it is to be alive and to be unable to say you are alive; to see that everyone is crying and to be unable to say you are alive.'" And how many people are buried just like this! There is nothing harder than being buried alive. One of the greatest misfortunes is being left for days and months in the earth and to be unable to detach yourself from the body; it's the heaviest prison—hell! If we were pure we would know when the spirit exits the body and we would never have such suffering. When the doctor says the patient is no longer alive people at once say, "pick him up!" They will make a beautiful coffin for him and carry him away with songs and music. Where is their love? This is the love of those close to us and society! Someone says, "I love you." How? The way a cat loves a mouse, or a wolf loves sheep? That's love too. But it's the kind of love from which the world suffers. The love that is needed in the world is to love others and help them be happy, just as we are happy. That's why Jesus said, "whoever believes in Me will do what I do, and whoever loves Me will love my Father, and We will come and make a dwelling in him." You say, "what will happen to Bulgaria?" I ask, "what will happen to you?" You don't know that the devil took all your property; he even sold your skin, and you ask, "what will happen to Bulgaria?" Bulgaria—that's you! You have to pray to the Lord to drive away this uninvited guest in you, to preserve your property, your mind, and your heart. The devil is the culprit of these sufferings. You shouldn't be distraught with him. I praise him only in one thing—that he's very industrious. He doesn't get discouraged: If you drive him out one door, he enters through another one. If he doesn't succeed one way, he looks for another, a third, a fourth. This is an excellent and praiseworthy trait of his. And God says, "take note of this: He is a teacher of men. He teaches them and he will teach all." When he lies to you, again and again, at last you'll say, "we know your lies. You can't deceive us anymore." Someone said to a friend, "you can't fool my monkey." His friend goes to the monkey and pretends to fall asleep; the monkey shuts her eyes too, but he walks away with the money. The master returns and gives her a good beating. The second time the monkey keeps her eyes wide open; she doesn't shut them because she knows there's a stick. With the experience we have in the world after suffering, when the devil comes, we'll tell him, "my eyes are open." When you suffer, say, "I still haven't gone through the entire process of the grain of wheat." And when your thoughts and your hearts transform and become exquisite, then you will acquire the image and likeness of God; then the Lord will resurrect you just as the sun revives the sown grain of wheat.

Lecture held on 23 March 1914 in Sofia

THE FOUR MAIN ELEMENTS

In life there are four elements for building the *Spiritual* life: Divine Love, Divine Life, Divine Thought, and Divine Will.

When children study arithmetic they have to learn four basic actions; when a chemist studies chemistry he will also encounter four elements. When Divine Love restricts itself, it manifests the Divine Life; Divine Life gives birth to Divine Thought; Divine Thought gives birth to Divine Will, and from Divine Will—our lives. If His life does not present itself in us, we cannot think.

When we want the Lord to live in us we must *create* His love—we must love Him, because otherwise He will not live in us. To create these four things, six more things are necessary that we need to know. There are three things that lie:

Taste—it wants to test the stomach to see what it needs. Perhaps some food may be cooked with bad meat, but flavored with seasoning; it deceives the taste buds. But when it goes to the stomach the latter rejects it.

The Heart—it lies to us; that's why we must listen to the soul. It doesn't lie to us. For the heart accepts adulation, but the soul rejects it.

The Intellect—whatever the attitude is between the heart and soul, the same attitude exists between the intellect and mind. They are controlled by the spirit. In order to reeducate the taste, heart, and intellect we must listen to the advice of the stomach, soul, and spirit-mind. And that's why we must know how to nourish the stomach, soul, and mind. If we know this we will be healthy.

Where is this necessary food? Our lungs do not look for air; if we open the mouth, it fills them. For mental food, we are surrounded by thousands of objects from which we perceive through the eyes and ears.

How do we apply these four basic elements? Through Love. People are unhappy because they are looking for love. And what is love? It is to be ready for self-sacrifice.

We love someone a lot because he gives us something. We love Christ because He feeds us, because He sacrificed Himself for us.

…the grain of wheat we eat. That's why it says: "…to eat My flesh and drink my blood." If you want someone to love you, you must be ready for sacrifice. To love means to sacrifice yourself, that is, to sow—we must sow love, so we may reap love. Our lives only have value insomuch as they can be useful to those close to us. Life is a force given to us by God. It can be taken away as it was given. We currently do not have life: We groan, we lie down, we toss and turn on the bed, etc. Man must have three things that are required for life: healthy and deep peace, and self-sacrifice for the Lord. Christ has shown us the path to life. First is self-sacrifice, and it means sacrificing the mind, heart, and property for those close to us. Christ put his life energies where they can grow. The first condition for our lives is to give up our many desires—impurities.

The river flows into the ocean in a clean state, but when it returns it carries impurities. We mustn't return with the unclean, bad desires.

To come closer to God, we must apply the Divine: Love, Life, Thought, and Will. When we apply them within ourselves we will have them in our lives and the Lord will send His spirit and we will be healthy and wise.

We need to let go of our sins and to stop repeating constantly, "God will use them as new soil to sow wheat."

The sun shines every day; the Lord is before us every day. The Lord lives above us, as the sun is above the earth; it sends us the necessary warmth and light to grow, removing the cold that pervades the universe and stops every advancement. In the same way the Lord, through His spirits, enlightens, warms, and develops us. As long as we are healthy, wise, and cheerful, the Spirit is with us, and the Lord is with us. For this life and this world, we need not a particular program. It's enough to fulfill what was given to us in the original Divine plan and we will be rich. We suffer because we are changing the Divine plan. We must break free from all false concepts, outward influences, and take counsel with the God who is in us. Let's listen to our inner voice—to consult with God who is in us. Let's listen to our inner voice—the soul.

God is in the soul—"I can," but the devil is [also] in the soul—"I can't," that is, in every Divine deed we must say "I can," and in every non-Divine deed it makes sense to say "I can't." The moment you say "I can," God will come and help even in the most difficult situations. When saying "I can," you will surely do it.

The devil is strong because we tell him "I can," when he tells us to lie and other similar things. Women make mistakes when they say, "I cannot please my husband," and mothers when they say, "I cannot discipline[1] my children."

Christ wants us to use two words: "I can" and "I can't." I can love; I cannot hate. I can speak the truth; I cannot lie, and so on. Thus two spirits appear with us every day. The good one tells us something, we reject it, but we are not free because the spirit of evil awaits us. Christ comes to teach us: When goodness comes, to say "I can," and when evil comes, to say "I can't." A cornfield cannot belong to two masters. It must belong to either good or evil; this too is mankind. The Lord teaches us everything that is good. Be faithful to God, who lives in you. We must have the four basic elements: Divine Love, Divine Life, Divine Thought, and Divine Will, so we may plant taste, heart, mind, and intellect in ourselves and develop our hearts, soul, and spirit. Let's not say "I don't understand," but only, "I understand"—then the Lord will give us a meaningful understanding of everything.

We must be faithful to God, to Christ. Christ—this is life,

---

1   The exact word in Bulgarian is "възпитание", which refers to an upbringing in the home. It includes things like good manners and the cultivation of positive habits that can be likened to "discipline."

love, living thoughts that teach nations to love each other. He is a *collective* of all sublime spirits that teach the nations how to live, giving them the laws and governing them. Christ is the One who delivers us from those chains in which we voluntarily entangle ourselves. If we do not see Him now, He will appear one day and ask for the tithe. He is our oldest brother. The day of His appearance is close; it's already late for those who haven't searched for Him. There is already light everywhere; the way of life is changing. We must be faithful to our God, our Christ, whom we already know. He gave us life and health and He will be with us and in us.

Lecture held on 19 April 1914 in Burgas

*Compiled from the notes of Mincho Sotirov, Ivan Garvalov, and Velichka Stoicheva.

KNOW TRUTH AND THE TRUTH WILL SET YOU FREE

Everybody in the world strives for freedom. By the word "freedom" we understand the breadth of our actions, thoughts, desires that are hidden in us, and the elimination of all constricting conditions.

Freedom is a quality of the *Spirit*. To deprive someone of freedom is a downfall. If the conditions for development are lost, there is a limitation in freedom. For instance, losing a part of the body—hand, foot; this is a decrease in freedom. Loss of mind, thought, sight, and in fact any of the senses is a complete restriction of freedom.

Truth is a condition to regain freedom of the spirit. Freedom implies three conditions: First, freedom of the *body*; second, freedom of *will*, and third, freedom of the *heart* to manifest feelings and thought. Christ says, "the truth will set you free." Truth will show us the way to freedom; not everything thought, desired, or willed brings us freedom. Every word is a grenade. Every word is a combination of thoughts. A bad word or thought can deprive us of freedom. The spoken offensive word produces its effect. We should always have a criterion to compare and measure our thoughts and desires. This criterion, this measuring stone is *Christ*. He must always be before us in our minds. When we are always with Christ, an abundance of thoughts, desires, and aspirations for work are born in us. This is a good sign, but not all are of the same quality. We need to know which one to choose from. Thoughts and desires are stones from a quarry, from which the future human body is built, and it is the spiritual kind. These thoughts and desires come from various directions. We must be able to choose the necessary stones for building. For building materials of our house we need, besides stones, also iron, wood, and other materials. There are spirits who sell us all kinds of materials either expensively or cheaply; when they sell them to us more expensively, they lie to us about the actual value.

Christ wants to set us free. We are bound by thousands of duties—the first of which are towards the parents, then to the siblings; next, when entering a marriage, toward the wife and children, and after that to society. The art is in knowing how to act in each of them. Freedom has rights and obligations. A society with only rights, or only obligations, cannot grow, but both processes are necessary and need to go together. Rights are limited according to our needs. If we want more, the opposite reaction will take place: Where there is more honey, more bees will come together to eat it; where there is more wealth, all the bad spirits will surround us. Wealth is necessary for freedom: When it gives prosperity, it also gives evil; a person may become lazy, arrogant, and so on.

In the doctrine of Christ, the value of the human soul depends on the inner qualities of being connected with God, that is, to be clothed in Truth, which is to be clothed in Love.

We recognize the sun because of its light and warmth. We know God because of the Truth and Love. When the Truth enters our minds we think, and when Love enters us we act. Truth is the inner seed of the soul. If we have it, we will always sense it growing stronger—there will be no aging, but constant youth; we will always feel lively. Hardships are a blessing; they are a condition to rise because we will struggle trying to remove them in order to gain prosperity.

All our organs, parts of the body that help us—they also limit us. That's why we must know their functions, so they may work correctly. Now the creation of the spiritual body will be subordinate to us. It leaves us and we separate from it. We must connect with all the spirits that make up, that live and help our bodies. And that means, says Christ, that we must connect with Heaven, and this connection is an obligation. Christ was connected to all the spirits. He didn't sacrifice Himself only on the cross. The existence of everything we know in life is from Christ, which is why we love Him. He left us wealth to use, but not to love it. He left it for us so we may use it, not to take and divide it. It's wealth for which Christ sacrificed Himself; if we don't use it, He will take it from us. He gave it to us so we can develop spiritually, and to prepare ourselves for an angelic life. After this world we will have to enter another one—the world of angels.

Christ wants us to use the touchstone, which is our Divine soul, and when we find it we'll be free. Christ taught people in the world how to find their buried souls—the buried treasure. Many of our souls are *pawned* and we have to find them. When man descended from Heaven to earth, he exchanged his soul for a deposit; that's why we must buy it back. All people who lived before us tilled the earth, adding soil, and we have to work with our souls on the same soil. This is why it's good to have conditions for measuring—the touchstone. Turning over, repenting, and so on; this is how the process of rebirth happens. To reconcile with the touchstone we must be free; to be free we must be grateful for everything that happens—good [or] bad—and this is Christ living in us. Then all positions are equally important for us: We will not be given a higher position if we haven't fulfilled the smaller one well enough. God also sends the angels to serve some sinful person so he can correct himself. We must always start with smaller things and move on to bigger ones, not to say, "now that we are free, we aren't entitled to do any work." The Lord created the earth, and when it fulfills its tasks, its particles will expand and the earth will end.

Every one of our actions is collective because we are connected to many souls. Every one of our thoughts is an obligation—a policy, and the spirit that has it guides us as we are in its hands. That's why we mustn't desire big things, because when we wish for them it's our right to receive them, but then the spirit will say, "now pay!" And when we cannot pay our debt [then] sufferings, deprivations, illnesses, and other things come.

Anyone [who is] angry is robbed, because he goes outside his body and the spirits rob him. That's why everybody must stay in his "house"—his body; that's freedom. If we enter foreign homes, we aren't free, because they can always drive us away.

The first important thing now is to distinguish our desires and thoughts: Whichever ones are for our benefit—those are the ones we should wish to fulfill. And then it's said, "the Lord intends them for us."

Lecture held on 26 April 1914 in Burgas

*Compiled from the notes of Mincho Sotirov, Ivan Garvalov, and Velichka Stoicheva.

THE MANIFESTATION OF THE SPIRIT

"Now to each one the manifestation of the Spirit is given for the common good."—1 Corinthians 12:7 (NIV)

There are many questions that concern the human mind, many of which humanity dealt with in the past. Such issues will exist in the future as well. I will give you a brief definition of the term "spirit." Many minds have a vague notion of spirit. Even the minds of people who have extensive knowledge, this concept is vague. You ask, "how is it possible for one to be learned, yet the concept of spirit so vague?" I answer: Very naturally; if you were deprived of sight and there was a picture in front of you, you would have a very vague conception of it. Consequently, even the concept of spirit can seem very vague to the erudite. When we look at this question, we need to consider whether we have the corresponding feelings and abilities to come into contact with the very reality of things, because we may have a concept of the world and its laws directly or indirectly, but these concepts of ours will vary in one case or another. I will give you a short translation of the word "духъ" [spirit].[1] In Bulgarian this word has four letters: If we take the letter "д", it forms three corners[2]

---

1   In the modern translation, the letter "ъ" is omitted and written as "дух." Many words used by Deunov finish with the letter "ъ" (pronounced "uh"). A modernization of the Bulgarian language took place during the Communist era in the mid 1940s when the language became more streamlined, especially in written form, removing much of what was thought of as unnecessary, including the letter "ъ" at the end of many words.

2   The letter "д" is based on the Greek letter Delta (Δ), which is why Deunov refers to it as a figure with "three corners."

and the letter "п" below. The three corners show the trinity of God, the three forces that manifest. The letter "y"—the two fingers, the index and middle finger, pointing up, show that the human hand is working on something. The letter "x", the cross, is the manifestation of that force that acts in four directions: one line that goes up and the other that crosses shows the human manifestation; the two forces that disagree, which cross. When pointing one finger upwards, it indicates that we are pointing toward God, but when a person comes to a cross-section, this is the other line of the cross; it means the spirit descends and defines this contradiction between God and His children. The letter "ъ" means the equilibrium of the human mind that wants to give people the basic laws. I draw this interpretation from the very letters of the word. Now, the other interpretation of spirit is the manifestation of its *essence*. Take, for example, the light that descends from above—it is the spirit. We don't know what the sun is: Scientists say it's located 92 million kilometers away from the earth; it may be so—we don't know. There may be a several-million kilometer difference in this calculation. If we decide to check, it's questionable whether we will find it on the spot that scientists determine for us. And what is the inner state of the sun?—something profoundly philosophical. Some say it is liquid, others—solid; maybe both are true. But regarding the light that comes down, we already have a real conception, because we see what comes down from the sun and reveals in front of our eyes the entire earth with all objects on it. Light is a Spirit that comes down from the sun and has direct contact with our lives. With this sun we can compare the Spirit too. It will not enter at all, because if it comes down—like the sun—everything we see around us will turn to dust and ashes, or it will turn back into a gaseous state. That's why God says, "I will not come down, but will project My Spirit through space, to offer the people My blessing." This is why God does not want to come down to us, but sends His Spirit—the light. This Spirit, this creative ability is namely what *builds* within us. Everything we possess is due to

Him. This intelligent power that God manifests, the scientists define in the form of laws, force, interrelationships between the elements, and so on. They give it various names, but it is an intelligent essence that works; it is a Spirit that creates laws.

The Spirit has direct communion with our souls. It is through the changes that take place in our mental state that we get a concept of its origin. Without the soul we would have no idea of the Spirit. The soul, with its own way of thinking, represents the Divine world in us. And if there is something Divine in us, it is the light-filled soul that thinks. This is why when we talk about man, we need to understand this. If you separate the intelligent soul from man, he remains a four-legged animal. In nothing else does he differ: eating, sleeping, having all the needs and weaknesses of the animal. The Spirit manifests in the human soul. Because of this, man, in contrast to other beings, walks upright. Why don't other animals walk upright? Because they are at variance with the Lord. Where they walk on four legs, it shows that their will is in contrast to the manifestation of God. Perhaps thousands of years will pass and they will reach the stage of human beings, to stand up and straighten. Compared to them, we rose and strive to rise higher, because we want to get closer to God and to be in accord with Him. There is a desire in us to walk along the Divine path.

Now, it is said this Spirit is given to everyone for use. What exactly is that use? The very word "use" has some meaning, because everyone works for some benefit. The worker digs a vineyard, but waits for a wage of 2-3 leva;[3] the woman works for her man but she also expects something for Easter, Christmas, for the big holidays, for the summer season—everyone is always working to gain some benefit. Some think life is very ideal, but what do they count as an ideal life? I understand the ideal life as follows: to have harmony, agreement in all our relations. Some want to live in Heaven, but where is Heaven?

---

3   Bulgarian currency

In the word "Heaven" I understand a state of complete order, where people respect their rights and duties toward one another. A person wants to progress, but you hinder him when you impose your rights, when you ought to realize that you have obligations toward him. The chapter I read about the Gospel shows what our relations should be. "But there's some meaningless things there," you will say. A Russian proverb says, "even in disorder there is order," and there's something dignified in disarray, I would say.

I'll make an analogy so you can understand from where distorted notions arise. For example, I give someone a walnut and tell him to do research on it. One person will study its taste: He'll try its green outer covering, bite it, and throw it away. I give the walnut to another person, and now, quite wisely, he removes the green outer covering, but when he tries the second layer he breaks his teeth and throws it away. I give the walnut to a third person, and even more wisely, he removes the top covering, breaks the hard shell with a stone, removes the kernel and eats it. If we take these three and ask them what a walnut is, the first will say the walnut is a bitter, pungent, poisonous fruit; the second—that it is a hard fruit that breaks people's teeth; the third—that it's something delicious and pleasant. This analogy can be applied to our mistakes: everything in the world is clothed in layers, and if we don't have enough knowledge, we won't find the essence. Food is necessary for the body, but food is also needed for both the mind and soul; that is, we need to eat two-fold. And when we say that it is not good to overeat, we understand that the body, mind, and soul must be equally fed. It's a whole three-fold circle that forms man. That's why those three who professed about the walnut are not smart enough. The one who ate the walnut thinks he's the smartest. No! I give the walnut to a fourth person, he takes it, but instead of eating it he plants it and in 10 or 15 years this one walnut makes thousands of walnuts. So we have four categories of people in the world who think: Some say, "the world is no good, corrupt; it's not worth living." Others say, "selfishness reigns there, it's the worst place," and the third kind—"the world is beautiful, pleasant." They are closer to the truth. And who are the fourth kind? Those who entered the Divine school and began studying, that is, to plant good things. The most excellent concept for man is to know that earth is a Divine school in which he is placed to learn; to learn to remove the top and bottom covering of the walnut, the shell, and not to eat the walnut, but to plant it. And when he learns the properties of all things, he will understand the very meaning of earthly life. And, like a master, he sends his servants to the vineyard to labor and gives them some bread and tools needed for work. In the same way, God gave the humans a brain as a tool for work. For what reason did He give it? To break stones or taste the bitter shell of the walnut? No, but to learn to plant the walnut. "Would I be better off if I just plant walnuts?" someone will say—"I won't get better." In the word "walnut" we have to understand good thoughts, desires and actions that we can plant in others. This work will bring you prosperity. When you encounter some resistance in your desire, don't despair, and don't throw it away: God clothes a thought in 3-4 layers—maybe one isn't beneficial, but the other one will be beneficial. If you remove the bad garment, if you plant your thought in good soil, it will give good fruit. This is how I see the world. Evil is plausible; it's the *outer* shell of things, and people seem bad. Not that they aren't bad—they're bad, but essentially they still aren't bad, because evil cannot come from God. Badness rises from some of our relationships in the world. Two families live in a house with four rooms: one family has more children, the other one, less. They start bickering, first about the rooms—who should get more rooms and before you know it, they're in an argument. I ask: Why this quarrel over rooms? It's a completely minute cause. And one family starts talking about the other family: "They're confounded people," and the other ones regarding the first—the same. In fact, both one and the other are misunderstood, because a well-understood person never argues. The word "argue"[4] originates from the Sanskrit root; to argue means to be in darkness. People who are in the light do not quarrel. A certain manifestation in our brains darkens our thoughts, and then bad desires follow. When we have noble thoughts, we are ready to live in peace and harmony, but if, however, a little darkness sets in, we're ready to change our attitude. So evil comes from the darkening of the human mind. Now, because God knows there is some darkness on the earth that causes harm (darkness always causes harm), if we lived in darkness it would atrophy all our feelings—eyes, ears, and so on, as there are known fish who live for years in underwater caves and lose the ability to see. He sent namely this Spirit to react in us, in our thoughts and feelings, in the body, so we may think correctly about things and form a proper concept for them.

First of all, we need to formulate a proper concept of ourselves, that is, what our attitude to God should be. According to my understanding, the earth is a school only for the individual human soul. If there is anything real in the world, it is the human soul. Some ask themselves, "what am I?" I am that which thinks, that which feels and desires. And every thought, every feeling and desire also has its own form. When you want to make a tool to kill people, how do you adapt it? You have some practical considerations; what it should be—it should be sharp, to be able to destroy. You make a ball for kids to play: Do you make it sharp? No. You make it round, smooth, so it doesn't cause harm to the child, because all sharp things are harmful. They say someone has a *keen* mind—yes, if it's necessary to do battle, he must have a very keen mind and explosive energies—wherever he hits, to bring desolation. But when a person lives in a peaceful society, what need and what use does he have of such a keen and sharp mind? And if you throw a dumb man at the front during war time, he's also not in the right place. We have changed

---

4   The phonetic translation of the word "argue" is "kara" in English.

the course of things: we put blunt things with sharp things or the other way around. I'm not saying there shouldn't be war on earth; in nature, warfare has two principles: one that destroys and another that builds. But there is constant exhaustion in both cases. We get exhausted, not only when we love, but also when we hate, because one who hates is breaking stones. And when we exhaust our lives in breaking thousands of tons of stones, what is the meaning of life for us? When we constantly think evil, we constantly crush stones. Of course, for the Lord, even this material is useful: He will use our labor to make smooth roads, and people will indirectly thank us for breaking the stones needed for their paths. Whatever we do in the world, our work will be useful, if not for us, for others. In one case, if we love, we work consciously; in the other case, unconsciously, and therefore the reward cannot be the same.

Therefore, if you want Divine Love to manifest, the Spirit must be with you. You must make way for it to manifest. But the Spirit is a very delicate being. Don't think it will come and knock loudly on your doors. No, it will knock gently on the door of your heart and if you open, it will immediately change your life; it will show you how to live. If it knocks on the door of your will, it will tell you what to do and how to do it consciously. And if you don't open, you will soon realize what you lost. When you meet an idiot, know that in the past, when the Spirit knocked on his doors, he didn't open. You say someone is stupid—why? Because when the Spirit knocked on the door of his mind, he rejected it. Whoever is cruel, you should know that the Spirit knocked on his heart—he too rejected it. Cruelty is like a crystal without softness. But you shouldn't think that there are no good people among the cruel sometimes, but overall they do not fit in an organized human society. So, we must always be ready to allow the Spirit to express itself in each of us.

Some say, "we want to see the Spirit." Well, the Spirit is the only thing you [do] see. It speaks, but because your ears are dumb, you don't hear, like when you speak to deaf people, they don't hear. You want to hear, alright! Tune your ear to pick up what the Spirit speaks. "I want to see the Spirit." Good, but if your eye is foggy, how will you see it? The only thing we see in the world, I repeat, is the Spirit. Here, this flower I'm holding—it's Spirit, and if you could see you would find the whole human figure in it. Now, why don't you see? Because your sight is limited. You see only the condensed parts, but not the incondensable. For example, some things appear round—the walnut, but if you plant it, will the stalk be round? It will immediately manifest its true essence. To know things, you must plant them in their own soil. And if you could plant this flower this way, you'll immediately see that it too is a wise being. And what does this flower tell you? Why this color? The color shows that life without love is meaningless. And for thousands of years it tells people what to do—they must love, that the mind should be neither too sharp nor too dull. In some cases it must be sharp, but when you find yourselves among smart people, sharp-mindedness is not necessary. When you find yourselves among enemies, the heart must be tough, but among friends—soft. You must know how to love. When you take a rose and smell it, two things become apparent: one, a delicate fragrance; the other, thorns. Every person has thorns, but they, of course, aren't the person himself. The thorns are for those circumstances in life, when one has to fight, to defend, when one shouldn't be too soft. Don't get together with devils; you must have spikes against them. But among friends your gunpowder must be damp. There are times when it must be dry and other times, damp. What will the husband do if his gunpowder is dry and his wife burdens him every day? When marrying, both must dampen their gunpowder. When exposed to the world, your gunpowder must be dry, in any need… I am translating an allegory, so you can understand all these things that exist in the world. You have friends and you think you know them, but until you see both the dark and bright side of your friends, you don't know them well. You want to be good at all times; you must be good under certain conditions, and bad under other ones. When you anger your friend you have to defend yourself, but to defend yourself you must know how to fight. If you struggle with an enemy, you are doing your job; if you fight with peaceful or unarmed people, you're doing something stupid. They say, "life is a struggle." And when the husband marries he says, "life is a struggle." And with whom is he struggling? With his wife, and the wife—with her husband. They have children, and the [children] read the slogan: "Life is a struggle," and they say, "well, with whom shall we struggle?—brothers against sisters." And the struggle begins; they grab each other by the hair and when they start crying they go to mommy and daddy. The people have a slogan! When they don't have a real enemy they create one—husband against wife, brother against sister, priest against his fellows, teacher against his pupils. Here you have people who don't understand life. Struggles must exist, however, with those forces of nature that must obey. When destroying some rocks in the mountains to make way for a tunnel, I understand these actions, but to use these energies in an organized society, I don't understand. This shows that people don't understand the existing relationship between themselves and their Spirit, or the tasks imposed on them by the latter.

Apostle Paul describes in the aforementioned chapter what the relationship should be. You might ask me a question: "Aren't there thousands of different relationships between things in the world?" But we must choose only those that are favorable to us. We need to know, for example, the relationship of water to us. If we put it in the stomach, it will have beneficial consequences. If, however, we put it in our lungs, it will produce entirely different consequences. If we bring air to the lungs, it will be beneficial to us, but if we put it in the stomach, it will produce exactly the opposite result, and so on. There are various relationships between things and parts of the body. We need to know where the water, air, light, sound, and smell belong. You will say, "well, we know these things—that light is useful for the eyes, and sound—for the ear." This is so. But do you understand the inner meaning of that light? In the morning when the sun rises, what do you say?—"Ha, the sun has risen." But when someone says, "the teacher is coming," what do the students understand? Everyone shuffles, takes up his books and sits at his desk. As soon as the sun rises, each of us must take his book and say, "the Teacher-Spirit comes," and sit at his desk and ask himself what he should do that day. The sun says, "I will listen to you, you will answer me; I will deliver my lesson, and you will deliver back." This is what the sun's rising means. If we could study the program laid out for us by the Spirit every day, life would flow very favorably. "But," you'll say, "today's sun appears like yesterday's—it rises the same way." No! I've never seen in my life two days exactly alike, and the sunrise alike. Every day differs from others and every day has its own program. And the light that comes is never one and the same; it differs from the previous days. In this namely is the greatness of the Divine Spirit, which carries countless riches, invisible worlds and reveals who God Himself is: He is grand. You meet a friend and say, "Ivan, how do you assess him?"—"He's one and a half meters tall, or 165 cm, has thick eyebrows, thick lips, likes to eat and drink." But that's not important. A day comes, you take a liking to him, and for you his thick lips, his outward, invisible deficiencies disappear. You start seeing something else in him, so you remove the first layer of the walnut; you see his mind. If you plant it, half of the walnuts that grow will be for you, and half for him. If you eat it, of what use will it be? Neither you, nor Ivan will be able to use it. So when the Spirit comes, it says that every day you must plant better thoughts, better desires. You meet a friend of yours, and sometimes you say, "I don't know what to say." You see people chattering a lot, but you don't know what to say, or you say too many things but not what you should be saying. First of all, you must plant the walnut and after planting it, you may talk as much as you like. Before planting the walnut, do not speak. Someone who works returns home and speaks: "I worked, I'm tired, I'm hungry." Speaking shows various relationships that exist between ourselves and our actions. The first thing you must do every day is to ask the question, "what kind of fruit should I plant today?" If you plant a walnut it will eventually bring its wealth in abundance. You would understand this parable only when you return, as you *will* return, to that world you came from; then you will notice how useful your good desires and thoughts were, which you planted—the good things you did for your loved ones, your friends, wife, and children. Currently these concepts are still foggy to you. Another example: You say to yourself, "this son of mine—I'm feeding him now, but who knows if he'll take care of me some day? I'm giving him an education now, so when I get older he can take care of me." Don't expect him to take care of you when you get older. Who knows, maybe you won't get that old. You might pass away sooner than him, without him having to look after you. The mother says, "oh, how I want a daughter, so she can take care of me in my old age." It's a very crooked understanding of life. Raise your children properly and do not expect anything in return. If you planted a good walnut in them, not only will they look after you, but they will love you. When a mother isn't loved by her children, this shows she was unable to raise them properly. The first thing (so your children may love you) is to receive guidance form the Spirit, to teach the children to love you.

    I will conclude my talk with a comparison. There are three relationships we need to keep: In the world there exists God, us, and a certain society. Some put themselves in first place, saying, "me first, then society, and lastly God." This is a very crooked solution to the question. Others say, "first society: I live for the people, for society; then me, and finally God." It too is a bad solution. Others say, "first God, the Lord, my Spirit, then me, the intelligent soul that needs to serve Him, then society, and finally myself." Here is the right solution. Any other solution will not be the right one. All mistakes come from the following: We want to know whether society is at the head, or [if it's] us. If we put three heads on one body, it won't accomplish anything! It will never agree which path to take. Sometimes you struggle what decision to make. This means you have three heads: cut off two, set the Lord as your head. Everything must be in place. Now, ask yourselves: whom have you set on your head? If you say the Lord, I will be glad. Put the Lord at the head. And do you know what your state will be? There will be no doubts in you; no fear, trembling; you will have willpower; you will be brave, determined, smart, good people. You will be rich in every respect—whatever you touch will turn to gold. Some are afraid of money. Only the stupid are afraid. Why? Because they are weak-spirited. You know what the story of righteous Job says? That he had worms, and when giving them to some beggar, the worms turned to gold coins. If you are like Job, the worm you give will turn to gold. You frequently unjustly accuse the worms, but they also do excellent work in the world. The modern world owes much to them. When the Lord takes them with His hand and gives them to you, they turn to gold coins. And what is this gold, this coin, given to you by the Lord? You acquire knowledge and experience. When a wise woman takes dirty wool, what does she do? She washes it, pulls it, spins it and weaves fabric. The stupid one, on the contrary—when she sees how dirty it is, [she] throws it out. How many times the Lord gave you Spirit, and you rejected it!

What does righteousness require? When you return from work in the evening, take off the backpack from your back and leave it in the entry-way; all the giving/receiving deal-making you're involved in, leave it in the entry-way too. Enter your room free, like there is no giving/receiving in the world for you, and say, "I thank the Lord for what He gives me." Eat well, thank Him again, and in the morning when you get up, take up the backpack or notebooks and head to work. What do we do? We come home in the evening and lie down with a full backpack on our backs; we toss and turn all night in bed. The Spirit says, "remove your backpack. This is not the place for it." We sit to eat, we feel burdened—because there's a backpack on our backs. We need to remove it and eat; this is the Spirit's message.

"Some people commit sin." Leave this question aside, in the entry-way. You think God doesn't know that people sin? Can we fix the world? There's someone to fix it. In the evening, when we return, we have to thank the Lord that He sent us among sinful people, so they can teach us good lessons. When we meet someone like this, we have to tell him, "you carry your backpack very well." He is a sinner, and in this condition he is a man with a backpack. One day it will come off his back. Someone is crude, sour—why? Because he hasn't removed the backpack from his heart. Another one can't think—why? Let him take off the backpack from his mind and then he'll think well.

Now I will give another example and conclude. There are two extremes, two opposites in real life, which we must always keep in mind. They are good and evil—two poles, the endpoints of earthly human life. In old times some king had two daughters: the older one was very beautiful and slender, but had terrible speech. The younger one was very kind in spirit, but very ugly in the face. Due to their outward and inward deficiencies, none of the surrounding princely sons wanted to offer a hand [in marriage]. Concerned about the future of his daughters, because he remained without heirs, the father decided to summon advice from the wisest people in his kingdom, to give him direction in this hopeless situation. Among all the good advice everyone offered, the oldest among them, that is, the wisest, gave the following: "You," he said to the king, "will make an inn available to all, and the first two young men that come in—they will be your two sons-in-law given to you by destiny." The good father thought that maybe fate would smile upon his white hairs and send him noble people from royal houses. When the inn was finished and opened the first visitors were in fact two young men. But to the great surprise of the father, one of them was blind and the other—deaf. Astonished by this, the king calls the old sage and says to him, "what is this? One is blind, and the other deaf? How will we arrange this? I don't see."—"I will tell you," replied the sage: "The deaf will marry the beautiful daughter, and the blind—the ugly one." So did the king. Indeed, the two marriages turned out happy; his daughters carried on well. At one point the sons-in-law began to feel embarrassed inwardly from their disabilities. When the wife of the deaf one screamed and cursed at him, he shrugged his shoulders and said to himself, "this is how it is when a person is deprived of one of his senses. I believe she speaks of Divine things, but since I can't understand them, it's my misfortune. I would give everything in this world just to hear at least one of her sweet little words." The blind, in turn, listened to the wise and sweet voice of his wife pouring out her soul, and said to himself, "what a wonderful being she is! How beautiful she must be! But I'm blind—it's my misfortune in this life. I would give anything to be able to see even for one moment the outward appearance of this Divine treasure." This reaches the king's ears and he calls the old sage to ask him if it is at all possible to change the fate of his sons-in-law, to liberate them from their disabilities. "It's possible," said the eminent old man, "but their earthly happiness and bliss will disappear."

If God unites you with the king's beautiful daughter and deprives you of hearing, do not despair that you cannot hear her voice. Enjoy her appearance and be thankful. Do not wish to hear her words, lest you become bitter and have contradictions within yourself. Two good things cannot come together in one place on earth. If the Lord unites you with the ugly king's daughter and deprives you of sight—from the temporary illusions of earthly life, be thankful anyway. Enjoy her good speech, her sweet tongue. Do not wish to see her outward appearance and image, because you will lose even what you have. Good things aren't always dressed with a royal mantle. Goodness and beauty are united only in Heaven. Here in this world, it's like this—good and evil alternate in human life. If in one life the Lord unites you with evil, thank Him. Do not be disturbed. You do not know the deep reasons why this happened. Know that the goal is for something good. In time you will understand the great Love in Heaven. If in another life he unites you with goodness, thank Him and do not wish to put on a royal mantle and to admire your appearance. Do not seek to reconcile good and evil within yourself: it is impossible. This is what you're given, so you can learn to recognize the profound things in the life of the Spirit. Your defects will disappear when your heart opens up, when the Spirit comes and your soul unites with it.

Lecture held on 3 May 1914 in Sofia

THE TALENTS

"And to one he gave five talents, to another two, and to another one, to each according to his own ability..."—Matthew 25:15 (NKJV)

I will speak to you about the 15th verse from the 25th chapter of the Gospel of Matthew. Without a doubt, you read this chapter many times; you stopped to ponder over the talents; maybe you made some conclusions, some of which are closer to the truth, others further. I will take this verse in its ordinary meaning.

When Jesus spoke a sentence or parable, he had in mind the underlying Divine thought, Divine law; that is, he did not speak for the sake of speaking, but spoke certain truths. Now we may ask ourselves the question: Why did he give five talents to one, two to the other, and one to the last? Is this random or thought-out? In nature, everything created by God is not random—there is nothing random. We speak about many things, that they happened "accidentally," when we are unable to explain them. We meet a person and say to ourselves that it's a chance encounter. One of the laws of life says our meeting is the condition of some preceding reasons that brought us to meet. When we don't know the law, we say we met randomly without any reason, but that is not the case.

What must we understand in the words, "five talents," "two talents," "one talent?" There are three types of people: some who correspond to the five, others to the two, and the third to one talent. Now, who are the ones of one talent? They are those who live only for themselves: "To eat three times a day, to drink, to lay down, so the body can become more comfortable, and to dress nicely—that's why," they say, "we came to this world." They are selfish people, unfruitful, seedless—people with one talent. And who are with two? A person who is married—he is one talent, and his wife—the other one. They gather by twos and gain two more talents—they beget children; now they are four, and say, "Lord, we used the two talents; we raised children and gained two more." This is the first meaning. In the second meaning, they are people who live for their homes, for society, for the people. Those with five talents have something more. The five talents correspond to our five senses: so, people whose senses—sight, hearing, smell, taste, and touch—are in place. They are people with proper reasoning and conclusions about everything that God created. They understand nature, they understand things, they understand causes and consequences. They are teachers of the world; they live for all mankind.

Now let's make a little calculation of the following talents: we have 1+2+5=8 talents. Is the number 8 random? No—it's the number of *labor*. Scripture says the Lord made the world in six days; He rested on the seventh day. After every break comes a new work day. We are in the eighth day. And God said to the people, "behold, I made the world, now your day begins, work and one day I will come to inspect your labor." We live in the eighth day, and because we don't know how to work we make mistakes. But God says, "work, move forward; of course, you'll make mistakes." Which teacher doesn't expect his students to tear books and stir up the school? Which woman doesn't stir things up while cleaning? Which painter will not get dirty while painting? Which person, who works, doesn't stain and tear his clothes? Along the path of our development we should not want the impossible. We must constantly expect change and wear-down. You're afraid of death. But what is death? Death is the shrinkage and tear-down of our garment. That's the law. The body gradually changes. Scripture says, "the Lord made man in his image and likeness." Yes, that's the Divine plan, but because He left us to work, to create a brain and heart, character, to educate ourselves; in the fulfillment of this Divine plan, the fact that we stir up and stain the surroundings means nothing. When a house is built there are scattered stones, bricks, sand—lots of things. But when the house is erected, all this is cleaned up and the people go to live in it. Therefore, we are now in the eighth day—we are building. And in this act of building three categories of people work: ones who have one talent, others two, the third, five.

Now, let's come together and gather the talents from the one who gained five more from the five—they become ten, two more from the two—four. They all add up to 14, and with the one buried in the ground—15. Okay, if we remove from this number the 8 that were given, how many were gained? Seven. What does the number 7 mean? Rest, as we said. Now we have the law, Christ's hidden intention; the intention perceived only by the one who knows Scripture—namely, that if someone wants to rest, he must work first; and whoever doesn't work must not rest, because when God worked six days, he rested on the seventh day. We often say, "when will I rest?" You haven't even started working yet. What kind of rest are you seeking? You barely got the pickaxe over your shoulder and you want rest! After you dig through the entire vineyard, then you may ask for, and get, rest. We have to understand the basic Divine law that rest is the result of work. Only those who work will be happy and joyful, and Christ says, "those who worked will enter into the joy of the Lord; every good thing I possess, they will also have." And what did He say to the one who didn't work but hid the talent in the ground? "Take his talent and give it to the one who has five, and throw him out in the darkness, to learn to work there." What is that external darkness? The worms that work down in the earth. If you don't learn to work, the Lord will turn you into worms and will put you in the ground to work in darkness, until you learn to work. All those who want to philosophize regarding the Divine law will see whether these words are right or not. I speak this morning about this basic law—we must work. And only when we work for God is it *real* work; when we work for ourselves, it's hardship.

Work implies knowledge; the one who took five talents has five senses—to him the Lord gave all abilities and necessary knowledge. And the one who has two talents has abilities according to his knowledge. I will make another comparison: With one talent—that's a person likened to a mineral [crystal] that cannot multiply—he always remains single. In him the sunlight can refract very well, but he cannot be a wise being. When your heart hardens like a crystal, you are a person with only one talent. And therein lies the hidden danger, because Scripture says, "and I will take away your stone heart." And this one talent must turn and start producing and developing. The other talents can be understood as the grain of wheat, or plant life, which stands a little higher than the crystals, and which multiplies and gains more. What can the beautiful minerals give us in life? We would all die if we were left to live off them. Thanks to the grain of wheat, which carries two talents; thanks to industriousness, and thanks to those other five talents—abilities possessed by our minds for a higher life, which shows how we need to develop the goods given by God—we can deliver ourselves from many troubles in this world. We have to ask ourselves what this means: "Every one according to his ability." It means that every one of us must know his ability. Frequently people say, "I want to have more talents, greater abilities." Ok; if you don't use the gifts you have—you haven't used them—you don't know how to develop them, who will give you more? Every one of us has so many abilities that if we were to develop them they would be enough to create a foundation for five talents. And few have five talents. I believe that most of you listening to me here have two talents. I can even positively say that all of you have two talents. But if you turn these two talents into four it would be different. And what does the number four mean? That you have to find the process of *purifying* your life. You need water, but it's muddy. You need to find a means to strain it, don't you? If you drink it with the mud, it will damage you. So the number four is a Divine process through which our desires and thoughts in the world get filtered. The one who has two talents must work until he makes a strainer…and do you know how much it costs? Ask a milkman: Go to a dairy farm and ask those who make cheese: what's left in the strainer? Only the whey can come out of it. Your strainer is your *critical mind*, which you must have for the things in life. When they say someone is critical you must understand that he has a strainer, and when he strains something through it, the valuable remains and the useless is discarded. It depends what you are straining: if you are straining cheese, it remains in the strainer, but if you are straining water, the clean, clear water will come out of the filter, but the mud will remain in it. Your strainer should have two essential qualities, meaning two talents: when you use one talent, the valuable must remain in the strainer; when using the second talent, the valuable must come out of it. I will make another comparison: The cheese strainer—this is your wheat barn; the water out of the strainer—this is your wheat, sown outside in the field, in life. The first talent should benefit from the fruit that God has given you, and the second talent you must sow—to work with it. You have different uses in the world; sometimes you're successful in your endeavors, other times you're not. This should not disappoint you in the least, because whoever has few talents and wants to acquire more needs to work more. This is the law. It's dangerous for the one who has one talent and hasn't worked with it at all. The first thing required of us is to know how to work.

I told you that you have two talents: you'll ask what they are. Your mind and your heart—these are your two talents. But you'll say, "for what can I use my mind?" Someone's car breaks down on the road; you pass by, you have knowledge, you fix his car; he will be grateful, and sometimes, in turn, he will help you. In this case you win too. The second talent is your heart. Someone is sick; your heart must tell you to go and serve him. The two talents—these are the roots of our lives. By "heart" we need to understand the roots of our lives, and by "mind," the branches and leaves outside. You know in nature there is a correlation between the roots and branches. Each branch corresponds to small roots down in the ground, and when a root dries down there, the corresponding branch dries up. The law you have to observe is this: know that if one desire withers, one thought will surely dry up. If two of your desires dry up, two thoughts will dry up. If three desires dry up, three thoughts will dry up, and one day, when your feelings completely atrophy, all the branches will dry up and you will turn into people with only one talent.

Take a person with five senses: sight, hearing, smell, taste, and touch: what role do these senses play in our lives? They are five doors through which one enters this world, through which we experience nature; five areas from which we can draw wealth. A man deprived of hearing, in the full sense of the word, is a stupid person. Being deprived of sight, psychologically, means to be deprived of the opportunity to see truth. To be deprived of smell, in a psychological sense, means being deprived of your intellect. To be deprived of taste means to be deprived of love, and so on. We can count off plenty of these things. Every one of our senses corresponds to a great Divine virtue, and every one of us must observe whether his feelings are in harmony with his heart, whether they are connected with the truth. If we look at this world, it is the garment of truth: the visible world is an expression of truth. In every leaf, pebble, spring, and rock there are great lessons; great knowledge is hidden there. Oh, what truths nature can reveal to us! We take a pebble, roll it and throw it, saying it's worthless. We haven't understood the meaning of this pebble. Or take a flower; we rip its leaves off and throw it away—it's worthless. We haven't understood the meaning of this flower. Let's come to our hearing: We hear the word "love." It's a flower. Have we understood the meaning of this word, what it means? No. "Why so?" we ask…"nevermind," and throw it away. We hear the word, "truth" and say, "it's an empty word." What, then, is most important to us? "A person should eat a little and after eating, have a glass of wine," some say. As far as the satisfaction of the taste is concerned, it's true, but not everything is about eating. Indeed, one should eat, but according to the law of five talents, with five kinds of foods. Every sense must be nourished with its own corresponding food. If we don't feed it this way, it atrophies.

You see that Christianity is a science; it's not for entertainment. And do you know what kind of science Christianity is? It's a great school with it's own departments, classes, universities, academies, and everyone who goes and listens there must understand what he is hearing. I don't want people with one talent who buried it. In the school where I teach I want people with two talents. Why? Because I don't want to waste my time with fruitless work. Would you like to breed lice or fleas? Those are the beings with one talent. All parasites are people with one talent: freeloaders, slackers, who live only on the backs of others, for whom a great punishment awaits. Test the spirits: when a spirit comes, first take the time to study it; if it has two talents, take it in and spread a feast. If it has one talent that's buried, don't let it in. If it has one talent—out; it's a flea, lice; it's a wolf whom you cannot ennoble. But some say, "you *can* ennoble this person." I say he can only breed fleas. How did the master act with the one who had one talent? He took him and threw him out, to teach him to work. We should never encourage the person with one buried talent. We must tell him, "you, my friend—life's greatest danger awaits you." We shouldn't lie to him, but must tell him the truth. We often say, "there's nothing to it." You have a child: if you see he has only one talent, drive him out. Let him go and wander around the world. You'll say, "isn't that cruel?" Take his talent, because he didn't know how to use it. You have a son with one talent, you send him to a foreign country to study philosophy or medicine or some art. He writes to you: "Father, send me 4-500 leva, because I need them for this-and-that," but he actually takes the money and spends it in the cafés. Two, three, seven, ten years pass by; the son returns. The father says to himself, "oh, this must be a very deep science." He spends 20-30,000 on him and expects a lot from him. After 7 or 10 years the son returns, but besides not gaining knowledge, besides spending so much resources, he returns 10 degrees below, totally rotten, debauched in his thoughts and desires, and then the father says, "why, Lord, did you give him to me?" Did God give him to you, or did you take him yourself? When a thief steals five cents whose currency is no longer in use, is the owner to blame? No, the thief who stole them [is to blame]. Often when someone steals from the Lord, he takes what has no worth.

Of course, with my talk I don't want to scare you, because that's not my goal. When a student is in school—when he enters a laboratory for experimental attempts, the teacher must explain the properties of the various things and tell him that if he's not careful, one attempt may cost him very dearly, because many have inadvertently lost sight and other senses.

Let's apply Christ's rule in societal life. They often ask me, "why is Bulgaria suffering?" Well, you place the head of government as prime minister with only one talent, and you want him to fix Bulgaria. How can he fix it? This person, as Christ says, must be taken down and thrown out. A person with five talents, not even two, is required for the post of prime minister. People with two talents should be policemen, soldiers; officers must have four talents; generals and ministers—five, and for the kings who occupy the highest seats in the country—they need ten talents. Bulgaria struggles because at the head of its administration there are no people with five talents. Frequently those with one [talent] are installed, and afterwards they call them in to judge them. As you see, even now they're judging them. Those who stole are stupid, but those who put them in power are even more stupid. A man honors an unskilled servant and expects good work from him, and afterwards wonders why the work is unfinished. We have to wonder about the master. And now in Bulgaria we need people with two, four, five, and ten talents. If we have them we will be the first nation in the world. There will be no hardships or obstacles for us. Even if all countries oppose the

Bulgarian people, they will not succeed. Then, I assure you, no misfortune will encroach on us. That's why you should pray for such people to be *created*. They will come. Let's put these talents—two, four, five, and ten—to work.

And finally, I ask: What is this mind for, which God gave us? First and foremost, it's a strainer. Did you use it to strain the milk? Do you know how to ferment and curdle it? Let's apply this law for straining in life. They often complain, "I don't have friends in the world!" Why don't you have friends? When you tell me, "I don't have even one friend," I would be suspicious and say that you are a person with only one talent. If you say, "no one loves me," I will conclude that you are a person with one talent who buried everything that is Divine in the earth. A selfish person who lives for himself deserves to be without friends, to be out in the dark. This is what Christ implied with these talents. You ask, "well, what is this starter we need to work with?" You have it, but need to know how to ferment, to curdle the milk. If the milk is too cold, can it ferment? It can't. If it's too hot, can it [ferment]? It still can't. You must observe one basic law during fermentation: you must have good senses, good desires; to ferment the person with a good yeast; to ferment him in such a way that he doesn't go sour; to ferment him with the truth, and if you ferment him with it you are people with two talents. Then you'll have four, and when you have four talents you are then saved people. It means you passed Christ's law, through the process of cultivation, the cleansing of bad desires. These are the two talents you need to apply in your lives.

You may have heard other sermons regarding the talents, that they mean money, abilities, strength: They are *objective*, not subjective. The talent is always a power brought from outside, which can be given and taken back. The talents can never be a possession held by man; they belonged to and still belong only to God, and He gives and takes them, according to our actions. You are born on earth, He gives you two talents and says, "work! If you gain two more, I will multiply them, I will give you five; you will enter My joy." Even when He gives you only one talent, there's a place for it in the world: If such a person says he wants to gain one more talent, he will be saved. And when we see that such a person makes an effort and suffers, this shows that he wants to gain one more talent, because when a person suffers, that original sinful creature in him struggles, which has only one talent. Such a person must pass through the single unit, from his "self," from his selfishness to Divine Love and sacrifice. A person who only has one talent must sacrifice himself to gain two. To cultivate the heart and mind—that means having two talents, and five—to develop all your senses to perfection. Do you know what the development of all these senses is? Many look, but don't see; they listen, but can't hear; [they] taste, but don't understand the good. For example, when a person tastes bread, does he say sometimes, "Lord! Thank you for the bread that you give me. Thank you for the life You bring through *it* in me." If you don't thank, it shows that you not only don't understand what taste is, but you don't understand why this mouth was made. It is useful for the life of Love to first enter, which is the foundation of everything.

Hold these thoughts in yourselves: If God gave you a talent, pray to Him to always be with you and give you two—therein lies the salvation. Christ came to save the world, to save more of those who have one talent. But do you know how many sorrows these lazy people cost Him? They're very expensive. If a person has one talent, leave him to the Lord. I tell you: drive him out. Why? Because only God is in the condition to heal him, to save him. You're not in the condition to do this. When I tell you, "drive him out," I want you to do him some good, so he can find God, because when he holds onto you, he will never work. When he finds himself left out, he will turn to God and be saved. Don't let him eat; let him go hungry for 2, 3, 5 days. Let him suffer a little—what's wrong? How so? How many times does a child cry during the day? If he doesn't cry, his mother will not feed him. People with one talent—there's no life in them; however much the dead body can work, that's how much a person with one talent can work. However much a miser can sacrifice, that's how much a person with one talent can help. I say to all of you who are here, who have two talents: If you start to look like this person and turn to one talent, you'll commit a great crime. You are people who can have four, and when the Lord finds you working, you tell Him, "with the two talents You gave me, Lord, I gained two more," and He'll say, "good rabbi, enter My joy!"

Lecture held on 10 May 1914 in Sofia

LOVE

"If I speak in the tongues of men or of angels, but do not have love, I am only a resounding gong or a clanging cymbal."—1 Corinthians 13:1 (NIV)

The word "love" has become very prosaic in people's mouths; so prosaic that it no longer makes any sense. When a word loses its meaning, it loses its *saltiness*, and everything that loses its saltiness has no power within itself, and as a result, a decline takes place. In the world of organs, when some food enters the stomach and cannot react properly inside, a condition forms which doctors call "indigestion" and which, in turn, produces some discomfort to the body itself. This law is true not only in relation to the physical world, but also in mental life: When a thought presents itself and cannot react in our brains, and the mind cannot perceive it, the same state forms in us. This is also the case with the human heart: When a desire enters into the heart of man and it cannot react (the heart, consequently, cannot perceive it) a similar condition forms.

Human nature has a threefold understanding of things. Take a fruit—a red apple, colorful, beautiful. At first, the form deceives your eyes. You will take it, turn it over on one side, then the other, and you will compose through the eyes—according to its outer shape and color—a certain concept of it. After your eyes finish this process you bring the apple to your nose, to see if it smells, and your smell will determine the quality of this scent. When your olfactory senses finish their work, your tongue and teeth will want to try the apple, and they will perform the last operation on the poor apple; they will ruin her beautiful garment, and from this colorful dress nothing will remain. The tongue will say, "this apple is delicious." In the same way, Love has a three-fold manifestation regarding people, and due to a misunderstanding of her correlation, a misconception arises that exists among people. Some say it is a feeling, others [say it is] a force, and the third kind [say it is] an illusion, and so on. Whatever the mind of man is, such is his condition, so to speak. Hence according to that condition will be his understanding of Love. To understand a person's rationale regarding some matter, see what he speaks and writes; to understand a woman, visit her, see the condition of her home; to understand a cook, go to her kitchen and watch what and how she cooks; to understand a soldier, place him in the battlefield; to understand a teacher, you must see him in the school; a priest—in the church, and so on. Every *thing* must be tested in its environment. Consequently, when you come to talk about the meaning of Love in a broad sense—of course, not all of you will be capable of understanding what I say, and to be able to convey this idea (so it can be understood) I must dress it in a simple form. I can speak in a language unknown to you, not because I want to be misunderstood, but because there are reasons why my language may be incomprehensible. When a small child is born, his mother first gives him milk, then, as he grows up, she prepares light food for him, then chews for him, and in turn he sucks and swallows the milk first and is very pleased. To give him harder food, however, he needs to grow teeth, otherwise he will damage his stomach. But before his teeth grow a certain process takes place: the child becomes sick. And then the mother says to herself, "the child is burning up. He won't die, will he? I will call a doctor." But when the teeth grow, this state passes. And in human life a similar state takes place: When they give someone hard food (Love) he passes through the process of suffering. Therefore, when we say, "sufferings are necessary," we mean the necessity of passing through them so our teeth can grow, so we can feed on this hard food. What are these teeth? Afterwards I can clarify, but now I tell you that once your sufferings in the world begin, it's a sign that you are teething. When you pass through this process you are then formed; you have 32 teeth, and are the age of Christ—32 years old.

Now, I will make a little analysis of how apostle Paul grasped Love. In order to understand Love, we have to compare this notion with its opposite concepts. When a person wants to describe an object, he needs to find its distinctive features; he describes, for example, a horse, a cow, a sheep, a wolf, and so on. He must find the marks that separate one animal from the other. In the description we usually analyze the outside, but we can make an analysis of the inner peculiarities when we highlight the differences that exist between them. In the modern world all people want to be eloquent speakers, because everyone knows that a speaker with the power of speech can influence the crowd. But apostle Paul says, "if I have all the eloquence that human language can achieve, even so, if I have the eloquence of the angels, but do not understand Love, I will have no use of it." The attitude will be the same as looking at an apple just on the outside. Now every one of us asks what will be his destiny and that of Bulgaria. If you could prophesy, everyone will come to ask you, and you will be honored if your prophecy comes to pass. But apostle Paul says, "and if I have prophecy, and know all secrets and knowledge, and if I have all the faith that I may move mountains, but have no Love, I am nothing." These things happening today do not constitute life. You can move mountains and cities, you can distribute whole kingdoms, but all this is just the outer part of life. And furthermore, apostle Paul says, "and if I give away all my property for the livelihood of the poor, and if I subject my body to burning, but have no Love, I have no use of it."

So even if we have all the gifts that apostle Paul reveals but are deprived of Love, we are deprived of the most important thing. Not that these things are without value, but they are only the outer part of man; they do not affect the human soul. And he goes on to describe the positive qualities of Love. The first quality is long-suffering.[1] And do you know the meaning of patience? It is the main pillar of life. If you have patience you can achieve everything; if you don't have it, you will achieve nothing in life. A person with patience is like a ship with an anchor; a person without patience is like a ship without a rudder. This is namely the distinctive property of Love. That's why it is said, "God is Love," because He is long-suffering. Long-suffering is a sign of the great Love that God exercises toward us. If He didn't have that Love, He wouldn't have tolerated us until now; He wouldn't have tolerated our ignorance and our baseness, and would have rid the world of us long ago. So whatever work we undertake, whatever goods we wish to acquire in life, patience is absolutely necessary for us. Many say, "patience is willfulness." No, patience is a great quality, and there isn't a more noble feature in human character. Man is not born with patience; he must obtain it. Love may come freely, but patience must be gained. And suffering is a process by which patience can be acquired: this is the method for gaining patience.

To be patient, we must be imbued with three basic qualities: Wisdom, Truth, and Virtue. Why does the mother tolerate some of her child's mistakes and still continues raising him? She foresees, despite his shortcomings, that he will become a great person, useful in his house and homeland in the future. Precisely when she foresees this, the mother says to herself, "for this child I will expose myself to all adversity, and will suffer all his weaknesses." And she acts wisely. The patient person is wise and foresees the future. Take a young lady: when she is still unmarried she keeps her hands clean; she doesn't even want to soak them in water. She rubs them with perfume. But when she gets married she's not afraid to smear them in the baby's lotion, and she even likes it. What does she find in this child? What attracts her to him? If

---

[1] The terms long-suffering and patience are used interchangeably in this lecture.

you weigh it—it'll come out to only a few kilos. There is a Divine soul in him that attracts the love of the mother inasmuch as, with her long-suffering, she is willing to please him; she cares for him in every way. If the man were left to care for the child, he would throw it out, saying, "this is not for me." Therefore, every task we want to accomplish in this world must ultimately be accompanied by Love. It is a great factor in the hearts of those who have it.

I speak to you about Love in a broad sense. I'm not talking about its essence. Some people consider Love a sensation, a pleasant disposition of the heart. This is not Love, because someone can drink half a kilo of wine and feel a pleasant disposition of the heart. For some pain you do some rubbing and feel some pleasure too, but it's not the same pleasure that Love gives. When a person loves you, he can sometimes cause you pain: Love simultaneously causes both suffering and joy—it's a characteristic. It's a force with two edges: It caresses all, but also punishes all. And how does it punish? When it separates from you, you become sad and say, "I'm unhappy." Why are you unhappy? From the absence of Love. "I'm happy." Why? "Because Love is present in me." But Love says something else: patience is the way by which it can come into the human heart. Long-suffering creates conditions for the manifestation of Love. Without patience Love cannot come to us. It's the first basic quality, innovative in its coming. When you acquire this patience in its broad understanding, you will see that it is a great force in the hands of the brave, the decisive person. This person has a great future ahead of him.

I will now use the word "benevolence." It's the positive, active side of Love, whilst long-suffering is the passive, protective side, with which you have to endure a certain burden. Benevolence is Love ready to build, to serve someone, whoever it might be. You meet a beggar who wants a favor from you—you do it. One of your friends has noble qualities and wants some favor from you—you do it, despite not being of the same belief and faith. We want people to be polite and love us, but we often violate this rule, and besides not having patience, we frequently don't show even the normal congeniality owed to people. Some say they love someone, but speak to others badly about him. The echo of this conversation will be heard one day, because whatever man sows, that's what he reaps. If he sows apples, he'll gather apples; if he sows thorns, he'll reap thorns. I'm not talking about what my relationship to you should be. I always look at what my relationship toward God must be, to Love—that is, what I am required to do regarding my brothers. How will I understand my actions? It's a secondary issue. It's important for me whether I'm prepared, whether I can fulfill the basic law that Love imposes: Can I be patient as it wants? Can I be kind as it wants? This is necessary for everyone, for the whole world, for those who actually have hearts. Those who do not understand this, I'll leave them alone. Some ask, "what will happen to the bad, the sinful people?" Whatever happens to the stones, the ants, with the little bugs. Do you really think the condition of ants is worse than yours? They are a thousand times happier than you: They don't feel those sufferings you experience. We must feel sorry only for those people in whom the Divine consciousness has awakened, who understand Love, [who understand] good and evil, who suffer and mourn. Some people say, "things are not going well for me in the world. I'm an unhappy person." I answer: because Love did not visit you, that's why you're unhappy. "Why doesn't it come?" Because you're impatient. "But I'm trying to be patient." Good, you started. "It's still not going well." Because you're not benevolent. You'll say, "these are very good things, easy for a person to do. We'll do them," but you don't do them. I tell you like a doctor: You are all sick, because I never met a healthy person in the full sense of the word. Only the saints and angels are completely healthy, who live in Heaven. The people are sick—of course, not to the same extent. When a doctor comes to your house he will tell you, "your house is not hygienic because it's facing the north. Get out of this room and move into the southern part. You need to keep the windows wide open, so clean air and light may enter. Change your sleeping mat. Pay attention to your food, and so on." And Love says the same: "Your room is facing north, it's unsanitary, you have to go and live in a southern room where the sun can warm you," that is, it's trying to say, "you have to be patient and benevolent." It says, "these are my two hands, with which I constantly work. They are the hands of Love." And do you know how much these two hands cost? They're priceless riches. When you have these two hands, you are in the condition to do anything. I repeat: for your spiritual hands to grow, you must necessarily have patience and benevolence. Once you give up these two qualities your outer organs cannot react, and your inner ones cannot evolve to express virtues. And why should you be virtuous? Because the virtues will bring you all necessary materials for building your house; [they] will bring you all those juices necessary for your growth. Virtue is not abstract, but something real that is always in the condition to build.

That's why those of you who can understand need to grasp what constitutes patience in the full sense of the word—not that patience where you endure insults (that's still not patience). The secret to patience is when a person insults you to find the positive side of the insult and use it. The insult is a very hard nut someone gives you. You have to crack it, pull the nut out and eat it. And if you can eat like this you'll become completely healthy. When people speak badly about you, when they slander you, they give you food, and if you can use that food, you'll be more than satisfied. People throw hard stones at you: you have to break them because there are treasures in these stones that you can use to enrich yourself. When you go home, start meditating and praying to the Lord to understand patience. Until now, many people occupied themselves with stupid things; many Christians want to be great, well-known, to have a lot of knowledge. Well, knowledge will come on its own, as long as you are people capable of perceiving and using it. It can also be a power that can benefit you and your loved ones, as long as you know how to use it properly; but it can also be like a backpack on a person's back.

Love doesn't envy. So, to see if true Love visited you, you must ask yourselves if you are envious. If you are jealous, you don't have Love. Love must be ever-present in our deeds: it's useful in this life, and in the next, and the one after; and the higher we climb, the deeper the meaning we will find in it. We must take this path now; there is no other path to Heaven. You'll say, "this path is difficult. Can't we do without it?" We can't; without *it*, we can go anywhere else except the Kingdom of God. Love doesn't envy; to unrighteousness it doesn't answer with unrighteousness; to evil it doesn't answer with evil. It endures everything. Of course, I'm not saying that envy or pride will never visit our hearts; sometimes they will come as guests, but we will not be judged for this. The point is not to make friendships with them. But sometimes we grab hand-in-hand with jealousy and tell people, "he's bad, you have to guard yourself from him," and we make the life of the person unhappy. Jealousy isn't something abstract. As you see, they are beings who acquired negative qualities. There are even people on earth who are the embodiment of envy.

Only after we learn these two qualities, patience and benevolence, we will learn the history of our lives; we will learn why we came to earth. Once again, I will bring up the example with the grain of wheat, because in the world, out of all the fruits of today there's no better instance than the grain of wheat: If you want to study the process of patience, see the patience of the grain of wheat. Without patience you will have disappointment. Many people will not believe you. You'll say, "people don't follow me." Why would they follow you? The people aren't born to follow you. They'll listen to your doctrine, but to follow you—never! You often ask, "whom do you follow?" You can truly be a follower of people, but sometimes you may be deceived. If you are followers of God only you'll never be deceived. There's one way, and Jesus Christ says, "I am the way." If people don't follow you, He'll say you are not on the path. Someone might say, "I don't believe," and take a different path, but one day he'll be convinced that this is the way; his life will show him, because it's a great test. But you'll say, "convince me, and then…" I don't want to convince you. I tell you that this bread I give you will feed you. "But tell me from what elements it is composed: With what kind of water is it kneaded?" I have no time. Will you take the bread to eat?—"I don't want to." I put it in the bag and go. You'll also ask, "what is Love? What is it composed of?" If you ask too much I'll put it in the bag, sling it over my back and go on my way; later I'll tell you. I don't have time now to discuss these questions. Life is something positive—try it, take some and eat from this bread and you'll see. Love is food for life; without it, one can't live and achieve anything in the world. Some people have a very vague notion of Love, whether in terms of trade, whether in learning, or in war. We must have Love everywhere; it's a great force. And this force, with which I lift this glass, is also Love. This same force can be placed inside a cannon, thrown from a grenade and kill lots of people. It can manifest in an earthquake. It can even destroy the entire world. It can create a world. It's a matter of use—how a certain force is used. Love is a force that can be used if regulated. People are self-loving—when Love comes, they want to shut it within themselves. But if it were shut inside us, it'll destroy our walls and go outside. It can't stay inside the dwelling where we wish to enclose it, and death comes. Death is a process of destruction of every selfish thought and desire. God uses [Love] to destroy every enclosure occupied by bad spirits. Our hearts and minds must have all the conditions to perceive it. It is quiet, calm, but at the same time with its actions it is a terrible force. When we are in harmony with it, the world is bliss. If we are not in harmony with it, there isn't a more dangerous force in the world than Love. And that's why people speak from experience when they say, "whoever loves much also hates much." It's as strong in the positive side as the negative side; that's why we must be very careful with it. When we have it, we shouldn't act negatively, because then it acts destructively—diseases arise, sufferings, a destruction of the whole society. Many say that God is Love, and as Love, He shouldn't punish. The Lord, being so kind, is at the same time demanding. When He sees us discontent He says, "put one kilo on his back." We ask, "why are they putting this weight on me?" But He, without answering, says, "add another kilo."—"But I can't carry…"—"Add another kilo." And when it crushes us like this we can't move. Then we say, "Lord! Forgive me."—"Remove a kilogram from him," answers God. We repeat the request—"Remove one more kilogram from him." The more we pray, the more kilograms are removed from our back. And when He removes all the burden, God asks, "well, did you learn the lesson?"—"I learned it well."—"If you don't want me to burden you anymore, you must be kind and patient toward your surroundings, toward everyone around you, just as they must also be kind and patient toward you. These little brothers of yours may do wrong, but you must have patience, just as I endure. The day you overstep the law, I will load you up again."—"I can't carry."—"You *will* carry." I told you how we can free ourselves from our burden; everyone must say to the Lord from his heart, "I am grateful in my heart and soul for everything You have given me," because God has given every person thousands of good things, yet, "he steps in water, but goes thirsty." Many merchants are dissatisfied. Why? Because they have 10,000 leva and it's not enough. When you give them 20,000 it's still not enough. You give them 50,000, [then] 100,000 they're still unsatisfied. Do you know what contemporary society is like? Perhaps you read about that fisherman who found a beautiful eye. They asked him, "how much do you want for that eye?"—"As much as it weighs."—"Weigh it." They put 10 grams [on the scale], the eye is dissatisfied. They put 20 grams—[it is] still dissatisfied. They put 100 grams—[still] dissatisfied. They put 1 kilogram, then 1,000 kilograms; 10,000 kilograms; all the gold. They eye remained still dissatisfied. "What should we do? We can't pay for it," they started wondering. Finally they called an old sage and asked him what to do. "It's a very easy task," replied the sage. "Take some dirt and sprinkle the eye." They did this and the eyelids along with the eye turned up. And one day, when God finds us dissatisfied, He'll say, "put dirt on his eyes," and we then become satisfied. Just as we often like to add salt to our dishes, so the Lord, when finding us dissatisfied, will put a little salt or pepper to make us happy. Because life is not in how much we have, but what we can *use* in a given moment, and being thankful for what God gives us. Then God will give us even greater goods.

We must apply this chapter from the apostle in our practical life: to begin work and to be helpful to our brothers around us. It's like we're in school, we study things. It's like we're in a flower-pot. Church is a giant flower-pot: you can plant everything there. School however is a garden in which one must plant only things that will be of benefit. In the schools we have to learn how to cultivate and plant the good and useful things. And in terms of school there is a connection between the heart and mind: we need not only plant, but cultivate and express the basic laws in which life should develop.

You say, "why didn't God give me more abilities, more power, more money?" I see many reasons for this. Because however many times He sent you to the field to work, you, your ancestors, instead of cultivating your minds and hearts, you busied yourselves with the taste of the forbidden tree, making ever newer and newer experiments that cost all your capital. However many times you reached these points of development, instead of working, you ran away and returned to Him and begged to receive something without any effort. You are like students whom the father and mother want to educate—they don't learn; they run away from school. Many of you ran away from this Divine school. You say, "this stuff is not for us, and we don't give a damn. Let's get out of here." You said this many times, and even now you might say it, but it's not a wise thing. Whoever wants to learn the Divine law, to take up a higher level, to rise to the level of the saints, where one can look upon life with clarity, and for God to look favorably on him, must surely finish the Divine school on earth with a final exam. In this completion lies everyone's prosperity. Unprepared in this world, you will drive horses, [you will] plow; you will break stones; you will make roads, until you learn what the horses, rake, stones, and roads are teaching you—to prepare for Christ's Kingdom. God sends the disobedient children to break stones; but to the obedient ones He gives noble occupations. You'll say, "this doctrine is difficult!" Yes, true—for the lazy, I agree that it's difficult. But for the diligent, hard-working and humble it carries hidden treasures. Do you know why the worm is in the ground; the frog in the water; the bird in the air; and man among them? These are four grand circumstances in life. But you'll say, "these are abstract things." They're not abstract. These are four great truths that reveal the narrow path—the path of God's thought. True, it's narrow. But there are profound reasons for this, which I cannot explain right now. They lie outside the boundaries of this world.

But to return to the word "love," which people have desalinated, corrupted. They've trampled her goodness, her beauty, and have ruined her harmonious sound to the extent that now only her hoarse sounds remain, which scratch our ear. And we say to ourselves, "love—these are life's illusions, empty dreams of young men and women who chase the elusive shadow of life." Yes, a shadow, but behind that shadow there's a reality from which the juices of life flow, from which the soul constantly quenches its thirst, like the wearied traveler before a cold and clear mountain spring. What invaluable wealth, what knowledge is hidden in this one word! And if the people knew how to pronounce it properly, like it was originally pronounced from the Divine mouth, everything around them would smile and tenderly listen to this Heavenly call. They would have the magic rod of ancient sages, before whom everything bowed down for good. Many will say, "how fortunate is the man possessing this rod!" True, it's the greatest happiness one can acquire on earth. And he can get it as long as he wants to strive for this kind of good.

Now I will tell you just this: if you first learn patience in life—to always suffer everything with humility and joy—you will find the truth. With your impatience and bad thoughts, you create a heavy atmosphere in your house. A woman is unhappy because the husband earned 150 leva; she wants this and that—desires, desires, desires. And who will work for you? Who else will supply them, and not you yourself? For example, if everyone wants to have full barns without work, where will they get them? Goods are acquired with difficulty, with hard work. That's why we should be satisfied with that which God (in His great Wisdom) is pleased to give us.

I don't advise you to ever listen to other people's advice. You may draw some lessons from them, but everyone should listen to the advice God put in his conscience. See what people say and if it agrees with what the Lord is telling you internally in your conscience, [then] listen to them; if not, don't follow someone else's advice. If you want to be free from mistakes, you must surely listen to the Lord. Everyone who doesn't listen to the Lord is not a smart person, but a slave to his external affections, to the people, to all.

You are looking for God—where? He is in you, in your mind, in your heart; He manifests through these two gifts. Hear your mind and heart well, by which the Lord speaks to you. But some will preach to you that the mind and heart are corrupt. It's not right. If our mind and heart were corrupt, with what would we know God? There are spoiled things in us, but not everything is spoiled. I ask you: If you don't believe your mind and your heart, who do you believe? If your mind and your heart are spoiled like mine, why would I believe you? In whom must we believe? In the Lord who lives in us. And when we believe in ourselves, we'll trust our brother too. Whoever doesn't believe in the Lord who lives in him can't trust other people. And whoever is not affectionate to those close to him is not pleasing to God. That's why God says to love our neighbors. Your neighbor is wounded, crucified, nailed to the cross. It's not your Lord in Heaven; you nailed Him. It's true; you read the Gospel. Your salvation will be no different, but through this nailing, patience and benevolence. Then your liberation will come. You'll say, "this is a difficult task." It's not difficult. Don't be afraid. To be nailed to the cross is something pleasant. The Lord endured this nailing for thousands of years. "Will we suffer?" You won't suffer. We don't want people who are afraid of suffering in our school. You have to thank the Lord for these sufferings. They are sent from Him. And those sufferings given to you now, you deserve them; you are worthy of them. If Christ didn't carry that crown of thorns, if He were not nailed to the cross, how would He have expressed that Love? Would you love Him today if He lived like a king? You love Him because He was nailed to the cross for our salvation.

Therefore from now on be courageous, don't be afraid of suffering, but say to the world that you are men, and that you are ready to carry not just one cross, but ten. Someone complained that the cross he carried was too heavy. The Lord said, "take it form him," and He took him to a large hall and said, "in this hall are large, small, golden, silver, iron, and stone crosses. Choose one." When the man walked around he found a small cross and said, "I want this little cross."—"Well, this is the cross you've been carrying until now. I gave you this cross," said the Lord. We often exaggerate our suffering, yet it is the way for us to come to God. And that's why when someone suffers, let us say, "he's a sinner who is saved." I'm sorry for him and I say to him, "brother, you are closer to Heaven. I would like to be in your place." When someone says, "I have never seen sufferings," I tell him, "you are still green." The green is nice, but when it starts ripening, suffering comes. Now take this idea in yourselves: I give it to you to think about from God's side: when suffering comes, rejoice and thank the Lord that He loves you and sends it your way. Suffering is a sign of God's Love, and let us all bear this cross. That's why the whole Bulgarian people, as a soul, received these sufferings from the Lord, to master these two great qualities, long-suffering and benevolence. "But," you say, "the Greeks and Serbs are such-and-such." So what?

Don't pay attention. You learn the lesson for your salvation. What they are is unimportant. Leave it. They didn't gain anything, but a time will come for them to learn this lesson too, which you were given earlier, for which you should thank and not grumble. "They crucified us."—"There's nothing wrong with that. You are closer to Me," says the Lord. "The others aren't. They are far away right now, but they too will come to this place." When they crucify you, then you'll enter the Kingdom of Heaven. So let's be glad that we have something more in this world. Let's all be followers of Christ and worthy enough to carry the name "Christians." What others will say, let's put it aside. Let us be long-suffering and benevolent, and to fulfill our duty to God as we understand it in our pure thoughts and desires. And in this great way we'll never stumble, but fight boldly, decisively, and encourage everyone who fights with us. This is the power with which we'll overcome the current difficulties.

Lecture held on 19 July 1914 in Sofia

JOSEPH'S DREAMS

"Joseph had a dream, and when he told it to his brothers, they hated him all the more."—Genesis 37:5-11, 39:1-23 (NIV)

In our lives, we often ask the question: Why do we sometimes experience misfortunes? It is generally believed that people suffer and pay off some transgressions from the present or the past, and seek the reason for it. We see that life unfolded this way for Joseph regarding two dreams he related to his brothers. Of course, they interpret the dreams to mean he had secret thoughts and ulterior motives, and to prevent them [from taking place], the idea of getting rid of him set in. And as you see, these aren't strangers but his own brothers. So at the first convenient moment they capture him and sell him to Ishmaelites, who re-sell him to an Egyptian, and then Joseph's trials begin; God tests his character. The life of man is nothing but a test; [trials] are the testing stone with which man's character is tested. The most precious part of the human soul is his character, which must pass through the fire, testing. And only when he passes through this fire and withstands all his exams, only then can we say that he is a man whose character has value—steadfast and everlasting. He has an eternal home to live in, character—that is man's home. We see that Joseph is plagued with difficult situations, one after another. Out of these situations from the two dreams came others, as outlined in chapter 39: since he was a handsome young man, his master's wife fell in love with him. She wants pleasure, but he tells her, "no, my master gave everything in my hands, and besides, you are his property, his right, and I cannot commit this sin before God." We see that the Lord reigns in the soul of this young man. Whatever he wants to accomplish, he first weighs it in, whether it is right, whether it pleases the Lord or not. He knew the troubles that would ensue from his refusal to fulfill the will of such a woman, but he preferred to suffer rather than sin. After this exam, indeed, he found himself in prison, but the Lord helps him here. If you look at the whole story in this chapter, you'll see that God doesn't leave him, but takes him out of prison by interpreting two other dreams of the Egyptian king. When we go through testing we don't know the *target* point God seeks. You want to go to Heaven, but if someone asks you what you understand under the words "Heaven" or "Paradise," you don't know how to answer accurately. You have some idea of Heaven, but for you it's so indefinite, like the two dreams in Joseph's mind were undefined. Indeed, what relation could the sheaves, sun, and moon have to him? But they showed the concurrence of certain future events: being sold off, being tempted by the woman, getting imprisoned, his deliverance and exaltation.

Now, what is this kingdom and this woman? Egypt is the kingdom in which we live, but the woman of the palace guard who tempts us, is the world. You are slaves who were sold, by being driven away by your brothers. You are in Egypt, and this palace guard's wife offers enjoyment with her: the world offers you some good things and tempts you. It's not bad for a person to enjoy himself, but there are forbidden things. When Adam was in Paradise, the Lord told him to eat everything. He only forbade him one fruit, and because of his disobedience came all his sufferings. And in this world there are things forbidden and if you try to eat forbidden fruit, suffering will surely follow. How many people like to touch other people's money? They need them for houses, for pleasure, for traveling abroad. Joseph, however, didn't see this question the same way. He could have had the indulgence of the woman of the palace guard, but thought, "I prefer to have God's favor, rather than a strange woman's favor." The world is a woman who doesn't belong to us. Tomorrow, after some pleasure, she might throw you out; she's attracted to your outer beauty. The modern-day deception lies in the following thing: When people honor our outer appearances, we fool ourselves by thinking it's because of our merits. If we have a famous, honorable singer, everyone honors only his singing talent, his throat. Should his larynx falter, they throw him out like a rag. All his respect is owed to a small slit in his throat. Similarly, we have a great violinist. Everyone respects him as long as he can move the bow. Should his hand paralyze, no one wants to hear about him. You may be a beautiful preacher, but everyone will listen to you as long as you have a sweet voice. When your voice becomes hoarse and raspy, they'll tell you, "we don't want a preacher without a voice." While the woman is beautiful, everyone walks around her. Should her beauty disappear, they say, "let another one come in her place." Joseph knew this self-deception, and he saw things only internally, long-lasting and eternal, which may always bestow peace to a man, and by this way he wanted God's favor.

We have to be careful with the small causes that lead to misery. If Joseph didn't tell his dream to his brothers, this misery wouldn't have befallen him. The question arises: wouldn't it have come in another case? Some exams are inevitable. I won't talk about these internal laws, but will say that there are things absolutely determined by God. If we decide to avoid the small ones, the big ones will come. To be able to neutralize the sufferings, we must learn form Joseph's behavior. In no way should we deceive ourselves, [by thinking] if we are well today, the next day will not change our lives and bring misfortunes we didn't expect. Faith or Providence determines the exams human life must go through, and these exams are necessary. Why are they necessary? I will just give you a comparison: To pass through a deep river you need a boat; to cross the ocean, you need a ship, which is called faith. And these tests and misfortunes are also necessary. They are the fuel, your travel ticket. Anyone who wants to change the path of the required law is a stupid man. Anyone who says, "why did the Lord give me these sufferings?" who murmurs, is a stupid man in the full sense of the word. Anyone, however, who says, "I want to learn their meaning," and is thankful for them, is a smart man. Notice: When Joseph suffered misfortunes, he didn't grumble, but greeted them with joy in his soul and thanked God when he rose in his master's house to a position where he had everything. He didn't become haughty. When the master gave him much greater goods, he wasn't seduced by those offered by the woman, because he said, "I have to fulfill one law. I mustn't falter." So pleasure in this sense is sin.

What is sin? Every thing that does not bear fruit or seed in itself is a sin. A woman who solicits and fornicates without giving birth commits a sin. Conception redeems sin. Every act that doesn't carry life in itself is a senseless waste of Divine energy. When someone makes you sin, he wants you to waste your Divine energy. You drink a glass of wine, the next day your head hurts. What did you gain? Did you become more noble? No. Why should we want and do things that don't add anything to our character? All of us must limit ourselves only to those pleasures that are allowed, legitimate and natural. For example, take a boy and girl, who play with horses and dolls: these things give them some pleasure, and on the other hand they also educate, preparing them for other *positions*. For the older ones there is some pleasure which can also be enjoyed. However, there are also pleasures that always carry with them the destruction of human feelings, human strength, human salvation. The unnatural life, the so-called hidden, illegal love that some men and women exercise, acts destructively on the heart and on their minds. You love someone; ask yourself: Does this please God? Does it benefit the one you love? Or do you corrupt his soul and his mind? Joseph was young, inexperienced. One lewd woman wanted to defile him, but he didn't succumb to her temptation and tarnish his name, which, if he gave in, no memory would be left of him. Notice: the woman, Eve, was the first to be put to the test and didn't resist, and after that, her husband. Now man is put to the test. That same snake tempted Eve in the garden: "Look, if you taste of this tree, what knowledge, what strength you will have. You'll become like God." Eve gave in and said, "for glory, I am willing, I can do it," because it was a form of cheating. That same snake appeared before Joseph in the form of a woman and said to him, "come with me," but he said, "no." Then came the sufferings, but also the exaltation. Man and woman represent two principles, two great forces—wise [ones], which act: we call one force *active;* the other [is] *passive.* One acts, the other receives, two processes in nature that alternate. God doesn't always give; sometimes He takes. He gives in one respect, and takes in another. On the one hand, the ocean sends moisture to the land, on the other, this moisture returns by the rivers back to the ocean. In this sense, man and woman are two principles at work: one principle creates, called man [or] God, the other is passive, called woman or the Lord; it's one and the same. Consequently, in life we have to be faithful to both principles. If the world requires us to obtain goods, we will attain them only when we withstand this exalted Divine principle. If you are faithful, all your dreams and desires on your mind and heart are attainable. You will attain them only one way, through God. Only He can satisfy your thoughts and desires. The mother feeds her child; the teacher educates the student: just as the child cannot be nurtured or grow without the mother, so the student cannot learn without his teacher. Joseph listened to the voice of his teacher, who lived in him, to the Lord, who taught him to observe the great law of movement and motion in life. All our aspiration in life must be directed towards this, to develop our character. How? The character is assembled with thoughts and feelings from positive forces. We ought not grasp life like some people, in their limited conceptions, as some scientist, or doctor, or philosopher—no. We must understand life through the *limitations* presented by God. Everyone sees things fragmented: modern science shows only one part of things; the genius of a talented musician captures only a small part of space; the mind of a philosopher [as well]. The strength of a strong man is limited only to his muscles. But some say, "strong in mind." A man can only be strong in mind when his power is connected to all Divine laws and when he is in harmony with all beings who surround him, from the lowest to the highest. Then his strong, powerful character can do everything because all beings cooperate with him. When we are disconnected from these Divine laws, a contradiction arises in our mind as well as all mishaps we encounter in life. Why do we fail sometimes? We doubt: we want to do good, without judging whether our actions are not good. We think we're so clever, that our idea is ingenious and will come to fruition. We turn it over, forward, backward, but it doesn't happen. Sometimes we wonder why we don't progress and why our memory weakens, why it becomes dull. We ourselves constantly stir our lives up. It's okay to stir the water up when you go fishing, but to constantly stir it up, even after you catch all the fish—you shouldn't. A wife is often angry with her husband and stirs up his water: "What do you want? A dress? Okay, here's your dress," says the man. The lake becomes clear again. The next day the wife wants to catch fish again, and stirs up the water again; now she wants a silk dress, a watch, to go for a walk. "Okay, here you go," the man replies. But one day this man goes broke; he has no money. What can he do? He picks up and leaves. So the lake dries up and loses its fish, even its water. What, then, will the woman stir up? To constantly stir up life, to disturb ourselves—that doesn't mean we understand life. We'll stir up, stir up, and finally we'll die.

Have you thought about death? What is it? It's depicted in the paintings: a person consisting of bones and hair in the hand. Have you checked to see whether this is so? "No, my mother and grandmother told me that this is so." Maybe it's true, but have you understood the meaning of these bones? Why is death depicted as a man without muscles? You have to be pure like the bones, which are white. That means you have to be *virtuous*. Everything unclean will be thrown out. Only virtue will remain untouched. You have, therefore, an emblem, so as not to be affected. If you step over the Divine law, you will always be affected. A person must fear punishment before, not after, transgressing. Crying doesn't save a man. Salvation lies in the organization of our mind, our heart, and our body; this is our task on earth. And that's why we have an outstanding example in the Old Testament, the greatest character in the face of Joseph. And when we read these chapters from Genesis, we must study the character of Joseph well. We mustn't think he was stupid; he was very smart, and that's why, as you see, his father loved him. Love is always due to Wisdom. But Joseph had a noble heart as well. His father sensed this, but his brothers thought that the father loved him because of some outer qualities and they sold him. But whatever circumstances they put him in, his character would have lifted him up either way, as it did. Due to his fine qualities, his master put him in a high position. Another test placed him in prison, but even there he rises, and finally God pulls him out of prison, where he spent—have you read how long?—two years, the determined time for testing. And what is *your* prison? Your current body. One day you have to leave this prison, which is dirty and unhygienic. Until now you have taken communion, but you don't know what the emblem [of] the wine represents? The baker had to be impaled, and the cupbearer [was] restored to his position—one of life's principles, the active one, must always be sacrificed. And the wine must come in to cool off life. It has great power, but because modern society is unprepared ahead of time, they become excited by it: they don't have the organism to use it. When the wine enters the bottle and begins to ferment, the bottle cracks.

But let us return to Joseph's character: We see that there was a sober, rational mind in him that understood the basic laws of life. He had a noble heart and didn't want to betray in any way the promise he made to God: "I gave my master, and the Lord, a promise to serve faithfully and not to betray Him." Therefore, he was not the kind of young man who followed bad inclinations and desires. In every case he followed noble aspirations and had a balanced heart and mind. In order for the Lord to live in us, our mind and heart must be in agreement and balanced. Should disagreement rise between them, the Lord ceases to live in us. There are places where anarchy lives, like in Serbia right now, and the whole world, because people's hearts and minds are not in agreement, since everyone wants to take more, and nobody gives. Everyone has a goal to rob his neighbor, and because of this there is always conflict between them. It's a common law, both for the small and large beings. Many want to live. Some are still with their fathers and explaining the kind of dreams they saw; others are in the second category—sold by their brothers in Egypt, in the court of that high-ranking palace guard, where they're exposed to his wife's temptations; the third kind are in prison. The best situation is to stand in front of the Pharaoh. But to stand in front of the Pharaoh, you must pass through three stages, which are three schools, three courses: the first is with the father; the second, with the wife that tests his chastity, and Joseph took the test very well—he left his garment and escaped clean. What does it mean to leave your garment? It means to leave your soul's shroud—the flesh. The world tells you like that woman, "come with me, I'm very beautiful; otherwise you'll go to prison." She tests you whether you'll be tempted or follow God's commandment. And you have to deprive yourself of all goods that seduce you, to overcome temptations and follow God's commandment. Trust in God; have faith in Him, and you can certainly expect a great future like Joseph. There can't be two opinions regarding this. I'm showing you here how one young man, who walks along the way shown to him by the Lord, rises from the position of an ordinary shepherd to the highest position in Egypt—not with thefts, lies, and murder, but with self-sacrifice in the face of sufferings and in keeping God's commandment. Therefore, the wisdom and knowledge you may have in your mind, the kindness you may have in your heart—only they can help you. Never deceive yourselves with external things that can entice your eyes, whatever they might be, black or blond. The state of your hands and face depends on your heart: whatever your mind and heart, that's the home you create; they're the *windows* you'll make in it. Through his mind and heart, man can always alter his outer social standing, from a poor man to become rich. But he'll only be able to alter it when complying with the Divine laws.

If we proceed to look at the second part of Joseph's character, when his brothers went to him, we see that he didn't take revenge, but wept with them and poured all his love for them. Therefore, if someone does us wrong in our lives, we shouldn't mete out to him the same measure. To think evil, to revenge, to gossip—that's not character. Forgiveness is character; only then can you rise to a degree of nobility. And we see this example in Christ: When he was on the cross and they mocked him, He said, "forgive them, Lord!" A time will come and they will ask you, "do you forgive those that brought you grief, who sold you?" A father told his son, "you will not become a man." The son went abroad to study. He returned and rose up in society, becoming a governor. His first task was to send several policemen to pick up his father, to bring him. The son asked him, "well, what do you think? Will I not become a man?" His father then said, "what you did—was it smart? Did you have to bring me here that way—to scare me? You are an unwise man who doesn't know what he is doing. You should have sent a carriage to bring me here." This is the method we use too; we want to scare people: "Let God give me power. I know how to rule—I'll hang them." The people used this method for thousands of years; everyone fights, and every home weeps. And is the world better off? Not at all. Only love can bring noble elements into the human soul. And punishment is used to the extent that love needs to uproot bad things. But the one who, via his surgical procedure, cuts healthy flesh, is not a smart surgeon, but stupid. Therefore, when you come into life, here is what you must do to observe the basic law: between your mind and heart there must be equilibrium.

Many doubt God's existence. Some of you will say, "we believe in His existence." But if they put you in Joseph's place, you would say, "if there is a God, He wouldn't have put me in prison. To take me from my father, my mother, and have my brothers sell me. Is that God? I don't believe." You must accept all suffering from God's hand, and when they come, you have to rejoice; sufferings are the stones on which you will put the stairs of your house. They will form your character; they are the thread that connects man and God. Only through them can one move from one world to another, a better one. And there is nothing better for your evolution in this world than suffering. Truly, you are averse to sufferings, but they are actually the greatest blessings. When a soul suffers a long time, the sufferings will give their fruit, and the soul will rejoice. If the roots of trees did not suck up the juices [of the earth], would we have sweet fruits? If the mother didn't suffer, if she didn't carry in her womb, would she have a child to give her joy? If the father didn't sacrifice his individual life, would he be happy? Can a teacher who doesn't make an effort expect to have students to respect him? Who, by laying on his back, was taken up to Heaven and placed there in a high position? From one end of the world to another, life is assembled only via suffering. They are like the chiseling of a sculptor who creates a statue. When we learn the deep meaning of suffering we will understand that it is a process that forms our character. And when we strike the last blows with our hammer, for the formation of our character, then we will end our anguish and the great statue of our life will appear. We prepare to go to Heaven. What will we take there? Our character, which is our wealth. You like being a beautiful man or woman, slender, with noble manners, but when you enter the world, what will the people say if your character isn't noble? Will they say that a person of virtue is expressed in your face? When one doesn't have a beautiful appearance, but has a good mind and a good heart, people cry, "here is a person with character." And that is the greatest praise the world can give us. If we have such a mind and such a heart, the world will need us. In Egypt, during Pharaoh's time, there were many eminent Egyptians. Why didn't Pharaoh put them first but chose a foreigner instead? For his nice features? No. For his mind and his goodness. If we are like him, the world will place us in the same position. If we are stupid, the world will also throw us out. The people of today rely on the opposite, saying, "one need not be virtuous, since virtue is foolishness." They don't know what they're talking about. Even foreign and strange things are taken on Easter. The character, however, will always remain with us as something of value. Today you find yourselves in the same exam-hall: You are worried like the Egyptians during Joseph's time. You don't know what to expect tomorrow. Fate, the future, is not in your hands. You can't predict how events will shape up. But fate would be in your hands if you have faith and trust in God the way Joseph did. Then you'll surely alter your fate, wherever you are, in whatever position they place you; like butter, you will float above water. The first thing is not to worry or be disturbed. You must have courage and determination, to be unafraid. Fear must give way to prudence. You should hesitate only when you haven't solved a certain question, whether it's right or not, but when you decide and believe it's right, you must surely announce it and assert it. Joseph addressed the question to the woman: "I cannot do this with you." Indeed, the bad consequences came: they caught him and put him in jail, but God was with him.

When building up your character, you need patience—it's the basis of things. And we see in Joseph's character great patience: he didn't worry at all in prison, but worked, learned, and was ready to endure anything. Patience is a trait of the character with which man is not born, but which is gained with effort. All sufferings in the world aim only to create patience in us, to teach us to endure, to be cool, to look upon the future with faith, and whatever discomfort and disappointment we have, to never be discouraged. A young woman may say, "my dreams are to marry according to my ideal [man]," but when she marries, she says, "my life is done." No, she's in the beginning stages of life. Some say, "I lost my money." So what? You're just beginning your life; you lost nothing. "I lost my health." You are beginning your life; you'll acquire new health. In whatever situation we find ourselves, we must endure and trust in God until the last minute. This faith must be ingrained deeply in everything. Some people want to be in good society, to be surrounded by nice people. Joseph, a foreigner, lived among strangers, but with his heart and mind he managed to find good friends among these people. But some say, "people are sinful." Make friends from these sinners—their souls are noble. The modern-day Christian says, "he's not a believer. He's still green." Well, unless he's green, can he ripen? Things that emerge from the earth are first green; they don't ripen immediately. Greenery is a process in which the juices are sucked up, and when they're absorbed, the ripening begins—"But he's insulting me that I'm green." It's very good that you're green. Nobody's insulting you. If you are a noble person, with hard work, one day you'll ripen. Whoever isn't green cannot ripen. If he's not green, he'll dry up, and there is no process of development in dryness. If you're green, I rejoice with you. Greenery is a noble trait. When you ripen, you'll turn yellow like gold. Everyone loves money, ripening. There are some people who haven't ripened. Do you know what money is? It means to be ripe. Life consists in a gradual development from greenery to ripening. This gradual process is called evolution in science, development. It's necessary, until everyone completes the process of development and acquires all knowledge and all the goodness of their hearts. When they acquire all these juices, God will send His grace and your fruits will ripen. Then the Lord will appear. When you're still green, He watches you from afar. When you ripen, He will surely come and pick your ripe fruits, because He needs them. When you begin to understand, to separate the essential from unessential things, the transient from the everlasting; when your character forms and becomes strong; when these fruits from your garden start ripening, then you'll be pulled out of prison and presented to the Lord of this world—to give your interpretation of the two dreams in life, and you will deliver the truth, not as prisoners, but as free men. Then the truth will be a wreath on your head, and the sheaves in the field will bow down to you, and the sun and moon, and the eleven stars of Heaven will greet you. And you will then understand the deep meaning of earthly life. Then God will appear, and the Kingdom of God will be established on earth.

Lecture held on 2 August 1914 in Sofia

THE LAW OF SERVICE

"Whoever serves me must follow me; and where I am, my servant also will be. My Father will honor the one who serves me."—John 12:26 (NIV)

Perhaps many will question themselves what meaning may be hidden in the words, "and whoever serves me, my Father will honor." The world has various aspirations: modern-day people aspire to gain knowledge, riches, lands, houses, honor, greatness, strength—they strive for many things. Jesus insists only on one thing: on service, for man to know how to serve. Servant: here is a prosaic word that depicts the lowest social position. But there are different servants: some are in breweries, in a pub, in some kitchen, in the theater, at the university, in the ministry, and so on. In a sense, everyone is a servant, but not all recognize this. So there are two types of servants in the world: the first kind, who understands his duties and knows how to do them, and others who don't know how to serve. We usually refer to the latter kind as *rulers*, who sit and wait for others to serve them, teaching others how to work and serve. Everyone wants to be in the first category as ruler. Christian doctrine, however, diametrically opposes this principle. It is precisely the principle that whoever wants to be a master must be a servant. It says that the Son of God didn't come to *be* served, but *to* serve. We are placed under the law of necessity to be servants. Someone says, "I'm the master."—No! He's deceiving himself if he thinks he's free, that he doesn't serve anyone. He serves his stomach at the very least, which puts him to work, making him fulfill tasks that may not always be pleasant—to cook really well and chew the food well enough, because, if he doesn't serve like this, the stomach will throw back the food and punish him, telling him, "you have to serve me well, otherwise I will fire you." Some think that only the master can fire his servants, but the stomach can also fire his master. Why don't you ask a doctor what the stomach does when you don't serve it well, just to see how he can fire his master. Service is a quality. How many misfortunes in the world stem from not knowing how to serve! When the mother learns to raise her children; when the teacher learns to teach his students; when the ruling powers learn to serve the population, to meet their needs, to create the laws necessary for their development—the world will have a different appearance than now. Today, modern civilization is placed in great trials: millions of people are called to serve in the army; some carry brushes, others put gunpowder in canons (firepower grenades); others carry small threads and when they stretch them out, they make an explosion; others keep horses: all this is a form of service. What fate awaits these servants? All these heads, legs, and arms will be dismembered, mixed up, and turn into a slurry. The people call this civilization, culture. With this, modern nations say, "we don't need God. Science will lift us up." But look at what it teaches us—to be callous, and to make guns and grenades. Yes, science brought us to this state, to make a dangerous experiment, and now Heaven tests us with service, which it commands us to fulfill. The world requires its own servants to serve, and God requires the same for Himself. Christ says, "whoever serves Me, My Father will honor." We are constantly trying to settle our affairs, and they always remain unsettled. We get sick, we call doctors to treat us, but death overtakes us regardless. We build a house, set up guards to protect our wealth, but they rob us anyway. Christ says, "you served this principle of yours for thousands of years, and you see the consequences. However, if you serve Me, you will find the meaning of your life." We have to serve like Christ, who didn't come to *be* served, but *to* serve. The people must serve the weaker, helpless ones. We mustn't let bad people serve the world. Do you know why modern society is spoiled? The mothers, who ought to raise and educate their kids themselves, leave this task up to spoiled and ignorant maids, while they themselves go to the theater, to balls, breweries, and other entertainment. What can the vulgar and indecent maids teach the children? Whatever they know. The maids raise today's kids, not just in Bulgaria, but in France, Germany, America—everywhere. I'm not saying all maids are vulgar, but the greater part of them are this way because of their masters. If mothers were servants (in the full sense of the word) to their children regarding their raising and upbringing, the world would have a different appearance. The same can be said if the father were to raise his sons. Since the father and mother let go of their duties and leave it up to vulgar and ignorant maids, who don't understand what life is about, to raise their kids, while they themselves go to enjoy worldly things, the results will be bad. The maid also cannot raise the child because she didn't conceive him and doesn't love him. She says to herself, "if the mistress of the house is at the brewery, why should I watch her kids?"

I will explain to you what service is, what qualities a servant must have: He must have, above all else, a noble heart; to be sensitive, responsive, humble, and to be flexible so he can adapt to all conditions. He must be industrious and not lazy. Life is demanding, and we must serve properly. When a modern-day tailor messes up a garment and cannot properly sew it, they return it back to him, and he pays for the cloth as well as all the losses. The same can be found in nature: it gives us cloth (the life we have is a type of cloth) and says, "assemble and sew this garment," and if we cannot sew well, it fines us. If we want to learn to serve, we must turn to Christ so He can teach us. The servant must be very wise: a stupid person cannot serve properly. The teachers and priests are servants too. If the teacher understands his vocation, he must first understand the *soul* of the child, to know how to guide the child towards knowledge. The priest has to understand the soul of his listeners, so he can give them the appropriate *food* for their hearts. We must possess another trait too: to have a lot of patience. Many people call patient people "bulls."

"He is," they say, "a bull." To be patient doesn't mean to be a bull. Patience is an act of reason. So we can withstand life's external adversities, we must have an inner balance of soul, heart, and mind. I'll tell you an example of a mathematician from previous centuries: He worked for 20 years on some calculations, which he kept in his room, written on small pieces of paper and scattered throughout, and always kept his door locked. One day he forgot to lock it. The maid went in to clean the room. Seeing many pieces of paper scattered on the floor, she picked them all up, threw them into the fireplace, and burned them, thoroughly cleaning the room. At one point the mathematician returns and asks, "where are the scattered sheets of paper?"—"I put them in the fireplace. Look at how it's now nice and organized."—"Do not do it again." This was the mathematician's answer. We serve like the maid, gathering the sheets of paper—"this is worthless, that's useless, now into the fireplace." That scholar, whose 20-year philosophical effort fell through, didn't act as we would have, but showed patience as an example: he didn't do something else, but just said, "do not do it again." Now you find yourselves in such a period: your house is open, the maid is gathering all the little papers. You'll see them one day burned in the fireplace, and when you find the house clean according to the principles of your maid, what will you say? I know there will be weeping: "Lord, am I the greatest sinner? Did you assign this destiny to me alone?" And we assume that we are people who understand the Divine Law! We must say, like that philosopher, "please, next time don't do it again." And, on our part, to take up the task of keeping our things organized, not to leave our room open to the fate of the servants.

Now Christ says, "whoever serves Me, my Father will honor." You constantly think of this world, about these transient things, wondering how to arrange your current family affairs, but you leave many questions unanswered, namely your relationship to your Master, Who will one day call you to give an account. And the day is coming. Do you know where you'll be in a few years? Do you know what will burst forth in Europe in this time? What will be the situation? You don't know. The modern-day world will be thoroughly *purified* and given a nice injection for creating a new life. The people coming to assist the civilization must apply Christ's principles, to learn to serve, and those who don't know how to serve thusly, as Christ wants, have no opportunity for development. Darwin's theory says that only the capable, healthy people survive. Indeed, only those who are *spiritually* and *morally* healthy will survive. And those with bodily health will also survive, if they have that inner, moral stamina. Do not deceive yourselves in thinking that health lies in the fattening of the face and body, in having a double-chin, a larger belly, to be plump, to eat more. How much food does a 100 kilogram person need to consume? I know of an English woman who ate 9 kilos of bread; another, who ate the bread and coffee prepared for 72 children. This is an unhealthy condition. I'm not against eating, but modern-day people think everything comes from eating. Indeed, it's one third of our lives, because from morning until night we only serve food: In the morning we think what to drink, whether to have tea or milk, whether to prepare the milk with cocoa in the German style, or with Turkish coffee, with froth or without. We barely finish breakfast and we're already thinking what to eat for lunch: will there be chicken or beef? With what will it be cooked? With tomatoes or zucchini? Should the meat be sliced? Will it have this-and-that? We finish lunch, then start thinking what to eat for dinner. Sometimes we feel satisfied, other times we don't. We are constantly modifying the food. Indeed, eating has turned into a whole cooking science, where people go to specialize. It's good, but it's not the ultimate goal in life. The power of a food that our stomach can use doesn't depend on how it's cooked. We shouldn't think that by adding more salt, pepper, or butter, the food will be healthier: this is all for our palate, for the mouth. To test whether a meal is good, we must see, when it sits in the stomach for half an hour, what will be the condition of the latter? If it feels a little heavy in the stomach, a little uncomfortable, the stomach is saying, "this food does not agree with your health. I can't secrete the necessary juices." Tomorrow we say, "why don't I add a little more, to boost the work," while the doctors say the stomach is enlarging. Contemporary people live exclusively for their stomach, and therefore their work is absorbed only by feelings and thoughts about it; the schoolteacher teaching at the school thinks how much money he'll earn—300 or 400 leva, and how much he will use for food and this-and-that. The whole question is placed on consumption, and afterwards we wonder why we can't progress as teachers and priests. We all seek to keep our body in a healthier state—the kind of food to eat, what kind of house to build for it: we all work for the outer state of things, but no one stops to think about the inner state of human life. Just as our home ought to be well-organized, so should our mind. If a sanitary home is useful for our body, then our heart must also be in the same sanitary condition. I don't regard someone as wise if he has a clean house but lacks the purity in his heart. So when we ponder over the extremities, we pay a lot of attention to serving only some outer things, when we ought to first and foremost pay attention to our mind and heart, and then afterwards to the body. If we establish our lives thusly, only then we will receive God's blessing.

Christ says, "if someone serves me, let him offer his heart." He came to earth to cultivate the human heart. In what does this cultivation consist? In all those rough defects in our lives to be removed. You've been Christians for a long time. You all follow Christ, but if He summons you over to test you now, how many of you would pass an examination on patience and humility? If He gave you the task, not only theoretically but practically; or on the other human virtues: Righteousness, Love, Truth, Wisdom. Do you think you wouldn't fail the exam? Whether others love you, that's on you; but whether you love others, you have not understood. If God requires us to love other people, in that love we must sacrifice ourselves. We often say, "those people ate me, they robbed me!" Well, didn't we rob the Lord, taking all those riches we found here on earth? Now God is descending to the earth and He tells all his servants who steal and lie, "that's enough stealing and lying! Now give an account of everything!" This is today's European war. God says, "give an account of what I gave you and how you used it." Many will say that economic conditions forced them into war: Germany has a little land and that's why it fights. If Germany has little land, do Russia and England have a little too? So it's not a question of land; there's something else missing in people. Everyone wants to become a master; every race that rises wants to domineer; every nation wants to reign over all other nations, and that's why they all come to a collision. If all people kept Christ's principle, to serve humanity; if everyone had his own sphere of work and would carry out his contribution to humanity, there would be no quarrels. Now everyone is armed to have dominion. We say, "how stupid they are to fight!" But what is happening now happens every day with us: enter a house and see what happens: two young people get together, decide to marry, and everyone is happy—"here's a couple that will live in peace and understanding." You see 2-3 months later the wife is disheveled, as is the husband. They fight at home: the wife wants dominion, and the man says, "I'm the master of the house." But they're both deceived; neither one, nor the other is master, but they're both servants. "But it is said that the man is the head." To be the head does not mean to be master. To be the head means to be a wise servant and as someone older than the wife, to teach her to serve, and for both to say, "we are servants to our Master. We may both be punished, but I will show you how this work should be carried out." This is an allegory, but it happens every day in the world. Let's leave the man and woman aside. Sometimes we are dissatisfied; we murmur against ourselves. Why? We say, "I have no will, I can't do this and that."—"Why don't you have the will? Aren't you your own master? What's the reason?"—"My mind is not working."—"Why can't your mind work? What's the reason for your mind to stop working? There must be some deep reason."

To what is this inner division in man attributed? It is due to the fact that we are in conflict with the Lord, with the Great Law. And whenever man comes into conflict with the Divine Law, inner turmoil rises up—this division; his mind is disturbed, he doesn't know what to do, and he's overwhelmed with bad thoughts and desires which don't constitute God's real power, and life takes on a different appearance. Do you know what bear trainers who teach bears to dance do? They give the bear a little bit of flour and put a giant ring around the lips, so when they pull, it will be obedient and not dangerous. We must put a little bite of food and a chain on the lower lip of *our* bear, and give it a little flour, so those dangerous instincts do not develop. Look at how many people go crazy over the desire to become rich: they gain a thousand, ten thousand, fifty thousand, one-hundred thousand, a million, ten million—they're unsatisfied. They gather and gather riches; what are they for? They have no inner meaning. To become wealthy, the people started learning new methods, through magnetism and suggestion to influence people, to affect their thoughts and actions. There was a time when bandits wandered through the forests with a rifle, now they're in the cities and carry with them other means for robbing their neighbors. They say that in New York three American hypnotists mentally suggested to a banker to sign a check for $15,000 and he gave the money. The methods for robbing have changed. Everyone wants to have this gift, this power in the world, but do you know the misfortune it brings? I gave this example another time too. In an old fable, it is said that a man wanted to have such power in his hands that whatever he touches turns to gold. He said to himself, "if I acquire it, it will be good for the whole world." An angel said to him, "if we heed your request, will you always be content?"—"It will be the greatest happiness for me."—"Let it be as you wish." And when he entered his house, the tables, books, cups—everything turned to gold. He went to the yard, and the stones, trees—they all turned to gold. He said to himself, "I will no longer be a servant, but a master. Woman, we are blessed people." The wife spread a feast, with soup, bread; and they called the children over to eat. The man grabs the spoon, it turns to gold; he reaches into the soup bowl, it too turns to gold; he grabs the bread, it too turns to gold; he touches the table, it turns to gold; he touches his wife, she too turns to gold. At one point he found himself in a dilemma and started praying that God save him from this great misery. Now you see how far greed and thoughtlessness can get you. We may have this power, but it will destroy our lives. Wealth is within us, not outside: it's not in our physical strength. Man's power doesn't reside in his muscles, but in that delicate and tender feeling which can develop all other abilities. And God created the world thusly, that nature obeys what appears to be the weakest visible power—Love. It is so tender and delicate, but actually controls everything. When Love enters man, it disassembles and transforms him. Take a man, who has beaten many maid-servants and man-servants. At one point, he softens and sacrifices everything to do good. What is the power that overcomes the man? That one principle that Christ describes: "Whoever serves Love, he serves Me." This is what Christ implies: "That servant will have everything I have." The people search for truth, and Christ put that truth in life, in that grain of mustard. If we put this leaven, Love, in our hearts and in the hearts of those close to us, to the rulers, it will transform the whole world. Disobedience to Christ's teaching created the current cataclysm in the world. In this collision and hitting, the Lord has put the milk in the can, and the people are turning up and down, until the butter rises to the surface. The milk will be used for eating, and the rest will remain as buttermilk. Some of it will turn to butter, the rest into buttermilk. The Lord will use both the butter and buttermilk for His purpose. Now, it depends on us where we end up, but the fate for most of us has been sealed—either in the butter or into buttermilk.

Christ turns to the Jews and asks which of them want to be His disciples. Some of them say, "I am a believer. I believe in Christ." Those who only believe in Christ are listeners. His question, however, is addressed to those who want to *apply* His law. If you could stop and think about the words, "I serve Christ;" if you could try for a full year to serve Christ, you would understand the great secret of these words, which cannot be spoken here. It's very simple, but you must have light. Christ must give you that light, the conditions required for its proper development. Only He can give it to you. I can give you little seeds, but the conditions required for their growth can only come from Christ. This feeling of love does not depend on our strength and desires. It depends on that contact we can have with Christ. Some ask, "where is Christ?" and expect Him [to come] from Heaven. Christ is already in the world, and the latter hear Him. He comes in two ways; He has two faces, one of which is kind—"I bring you peace," and the other is a scowl—with fire, guns, and cannons. Now He calls you: "Bring those who did not heed My teaching, to witness the bitterness of disobedience. They don't want to serve Me. Let them try all the bitterness of their deeds. Everyone must reap what he sows," just as we are unable to forgive a criminal who killed a bunch of innocent children, and we punish him.

Christ turns and says, "if anyone serves Me, let him follow Me." And you say, "it's easy to follow Him. We can follow Him and call Him 'Teacher,'" but He might reply, "you don't say this because you want My teaching, but because you ate the bread and fish." He will ask you, "have you helped a sick person? Did you cure him?" For a man to serve the Lord, he mustn't seek Him to serve *Him*, but his "smaller brethren." The people want God to make their wives and children healthy, to give them money and a high position. This is the form of service to God from the past 2,000 years. And now He asks Europe regarding this: "What have you done for Me after all these years?" And if Christ appears, what will you tell Him? Think about what you would tell Him regarding this—what you have done for Him. We can be calm during these events that threaten the whole world. It is important for us to know under what category we will fall. Many of you wanted to see Christ. The day is coming when you will see Him—some from up close, others from far away, and others only up in the clouds. And that's why I say: the moments you are experiencing are the most difficult for you. If, from now on, you have the illusion of achieving this or that, you are very much deceived. I'm giving you advice: in the short span of time that is left, learn to serve Christ, lest He find you unprepared. Do not think that there is still time. There is no time! For this entire generation there is no time. Children, elders, priests, rulers, and kings—all must learn to serve God; if not, they will turn to buttermilk. The milk is already drawn from the cow. What do you understand? What do you think I'm trying to tell you? That the milk is already drawn out of the flesh and that God is ready to remove the butter. All of us see this cow; the dairy cow—that's us. If the Lord has been calling us for thousands of years, how should He find us on earth when He returns? When the father returns and finds his children at home, pulling each others' hairs and fighting, what will he think?—That the mother did not raise them well. Everyone has some grudge against someone: the people are constantly judging; ordinary citizens, teachers, priests, liberals, conservatives, narrow and broad socialists; amongst religion and teachers and science—there is a division in views everywhere. But we have to convince ourselves to reject everything that poisons our life, and in that moment at least to be reconciled, to become quiet and still, to await with humility the great event that is coming. Until now, the people asked if there is another world or not. A moment is coming when the Heavens will say whether spirits exist or not, whether angels exist or not. In about a year you will see whether there is a God or not. You will see whether God can fix the world or not. If someone doesn't believe, let him wait and he'll see. I will not speak to you with arguments right now. The wise will understand what I say. Whoever doesn't want to will wait for some time in the future to learn again.

Now, the question for you: Christ wants all of you to serve Him. Those who want to be His disciples must serve Him in a broad sense: Let them serve those who are suffering, people who are disturbed, saddened, to lift their spirits. Some people are in despair and they're asking themselves, "what will happen to us?" Show them the real way. I will give you an example and conclude. A traveler stops to check in at one of the big hotels in the city of New York. He enters a room in which there is another traveler who had the habit of sleeping very deeply. During the night the hotel caught on fire. One of the travelers got up and went to the sleepy one, saying, "get up! The hotel is burning." The other replied, "get away. Let me sleep in peace."— "Get up, I tell you! The hotel is burning," the first one insisted. The other one got up and threw him out, closed his door, and continued sleeping. The fire consumed the hotel. Finally, they see him on the roof, screaming for help, but there's nobody to help him. And I tell you: this hotel, in which you live temporarily, is burning, and I advise you—save yourselves, because then you'll climb up on the roof and call for help, but nobody will be able to help you. When they tell you the hotel is burning, dress and go outside. Everything that burns will collapse. All those things that hindered human progress will collapse, and then, on top of the rubble the Lord will build something good. Do not think that life will end. An epoch is coming, more advanced than the one we had until now, and we can happily await this bright future. From these storms, which are coming to disinfect, to purify the world, we mustn't be afraid at all. We have to thank God they're coming. And there is no reason to try and stop them, not that we can stop them at all. They'll pass and bring their good tidings. We just have to be ready when Christ comes, Who *is* [indeed] coming. For some He has already come, for others He is yet to come. When He comes to tell us, "whoever serves Me, let him follow Me," to follow Him. Will you follow Him or not? In that following you will find the ideal of the individual, of the home, of society, of the nation, and all of humanity: it's the meaning of human life here on earth.

Lecture held on 27 July 1914 in Sofia

THE IMPORTANCE OF SMALL THINGS

"See that you do not despise one of these little ones. For I tell you that their angels in heaven always see the face of my Father in heaven."—Matthew 18:10 (NIV)

Generally, people from both genders aspire toward great things, toward big things. Everyone, due to an inner weakness, despises small things. They give you a *stiver*[1] coin, you say, "it's worthless. If it were a thousand, ten, one-hundred thousand I understand, but a stiver? Am I a beggar?" When we strive for big things, we seek acquaintance with high-ranking people; with kings, prime ministers, chiefs of staff, scholars, philosophers. For lower-standing people in society we say, "he's ignorant, a simpleton!" From one end to the other, in our life we see contempt for little things and search only for big things. But Christ turns to his disciples and warns them not to despise the little ones. Why? "Do not despise them because you offend their angels who serve them in Heaven. If you despise these little ones, you despise the angels who guard their little ones like their own children." When we want to cut down a tree, we first lodge small sharp wedges, and when they open the tree up they make way for bigger ones. If the wedges are large and dull to begin with, how will they cut into the tree? So, little things make way for larger ones. And in the world the entire process of development begins with these little things you despise; all the progress in this universe is owed to them. We say that the wooden plough feeds the whole world, that when the plowman plows the field well and sows

---

1   A coin of very small value.

it, it becomes very fertile. This is so, but we shouldn't forget the role of those billions of worms who also plow the field. Because we are brought up to despise the weak, as Christians, we carry under the sheepskin the instincts of a wolf. And once in a while under that innocent garment we show our nails: we haven't forgotten our old habits. If someone takes even a penny from us it becomes a court decision. If he steals five to ten thousand leva—"Ah, bravo!" we say. But the one who steals a lot didn't acquire this habit at once. First he took a stiver from his father, then a copper coin, then a penny, five pennies, ten pennies, and so on. This law is true in every respect. When we despise small causes, we make way for great consequences in the work at hand. I can say that all our current misfortunes, societal and personal, are due to that contempt for small things in the past. And that's why Christ turns to his disciples and tells them not to despise "those little ones." Now, what are the "little ones?" Maybe someone might say they are our children. It's true that they are our children. But when it comes down to fully applying Christ's law, we see there are many things that shouldn't be despised. "Do not despise these little ones!" I will explain the meaning hidden in these words. A Hindu gives his son a walnut and tells him to study it. The son breaks the walnut and eats it. "What is contained in the walnut?" the father asked. "Nothing special. Some nuts, pleasant-tasting." The Hindu asks his son again: "Didn't you find something else in the walnut?"—"Nothing."—"Son, great power is hidden in that walnut and if you didn't eat it, but planted it in the ground instead, a big tree would have grown from this small thing, which is the seed of a great thing." The Lord sends you a small thought, an apple seed, you say, "it's nothing," and throw it away. But God says, "see what power it holds. Plant it, and you will see what tree will grow from it." It is precisely because of this constant contempt for small thoughts that we have come to this state and say the world is bad. And we are the smartest!

Christ says, "do not despise these little things. Do not strive for big things. Learn to recognize what power lies in small things and use them. They will help you acquire bigger ones." Aren't your houses composed of small, microscopic grains, compressed together? On these little things—like the grain of wheat, fruits, and other things—our daily life rests. This is in relation to the body, but also in relation to the mind: small thoughts and desires cause happiness and joy in life. Sometimes we laugh at children, because they're entertained by little thoughts. Not the thoughts, but the *grains* that help in the development of great things—they are small.

And why should we avoid contempt for the little ones? Because we shouldn't overstep God's second commandment, to "love thy neighbor." Any living creature that has a relation to someone, and benefits him, shouldn't be despised. That creature may be a pigeon, a chicken, a sheep, a bull, a horse, a donkey; for every one of them there is a book where it is written, "today you loaded your donkey with this much, tomorrow with that much." It's written there, and when God calculates 5 leva per day for the donkey, in 100 years, let's say, it will have served you all your life. What surplus will you have to pay it? One day you will find yourself like that debtor whom you owe 10,000 talents. You'll say, "I don't remember," but God wrote in the book that you owe this much. So we all owe these little ones. Our current development, our current thoughts, our current desires are owed to these little ones of whom Christ speaks. And, consequently, since we owe them, we must love them, knowing that they worked for us and we must now work for them. And I'll say something in regards to a conundrum. I am often asked, "why do the angels care about people? What connection lies between them?" One time, when the angels were in our place, as people on earth, we were in the position as animals who served them. They owe us a lot, and now God makes them repay us. Also, the more advanced angels do not despise their smaller brothers, because the latter worked for them. You may have an ignorant servant, but you don't know the relationship between the servant and yourself, why the Lord brought him to your home. Your connection with him is not from now. This servant has been in your home many times. You don't know, but God knows. He, perhaps, saved your life many times from destruction. Therefore you must have all the love and kindness for him. And then we can explain the great Divine Law—to have love for the smaller ones. Love is not for great people, for the angels, or for the saints; it's for the small ones, the tiny ones, the poor, the fallen brothers. This is why the mother develops such a strong love for the child. She loves him by virtue of this Divine Law, which states that she has to love him. She loves him just as he is, because of that internal fire, because the Lord entered into him incognito. You want to see the Lord, but when He comes in this child you say, "why, Lord, did you give me this child?" You cry to the Lord every day, and you chase Him away every day. And you call yourselves smart people! You're not the only ones who have this attitude, but the whole world does too. The Lord tests your mind every day, to see how much you love Him and whether you speak the truth. One time, when the world turned corrupt, word got out that the Lord walked on the earth to see how the people live. The latter said, "there is no Lord in Heaven anymore, so there is nobody to restrain us. We can live more freely." God sees a person somewhere, selling a blind horse, telling the buyer, "believe for God's sake, it's not blind."—"Since you trust in God, I will believe," and buys the horse. God walks past a house and sees a man demanding from his wife: "For God's sake, forgive!" He forgives her. These two appear in Heaven afterwards and say, "we, Lord, preached Your name on earth." So modern-day people call the Lord when they want to sell a blind horse, or when they want to beat their wives. The priests cry, "believe in the Lord," but what will God say to them? "I don't know you, because you used My name not for My glory, but to lie to the people, to commit some transgressions and to cover them." It's these small things that create misfortunes. You have a blind horse and want to sell it in

God's name, but watch carefully and be accountable for what you are doing. Do you know what this blind horse means? It's your body, and the people are constantly accusing it, and punishing it. Everyone says it's corrupt. The body is not at fault. Someone got drunk at the pub and said, "don't feed the horse." He's doing wrong, but punishes the horse. Don't despise the body and don't mix up the flesh with your desires, your lusts. You must renounce *them*, not the flesh, because that would mean renouncing every thought and desire that happen through *it*. And you shouldn't torment your body, this temple created by the Lord. Therefore, you must be very kind to your body, because while it's healthy, you can work.

Now, when Christ says, "their angels," he's implying those wise beings who hold us accountable for our actions. What we call "conscience" are those angels who live in us and mark every act—good or bad—and who say, "you did well," or, "you did wrong." You insult someone and his angel tells you, "your act was unrighteous." You start apologizing: "But excuse me, I was a little nervous, ill-disposed; these were the conditions." That you are in that state has nothing to do with the rule that you should not despise these little ones on which the Divine Laws rest.

These small things can sometimes bring great benefits, as well as great harm. A wolf told everyone he was a hero and, among the animals, that he's a king. The fox told him, "don't boast so much, because if a mosquito enters your nose, it will sting you and you can't do anything to it."—"When I blow with my nose, it will fly out," the wolf replied. One day, a mosquito entered his nose, stung him, carrying a disease with it, and the wolf died. And in our lives, small causes, in one respect or another, may contribute to our development, but they may stumble us too. The causes that make us good or bad are not bad in themselves; their *use* is bad. Take the air as an example: if you put it in the lungs, it will purify the blood, and the person will feel good from this purification. But if you put it in the stomach, it will cause a stomachache; the same thing in both cases produces two opposite reactions. If you put charcoal in the stomach in a dissolved state it will feel nice, but if you put it in the lungs, it will poison. Consequently, under these little things, of which Christ speaks, that we shouldn't despise, He understands human life as a whole, with which we are closely connected. For instance, if I asked you: Can you say how your body, your heart, and your mind took form? Can you say how these things happened? Originally, when man appeared on earth, he wasn't huge, but microscopic. But, under some conditions he developed and became a man who is now a million times bigger than he used to be. His power was initially hidden in the fetus. In the same way, in our modern life, *thought* holds a great Divine foundation, and if it falls on good soil, *it* can revive our lives. What we refer to as "revival," exists as a law of the spirit. It is that inner Divine process that uplifts and renews the human heart, human mind, human soul, and human spirit. This is a process of rising from the bottom and moving upwards. And in that Divine aspiration, we produce our rising, deliverance, and salvation. This is why all beings, from the biggest to the smallest, strive to renew themselves, to rise. And in youth is hidden the flowering of the human soul.

When we say we shouldn't condescend the little ones, it stems from the principle of not hurting the Lord, because when we hurt someone, we don't hurt just him, but the Lord who is in him. And even when we do good, we help the Lord. When we help someone, his angel in Heaven will be at our service. Therefore, if we want to have friends in Heaven, we must serve the little ones, and their fathers (the angels in Heaven) will take us into their home and will offer their hospitality. We'll feel at home; a favor for a favor, love for love—that's the world.

Now, do you know why Christ stated this idea to His disciples? Contempt: this state must be driven out of your soul. For example, you meet a person you don't know; contempt arises in you, because he might stand lower than you. If you only believe ignorantly but help him it's a different matter, but if you despise, you poison. Contempt gave birth to modern-day aristocracy and the castes: some are nobles, others aren't; some are rich, others are poor. If we understand the relationship between things, we will see that we should not be ashamed of poverty because it is a position given to us to carry out: we have to be small, we have to be poor, so we can become rich. They are two opposite poles, among which lies development. And the movement is always from the bigger to the smaller, i.e., the Lord always strives for the little ones. He doesn't bother with great things. He made the world, but managing the whole world doesn't give Him as much pleasure as working with the children. His job is, when He sees people doing wrong, to teach them. And with this He gives us an example too—not to despise the little ones, but to endure and teach them—that's our rest. When a teacher deals with his students, it makes him happy, and he praises the students when they learn. The saints and priests deal with sinners, to turn them to God. And the task for most of us is to turn our attention to the weak people and small things. When someone says, "I can't get any rest," I understand that he's dealing with big things, big thoughts. How can he rest if he puts on his back a backpack too heavy to carry, with 10, 20, or 50 kilos of gold? When he leaves just a *napoleon* in the bag, he will see how [restful he will feel]. And now God comes to say, "put the backpacks down!"—to free the world from them. Down with the weapons, which destroy your minds and hearts. "You must become as children, not to despise the little things that I created." The Lord wants to turn back the people to that pure, original state, which people call "div,"[2] but which is not actually wild. I wish for the people to become wild like this; "div" in Sanskrit means "pure." Let's become pure and get closer to God, instead of becoming coarse and evil. I

---

2   The word "div" is a phonetic translation of the Bulgarian word "див," which means wild.

would like the whole world to become wild sooner, to become pure, noble, not to despise small things that God loves, and to put Love, Righteousness, Wisdom, Truth, and Strength on that high place where they should stand. Therein lies salvation.

Lecture held on 3 August 1914 in Sofia

PEACE BE WITH YOU

"On the evening of that first day of the week, when the disciples were together, with the doors locked for fear of the Jewish leaders, Jesus came and stood among them and said, 'Peace be with you!'"—John 20:19 (NIV)

Immortality: this is the aspiration of the human soul, an ideal for which it strives and constantly wants to fulfill. The human soul lives on earth to find the path to immortality. Immortality is governed by a great Divine Law, a law that man must examine and apply in all areas of his life. And, in this sense, we must constantly learn to find the conditions in which immortality can exist. One can be immortal and lose his immortality; one can also be a mortal and gain immortality. Death and immortality: these are two conditions. In scientific language, immortality is the equilibrium of things, of the forces that act in nature. Death is the loss of this equilibrium. Immortality holds unification and harmony within; death—disunity, disagreement, disharmony. When people desire immortality, they must know exactly what it contains within itself. When you enter a modern-day concert hall to listen to a symphony orchestra, if you have the ability to observe, you will see that first and foremost, when the musicians come with their instruments, which are mostly stringed, they remove them from their cases, after which they tune the violins, determining the tone of the strings, some of which are tightened more, others less. And after they tune their instruments according to a general tone, then they pick up the bow and start playing. Do you know how long it takes for a violinist to enter a symphony orchestra, to be able to master his instrument, his bow?

He must dedicate at least 12 years of special training. In Bulgaria they usually say that whoever plays the violin is a gypsy—that's the byname for violinists. But that instrument holds a special emblem. We can say that the violin is the most perfect instrument which, in the 300 years since the great craftsman, Stradivarius, created it, has not been modified, because it has almost reached its perfection. The violin can be likened to the human soul: it has four strings and a bow. The violin *is* the human soul. The strings: these are the four human *temperaments*. The human *will* is the bow. When a violinist goes to buy strings, he'll say, "give me such-and-such a string: 'Mi, La, Re, or Sol,'" and when he returns home he knows where to put each individual string. In human nature there are, as we said, four temperaments: choleric, phlegmatic, sanguine, and nervous; these are four states in man. They correspond to the human soul, mind, heart, and life. These are four main strings that we must know how to wind up and loosen. And when we tune our mind and our heart, we have to know how to tune them in the same tone. On the violin, the four strings are tuned to four different tones, and between each string there are also four different tones; that is, each subsequent string is tightened four tones higher than the preceding one. When you tune the whole violin, you have 4 X 4 = 16 tones—*steps*, on which the strings are set. When the violinist tunes his violin, he takes the bow and starts playing. And the violin is the only instrument which is played on a cross, an instrument that creates the most pleasant music, which, with its tones, comes closest to the human voice. Therefore, when you tune your violin and take the bow, you form that cross, from which you now constantly weep and say, "why, Lord, did you give us this heavy cross?" I tell you that the Lord has given you a wonderful tool, but you don't know how to tune it, and that's why you carry it on your back as a heavy load. Get it down and start tuning it to play. And when apostle Paul says, "I will praise the cross," what do you understand? I see people who carry these crosses everywhere. I see them in churches and everywhere else, but

I haven't seen someone play on his cross. You go to a concert hall and see that people clap for playing on the cross, without perceiving that they too have crosses—sufferings, that they also play.

But the most important thing in this cross-playing is keeping tempo. When the conductor lifts his baton and waves it around, everyone must take heed and be guided by him. And the movement of bows gives us some pleasure, because the bows move according to certain rules. So when we reach the deeper meaning of life, when we tune its strings—the mind, heart, soul, and life—and when we put the bow to work (the human will), through the Spirit of the conductor, who will lift his baton, we will create the most pleasing music in our lives. Notice that the cross is a great blessing with which the Lord visits us on earth; the greatest symphony, music, and singing, which is called salvation, comes from *it*. In *that* singing is salvation. When Christ was suffering on the cross, the angels above, in Heaven, didn't cry, but they sang. All the prisoners in hell were glad that their Savior was coming. Also when He was born on earth, the angels came to announce His coming, again with singing. So, when this instrument appeared, these strings, this bow—our faith, the angels sang above in the Heavens. The modern-day Christian says, "woe to us! The earth is a weeping-place. Life is a burden. There is no meaning." For stupid people, who do not know how to tighten their strings, who do not listen to the conductor—for them, life is truly without meaning. But for those who can tune their violins and play, for them life has much meaning. And the violinists who play so wonderfully get a very big salary: 4, 5, 6, 7, or 1,000 leva a month, just by moving the bow. Christ often comes to you and asks, "do you know how to play?" When I ask someone, "do you know how to suffer?" I mean, "do you know how to play?" You don't want to suffer; that means you don't want to play. Those who don't know how to play are grim. I have no hope for them. They say, "a man who sings and plays, thinks no evil." A man who suffers means he sings and plays in life and is saved. Does a violinist, who plays, ever go hungry? Whoever doesn't know will end up begging. Whoever knows and sits somewhere to play, he gets paid a salary from the people. Whoever knows how to suffer will never go hungry. And notice: people also rush to help someone who suffers, just as they give to the violinist. When I stand and listen how someone plays, while others just watch the bow move, I also hear the voice of the violinist and see if he knows how to play or whether he is just now learning. If he's still learning, he's a novice; he's just now taking lessons, but in 12 years he'll be in a symphony orchestra, and then you'll pay a lot for a ticket to listen to him.

Now, when we learn that great law, to sing and play, as we say in the modern language, or to suffer, in the Christian sense (these words mean one and the same to me). Through suffering we will encounter that great law, immortality. It holds all the harmony; it has no disharmony. Christ, who came to earth, came to teach people how to sing and play. He will teach you how to tighten the strings of your soul. The soul's string is "Mi," the highest string; of the mind, "La;" of the heart, "Re;" of life, "Sol." This is the first lesson that Christ will give you. Many times people ask themselves, "why did God give me this good-for-nothing heart?" Is your heart defective, or are *you* defective? They say, "why did God give me this stupid mind?" Is the mind stupid, or are *you* stupid? "Why did the Lord give this meaningless life?" Is life meaningless, or do *you* not know why it was given? Sufferings: these are the laws through which God acts upon our development. We have to sing and play—to feel and think. To think means to play; to feel means to sing. Now, if two neighbors tune their violins and start playing, it will be very pleasant. A year ago I visited a family: the father, the wife, the son, the daughter— they all played. The father played the violin; the son, the bass, and so on. They all have something to do. Most modern-day people—the husband, wife, and children, don't know how to play and when they have nothing to do, they start fighting. For them, of course, life is meaningless. Christ says, "tune your violins, pull your bows, learn to play!" When you gather in the evening, start playing or singing a song in tempo, then another, a third, a fourth. Eat, start again; go to sleep. The next day: start life's work, then again.

Now you'll say, "how does this relate to Christ's resurrection?" The modern-day Christian considers the question of the resurrection and says, "when I go to Heaven, I will learn everything." That's for the other world. But what should we do in *this* world? Therein lies the illogical nature of people's thoughts. Regarding this world, we're very smart, but in regards to the other one we're not. When a young man wants to study at a university, can he fly away from his house and enter directly into it? First he must pass primary school, then go through the departments, high-school classes, to prepare to understand higher education, and finally he can enter the university. Now, why did God send us to earth, and what is it? It's a primary school, a department of a school which we must pass through. If we don't pass, how can we get into any classes? When we go to the other world, do you think they'll accept us in their classes? No way! The word "resurrection" holds a great concept within itself. It holds Divine secrets. To resurrect means to be the master of all elements, all forces, all thoughts, all desires, all of one's actions. And how can someone rise when he's not the master of all these things? When a frog, or a little snake scares you, how can you be ready for a resurrection? When you cannot bear even the smallest pain here on earth, and serve the Lord, how can you rise? If a violinist has to spend 12 years, 1-10 hours of hard work per day, just to learn to play, how much should we Christians play to learn Christ's resurrection? One of the weaknesses of the modern-day church lies in thinking that everything can be obtained freely. The Lord can give us a violin, strings, and a bow freely. He can even give us a teacher and pay for him as well, but we'll have to spend 10 hours a day to learn to play: the effort must comes from us. And whoever cannot exert himself is a lazy person, incapable, undeserving of Christ's Kingdom.

When Christ tells his disciples, "peace be with you!" if I could interpret this phrase in its broad sense, it means the same as when the conductor takes a symphonic aria, waves the baton, and everyone at once listens and starts playing. And when Christ says, "peace be with you!" everyone must prepare with his violin, his bow, and listen to this Divine tempo, which continually moves from one end of the world to the other. Everyone sings and plays before the Lord; He inspects them. The one who didn't learn to sing curves his mouth. Weeping: it's crooked singing. In laughter the mouth lifts up a little, but in weeping it curves down. The one who weeps is young: He still hasn't learned to sing. And so, weeping is crooked singing, which, in fact, is preparation for good singing. It's not bad to weep, because after awhile this weeping will turn into very good singing, but it's hard for man. We must be lenient; he will eventually learn to sing.

With that new energy, which Christ brought to the earth with His resurrection, He showed the way for this Divine art, salvation. And that's precisely why we must study the Gospels diligently. You say, "I don't understand this, I don't understand that. This is useful, that's not useful. This is right, that's not right." I ask: What's right? Some people don't want to suffer, don't want to sing. Others don't want to work. What, then, do they want? Weeping is an exercise: it's a process that leads to singing. The pickaxe also has its own tone. To work with a pickaxe, picking it up and putting it down—it means to beat a drum. And the drum needs to be played. You lift the axe and set it down: it's the bells in music. And when you lift the pickaxe and dig, you have to think too. You have to say to yourself, "the Master is watching me. I need to know how to set this pickaxe down rhythmically." Chop wood, but chop it according to all the rules in art. We say, "this is pointless, that's pointless." Then what has meaning in life? The smallest visible works, of which we give the least importance, hold the greatest meaning within.

Resurrection is a process carried out in our lives by the Spirit of God—a grand process through which God restores that original harmony. One day, when your ears open and you begin to hear a little more, and from further away than you can hear now (they're very thick now). You don't even have musical ability. You catch only the crudest tones. You'll notice that certain tones move through the entire universe, which some objects, like the wellsprings, trees, and leaves give out. And you will hear a great music that travels from one end of the world to the other, and then you'll understand the inner meaning of life. And Christ, through His resurrection, wants to bring you to that concert hall. He will pay for you: He will give you a ticket, but will you have the ear to grasp this Divine music when you enter the hall and see the concert, the playing? This is the inner, deep meaning of Christ's resurrection. This is the life that develops among the angels, from the lowest to the highest. This Divine manifestation is everywhere in the world, and because we can't find that inner link, we assume there's no connection between all phenomena. And when you hear the words, "peace be with you!" you must be ready for whatever the conductor will command you to play. Will you sing or cry? When the Lord lifts his baton and says, "peace be with you!" the husband, who doesn't know how to sing, starts yelling, and his "singing" is then called beating. And he's beating the drums, but he's hitting them the wrong way. The wife sometimes beats the drum the wrong way too. The Lord says, "you haven't learned to beat the drum. You're not playing such-and-such a tone correctly. You haven't fixed your voice. Tighten the strings of your life, of your soul a little more." Then He says again, "peace be with you!" and you start to play…"Wait! You're not placing the fingers on the violin correctly," He'll stop you again. You'll say, "I'm tired already!" But you have to understand that artistic ability is acquired with great patience and hard work, and that there is no Heaven for lazy people. That's why the Lord says, "if you don't become receptive like children, you will not enter the Kingdom of Heaven," because children have the desire to study things, but adults say, "we don't need this, we don't need that," and finally they hunch over like a question mark, the earth pulls them down, and they get buried under it. The Lord says, "because this violin isn't well-made, put it down and re-make it." They will re-assemble it, and it will come back into the world to start learning again. The Lord decided that every one of you must learn to sing and play. He doesn't want children in Heaven who don't want to learn to sing and play. And apostle Paul says he went to the third Heaven and heard something ineffable which cannot be put into human language. He heard singing and playing. John also said he heard singing and playing.

This is the thought I want to leave you with: Do you know the *fundamental* tone of your soul? Do you know how to tune your violin? Learn to tune it. Every morning, when you get up, tune your nervous system. You are a little upset, worried: that shows that your violin is out of tune. Stop, tune it. And like that, when you tune it gradually, your worries will disappear. How will you tune your nervous system? You'll go and pray; prayer is tuning. Some ask, "why should we pray?" To tune your violin. If you tune your violin this way, you'll say to the Lord, "my violin is in tune," and the Lord will say, "start your work for the day." And peace will enter in your midst, and your work will go well. And some days the woman doesn't tune her violin well, so she starts beating this child, then the other one; of course, that day the music is not going well. She says, "why did God give me these kids? They're so ill-behaved." Are the kids misbehaved or the mother? It's questionable. Another day, when her violin is tuned, everything goes well, but the kids are just the same, so there's something out of tune. That's why the first thing we should do in the morning is to pray, to tune our mind, our heart, our soul, our life, and to appear before the Lord like this, ready for work. We should be thankful and say, "today we learned our lesson in singing and playing well, and when our Father returns, He will be grateful to us." Christ came to see how we sing and play on earth. He's nailed to the cross, and 500 million people today sing and play on this cross, which, since He came, gave a perfect civilization.

And so, Christianity is Divine music, Divine singing. Learn to sing and play *it*. Tune your violins well, move the bow correctly, and listen to the conductor's commands. The whole world will follow this Divine Law, and you'll prepare yourselves for the next world, the other life that is about to come.

Lecture held on 11 September 1914 in Sofia

THE NEED TO KNOW GOD

"Now this is eternal life: that they know you, the only true God, and Jesus Christ, whom you have sent."—John 17:3 (NIV)

Life is the most natural and strongest pursuit of the human soul; this is the wealth [the soul] wants to acquire. This aspiration exists not from now, but from thousands and millions of years, and not only in man, but in the other mammals as well, in birds, in fish, and even in plants. The difference is only in the methods for obtaining life in these various beings.

When it comes to man's aspiration for life, which affects us, it's important for our development. You enter, for instance, a music school, not just to listen, but to learn. They give you a violin, they give you a bow, they attach strings on the violin, they teach you how to tune it, they give you a teacher to teach you the basic rules of music, and you start exercising your mind, your hands, and your fingers. And in this way, in the course of time, you master the art of an excellent violinist. By the same law, the Lord wants to teach us the method, the way to attain life. At one time, man possessed eternal life, but he lost it. He lost it for a simple reason, and now he's trying to make up for his mistake. This error caused death, and only when one begins to experience the constant destruction of his spirit, his mind, his heart, his organism, and everything he builds, only then does he understand what he lost.

In the first chapter of Genesis, it says that God put man in paradise and told him to cultivate the land and use everything in it, but he forbade him to go near only one tree, the tree of knowledge of good and evil. Man, however, wanted to experiment with disobedience, and in this attempt, it was the woman who started first. It is said in this chapter that the snake coiled around the tree of knowledge and began conversing with Eve, asking her, "how can you, as masters of paradise, who use all the trees here, not use the tree which holds a great secret within itself?" The woman asks, "what secret?"—"If you eat from this tree, you will have the knowledge of God, you will know why you live, you will know good and evil, you will be very powerful on earth, as powerful as God." And at that moment, the woman becomes vain and says to herself, "my strong desire is to become like God," and plucks off the forbidden fruit, tastes it, and then goes off to convince her husband, and he also tastes it. And as a result, the Scriptures say that they both became naked, they saw themselves naked. When do people become naked? A wealthy father dies and leaves his son money, farmlands, and forests. The son befriends some people, begins a life of leisure and festivities, spends everything and ends up naked. He doesn't end up naked just like that, but from eating, drinking, and laziness. This leads us to the idea that Adam and Eve ate from this tree for a long time, and they're starting to rely heavily on paradise, then the Lord tells them, "what are you relying on? Is this your property? Get out right away! From now on, with labor and sweat on your forehead you will earn your living, so you can learn this great law, to appreciate the life I give you." Man can easily become impoverished. An American millionaire, the father of whom left an inheritance of 20 million dollars, had a weakness for flowers. He began collecting all kinds of flowers from every corner of the earth, even sending a special expedition for some especially rare flowers. A couple decades later he spent everything he had, and when he died, his funeral was financed by the local municipality.

You'll ask, "how can someone lose his life?" I will tell you how: You have a son, healthy and sound, educated in a foreign country, but an idea rises in him to become great and glorious, to attain the Georgian cross. He says to himself, "I will go to fight for glory," and he goes. A bullet hits him; he gets the glory, but loses his life. Adam and Eve wanted this type of cross, and God sent them to the battlefield. They exit paradise, try to conquer the world, but lose their eternal life.

Now let's go back to Christ's thought. Spending money, losing one's life, we know that. But to gain back our life—we don't know. Christ came precisely to teach us how to attain the life we lost. I will expound particularly this idea for you. Christ says, "I am the life." How does life differ from other forces? It's a force that builds, elevates, combines, unifies, gives joy and happiness to the human soul. In the last verse from the chapter that I read to you, three words are important: "life," "knowledge," and "God." Life is the goal we seek, knowledge is the method for achieving that goal, and God is the environment or the conditions from which we can obtain this life. This question has a double meaning. I can illustrate for you its purely philosophical side. I can explain its biological origin, its physiological or psychological manifestation, and so on. But that will be of no benefit to you. If I don't give bread to a hungry person, but start explaining how the bread is prepared, the kind of flour it's composed of, the woman who kneads it, how she baked it, the kinds of elements in it, how the chemists found them in their labs, and so on, the person will say, "I'm hungry. Let me eat. I don't need to know that a woman kneaded it. That it has such-and-such elements, I also need not know. The only thing that interests me now is satisfying my hunger, then afterwards I can listen to your explanations about these things." We'll also say to the philosopher, "we need not know the elements that make up life, how and from what it's composed, how it originated. We want to eat, to feed on eternal life, then afterwards we can discuss these things with you as much as you wish. Now we want to liberate ourselves from this death." And I think this is the proper solution to the question.

How can you acquire eternal life? You haven't lived yet. You think you live, and you say, "I live." You really have life, but it's not yours. It's a life *loaned* out to you. Tomorrow, the one you owe will show up, presenting the policy of your debt. He'll throw you in jail and take your life. They'll put you on a stretcher, and along the way he'll just come to confirm the sentence by reading you a prayer for peace, so the Lord will remember you in His Kingdom, that is, to be merciful toward you. After that, the singers will sing the assigned song and they'll bury you. What does it mean to bury a person? It means to lock him down in the dungeon to pay off his debt. Anyone who, instead of going to pay off his debts, goes off to search for the Georgian cross, will be buried in the earth to pay off his debt first, to learn to acquire his life. Everyone cries when one of their relatives dies, but crying doesn't save. The one who needs to collect from us will have no mercy, no matter how much we cry, but will say, "pay the debt." Now, it's necessary to understand the basic law of life to liberate ourselves from death. I will give you an example to clarify this. During Bulgaria's slavery, at the time of the janissaries, a Turk, Dahlia Pekhlivanin, conquered an entire area and kept the inhabitants in fear and trembling. Whoever and wherever he caught, he beat, shook, wounded, and killed. He boasted everywhere with this, by keeping the *gyurs*[1] frightened. None of the local population dared to raise their voices. Everyone prayed to God to release them from this evil. All the men carried the marks of the Turkish Dahlia. But nobody dared to lift his head. Everyone carried his own yoke out of fear. One day, a young Bulgarian shepherd was passing through this place, [looking] neat and well-dressed, with a staff in his hand. Entering a forest, the Turkish Dahlia saw him from afar and called: "Hey, *gyur*, stop! Who gave you permission to pass through here?"—"I'm a shepherd. I'm passing through here with my flock."—"Why don't you throw that staff down."—"But I'm bringing it to you as a gift. It's full of gold. My grandmother said that my grandfather

---

1   A "gyur" is a derogatory word the Ottoman Turks used to refer to Bulgarians.

got it from Heaven. It never lied to me and guides me along the way."—"Look at that stupid *gyur*, what nonsense he's speaking! I'll show you from what Heaven it came from, from yours or ours! I'll stick it in your head!" But the brave shepherd broke Pekhlivanin Dahlia's sword in two with the first blow. With the second blow, his right arm completely drooped. The third blow broke his left leg in two, and Pekhlivanin Dahlia dropped to the ground. "Didn't I tell you that my staff is always right, that it came from Heaven? For now, these three words you learned are enough for you. God repays well. The second time I pass through here, my staff says, I'll tell you three more words and crush your head."—"I believe," replied Pekhlivanin Dahlia, "in your staff. I will apply its words in my life. Can I oppose such a staff that comes from Heaven and always speaks righteously? May the people be free from now on. Such is the will of Allah."

I expound this poetic narrative to explain truth in folk form. This Turk is *death*; the people—that's us. Is there a place on earth where this Pekhlivanin didn't enter? Is there a home he didn't visit? What do the crosses on the tombstones say? Everyone in this world speaks of Pekhlivanin Dahlia. Mothers and fathers speak about his feats. There are entire volumes written about his history, his power. Everyone sings the same song: Pekhlivanin Dahlia is invincible in this world. And if someone tries to say that it's possible to free ourselves from him, we immediately hear the words, "are you crazy? Are you in your right mind? That's impossible. We don't believe. These are empty words, stupid phrases, and naive illusions of the youth." But all it takes is a young Bulgarian shepherd, with his staff from Heaven, which doesn't lie, and with three blows—on the knife, in the right hand, and Dahlia's left leg to refute the false theory that Pekhlivanin Dahlia is invincible. However, courage is necessary. Will power is needed for this gigantic struggle. But someone will object and say, "I don't see a profound meaning in this simple example." Yes, you are right. From your viewpoint, because you don't bother to organize these things in order. But, if in that formula is hidden the following truth, then what would you say? Suppose this young shepherd represents the wise, unconquered man. If his grandmother represents Divine Love, which constantly speaks to our soul that freedom is a human right. And if the grandfather represents Divine Wisdom, which carries the staff, that is, the Divine Laws, and entrusts it into the hands of this wise being, to defend his soul from enslavement. And if the knife represents the natural forces in opposition to human progress; and if the arm represents the corrupt human will; and the left leg, the corrupt human heart. We think that by reacting to these forces in a given direction, we can remove the destructive actions.

In this sense, it is necessary to understand the words, "he who endures to the end shall be saved." Victory is a condition for acquiring life. And Christ's words, "when the stronger one enters the house of the strongman and ties him up, only then can he plunder his home," imply the same idea. That is why we need that knowledge that can inform us of the process for acquiring life. A woman who wishes to weave cloth must first know how to wash and pull apart the wool; to prepare her loom, her harness, her reed, take-up rolls, and after that to create the pattern and to roll it through the heddles, to pull it and begin to weave according to the established rules of this art. The shuttle must constantly be thrown to the left and to the right side, carrying the yarn of the *warp*, which, when woven through the base, forms the desired fabric [the *weft*].

The painter who wants to paint a valuable painting must first understand the laws of this art, to understand how to combine paint and to master his brush. The sculptor who wants to make a great statue must be a master of his hammer. Whoever builds a house must know how to build it, raise it, and put it together. A physician who wants to be well-known and useful must know the elements that treat the sick from up close. A teacher who teaches and educates must have a basic familiarity with the human soul, the human mind, and act accordingly.

Now, the Christian man who wants to acquire eternal life must know the foundation of this life and to apply the laws through which it comes together. Life can be likened to a fabric, which we must first weave, and wear afterwards. It's the first garment that must clothe the human spirit. When we wear out this fabric, we become naked outwardly. This nakedness is referred to as a moral downfall.

Christ clearly states, "eternal life is to know God." To know Him is the secret to acquiring eternal life. But, you'll ask me, "don't we know God?" If you knew Him in Christ's sense, you wouldn't die. But, you'll object to me: "Who doesn't die?" Well, this is what defies the people's claim that they know God. But you'll tell me that Christ died too. No, He didn't die, but He rose and appeared before His beloved ones. When you die, will you rise to appear before yours? That's the important question for you.

You may have a notion of God as a philosopher, a pantheist, as a materialist, some clergyman, but it will not bring you eternal life—that eternal origin, that eternal goodness we seek, which constitutes our goal. Away from this [conception], you will be in the condition of a sick person who, during night time, runs outside towards the moon and expects it to give him warmth; or a hungry person who observes the nice loaves from far away; or a thirsty person who, from a distance, imagines he's drinking clear water and says, "I know *it*." I tell you: This is not knowledge. It's a notion of the outward shadow of things. When you acquire the real "understanding of God," your soul will achieve eternal life. Then you'll meet death like that young shepherd. And there won't be an inscription over your grave that says, "here lies a young, green person touched by death."

But let me return again to the subject and clarify the matter with a small analogy. Every living being wants its own environment and conditions in which it can live: plants need soil, moisture, light. For fish, water is necessary, outside of which they cannot live. For the birds, mammals, man, the environment for their lives is air. This analogy is also true in terms of human external feelings. The environment for the human eye is the light; for the ear, sound; for the nose, smell—the flowers that constantly release those etheric vibrations, which make up the "food" of that sense. The environment for taste is food—all those organic substances, juices, that constantly flow in and give life. If we now climb even higher on this beam, we will notice how this great law works. The environment in which our heart lives is through desires. The environment in which the human mind can live and develop is through thoughts. Without thoughts, the human mind atrophies; without desires, the human heart as well. The environment for the human will is strength, productivity and the energy for work: without work, the will atrophies. By the same law of comparison, the environment for the human soul is God. That's why the Scripture says, "in Him we live, we move, and exist." Through Him the soul can acquire its original life, to clothe itself with immortality. Therefore, God is an internal environment, an internal condition, an internal power, from which we must constantly draw. For example, just as our eyes are connected to the light; our lungs, to the air; just as our stomach is connected to the mouth, so it can eat; so our heart and our mind are two means through which the soul can take in life. These are preliminary environments for the Divine environment—the universal Divine consciousness, in which our soul is submerged. It is true that whenever a being loses its connection to its environment, it is exposed to death, regardless whether it is a plant, fish, bird, mammal, or a human being—the law acts the same way. Christ, who deeply understood this law, insists that we need to know God, or, in a scientific language, that we need to be connected to our environment.

But, you'll say, "we will know Him when we go to the *other* world." The other world is God. People who think they'll go to the other world after death resemble that criminal son who, when locked up, says to himself, "I'm going to see my father." Will you see your father in prison? You will go the place of judgment. In the other world you will not go to your Heavenly Father. To go there, you must conquer death, to get out of prison, to be free. That's why Christ says in the above chapter of the Gospel, "I am the door," and elsewhere, "the one who enters and exits through Me, will find pastures too."

Tell me now, have you entered through this door, and have you exited out of it, and how did you do it? If I ask you about your friend's house, you'll say, "the outside gate to his house is to the west, but the inner one, toward the north, or south." You'll also describe how big it is, the paint that covers it, and how it closes. All priests say, "Christ is the gate." If Christ is a gate, why don't you enlighten us: what is it made of? From wood or iron? From gold or from silver? With precious stones or something else? What kind of chainlink adorns it and what is the foundation on which it stands? "But," you'll say, "it's in a figurative sense." Good, then make an interpretation of that gate. What is Christ, and in what sense is He a gate? You'll say, "Christ saved us." How did He save us? "He died for us." Can a dead person save? "But he rose." How did He rise? "By the Divine life." So Christ was united with God, He knew God, and by means of this knowledge of God He overcame death, rose, and came to our souls. Now He is with us. For 33 years He was imprisoned with us, and He taught us how to get out of this prison, how to conquer death and evil. Christ is now out, [He's] in the other world with the Father of Light. He comes to visit our minds, our hearts, and the world will see Him after those three blows: against the knife, in the arm, and the leg. He will break down all those false teachings. What are these false doctrines? They are those elements, thoughts, desires, and actions that destroy human happiness, the human mind, the human heart, the human soul, the human spirit, which lead to death, anarchy, and bondage everywhere and drive a nail through our lives. And what is the doctrine of life? It's all those elements which give happiness, goodness, enlightenment, which raise the human spirit, the human heart, and bring love toward everything—that is the living Christ. That's why He says, "in order to have these essential elements, which bring eternal life into you, you must know God." One must fight in the world. But with whom? With death. However, this art must be understood correctly. Otherwise mistakes will constantly follow us. I will tell you how: A Bulgarian mother sent her son to Germany, I think, to study. She was a rather well-to-do woman, sending her son up to 3-4-500 leva monthly, but it was too little. The money wasn't enough for him. One day he writes his mother to send him 1,000 leva. She, however, replies, "I don't have money. You should look to find some part-time job." But the son states, "if you don't send me money, I will kill myself." Then she, indignant, writes this: "Kill yourself. I'll spit on your grave. I don't want a son who is a coward, who doesn't want to work; who is afraid of working in the fight for life and wants to live like a granny." These are not the exact words, but they are in that context. The son comes to his senses. And that telegram sits today in a frame, and when questioned he replies, "she saved me." So you have to fight the elements of death in the world. And how will you win? Only one way: when you know God, the beginning of life. But you'll ask me again, "how can we bring ourselves closer to this beginning?" It's the easiest thing. Let's say you're suffocating. What do you do? You open your mouth and breathe. You have to take in air through the nose. So, in order to have life, we must have knowledge, and in order to have knowledge, we must have a fresh mind to perceive, to move. And when you constantly perceive those noble, elevated thoughts with your mind, just as you constantly take in air through the nose, you are on the path to eternal life that you seek. If you make a small attempt, to strengthen your will every day—when bad thoughts and desires come, to chase them away and perceive only the good thoughts and desires—in one year or more you can do miracles. There won't be a stumbling block which will not obey this effort from your will. Now, of course, whoever wants to acquire immortality must have a strong will in the true sense of the word. But, you're saying, "I can't." Whoever can't will go there, to prison. This is how it's written in the Divine Book. When you say, "I can't," God says, "lock him up. I will teach him how he *can.*" There's no other way out; this is our destiny. If we want to unite with God, to live with Him, to obtain eternal life, we must surely serve Him. Otherwise, service will still be required, but to whom? To the devils, the princes in this world, who will force us three times a day. The devil will take the whip and say, "let's go!" You don't want to work for God?—whack! Finally you'll say, "there's nothing else to do. Work has to be done." Of course, because otherwise there's a stick, a whipping. If you stop, the whip starts cracking again. These are the two paths. "I don't want to serve the Lord." If you don't want to serve the Lord, you will have another god. "I want to be free." You're deceived. There is no freedom in this world. Freedom belongs only to the one who is united with God, who lives consciously; he is free. Some of you say, "I was angry. I told him this and that." You think you acted very wisely. You outtalked someone! Who outtalked who? Whom will you outtalk? "I beat him up." What did they pay you for this?—Nothing. Tomorrow, however, they'll beat you up. What kind of freedom is this? Today you hit, tomorrow they hit you. Today you strangle, tomorrow they strangle you. This is not freedom.

Christ says, "you must acquaint yourselves with the basic principle of knowledge." I want you to apply what I will tell you. You go to church, straighten up, cross your hands, close your eyes, carry away and pray to God. You get out of church and you forget everything. From the outside, people say, "that person goes to church, he's pious. The moment he goes out, his life is different." So you haven't found the proper, real way to salvation. But they say, "Christ came and saved us." Christ saves the wise and good ones. He never saves evil and stupid people. He saves the smart and good, who listen and obey His teaching. First of all, Christ teaches us how to work for ourselves. He says, "I am the way, the truth, and the life." The way—that's the method. Truth—that's your mind, through which you must familiarize yourselves with good and bad things. Life—that's an art with which you already know how to make fabric and to clothe yourselves with it. Make a small attempt with yourselves. You're sick, you're nervous, you're indisposed, your children aren't nice. Leave the children aside. Don't worry about them. Think about yourself a little. Why are you nervous? Why are you indisposed? There are deeper reasons for this. If you tell me, "I'm thirsty," I'll tell you, "drink."—"I'm hungry." Eat. "But how will I drink? There's no cup." Kneel down at the foot of the mountain spring. That's the element that can satisfy your thirst. "I don't want to kneel." You will kneel, otherwise you'll stay thirsty. "But I will sully my trousers, which I just bought." If you want to salvage your new trousers, you'll remain thirsty. It's better to kneel, to sully yourself, so you can taste the pleasantness of the water. "I'm hungry." Come with me. I take him to a room: Here's some bread. Sit on the ground and eat. "But the people will see me. It's embarrassing." If you're embarrassed, you'll remain hungry. If you're embarrassed to go to school with a school-book, you'll remain ignorant. So, when someone is called to follow Christ, he shouldn't say, "what will the people say?" But he must come closer to Christ, to apply His teaching and he will become strong. The devil comes near because we are weak. I don't want you to be weak, but to feed yourselves. How? To feed your mind, your heart, to acquire eternal life—that's what it means to understand how to feed not just your body, but your heart, your mind, your soul, your spirit. It's a method for eating according to the profound teaching of Christ. And this morning I will give my lecture the title *Learning How to Eat*. You only know how to chew and you exercise this ability very well. From now on, throw away the dish and feed your heart, feed your mind, and feed your spirit. And when you eat like this, I'll tell you that you're very smart, that you've digested Christ's teaching and that you'll gain eternal life, because you know how to unite with God.

I put this question on practical grounds, as I speak to you about things I understand, about things that I tried myself. The only thing that hinders you is hesitation, philosophizing: "How does this work?" When it comes to practical life, there is no philosophy. Have you ever called a woman over to teach you to weave and spin?—"But I can't." You'll be able to. In the beginning it won't come out the way it should, but gradually, day by day, after a week, after a month, your yarn will become finer. After this, you'll learn how to sew, and afterwards the weaving will come by itself. Don't think that everything will suddenly go smoothly. You'll have stumbling blocks, but if you persist you'll learn. Your first attempt should be as follows: Try for one or two minutes to keep your mind free, not to think about the usual worn-down things from everyday life. You say, "I stopped thinking. I don't think about anything." But in your mind pass thoughts about your grandmother, your children, chickens, bulls, wood, stones, and you think you're free. There is chaos in your mind, where you can find your grandmother, your mother, your children—everyone. Finally say, "I want to be free. I will think about God today, the great Love in life. Everyone out, to the yard where you can play and leave me free, because I have a very important task." Try it the first time for just two minutes…"But the kids will come, they'll fight, they'll cry." Let them fight; let them cry. Forget them for two minutes and devote this short time to think only about the God of Love. That's the art, the least [you can do]. "But," you'll say, "that's a very easy task." It's not easy. After this, try 5 minutes, 10 minutes. First and foremost, Christ wants you to expel the oxen, the hens, the horses, the wolves, and the foxes who have stained your sanctuary. Do you know who these wolves and foxes are? There are foxes and wolves in you. I see them, with long tails, with red fur, with big teeth and nails. Your hatred—that's a wolf; your hypocrisy—that's a fox. Why do you need that fox? What use will it be to you? None. Expel everything outside and put everything in order within yourselves. Then you will call your priest: "Come, servant of the living God, put on your garment, take the censer, which you use to deliver your incense to God." You'll also call the bishop of your life. And who is this bishop? Your spirit. You'll also call the singers. Who are they? Your noble feelings and desires. You'll say, "let's come and sing, to serve the Lord in this erected temple." And then Christ will come, and when He finds this assembly, free from those who sold doves and the like, He will say, "peace be with you! The day of your resurrection has come. Today you will be with Me in paradise." Do you know the deep meaning of the words of that robber who was crucified on the right side of Jesus?—"Lord, remember me in Your Kingdom!"—He was a man who expelled with his whip all the vermin, and that's why Jesus said to him, "you are the man who will be with Me today in paradise." Expel from yourselves all vermin, swine, foxes, and wolves. But what did the other robber, on the left side of Christ, say? "If you really are the Son of God, come down and free us." How can He free him when he hasn't driven out all the vermin within, when he's a slave to his selfishness?

I think you understand me: I'm speaking very clearly to you. I want to speak to you in a way, perhaps, nobody has ever spoken to you before. The first thing is to learn to love the Lord, and that love will connect you with Him. You have a thousand occasions to connect with Him and to make your life joyful. And when you unite with Him and enter eternal life, everything in you will transform and everything will come into place. So, charge yourselves with the task, first for two minutes, then for five minutes, to expel foreign thoughts from yourselves, and when you remain alone, begin in that deep meditation, to contemplate this great puzzle: why are you on earth? Why are you indisposed? Why don't you have noble thoughts and a noble heart? Why don't you have the will to solve a certain question? Christ will answer you. He will answer in this form: "I am the way, the truth, and the life. When you expel everything outside and accept Me within yourselves, when you know the Lord, My Father, Who lives in Me, Who gave eternal life in Me, He will give the same to you as well." We must accept Christ in ourselves so we can connect with God. And only then does Christianity have meaning, when we learn to conquer *this* life, so we can acquire the *other* one, which, namely, is valuable to us, because it brings knowledge, strength, noble feelings, happiness; it gives power to the spirit to overcome all. Let the fear of poverty stop in this world: it's Christ's doctrine. You're afraid of death. Meet it by saying, "we will fight it." They might want to throw you in jail. Tell yourselves, "we will fight against the one who brings death, through the power of Him who lives within us, through the One True God." The whole world may confront you. They might scare you. Do not be afraid. A person who is afraid cannot become a citizen in God's Kingdom. You now fight in the world and when you go to Heaven, they'll give you a Georgian cross, which will be a *living* cross. You'll return, and then Christ will say to you, "come, you, good servant, who fought on the battlefield." Man suffered for thousands of years, but he didn't suffer for mankind, for Righteousness. Until now, he suffered always for himself, for oxen, horses, and the like. Finally, he must suffer for Christ. In this suffering you'll find the real life. And that's why apostle Paul says, "if we liken ourselves to Him when we suffer, then we will liken ourselves to Him in the resurrection," because God, in the same way as Christ rises, will also raise us if we live for Him. Let the Spirit of Christ dwell in us, so we may know the True God and gain eternal life. Then we will go out to work for our younger brothers and sisters, and they will learn the art of acquiring the riches of this Divine life.

Lecture held on 21 September, 1914 in Sofia

HOW MUCH HIGHER MAN STANDS FROM SHEEP!

"Of how much more value then is a man than a sheep? Therefore it is lawful to do good on the Sabbath."—Matthew 12:12 (WEB)

We must thank the Hebrew Pharisees for provoking Christ to say such a great truth, otherwise He would not say it. People who are extremely formalistic, who strain at a mosquito but swallow a camel; specialists and virtuosos at faultfinding in others—the Pharisees could not explain how the Sabbath could be violated. According to their belief, according to the law of Moses, the Sabbath had to be spent in rest and *inactivity*. The Hebrews understood rest as it is, the way Bulgarians understand Sundays. The Bulgarian will bring his oxen to the barn, he'll leave the plow by the granary, he'll dress nicely, he'll put on his cap and go to the tavern, where upon entering he'll shout, "give me half a kilo of wine. It's Sunday. We have to work for six days, but we'll drink on the seventh. We'll be joyful." The Jews had similar views regarding the Sabbath, and Christ rebukes them by making a comparison: "If your sheep," He says, "falls into a pit on the Sabbath, you will take it out. Not, of course, out of love for the sheep, but not to hurt your interest. But if you have to do good for someone who needs help, you raise a big issue that he should not have his hand restored on the Sabbath." Christ adds something more: "And how much more valuable is man than a sheep?" That is, how much higher a wise being stands from the unwise one. If you cook for your stomach 4-5 hours a day, to treat it well, because it constantly *bleats*, and say, "I don't want to make it suffer. Let me feed it," why, when it comes to the intelligent being, man, to raise his thoughts, his heart, do you say, "this does not happen on the Sabbath; there's a time for that, let it wait?" Christ sets two conditions when He says, "just as you take care of your sheep, by the same law I must also take care of the intelligent being. As you bring your sheep out of the pit, I have come to earth to free these intelligent beings, to bring them out of the pit."

That man's hand was stiff. Do you know what a stiff hand means? His will was paralyzed, and Christ says, "I want to restore his will, so he can act freely, to apply his thought, his senses, because he's sent on earth to work, whether it be on Monday, Tuesday, Wednesday, or Saturday. Whenever it is, I will fulfill My mission." And such work, which doesn't violate the Divine Law, can be done by everyone because rest is intended only for the body, not for the spirit. On earth, only the lazy ones rest, and they rest every day. And the diligent say, "when Christ returns to us, then we will rest." The true Christian must understand work in this way.

There's a basic principle that we must bear in mind; there are some laws we must understand, and not just understand them, but apply them in our lives. Without this application, every teaching, any religion, whatever it may be, is fruitless. For a plant, it's not enough to just sprout, to grow, to develop, to bloom, to give fruit, but this fruit must also ripen. Only when the fruit ripens does the plant achieve its purpose. Therefore, according to the same law, man can be born, develop and bloom, but if the fruit in him does not ripen, his life is fruitless. Christ loosened the man's hand, He restored his will.

If you read this chapter a little further down, you will notice that they brought to Christ a madman, a blind one, and a mute, and that He healed them. These things are connected. Who are the madman, the blind one, and the mute? You may say these things occurred only during Christ's time, but they exist in our time too. I'll stop for a moment and give an example, and with it I will explain the meaning that Christ put into these words. There's a story about King

Solomon, in which it says that Solomon called a wizard, a prince of spirits, to assist him in building the temple. That prince, however, after teaching him how to build the temple, wanted to get his throne. When Solomon found out, he caught the spirit, shut him in an earthen jug, sealed it with his seal, and threw it into the sea. After spending ten years in the sea, this prince promised to the one who would open the jug to give him the nicest woman in the world. No one opened it. One hundred years passed, he made another promise: The one who opens the jug will receive not only the nicest woman, but also the best children. Still, no one came near. One hundred, two hundred, three hundred years pass; another promise: to the one who pulls him out, he will bestow not only the nicest woman in the world and the best children, but he will make him the wisest man. And luckily, nobody appeared. He makes another promise: whoever frees him, he will not only bestow the above-mentioned things, but will also make him a king on earth. Still, no one appeared. After 500 years he said, "whoever frees me from now on, I will kill him." Some time passes, a fisherman goes out to catch fish. He throws his net and the jug gets caught, which he pulls out. He thought to himself there must be a priceless treasure in there. He started to unseal it and when he opened it, a black smoke started to come out. At one point the figure of the prince appeared, who said, "I promised to kill the one who pulls me out of the jug. Earlier I promised such-and-such, nobody appeared. Who is to blame now? This is your fate." The fisherman pondered, "why did I have to unseal that jug?" But at one point he said to the prince, "I don't believe you came from the jug. You have to first prove to me that you came from the jug, and then kill me."—"I was in the jug."—"You weren't in the jug."—"I was in the jug."—"You weren't."—"I was."—"Prove it." The spirit started to go back into the jug, and when he went in completely, the fisherman immediately sealed the jug and said, "if you promise the first things, I'll let you go."

That's life: You come to this world, it's a sea; you throw your net, you catch fish and gain something. When you have these favorable conditions to catch fish, you're not there. When conditions that cause suffering, disaster, come you then throw your net and pull out the jug with the evil spirit. In that story you'll notice a contrast. Despite being a story, it shows that every life has favorable and unfavorable conditions. We have to understand the laws so we can make use of the favorable circumstances. If we are caught, like that fisherman, in unfavorable circumstances, we will reap death.

Let me return to Christ's words, who Himself said, when they brought to Him a madman, a blind one, and a mute. The madman, the blind, and the mute are within us. Here you all look like angels; how beautiful you are, pious, but when some madman enters you from one day to the next the crying starts and then the gnashing of teeth. The husband, the children, they run away: "Your mother is going mad!" You wise ones must extend a hand so you can cure the madman, saying, "peace be with you!" Just like the one word from Christ, where the madness came out of the man. In the same way you can say these words and cure the sick. When you start feeding your horses in the stalls, they start kicking without realizing that there are children around. What should you do? You have to say like the Bulgarian, "pshhh!" and to pull it by the bridle. The bridle: that's a law. Every unwise being must have a bridle. The wise one is given the power of speech, to speak. Therefore, you have to cure that madness in you. That sheep has become too stubborn, it's mad. You have to cure it, it's blind. The people say, "but we're not blind." I believe you. Maybe you're not, but there are many who are. They asked a woman who couldn't read, who didn't know how to read, and she said, "son, I'm blind, blind!" Can't you open that woman's eyes? Open them. Teachers are people who open blind people's eyes. They are wonder-workers: you send your son to them and 15 years later he returns with his eyes open. And you must open the ears of the deaf, to hear and perceive. For man, this is easy because he has reason. That's why Christ says, "how much higher man stands than a sheep!" What

HOW MUCH HIGHER MAN STANDS FROM SHEEP

is the life of a sheep? To graze grass so it can cover it's back with a little wool, and to give milk, and sometimes to bleat in front of you. You'll say, "there's something wise in the bleating." Some modern people are like sheep. They're constantly bleating: brothers complain about each other, servants complain about their masters, and masters about their servants. They sing the same song for 365 days out of the year. Isn't this life a constant bleating? Christ says, "how much higher man stands from a sheep," because man can think. His hand must be loosened, the madness in him must be cured, his blindness must be removed, and his hearing should be restored. That's what Christ is trying to say with these words. He says to the Pharisees, "you don't understand the basic Divine Law, and I know why you want people with withered hands. Your interests dictate the need for disabled people. You tell the blind, 'it's better to be blind so he doesn't see our transgressions,' to the mute, 'it's in our interest to keep him ignorant.'" And if there are people who don't like enlightenment, that happens because of some practical interest. Christ, however, claims the opposite: He says that the crippled must have their hands loosened. The mad, blind, and deaf must be cured. He wants wise people who understand and do God's will. The Bulgarian word, "man," has a profound meaning. It stems from the Sanskrit word, "manas," which refers to a being that thinks. That's why people say, "be a man," that is, a being that thinks, reasons, which has the will to do what is good. That's what it means to be a man. And be confident in this law, that man cannot have will if he doesn't do good. Some say, "I have will." If I drop a wheel from Mt. Vitosha it will roll down, but it can't go up towards the mountain. From the mountaintop, a creek winds down, but it can't go up. In the same way, most people roll and walk downwards. And only a person who can climb up the mountain, only this kind of person has will. He can remove and overcome some stumbling blocks and obstacles. And Christ turns to the Jews and says, "you shouldn't be like sheep. You shouldn't be like creatures who can only roll down, like rivers and rocks. But you have to be people who climb up towards God, meaning, to do His will." That's what He wanted to tell them. They understood Him. And in contemporary life, people constantly go down; they roll down from Vitosha and wonder why they're unhappy. Everyone who rolls down is unhappy. A person is happy when he starts climbing. Until a person starts thinking and reasoning, he's unhappy. The moment he starts thinking and reasoning, he becomes happy, and the previously impossible things in life start becoming possible.

The hidden idea that Christ puts into these words has great significance for you. When God says, in the first chapter of Genesis, that He made man in His image and likeness, He wants man to think and act the way God thinks and creates, to have will. And "likeness" means to *liken* things, that is, to differentiate between good and evil, to produce harmony. To think and act is a Divine principle that God put in us. And everyone who doesn't think and act the way God asks from him doesn't have God's image—he's a sheep. We're not saying the sheep is bad, but that the sheep's purpose is to graze and give milk and wool, whereas man's purpose is completely different. He's designed to manage all beings, to regulate the atmosphere, to regulate all other elements, to organize the earth. He must become a good master, and he can become one only when he understands what God put in him.

Nowadays they frequently ask, "are you a Christian?" What do you understand by that word? Do you believe in Christ? I believe Christ came. I believe it, the same way I believe the King of Russia once came to Bulgaria. So what? Do you believe that your student went to school today? "I believe." But this belief must go a little deeper. I would ask the student, "did you listen what your teacher taught you today?"—"I didn't." I would tell him, "I listened to his lecture and know more things than you." And that's why he'll say, "you understood the meaning." The people say, "we believe that Christ came to save the world." Fine. You preached this for 2,000 years. But *how* will He save it? "He shed his blood to redeem the people." Well, good. When a Bulgarian farmer buys from the market a pair of oxen, what does he do with them? He puts on a halter, places the yoke around their necks, takes the plow, and goes to the field. You believe in Christ, but if you're in the position of a sheep and don't get to work, do you serve Christ? You believe He came. That's good, but do you listen to Him? No. I recommend you go and listen to Christ when He speaks in His school, to understand His teaching and to apply it in your life. The last thing I want from people is to throw away what they have. This is what you have right now: you're still in elementary school, and for 30-40 years you're constantly reading the alphabet books, and that book has already turned to rags. Put the alphabet books down and take up the chapter books. I understand if someone takes up the alphabet book for one, two, or three years, but for 100 years to spell words out-loud from the alphabet book, I don't understand. "The chapter books," says Christ, "take them up now." And for those who finish the chapter books He says, "put the chapter books down! Take up the grammar, arithmetic, physics, chemistry, God's Law and go forth. Enough with the bleating."—"Do you believe Christ came?" Something more is required of you. Listen to what Christ is saying and understand what He brought. Only then will you learn about the profound meaning of this life. And when you have the ability to think, to act, and create, you have an advantage hidden in you. You have riches, a mine which you have to excavate—your mind, your will. I ask you now: Have you worked on your mind and on your will, or did you just bleat over your alphabet book? If Christ, who is coming, visits your homes, He will check to see if you really made yourselves useful. I don't mean those ordinary houses you made, but the ones in which you live right now, with which you have now come here. Christ will see whether in those little cells, in those rooms, there is rational human thought and action, or whether there's sheep excrement. And that type of manure is good, but it's a sin for man, whom his father sent to school, to whom he gave all conditions to become a wise being, to remain outside and bleat. And when the angels come down and return back to Heaven to report about the people, what will they say up there?—"They're still bleating down there." This bleating will turn to speech at some point. And now, when Christ wants to make this sheep wise, since it has the conditions to become thus, He puts these two principles side by side and says that from sheep's wool one must spin it and make cloth with it. Anyone can shear a sheep, but the wool must be processed. And if the wool is not sheared at the right time, it will fall, like leaves on a tree. So the wool must be collected, processed, and spun into cloth: Our thoughts and desires must turn into actions, and then they can clothe naked people. When did man become naked in Heaven? When he became stupid, when he became a sheep and started bleating; when his hand withered; when his wife succumbed and left the virtuous life for the shiny outer appearance of things, and he himself followed this example—so both of them gave into a licentious life. Then they became stupid, lost their sight, their proper judgment. Now Christ says, "I came to earth precisely for the man made in God's image and likeness, to untie his hands, so he can execute God's Law. You, who have hitherto herded swine, after they even forbade you to eat the carob pods, what do you expect now? The song of the singers? 'Lord, bring peace to the soul of your rabbi.' You want God to bring peace to your souls among the swine, amidst the carob pods of this world? No, take your staff, take your bag, and go along the path to your Father's house, toward your Father's school that God prepared for you." Christ advises you to put aside your alphabet books and to take up the grammar book. That's useful knowledge. It teaches us how to speak and read properly, where to place "Ѣ," or "Е," or "А," "Ъ," or "Ж." Proper thinking is required from everyone, as is proper judgment, proper feeling, proper action. Our life must be beautiful and nice, in its outer form as well as in context, and, as it was said 2,000 years ago, "be perfect, as your Heavenly Father is perfect." Here is the slogan for the new life for which we should strive—it's a Divine Law, but in this respect a little more effort is required from us. And I commend worldly people in one respect. Watch a lady who prepares for a party, or a ball, or the theater—how much effort she exerts in her dressing room: for a whole hour she turns here and there, looking at her face, her nose, her hands—everything must be in order. I commend her. But you, Christians, how many times have you sat in front of your mirror looking at yourself to try and rectify your character? You say, "I can do without a mirror." You need a mirror. Take an example from that worldly lady. I uphold the mirror, but the mirror of the heart and mind: when you look at yourselves in it, everything should be rectified. Only then should you appear before the Lord. Don't think the Lord will accept you in Heaven as you are. No! Worldly people understand this much better. That's why Christ says, "the sons of this generation are wiser." Not only should we avoid judging them, but we should take a very good example from them. In every respect I prefer worldly people, because they give an excellent example, both in their ability to comprehend, and in terms of energy, and in preparation. If we would take example from them and apply it in the spiritual world, we would stand higher than we are right now. [Religious people] say, "their things are stupid. We don't need this. We don't need that." Well, what do you need? Heaven? But Heaven doesn't want stupid people. If you can't build a house from stones, how can you build character, which requires a great deal of effort? You don't have 1,000 leva to build a house, but you want to build a splendid character! And when God says not to pay attention to worldly things, He means this: when you build one, two, three houses, He says, "that's enough. You're a specialist. Now I want you to build the home of your heart. Build the house of your mind." By analogy, the same law must work from bottom to top. That's why Christ says, "how much higher man stands (who thinks, who can develop his character) than a sheep that constantly grazes and bleats." The modern world *wants*, [saying] "bread, bread!" This cry is heard everywhere. And we need sheep, because they give us wool. But if the whole world were overrun with just sheep there would be no harmony at all. I understand that, in us, the element of reason must take a higher position than the unreasonable: the human side must replace the animal side. The saying is heard everywhere: "He's an animal." It's not bad for someone to be an animal, but there's something higher than the animals. It's natural for a sheep to be an animal, but not for man. And the Scripture refers to the "living spirit" and "life-giving Spirit" that wants to teach, to ennoble, to save humanity and its disciples, who are called upon to do this, to co-create with Christ. He wants wise people to help Him, people who understand well enough how to build according to all the rules of the Divine science; people, in whose minds the glory of the Kingdom of God sits in first place. Now we need the kind of people who cannot be tempted, nor can they be deceived by the outer appearance of things. I recognize that some priests don't do their job properly, but I don't judge them. That's their understanding, but I myself should do what is required of me. If we constantly stand in the same place and judge them, and we ourselves neglect our duties, of what use will that be? None. It would be like a teacher who doesn't deliver the lesson to his students, and therefore wants to punish them. Let us pass into a stage of intelligent life, which aims at the improvement of all nations, of all mankind. We need to have in mind the human soul, the home, society, the people, humanity; Christ includes all these categories. All this forms a whole. The home is a larger individual; society [is] larger than the home; the nation is even larger than society, and humanity [is] even larger than the nation. That's why we strive from smaller things to the larger, that is, from the animal toward expressions of reason. When Christ puts this idea before you, "how much higher man stands from a sheep," He assumes that man is more capable of building and constructing his life.

The first thing, upon returning home, is to start healing the madman; the second you should do is to open the eyes of your blind man; the third, to unplug the ears of your deaf man; the fourth, to untie the hand of the one whose hand is tied, to put your mind in action. It's a serious task. You have rules. You'll make the decision. Of course, one, two, three days may pass, but if you persist, you'll solve it. And when you're solving it, the results will show how the work should unfold. If a teacher constantly solves his student's equations, the latter would never learn to add. The teacher sets one, two, three, four, five equations and says, "next time you will bring me these equations fully solved." And the whole world around us is nothing but equations that God put forth for us to solve. In the chapter I read to you, Christ set forth many equations. I stopped on one. The others are much more difficult, even harder than proportional equations. I'm now giving you an equation with just four basic operations: addition, subtraction, multiplication, and division. Once you step into the difficult proportional equation, there the task is a little harder, but with the four basic operations you can solve it quite well. Some of you say, "we don't know how to add." You'll learn. Two apples plus two more make four. You don't know with whom to get along, to add: the man doesn't know with which woman he should come together. Then comes subtraction: the man marries a woman, doesn't like her, wants to abandon her: he doesn't know how to subtract. Now is not the time to subtract. His children multiply, he wants to kick them out because they're not smart. He has to teach them. What a great law is hidden in these four rules: to know how to add, how to subtract, and so on. It's a profound science that faced mankind for thousands of years. We learned only the *mechanical* aspect of arithmetic. When we start coming together with saints, with angels; when we come together with God, then we'll learn the *real* addition. One coin and another coin make two coins, but what if the addition holds both a plus and a minus? Someone says, "I can add." But how? With plus or minus? "I have," he says, "minus 2,000 leva." Ah, you're a rich man. You are a capable of doing good for others. This is the basic law of Christ. You'll bring this sheep in and you'll subtract. It'll give you the elements. If you visit a shepherd, he'll teach you the basic law of addition and subtraction: when turning the milk into cheese, he'll gather one part, and remove the other. If he knows how to remove the unnecessary, he'll win; if he doesn't know, he'll lose. And you, if you know how to curdle your cheese, how to add one and remove the other, when the time comes to balance your bill, you'll say, "now we have a profit." If you have a loss, that shows that you didn't use that one principle of wisdom from Christ, but you were a sheep, just grazing and bleating the whole time. When the sheep sees a wolf, it clatters with its hoof. It wants to say, "you have to get out of here. Don't you know that I'm grazing?" But [the wolf] jumps on the sheep and eats it. That's how smart it is! And when you see the devil, don't clatter with your foot; he's not afraid. He only fears people who have a mind and a will, whose hands are untied. That's why Christ came to untie the man's hand and to give him the strength to fight with the wolf, with the devil. Wolves also have the right to roam the earth, to use their teeth, but we too have the right to use against them our mind and will. They have the right to eat, but we also have the right to remove their teeth. They have the right to use their nails, but we also have the right to cut them. Remove the devil's teeth and chop off his nails! And when you turn the devil into a sheep, to give you wool and milk, don't worry. Perhaps the next thing for you is to turn him into an ox, to throw a yoke over his head and make him plow. And Christ says in another comparison, that the spirit, after coming out of the man, was very restless, and if he returns back he would become seven times worse than before. All those stupid people are also seven times worse. And therefore Christ says, "I have come to save the wise." Not for the animals, but man. It is namely this salvation of the profound Christian doctrine that we must apply in our life, to be models with our mind and our heart. Our home must be an ideal garden; that's the task of our life.

That's why you must begin your work, and everyone should work within himself. When a Bulgarian receives a friend as a guest, he gives him a tour of his farm, showing what he has, how it's organized, and his friend praises him and feels happy. One day, God will come down from Heaven: where will you take Him? Your barn and your granary are torn down, as are your church and school. If He finds everything in order here, He'll say, "here is a man who labored wisely." That's the idea that Christ presents to you this morning—"How much higher man stands from a sheep."

Lecture held on 28 September 1914 in Sofia

PHARISEE AND TAX COLLECTOR

"Two men went up to the temple to pray, one a Pharisee and the other a tax collector." —Luke 18:10 (NIV)

Perhaps you'll ask what is so marvelous about two people, one a Pharisee and the other a tax collector, entering the temple. Indeed, there is nothing marvelous to those who understand things, but for those who don't understand, everything is marvelous. For those who understand, everything has meaning, but for those who don't understand, everything is meaningless.

I will take these two people, Pharisee and tax collector, as the subject of my lecture today. These two people are prominent representatives of a very old culture. Let's compare their distinctive features side by side, so you may be enlightened regarding their beginnings and spiritual character.

The word "Pharisee" derives from the Hebrew word "parash," which means "to divide." There is also an Arabic word, "Farsi," which derives from the same root and means something perfect in form. To know a "Farsi" language implies to know it very well. Christ presents in this chapter two distinctive types. A talented artist, familiar with knowledge of man, would draw these two types with all their distinctive features, and such a fine painting deserves to hang in every house to serve as a model. What are the obvious features of the Pharisee and tax collector? It's not enough to say, "he's a Pharisee," or, "he's a tax collector," but we must know the outer marks of their faces, their hands, their bodies, the structure of their heads. Then we have to get to know the details of their mental state. Only in this way can we clarify the idea presented in the text and use it. Christ was a great artist, giving two distinctive features of these two characters, and based on them I will describe the Pharisee and tax collector. But you'll say, "how can you describe a person using only a few words about him?" This is a science; it *can* be described. There are scientists who spend a lot of time doing comparative anatomy, studying the structure of animals so well that if you gave them the smallest part of some prehistoric animal, they can describe its height, they can rearrange all its bones, they can recreate the muscles and tendons, and in that way, they can restore the lost form. If you give an expert botanist even one leaf of some plant, he is capable of describing the entire tree. By the same law, I will try to describe to you the Pharisee and tax collector, to show you what they are. But you'll tell me, "what do these two, who lived 2,000 years ago, have in common?" There are two types of people living in the world, Pharisees and tax collectors. Many others descended from them, but they remain the main ones. You can fall into either one or the other category, regardless of whether you are a priest or not, whether you are a nobleman or not, whether you are a scholar or not, whether you are a philosopher, man or woman. These two characters intertwine and stand out in everyone's lives. They will always remain the foremost distinctive types in human history. Christ's art consists precisely in the fact that He, with very few words, was able to express and present them so clearly.

At first sight, the outer appearance of the Pharisee is presentable. He is a pleasant-looking man, well-built, slender, tall in height: 175-180 centimeters—above average; hands and fingers elongated, long thumb, symmetrical—a sign of established views, the presence of will and intelligence; index finger as long as the ring finger—indicating that when an idea arises in him, he sees it through to completion. His digestive system is exemplary: he has a sober approach to eating and drinking, lacking the weakness of a glutton and wine-drinker. His taste is refined. His waist is thin. He passed the four age-periods on time, and is now entering the fifth, that is, he's 45 years old. Shoulders are slightly rounded, the face slightly elongated and pear-shaped, with a developed nervous system. The lower jaw is well-developed, with an elongated and sharp chin—a sign of a person with an active mind that can grasp well. The mouth is average; lips are neither too thick nor too thin: the ends of the lips are a little raised, with a smile of contempt—"The people, they're the masses." But he never mentions his inner contempt. Eyes are ash-gray; eyebrows form an arc, a little bent over, like the branches of an old tree, a person who lives a long time and who has life experience. Forehead is nice, elevated: at its base, above the nose, it sticks out—a sign of a person with strong individuality, with an observational and practical mind. The area of the temples is of average development. The ears are upright and close to the head—a sign of material order. The follicles on the beard are a little scarce and reddish—a sign of impulse and persistence. The head is rounded, the circumference above the ears being 56-60 centimeters, with strong development and upraised parietal area—a sign of a person with great self-control, self-esteem, pride, exactingness, and vainglory. He possesses strong religious sentiments, but biased ones. He shows compassion, but only toward himself and his loved ones. The face is on the pale side, with a nose of Greco-Roman type. He's a person with an aesthetic taste, but without poetry or love of nature, for the lofty and ideal. He's a person with strong faith, but only in his own mind; with great hope, but hope only in his strength. He has religion, but in that religion he honors and loves only himself. If we enter his temple we would first find, not the image of Jesus Christ, but his own portrait; and in place of the Virgin Mary, John the Baptist, and the other saints, his ancestors and forefathers are lined up, for whom he burns incense and offers prayer: "Our family is great and glorious." He's an intelligent person who accumulates life experiences, is very familiar with the Jewish Kabbalah and the principles of the civilization of that time, and if he lived in our time he would be a prominent writer, philosopher, artist, statesman, and spiritual leader.

Why does Christ single out this type [of person]? What's wrong with [the Pharisee's] prayer? The Pharisee has a philosophy that has long since outlived its time—a person who lives only with the past, and loses the present and future; a man who has fallen in love, like a young man or woman, with his own image, who, wherever he goes, sees only *it*. It's strange when a person falls in love with his own image. I once watched a Bulgarian writer: he sat in a conspicuous place. There was a mirror next to him. He started smoking a cigarette, turned and looked at himself in the mirror, as if he were saying to himself, "I'm beautiful. I make an impression on people." He'd smoke again and pose in front of the mirror. If that mirror shatters one day, his happiness will shatter too. The Pharisee is like that type [of person]: he's in love with himself. And you see, when he turns to the Lord, how interesting his words are: "God, thank you that I'm not like other people. I'm something more." But his philosophy is wrong here because God created all people. "I'm not like other people." Well, what are you? You're not an angel. You're built out of the same house, and the same blood flows in your tendons. He wants to deceive both himself and the Lord. Here is the first lie he adopts, and God tells him, "you don't speak the truth." The beliefs of the Pharisee are negative: he doesn't compare himself to those who stand higher than himself, with the angels, but with the lower types, with the criminals, because he's not like them. Let's assume that I compare myself with vermin and say, "thank you, Lord, that I'm not like these bulls, donkeys, dogs, lizards, and snakes." How can I compare myself to them? This is a weak feature encountered in all people. Years ago, there was in Bulgaria some movement among high schoolers and students, when examining the lives of great writers, like Shakespeare for instance, to absorb his shortcomings, because they don't have his positive attributes: "Wait, do I have them too?" and when they find them within themselves, they say, "I'm a genius like Shakespeare."

They explore Schiller's character and look for his eccentricities, and upon finding it within themselves, "I'm like Schiller too." When they study a series of writers like this, they say, "we are great men." Yes, great, but in a negative sense: great ones, who have minus one coin. I prefer a person with zero coins, because he neither takes any, nor does he have to give. And the Pharisee makes a comparison and says, "thank you, Lord, that I'm not like the other one, a robber." The Lord says to him, "if I put you in his place, what would you be?" Once an angel watched from Heaven how a person committed sins, then turned to the Lord and told Him, "how can you tolerate this lowly creature? If I were in your place I would wipe him off the face of the earth." The Lord sent the angel to earth to incarnate, putting him in the same position, and the angel committed twice as many sins as the man whom he judged. So, a person should not condemn people for their deeds based on the current place where one stands, because in *their* place he would commit them too. Many come to me and begin like this: "We're not such bad people. We're civilized, because we hail from a prominent family." I have no doubt in your words. Deep down in my soul, I believe what you are telling me. We're all from a prominent family; I support that. But your ancestors and forefathers, as well as mine, weren't as noble-hearted as you and I think. Many of them were great scoundrels, criminals, evil-doers, and the worst vagabonds. The testimony the Lord wrote about them is carried by you and us from above. Things may appear to have some kind of goodness on the outside, but they don't have the matching content from within. The fact that our ancestors and forefathers weren't as pure as we assume is revealed in the bad traits we inherited from them, which we manifest at least twice a day. If your grandfather and grandmother, father and mother, were pure and good like angels, where do these traits and bad manifestations come from in your life? If you pour a little acid or poison in some liquid, it will be noticeable and it will reveal itself; it will be known that in the good there is something bad mixed in.

So people who hold the philosophy of that Pharisee can be called *conservative*, from the conservative party; people who have a high opinion of themselves. It's not bad for a person to have a high opinion of himself, as long as it's right and there's no acid mixed in. The greatest conservative and regulator in nature is *nitrogen*, which stops every kind of combustion, suffocates all life. Nitrogen is the oldest, most balanced element in nature. But if nature were left with it alone, everything would be dead. Still, the organic world must be very thankful for it.

The Pharisee turns to God, not to ask for help to iron out some of the roughness of his character, not in the least. He's just thankful that he's not like other people—a burglar, a robber, a killer, an adulterer. As a scribe and philosopher he should have stopped to ponder over the causes leading to burglary, robbery, murder, and adultery. When we meet some people who stand, let's say, lower than us, according to Christ's teaching we shouldn't judge them in our own soul, but extract a lesson; to find the causes that lead them to their lowly condition, and if there's some part of it in us, to uproot it. Because the one who set the great laws of life says, "do not judge, so you may not be judged." There is profound meaning in these words, and whoever understands them comes close to the great Law of human goodness. Modern zoologists study the animals and have given to the world many valuable things, but nobody studied the deeper reasons for their appearance. So, why, for example, do some have horns, and others don't? Why do some creep [on the ground] while others walk on four legs? Why do some eat meat while others graze grass? Why are they deprived of human intelligence? And for this there are deep and underlying reasons. It's not as arbitrary as one might think. When the people understand these deep reasons, they will reach that wise philosophy, upon which the future social order will be built, "the dawn of the new civilization." The entire contemporary civilization rests on the views of the Pharisee—it's a *Pharisee* civilization. *That* civilization, where the people differ in form, outwardly, in etiquette, arose in the distant past in Egypt, India, Babylon, China, Persia, Judea, Greece, Rome. It can be found today in Europe, dressed in a beautiful Christian mantle. I'm not saying it's something bad in its foundations, but I say the form must always have some content in it. Out of this form remains a simple shell in which only parasites can live. They say, "he has marvelous eyes." So what? "They're beautiful." What constitutes their beauty? "But they shine, they're nice." What exactly makes them nice? Someone has a nice nose, decent-looking. What constitutes this beauty? His mouth looks nice, well-formed. In what respect? The people grasp some things they cannot explain, namely in black eyes, or in blue, or in the grayish, or in the greenish, or in the hazel, [where there] are some hidden powers. If you look at a person with black eyes, you will produce some idea; if he looks with brown [eyes], some mood, and so on. People with blue eyes are cold. They're like a clear but cold sky. These kind of people don't belong on earth. They have faith, but they were born prematurely. Perhaps they're the people who are just now arriving. I'm talking about those blue eyes that are an expression of the sky. Scripture says that Christ had such eyes. They say about somebody, "his mouth is beautiful, like a rose." What is the mouth? It's an expression of the human heart: is it someone with a soft or hard heart? It shows how intense and honest a person is. In those who have a good appetite, you'll notice the lips are thicker. It's a physiological law. More blood flows through, that's also why they're fatter and redder. When they taste food, they say, "oh, that's nice," and their face shines, giving a delicate, barely noticeable smile: it announces that the soul of the person is well disposed. If we take a person with a beautiful nose, it's an expression of human intelligence. Whether the nose is straight or curved, whether it's a Roman type or Greek type—this is of great meaning. The outward appearance of the face is not irrelevant, and it's an expression of the external life of man. If we peer into a human face and see that it lacks symmetry, that one of his eyebrows is not like the other one; one is more developed, the other one protrudes; if there is some asymmetry, this indicates there is something unbalanced in him. When you place a straight line over your nose, you will see where it stands. The nose is a barometer, a heat meter that shows the state of your mind. When machinists drive a machine, there's a device that shows the atmospheric pressure in the boiler, and according to this display they either add more coal to increase the steam, or, if it's unnecessary, they release it. Have you ever stopped to think, like the machinists, to see the state of your steam, your heart? That's why the Lord gave you a nose. Go in front of the mirror, ask your mind, and it will tell you the state of your heart. By looking at your eyes, you will see the condition of your soul. The only thing that never lies and cannot be hypocritical is the eyes. That's why when someone wants to lie, he blinks or puts his hand on his eyes. The child realizes that his mother, by looking at him, will know if he's lying, so he puts his hand in front of his eyes.

When the Pharisee prayed, Christ looked at him and said, "your spirit stands on shaky ground. Your ancestors didn't live as pure a life as you imagine. You think you're unlike other people, but you *were* like them in the past, and even now you're not very far from their way of living." However we interpret this fact, whether according to the Hindu philosophers' teachings on reincarnation; or according to the teachings of Egyptian sages about transmigration; or according to the teaching of Kabbalists and occultists on the emanation (outflow) and perfection of the soul; or according to contemporary philosophical doctrine of heredity, it's indifferent. These teachings and theories are only to help clarify some things a little more, to make the phenomena of human life clearer and more understandable. But the main principle, standing at the base of everything, still remains one and the same, however we explain and interpret its manifestations: The great law of cause and effect, of deeds and retribution—it never lies; it always speaks the absolute truth. If you're good, it's written in the book of life that you're good; if you're bad, it's written that you're bad. If you speak the truth, it's written in the book of life that you spoke the truth; if you lie, it's written that you lied. If you help your neighbors, you sacrifice yourself for your people, you work for the good of mankind, you serve God with love—this is written in the book of life. If you violate your neighbors, betray your people, hinder the development of mankind, are unfaithful to God—this is written in the same book. He writes mercilessly his testimony on human actions: on the forehead, on the nose, on the mouth, on the face, on the head, on the hands, on the fingers, and on all other parts of the human body. Every bone is a testimony for, or against us. And we read this story of human life every day. In the previous pages, the lives of all our ancestors are marked out: regarding some of them, it's said they were terrible criminals, thieves, and robbers. When we browse its pages and follow the line by which they came: Abram, Isaac, Jacob, David, Solomon, and many others, we find their actions well documented. Regarding Abram, we find that he was a righteous man, very wise, a man with a big heart, with great faith, with an exalted spirit, familiar with the profound wisdom of the Divine order for the great future of mankind. Regarding Jacob we find that he was originally a two-faced man, cunning, selfish, and deceitful who, by lying and deception, succeeded in taking his brother's birthright, and only in his thirty-third year was there a transformation, after serving his uncle Laban for 14 years for his two daughters; then he experienced a change for the better. Regarding David, we know he was a brave man, determined, with an excellent and natural poetic ability, but he had a particular weakness for beautiful women. He took Uriah's wife by deceit, and his trials began from that day. And the bold prophet Nathan didn't hesitate to expose him directly to his face and show him the bad consequences this law will write about him in the book for his future offspring. Regarding Solomon, it is said he had an excellent philosophical mind with a good but corrupt heart, with extremely strong feelings and passions, much vanity and weak will, and was a first-class Epicurean in eating and drinking and enjoyment with women. Christ knows this; He knows how his ancestors lived, and when the people say to Him, "good teacher," He replies, "why do you call me good? Only God is good." He's trying to say: "The family I was born into isn't as noble as you think. Because God has another measure that you miss. He requires total purity in every respect. Many from this family didn't live in a way that pleases the true God, Whose will I do." So that's why He turns to the Pharisee and says, "you're lying to yourself, and to the people, and to God: many of your ancestors committed crimes, and therefore you have no right to say, 'I'm not like them.' And because there's no humility in your spirit, your prayer cannot be accepted, and you cannot be justified. You Pharisees have distorted the Law of God by placing hypocrisy above Him as a cover. Stop presenting yourselves for something you're not! Because God is not a man who can be fooled by external appearance. He sees your heart and judges accordingly."

Now, let me turn to the other type, to the tax collector. You have a person of average height, slightly rounded (chubby); short legs, fat hands, fingers also fat and sharp, a round face; the digestive system is well-developed—he likes to eat and drink more. "I have a long way to go, I must have food:" That's how he philosophizes, and therefore becomes a tax collector: he'll mooch from here and steal from there, filling his sack. "You do as I do. If you'll excuse me, you might think of it as stealing, but I need it. You don't want to give it to me, but I'll take it by force or steal it." I said the tax collector has a round face, thick eyebrows, a chin wide at the bottom—whatever he undertakes, he achieves with success. He's between 40-45 years old. The beard is covered with black curly follicles, as is the mustache—a sign of great heat; developed nose, slightly short, thick, wide at the nostrils—a sign of a good respiratory system; a person given to feelings, impulsive, like a child. He can always express his joy. When he drinks half a kilo of wine, he can jump and rejoice. When he sobers up, he starts crying because his wife is sick. The area of the temples is well developed: large ears, almost like Tolstoy's, like a man who steals; he takes, but also gives—"Father and mother stole, why don't I give and do good? Hopefully the Lord will forgive our sins." He has brown or burgundy eyes— a sign of natural mellowness and good spirit, which await their time for expression. The head is properly developed, like Socrates' head. He has well-developed domestic and societal senses, a strong religious sense, a warm-hearted sense for compassion, a proper understanding of life, an outstanding mind free of sophistication, a highly developed conscience that reveals his mistakes, and he's not embarrassed to confess them even to God, and to the people, and to himself. He doesn't have pretentious views of his own noble character. He has religion, in which he places the image of the *Good* God, and not his own. He always trusts that the Good Lord will guide him to the light. There is more faith in *Him* than in himself. He has a proper philosophy: he doesn't compare himself to the lower-ranking thieves and vagabonds, but says, "Lord, seeing You, the angels, the saints, what am I? I need to rise. I need to be as You [want]. I'm a sinner. My fathers, ancestors, and I are no-good people. I eat and drink, and I've turned into a pig. Forgive me for being unable to use the good things you've given me." And what does Christ say? The person who is aware of his mistakes has a lofty ideal. One day, he will rise higher than the priest. How can this be? Rich people rely only on their rent or income; they don't work, but only discuss politics and the social life. Others that get up early, work for 10 hours a day, experience failure after failure in life, but persist, and after years they acquire knowledge and become prominent people.

Now, among you (if you'll excuse me) are both types. But because Christ gives both opposing poles, I say: Take the good from one and the other and create a noble Pharisee and tax collector at the same time. Create the third type of Christian, the new person. This is my idea. You say, "am I so sinful in my life? How can I be a Pharisee? You insult me." I will tell you a truth: When misfortune appears in life, you say, "why this misfortune, Lord? There are others who are greater sinners than I am." Aren't you, then, in the Pharisee's place?—A person who argues with the Lord. The Lord will tell you, "you're so righteous, but do you know how many disgraceful things your fathers committed, with whom you partnered at one time? Here you have a signed document from so many years ago, which you have to pay off."—"But, I don't remember."—"It doesn't matter. It's marked in my book. It doesn't lie." Misfortune comes to you, be grateful—"It's small." Then you'll be in the tax collector's place. And Christ will tell you, "you'll go to your Father's house." You sometimes judge the Pharisees: "They're insincere people," but do you know that you, who judge the Pharisees, are modern-day Pharisees? Learn a lesson about yourself from the character of this Pharisee so you don't have his negative traits, or if you have them, to uproot them, so you don't walk along the path of negativity in life. What your grandfather, grandmother, father, or mother achieved is of no use to you. You know the story of the geese who were led to the city: "What a disgrace! This gentleman leads us like a flock and doesn't know that our ancestors freed Rome at one time."—"And what have you done?" said the traveler. "Nothing."—"Then you are worthy of boiling in a pot." Your grandfather and your father were such high-born, noble people, but what are you? You don't have a noble character—acquire it. Your grandfather and father may have left you some capital, but you could spend it all, lose it.

And in religious terms, if we stop, we'll find religious Pharisees: "I'm from the Orthodox Church," "I'm from the Evangelical Church," "I'm from the Catholic Church," "I'm a freethinker." I'm glad you're Orthodox, that you're an Evangelist, that you're a Catholic, that you're a free-thinker, but do you have the noble features of Christ? "I don't have them." You're neither Orthodox nor are you an Evangelist. You're nothing. Acquire them so you can become one.—"But I'm a freethinker." Do you have the noble traits of those honest freethinking people? In the word "freethinker" I understand a person who is friends with *Truth*. If you're not such [a person] then you're a first-class liar. People often say, "you're an outstanding person." The people of modern society gather together in a group of three or four in one place and start praising themselves with noble characteristics, distinction: "We read and are enthusiastic about your work." He leaves, they start: "He's a first-class fool." The second one leaves, they say the same about him. The third one leaves, and he too is such-and-such. When the last one remains, he, of course, wouldn't say anything bad about himself. Don't be fooled by what people say, because they could just as well say many bad things about you. Nobody speaks the truth. Your enemies will tell you, "you're a vagabond, a liar, a good-for-nothing." They are closer to the truth than the one who flatters you—"you're noble." You may be good, but not that much. Don't think that you're excellent. Sometimes you walk upright, waving your arms and cane around, as if you solved some great Archimedean problem. You think there's no other person like yourself. If you're a tax collector you say to yourself, "I will rule the world." Christ says, "listen, many years ago your fathers and ancestors ruled. I remember. In my notebook it's written that they committed crimes. You could go down that path too. Don't get ahead of yourself." Therefore, in whatever situation we find ourselves, we must keep only the Lord as our ideal. In this world we will come across many bitter things. We may encounter a friend who loves us and can tell us some truthful things. I'm not saying to suspect everyone is a liar. No, but if 100 people praise you, among them only three will speak the truth. The others will tell you the truth either very roughly, or in a very flattering form—two extremes. The truth is not there, but in that middle way, when you take the positive traits of the Pharisee, his excellent mind, perceptiveness, and organization, and from the tax collector—his compassion, deep religiousness, his inner consciousness to recognize his mistake, and to strive to straighten out his life. And we find this Pharisee and tax collector in families: the husband is a Pharisee, the wife is a tax collector. The husband hails from a high-born family: rich, tall, and beautiful, a noble man, as they call him, and the wife from a simple family: her father and grandfather are uneducated, stupid people. When he looks at her he says, "do you know the situation from which I rescued you?" and she curls up. There's nothing she can do except to curl up and cook: any motion with the Pharisee's finger, about not having cooked the food well enough—"I don't want such a simple, ill-mannered woman," forces her to cry and listen: "I don't want this tax collector in my house." In another situation, the woman is the Pharisee, while the husband is the tax collector: She comes from a wealthy family, her father supports her husband who apprenticed with him: "Don't you know the grace I showed you by taking you in? Don't you know how to dress, how to put on a necktie, how to blow your nose?" These Pharisees are terrible formalists when they list [one's faults]. Now both of them, just like one, the other as well, need to rectify their lives. When Christ says that the tax collector is more justified than the Pharisee, He wants to say that the tax collector also isn't fully righteous, but in his outlook on life, he has a better grasp of the Divine order than the Pharisee. He wants to say that one day this tax collector will stand much higher than the Pharisee. If you don't want to humble yourselves, the Lord will humble you, because He humbles the proud and lifts up the meek. Pride and humility are synonymous with these two people, the Pharisee and the tax collector. You know what can happen to you in the future: All your noble features and all your ancestors cannot save you. Some years ago in England, in London I think, one of the richest and most prominent Englishmen entered his underground safe to examine his treasures and by chance he closed the door, leaving the key outside. After taking a walk-through of all his treasure and rejoicing over it, he wanted to get out but found himself locked out. He sat there for a day, then two, three, with gold all around him, tremendous wealth, but he could neither get out, nor could he call out. Finally he was forced to surrender his soul in that place, leaving behind a note: "If there was anyone who could give me a piece of bread, I would give him half my wealth." If one day you happen to find yourselves locked out like that rich man, in the underground of your noble fathers and ancestors, a piece of bread could save you. That's why Christ says, "the bread can save you, and not those things you fight for." And do you know that a lot of people die like that, closed within themselves? People in despair commit suicide. And who commits suicide? Tax collectors don't commit suicide, but it's always the Pharisees. Poets, painters, and statesmen say, "the world cannot appreciate us. It cannot appreciate our creations, our works, our paintings," and they commit suicide. It's always these Pharisees, these noble-minded, with proper facial features and red beards; they're the ones who commit suicide. The Pharisees in Bulgaria don't have red beards. I'm talking about the Jewish Pharisees. They're the ones I'm describing. I would describe ours differently. The Bulgarian ones also resemble them, but they differ in some things. But because my talk isn't about the Bulgarian ones, but the Jewish tax collectors, you can make conclusions about the Bulgarian ones and look for those types. How will you look for them? My lecture is for you to apply this practically in your life.

Modern people preach that in order for a person to succeed, he must have will power. There is a threefold manifestation of the will. The will may be: 1) Self-will; 2) Will that takes into account only our interests, only our nation's interests, and 3) Will that takes into account the interests of our society and nation, and man, and God. The last will, which encompasses all the obligations within itself, which we have in this world; that kind of will, that there is no force that can divert us from our duty—that's a good will. The will to work for the glory of God and mankind, for your nation, for your home, and for the elevation of your character—that's will. Some say, "you must have a noble mind." A mind that conceives its relation to God; a mind that busies itself by trying to apply exalted thoughts in life—that's a noble mind. You have all the potential for this. "But my nose isn't the way I want it to be." It will develop. Look at the little birds in their nests, who don't have feathers yet, how they await their mother and the moment she shows up, they open the mouth, saying, "chirp!" and plonk!—their mother drops a worm in their mouth. And 20 times a day, "chirp!" and they open their mouth again. The more these birds pray, "chirp!" the more worms fall into their mouths. And now their wings start to grow, and finally they fly away. You too must walk according to the same law, opening your mouth to pray. If you don't open it, you're a Pharisee, and Christ will tell you, "the world is not for you, the Kingdom of God is not for you, the future is not yours." That's what Christ wants to say. There are people who don't like to open their mouth, who just keep silent. I understand silence, but when? When you're angry, when you want to insult someone, when you're jealous; but when you're joyful, when you have to say a comforting word, open your mouth and say it. Do you open your mouth when you're going to discipline your children? That's the question set before you. You discipline your children like the Pharisees: to avoid touching the cooking utensils, to not stain themselves, even not to soak their hands—the mother will wash them: "Let the father buy them new shoes, watches, little fasteners." The father must become a slave to this Pharisee. When he comes home at night, they frown at him: "Soon we want this and that," and he curls up. Why did Christ say, "woe to you, scribes and Pharisees?" In homes, with our children, and in churches, everywhere we manifest these traits of the Pharisees, and we wonder why the Kingdom of God doesn't come. And on top of it all, we blame: "Good-for-nothing world, no-good society, the priests are such-and-such, the teachers are bad, the statesmen are bad," and who is he?—a saint! You're also like the ones you blame. Stop and let go of these things because your mother is with you. When you say "chirp!"—plonk! You will receive food. These things may seem funny to you, but they're great truths. They're small things, but we must draw a lesson from the example. In comparison to Heavenly life, we are beggars, and the Lord constantly sends our mother with these worms. Greet your mother because she brings you food. She traveled so much just to find a worm! How can we thank God, Who thinks about us every day and brings us food? Every morning we should say "chirp!"—to pray to Him. Do you know what it means? It has a profound meaning. What does this "chirp" mean? If you knew it, you would know the words Heaven uses to speak. It's a very short word, but meaningful. And now you're in the temple; Christ turns to you and asks, "how do you pray? Like that Pharisee, or like the tax collector? How will you go out into the world and start work? Like the Pharisee, or like the tax collector? You're from the same clay." But Christ wants to tell us not to be Pharisees. My head is bursting from these Pharisees! If there's something disturbing in this world, it's these Pharisees. "But, so-and-so has these traits." I know. What should I do? Wait for me to cleanse myself, then the people. Wait for me to get rid of my fleas, then I'll help the others. Because otherwise, if I go to him, the one who has fewer [fleas] will catch some of mine. "But we have to discipline him." Wait for me to discipline myself first. "But you should preach." If I preach ahead of time, I will fill the people. "Go out and say such-and-such." What will I say? Should I lie to the people? When you go out, you have to speak the Great Truth with words, and with your life. That's what Christ is implying. When we start studying, we have to work simultaneously with words and with our life. I really like those modern-day teachers who, when teaching a subject, physics or chemistry, they immediately begin with examples: "Oxygen is derived in such-and-such a way, this happens like that." You enter the wood-shop, the teacher explains in theory and in practice. You go to the tailor—the same happens. Christ tells the Christians, "enter and take up your yardstick and scissors." Some need to take a needle, then the scissors. What are scissors? It's our tongue. When you begin to sew and cut, there are no better scissors than your tongue. When you start cutting left and right without thinking, you're misusing your scissors. Because if you speak out of place, you're cutting without thinking—the cloth will go to waste.

I'm not telling you all this to discourage you. I'm not telling you that you're born a Pharisee, but that you have the *disposition* of the Pharisee. Everyone has it. And it's good that you have it to some extent. But when you start saying, "Lord, thank you, because I'm not like the others," the Pharisee lives in you, and it's hard to free yourself from him. He lives in the neck, in the crown of the head, in the ears, in the head, in the nose, on the inner side of the eyes. Where will you find this Pharisee? In all your traits and manifestations.

Now Christ asks us, "what is the best way we can offer our prayer to God?" His implication for this prayer is in the broad sense, for the benefit of life in society. Some believe that true prayer can only be offered in church. Examine the prayer offered in church: does it have some connection to family life? Can it help you? And you have to find that church. Where is it? The teacher first teaches the students about some elements and leaves them alone to solve the problem, to find the relationship of a certain law. In one part of the Epistles, it says, "you are the temple of God." If we are temples of God, when we enter into the secret room before God, how should we enter? If we enter like the Pharisee, Christ will tell us, "you haven't reached your goal." If we enter like the tax collector and acknowledge our mistakes, and promise to rectify them, we will succeed and hear Christ's answer: "You are justified. You have a future." Maybe if the teacher finds many mistakes in the notebook, the student shouldn't say, "how petty-minded he is. There's just three mistakes!" He can even smudge it; he can scribble 4-5 words, and the student might say, "he ruined my notebook!" Yes, but if you want to be perfect, you need to thank him for giving his attention to even these mistakes, because the three mistakes can become more. Rectify them, don't leave them. Because the mistake is like a flea: if you leave it, in one week it can breed thousands. One mistake is enough to send a person to the pillory. By the same law, a single virtue is enough to lift you to Heaven and to place you among the angels. Given the conditions, if one of your actions is wrong, it will pull you down. If it is virtuous, it will pull you up.

Therefore pay attention to both virtue and wrong-doing. If there is only one virtue in a man who led a wicked life, that is the rope thrown into the stormy sea of life, which if caught, can lead back to the shore. Therefore the last remaining mistake that is still left is very bad and can destroy a man, just as the last virtue is strong enough to save. They can alter our lives; it's a law. And that's why Christ says, "don't be negligent." The Pharisee possessed many noble characteristics, more than the tax collector. In many respects he stood higher, but he had one final flaw—pride, which could bring him to hell. The tax collector was a great sinner, but he had the last virtue—humility. And he said, "I will work for my salvation," and that's why God blessed him, because he hoped to correct it in the future. I ask you this morning: Where do you stand? With your last mistake, or with your last virtue? If you're with your last mistake, I'm sorry for you. Beware: You're at a dangerous point in life. If you're with your last virtue, you're safe. I congratulate you. You stand securely on the rock. Hold on to that last virtue and Christ will walk with you.

Lecture held on 5 October 1914 in Sofia

THE CONDITIONS OF ETERNAL LIFE

"And this is eternal life, that they may know You, the only true God, and Jesus Christ whom You have sent."—John 17:3 (NKJV)

When a young Bulgarian man, pure as dew, meets his *ideal* [woman] on earth, he stops and says to himself: "I found her. She's the one. Now, like Archimedes, I can determine the relative weight of bodies, to figure out how much silver, how much copper, and how much gold is in the King's crown. Now, like Newton, I can say why the apples ripen and fall; why the rocks roll from high places; why the mountain springs roll downwards, hopping, rumbling, and flow so fast; why celestial bodies move in space and revolve around their central axis. Now my mind, my heart, are revealing this great mystery of movement in life. I can tell you about eternal life; I can describe its properties, qualities, conditions, and elements. I found them! I found the philosopher's stone. I acquired the elixir of life. I can be brave like a lion and patient as an ox; I can fly like an eagle, and be wise like a man." And it is properly said, "you have revealed it to babes."[1] This young man isn't far from the truth. He understands the original language spoken by the Lord. His conclusions and grasp [of this matter] show that he understands the original, from which he draws inspiration. He speaks, thinks, feels, and acts properly, in a grammatical, logical, and philosophical context. There's peace and accord in his soul. There's no dispute about the word "eternal," whether

---

1   At that time Jesus answered and said, "I thank You, Father, Lord of heaven and earth, that You have hidden these things from the wise and prudent and have revealed them to babes."—Matthew 11:25 (NKJV).

it should be placed in front of, or after the word "life."—"That's the outer shell of these things," he says. "What matters for me is that it's in my mind, in my heart; to have it penetrate deeply in my soul, and to sustain my spirit with its Divine fire." His answer is true.

Years ago, it was common for the coachman to sit in front of the carriage while the master sat behind. In recent times, the custom changed: the master sits in the front while the coachman sits behind. In front or behind, it's all the same. As long as the reins are in good hands, the horses are strong, the carriage is strong, the coachman is sharp, and the master is wise and good, then the goal is achieved. But someone will ask, "what are you trying to say with this?" Nothing more. It's simple and clear: the master and coachman must be in their places. "What more?" Can you say like that young man, "I found her, and I found *it!*" That's the important question for you. When you answer it, the world, and life, will take on another appearance. But back to the subject: When Christ said these words about "eternal life," in the presence of His disciples, He revealed to them a great law in life, a law through which two elements can be distinguished and defined, which enter the temporal and eternal, in the conscious and supersensitive life. Now, people who don't understand the profound meaning of the original language can translate one way or another by displacing words. Yet there are some laws that regulate human thought and don't allow a kind of shifting. Until one learns to think properly, he will make mistakes and redeem himself through a number of sufferings. The written things in the great book of life are for wise people; they're not for the inferior beings who don't understand these laws. Now, if someone reads "eternal life," or "life eternal," he will ask what we can understand in the word "eternal." This word has internal and external meaning. In "вечен живот,"[2] in our country they understand a long, limitless,

---

2 The phonetic pronunciation of this word is "vetchen zhivot," which translates to "eternal life."

and uninterrupted life. In English it's "eternal," but the root of this word is of Sanskrit origin, meaning land, and "land" in Sanskrit implies a being that conceives and gives birth. Frequently, "eternal life" is mixed with the existence of man, but man *can* exist without living. The metaphysicians argue over this subject, but when we enter the realm of experimental philosophy, where we examine the Divine laws, our conclusions must be based on truth and the results [must be] correct.

There are three basic elements in human life that never change, three main principles on which this current life is built: They are built into grammar, logic, and mathematics. For instance, when children first learn sentences, they say that the sentences have a subject, a predicate, and a link. There may also be definitions, additions, and so on, but the basis is in these three words which produce thought. If I asked you, "what is a subject?" you would say, "the word that refers to the object of which is spoken in the sentence." And "predicate?"—"The word that expresses what is being said about the subject." Good. If a teacher gave you the grammatically-read verse to divide, showing the most important words in it, all would turn to the words "God" and "Jesus Christ." But here the basic thought is "eternal life," and "Jesus Christ" is an addition to that thought. God and Jesus Christ are both the beginnings of eternal life, or the two supporting columns, the two pillars upon which he sustains. Logically speaking, "God" is a great prerequisite; "Jesus Christ"—a small prerequisite, but "eternal life"—the conclusion. To make this idea even clearer, the words "eternal life" imply the wise movement of souls; the word "God"—the potential of the spirit, the conditions, forces, laws of nature, on which this great order of things is built and sustained, and "Jesus Christ"—the intelligent beginning that arises from the One God, who guides and preserves all living beings. Now you might think that by saying "eternal life" you understand what eternal life means. But what is the main element of understanding? We understand only the things we can experience and do. Every thing we can't experience and do, we don't understand. For these things, of whatever nature they are, we have nothing more than an idea and can only guess. If they give you cloth, you'll say, "I know how it's made," but when they tell you to make it, to spin the yarn, to lay the foundation, you'll say, "I don't know."

Science says that every being, in order to live, requires an environment and conditions. For instance, the environment for fish is water. What should we understand by the word "environment?" "Environment," "foundation," and "soil" are things that have many similarities. In Bulgarian and other languages there is no word that shows the essential difference between these three words. The first element in "eternal life" is that element in which the soul is submerged, like the fish. We call this element "environment." When we build a house, we call this environment a "foundation." Upon the foundation we raise walls and add a roof. When putting a plant in the ground, we call it soil. We put various seeds in the soil. In the very beginning of everything, we must find the environment. What is the environment in eternal life?—God. But there are two other transitional elements, or conditions. Some mix "conditions" with "environment." There is a difference. In order for a railway to pass from Sofia to Varna, it must meet certain conditions, which are: railroad tracks, coal, and water. And when we turn to man, what are the conditions of his life? *Air* is the environment in which man lives. He is immersed in it. But air is not the only element necessary for the existence of man, fish, and birds. There is a second element: food. But we aren't immersed in food. This element is *transient*. It comes from outside, enters us, and comes out of us, leaving its influence behind. The third element for man is that in which the fish are immersed: water. It's the environment for fish, but only a *condition* for man. If we immerse man in the same thing in which the fish are immersed, he'll die. Consequently, water is a condition for the existence of man. Let's take air, which is man's environment: if we deprive him of air, he'll die. Air is a condition for the fish. This condition is found in water itself, and when it passes through the gills of some fish, this air goes into its respiratory system and purifies the blood. The environment for fish is water. The environment for man is air.

But the environment is only one third of the truth. Where do false ideas come from? When we use an analogy, for instance, we have to know what dose of truth it holds. We always have to be sincere, and not only our conclusions must be true, but at the same time the small and great premise must also be true. One of the premises may be true, but if the other one isn't true, your conclusion will be inaccurate. And when the mathematicians and engineers make certain calculations on buildings, they take into account all the circumstances to avoid possible mistakes. By the same law, you have to build things in yourself when you want to build your character—your mind and your heart. You have to know how to build it—to know what is the environment, what is the condition, and what is the element, because there are elements. The elements regard the maintenance of life, and the conditions—the *existence* of life. For instance, the fields, the gardens, vineyards, and so on, make up the conditions for life, from which the elements of life are derived: the wheat, fruits, and so on. Light is a necessary element for life, but it's the fourth element: the air, food, and water are the first three elements. If the fish said: "The water is enough for me," because it finds all its food there, and if man also wants to live in the water, he would find himself in contradiction with the basic laws governing his life, because he cannot enter the water and live in it like a fish. It is precisely from these conceptions that errors occur in all modern philosophies and religions. In them are many dogmatic questions that are half true.

Let's return to the word "eternal." It refers to the spiritual world, implying the materials from which a life of immortality can be built. The word "life" implies the organic life in matter that grows and develops and can't be continuous, constant. Its form can be altered, and we call that change death. However, the notions of death vary. To die doesn't mean to lose one's consciousness, not in the least. But it means one can lose those conditions in which life manifests. The consciousness can remain, just as one's bones remain when one dies. Consciousness: it's the spiritual backbone of a person. So, upon that backbone, like the human backbone, the entire nervous system rests, along with the organs that function together with the other senses and abilities. When we come to God, He is the ultimate power, or, the necessary environment in which man is spiritually submerged. To explain that analogy: When we say that light is necessary for the human eye, it means the cells in the eye are submerged in the light, and that it is necessary for maintaining their life. The human soul must also be submerged. You haven't submerged it, meaning that you're out of your environment. You'll live like a wheat-germ, like many grains of wheat that rest in the Egyptian pyramids and graveyards for 5-6,000 years in a dry place, and they wait for conditions to be planted so they can sprout. These grains of wheat have recently been taken out and planted, and they gave an excellent result. And the human soul, like a grain standing in the Divine granary, awaits these three necessary elements that have the conditions, forces, and laws, in order for it to begin its life again. In the Christian sense, we have to find the conditions in which we can immerse ourselves and live in God. In this sense, the effort of every conscious person must be directed to achieve this state. You live, you exist, but this life and existence is just vegetation. Your existence consists of only one element and is limited by the Divine Essence, which created you as grains of wheat and fruit seeds. You can't avoid your existence. You can't destroy yourself. Your *being* is beyond time and space. The human soul existed in that state for billions of years, in the bosom of Divine Consciousness, but during that time its life was of a different nature; it wasn't individualized, it didn't know individual life of the individual spirit. It lived in the contemplation of Divine bliss, in a sleepy state. But now, with its awakening, it comes to earth to learn the inner meaning of this life, the life of individuality, to acquire its own immortal life by itself and to become a citizen of Heaven with certain rights and duties. That inner striving is a condition imposed on it by God. Now, some want to incarnate and live as God at the same time. But to live as God is a contradiction, because in order to live as God, there's no need to come out of Him. What is the need for this Divine Consciousness to separate, to seek some other life? This shows that the human soul always existed in God, and its eternal aspiration is to seek Him in all His manifestations and to imitate Him.

But let's return to the scientific side of the subject, the possession of these three basic things: environment, conditions, and elements of existence. In the church, this idea is expressed in the "trinity" of God. What does this word mean? Three different beings who have one thought, one will: Father, Son, and Holy Spirit. They are in grammar: subject, predicate, and object; in logic: a great premise, a smaller premise, and a conclusion. The environment for all beings, and for our soul, is God. The element that carries life in itself is Christ, and the conditions that help manifest life are in the Holy Spirit. When you alter the course of things, you must simultaneously alter the laws too, which regulate the forms of things. You can dip in the water, but in order to live in it, you must alter your human form into that of a fish. That would be a degradation in life, because you make the environment (in this case the water) your environment. But in order to elevate life, you have to make the environment a condition. In one case, and the other, the form of the being must necessarily be altered. We can change the form of a fish only if we change its environment. If we gradually remove it from the water and bring it into the air, it'll surely reorganize itself and its entire organism. It'll become a bird, adapting to the air. Then the water will become a condition for its existence, just as food and light are conditions. When Christ says, "this is eternal life, that they may know You, the only True God," what did He mean to say with the words "the only

True God?" That Supreme Power, which constantly moves in us, which carries life in itself, creates the conditions through which we may come to know *it*. A being immersed in a certain environment cannot know this environment. For instance, the fish cannot recognize the water where it is submerged. Some want to know God. If you are immersed in God, you will not know Him, because you are within Him. Then you only live in Him without knowing Him. But you have to come out of Him and make Him a condition for your existence if you want to know Him. Let's assume you talk to a cell that lives in you. Human cells are intelligent beings. They have some sort of intelligence. They are like birds and fish. This may seem strange to you, but that's how it is. You can try to talk, and these cells will understand you. And when you speak to them in their language, they'll do their job well. You can also scare them; they'll curl up. Now, if a cell says this: "I want to know what a person is," it would be the same as when people say, "I want to see what God is." Then God would no longer be the environment; man must come out of Him. "But, is that possible?" It is. You just have to alter your form. "But I can't!" Wait until you alter it. That's the philosophy of the question. And the cell, in order to recognize what it means to be human, must pass through billions of conditions, through all tissues: in the stomach, in the heart, in the lungs, in the brain, and so on. Only then can it stop and say, "I formed my opinion of what it means to be human." And now we, the philosophers of this world, after traveling everywhere, stop and say to ourselves, "come, let me tell you the nature of God: He's omnipotent. Now do you understand?"—"I understand." You don't understand anything. Only when you come out of that environment, when you pass through the door called "death," when you "die," only then will you recognize what God is. That's precisely why people are "dying." And when someone has the desire to know God, he must "die," saying to himself, "I have to die to know God." That's the most proper definition of knowing God. Those who wrote the Gospel were very wise people. Some think that the writers of the Gospels were like fishermen, simple and uneducated, and that Jesus Christ was simple and uneducated. But that's not the case at all. Christ studied at the Divine School. He didn't need to study on earth. I wonder why this superficial conclusion where a person who never studied at all was able to turn the world and take people to God. The materialists and pantheists say, "you Christians are such fools. You have no logic: You rely on a simple, uneducated man and trust Him to lead you to God. When we reason," they add, "we take all things into consideration." Someone once preached in a church that Christ, with 5 loaves and 2 fish fed 5,000 people. To make sense of this miracle for the listeners, he said, "don't think that these loaves were ordinary. They were as large as the hills." Upon hearing this, a shepherd whistled and said, "why do you speak like that? I'm not surprised that the loaves were so large, but I wonder how big the mouth of the oven may have been to be able to bake these loaves." Herein lies our illogical, our superficial reasoning. The first thing a Christian must do is to free himself from all false conclusions, false thoughts, false desires. And he can do that. A logician can do that. A logician can immediately release himself from them. And a disciple can check the extent of their correctness. Take this proposal, for instance: "Man is a two-legged being; every being with two legs is a man; consequently, the chicken has two legs and is a man." The conclusion is very correct, but two legs are not things that characterize the person—he can also walk on all fours. But what characterizes man is his mind, his heart, his soul. These are three elements. The legs and hands are just a by-product or an external physical product for human activity. When a person must be active, he has to have hands and feet. The conditions will create them. You will ask what they'll be. They'll match the environment. We say that certain organs are impossible to change while the being lives in the same environment. If we take the fish, we'll say that the fins it uses to swim are necessary in the water, and that they cannot change. But if the fish comes out of the water; if it can do this and desires to become human, the fins must turn into hands and feet. We, who want to pass over to the spiritual world, are like fish immersed in an environment. If we want to get to know the conditions where the angels live, the latter will tell us the way we say to the fish if it wants to get out of the water and enter our environment, to think and act: "First and foremost, you have to alter your gills, to form lungs and learn to breathe." The fish that teaches another [fish] to make lungs will be the wisest fish. Now I also recommend this teaching, to make lungs for the other world, because if you lack them, you won't go there. You have to be prepared, because your life will continue upwards after leaving the earth.

Now let's turn to the word "познание [knowledge, understanding]."[3] In our written language, the words are composed of certain characters, the letters with which they are written. For instance, let's take the Bulgarian word "познаване [to know, to recognize]."[4] We first have two lines descending from top to bottom. When we put another line above, it becomes the letter "П." We want to make "О." We draw a circle and place it next to the "П," becoming "ПО." For the letter "З" we take the two halves of the letter "О" and place one on top, the other on the bottom. For the letter "Н" we also take the vertical lines of "П" and place the top line in the middle between them. We have to write "А," taking two lines touching above, and joined by a line through the middle. For the letter "В" we take a straight line and stick the "З" sign next to it, and so on. But the one who created these signs had some idea within himself. I think analogically about plants and flowers in the following way: When the flower grows, it stands like a cup opened upwards, until it embraces the things it receives. The moment it receives, it starts turning downwards and finally it hangs, forming the letter "П." And I say, in *knowing*, the cup is turned toward God so He can pour something in it, and upon receiving it, it wants to experience within itself what this is—creating the experience. Or in an organic sense we imply that this flower has already bloomed and that the fruit must ripen.

---

3   The phonetic translation in English is "poznaniye."

4   The phonetic translation in English is "poznavane."

So you can't know until you conceive. Otherwise you'll be an empty soul turned upwards. When the soul turns downwards, we'll say the Lord put something in you. This fruit may fall prematurely, but then it must repeat the process of development again and ripen, because without pain there's no success. The "O," zero, they say, is nothing. But in mathematics it has the power to increase and decrease by ten, if we place it in front or behind some number. If, for instance, after 1 we put 0, we get a number ten times larger, and if we put it in front of 1—ten times smaller. So, even nothing is something. How can that, which has nothing within itself, increase and decrease things? In my understanding, in *nothing* exists time and space like two elements for our natural development: light and heat work in space. So, when we put a zero behind the "Π," it indicates that the flower has conditions to develop. But we descend into this tree, which has a double life—up in the trunk and branches, and down in the roots. We say that the fish is submerged in the water, and man, in air. It's half true. There are other elements, without which life would cease to exist. Fruit plants have two environments: soil for the roots, and the atmosphere for the branches and buds. Then "knowledge" implies the understanding of soil as environment for the branches, and for the roots, as a condition for acquiring food for the branches, the leaves, and the flowers. You are, let's say, down in the roots. When traveling upon this tree, the tree of life, there exists a double-life: material in the roots, and spiritual in the branches. They are like subject and predicate. The world of spirits, of angels, which some call the astral world, is the connection between the human world (the physical, the material), and the purely spiritual or Divine world. The one who speaks is God—He represents the predicate, a fountain of knowledge, power, and life. Man is the subject, the soil that prepares life's juices, and the auxiliary verb, "is," represents the spirits, the angels, who connect the physical world to the spiritual, and who apply the laws of harmonic action in these two worlds. You may have a subject, and you may have a predicate, but if you don't have this connection, you don't have a sentence. The angels, in fact, bring us the knowledge of God, without which we cannot have any life within. I'll make an analogy: Let's say you go out at night during the winter, shivering, and you warm yourself by the moon. Someone asks you, "why are you sitting here?"—"I'm warming myself."—"But there's no sun."—"You're a blind man. You're deceived. Little by little, this sun will warm me." When you have no idea of God, it exposes a gap between God and yourself, a certain barrier that crosses your life and the Divine. Now, I notice that in this speech there's something vague in your mind. Do you know why? When I travel from this world to explain things from *that* world, there's a gap. If I tell you about music, I can say that one can grasp with his ear at least 32 to 46,000 vibrating sound waves per second. When it comes to light, it appears immediately as a red ray that produces in our eye 428 billion vibrations per second. As we climb higher on this bar, between the red and violet rays are 739 billion vibrations per second. Our speech can only be logical when we restrict ourselves to the narrow circle of things that we can grasp, which we can try and understand. As we move abruptly from sound to light, we can't always be logical, because between sound and light are some vibrations that we haven't taken into consideration. We pass from sound to light, but we miss some areas, of which we know nothing. We travel to *that* world from 32 vibrations and we reach 46,000 vibrations per second—the world accessible to our ear, and we say, "this is as much as we know." But when we continue from here and go further, we're in the dark and say, "we don't know this." When we reach the red rays, we say, "thank God! We passed through that desert." And that desert encompasses an unimaginably massive space between two boundaries of 46,000 and 428 billion vibrations per second. All those things people don't understand are a desert for them, in which nothing grows, nothing happens. When Christ spoke of "eternal life," He was very careful. He filled the gaps, united the worlds into one whole: the "spiritual" with the world of angels, the "Divine" with the world of the Trinity, the "physical" with the world of people, the souls. That's why He says, "I am the way of Truth in life. I connect these two worlds and lead equally to the world of angels, and to the world of God, to the Truth. Therefore, whoever follows Me and goes on this path, which I will point to, will find the necessary goods for his soul, Divine peace." That's why He says, "I give you peace, I leave you My peace." And peace is a child of Heaven; It is raised in God's dwelling. From the above we conclude the following: The Way: this is the movement of the Spirit in the rational application of laws in nature. Life: this is the harmonic organization of elements and development of powers in the Divine Soul. The Truth is the manifestation of the One God, who creates the conditions in which the human spirit and the human soul can strive for something better and brighter in this vast world.

Let's look at "eternal life" as a spring flowing from some mountain peak of the Divine, beneath some cliff. Water is the life-bringing element. The flow of the river [is] the path of descending to a lower level, toward a lower world. That's why Christ says, "I come from Truth—from God—and descend to the material world, to help the people, to quench them with this living water." That's why He says elsewhere, "I am living water." These three things of which I speak, Eternal Life, God, Jesus Christ, Way, Truth, and Life, are interconnected. If the water doesn't spring out of the mountain peak, and if it doesn't flow along the path of the river bed, of which Christ speaks, it cannot carry the expected goods. And from a purely Christian viewpoint, we ought to be near this spring. The living Christ is the spring. One only needs to know how to drink from the water of that spring. I'm not saying you don't know how to drink, but you drink 500 or 1,000 kilometers away from the spring, and then you say that you know the essence of Christ. And you don't know how many other elements entered into that water, sullying it, deceiving your taste buds. You have to go up the river. The path is a little long, your feet will get calloused, but when you reach the spring, you'll say, "that's what I call water!" Those who can't go to the spring will drink muddy water. It's muddy, but without water is even worse. I tell you, even though you'll get callouses on your feet, go to the spring and drink the pure water. Upon returning, you'll have a clear and fresh mind, a good heart and a broad outlook. A lot of effort is necessary, a lot of work upon oneself, in order for one to apply Christ's teaching, to obtain those beneficial results which will one day raise him up and make him a fellow citizen of Heaven, to live among saints and angels.

Now let me get back to the question. When we talk about eternal life in the sense of immortality, everyone will say that such a life is not possible here on earth. Indeed, when someone "dies," can he acquire life? The conclusion is correct, but not all correct conclusions are true, because how do we know that man really "dies?" When someone doesn't work during the spring, the summer, or the fall, but says, "I'll work in the winter," I would tell him: You don't have conditions for work. If you didn't work during the spring, the summer, or fall, how will you get wealthy during the winter? If you didn't work when you had the time, how will you acquire eternal life? You can acquire eternal life now, today! As long as you have the courage of that Bulgarian shepherd, properly carrying your staff and knowing how to wield it, how to strike. When translated in scientific form, striking means the conditions in which you can react when exposed to some misfortune in life. You often say, "whatever the Lord says," but God says that such a coward should have his sheep taken away. He'll be a slave, sitting like the Jews in Egypt, forced to make bricks. And truly, all we do is make bricks and houses. We build and build, making a house; then the Lord comes and kicks us out. We start again: 5, 10, 15, 20 years we save, and after a few years he takes it away again. Why this fruitless effort? I'm not trying to say we shouldn't work, but we must work *wisely*, to gain something that is ours. When I preach this, someone will say, "but you're teaching us not to work." I teach that you have to work. The one who comes, the tax collector, takes away your property and heart and sells them, but he never sells your mind. How many hearts, how many souls are exchanged and sold! And the people say they're owners. We see many who don't know how to think and act. They can hate, but they can't love. All these people with their corrupt minds and hearts create karma, and see, in the future, the whole population draws and weeps over the laws issued by their elected ones. Go and ask your legislators, ask your chamber of deputies what laws they're making. Some chamber-member says, "I'm crafting laws where in the future God's Laws will no longer be taught in schools," and another one: "God will be thrown out. It's something anachronistic. No-one will go to church. The new ideas will be followed, and whoever doesn't follow this law will be fined with such-and-such amount of leva."[5] You say, "there's nothing we can do. These are the deputies we sent to make laws; we will obey." But you will also say, "the law they drafted and put into effect is not fair." Now you will have to drag in other deputies who will prove your right to create another law. Whatever happens in the world happens inside us as well. Christ says that in order to obtain eternal life, one must first learn to think and act properly. You now say to yourselves, "we know. When we return home, we'll start applying the law accordingly." What will you apply? The old law, all over again? The smallest annoyance will drive you off the rails, and you'll forget about eternal life. The servant burns the meal, and you start yelling and arguing. You lose your mind and heart over one meal. Do you know what you resemble? Many times, wise people leave stories for certain cases. For example, a dog passed over a bridge, and looking over the water, it saw another dog carrying a bone. Dropping its own [bone] it threw itself in the river to grab the other bone, losing its own. Oftentimes we too, in the same way, leave the *civilized* to chase the *wild*. Let the servant burn your food. Don't let it disturb you. When

---

5 Deunov is most likely referring to the Communist party.

preparing eternal life for yourselves, have the patience and self-control of that philosopher who, after working 20 years on some mathematical equations, which he wrote on little papers, didn't get angry at the maid after returning home to find that, during the house-cleaning, she threw all his little papers in the fire. But you have to keep your little papers safe. Now you frequently gather and collect all these little papers which God wrote and say, "what are these rags?" and you throw them in the fire. When God comes and asks, "where are your books?" what will you answer?—"We cleaned the room."—"This should not happen again." In that way, you shouldn't clean your Divine room. These books are the various centers in man, in whom God wrote much, and which are very precious to you. Everything must be put in order. There are many things scattered about the building that the Lord is constructing: there are scattered bricks, sand, stones; all these materials will be used to construct your new home. You must prepare this material yourself. That's why Christ says, "when you know within yourself the One True God, who builds, who is an environment, an element for you, you will acquire eternal life." And now I want to leave you three things you have to think about: environment, conditions, and elements. Whoever cannot ponder over these, let him ponder over whatever he can. But to those who think, let them see whether they're submerged in that environment which is called God. Do they have the conditions and elements? Is their air clean? Are their windows open? Are the eyes and tongue in place? The tongue isn't as small as it appears, that little tongue. This little tongue, which creates and brings down in the world, barely shows itself. It's invisible, but what a hero it is: it breaks bones, it brings people together for battle. If the tongue isn't in place, you need to tighten its screws so it's not loose, because when the Lord comes, He'll inspect whether all the screws on your tongue are in place and whether the tongue functions the way He made it. The screws are broken somewhere—chatter. "Soon you must give the screws here!" I know so many lost screws! The lost screws, the rings, all the parts of your tongue, your mind, your heart—you'll bring them all. All this has to be put into place. That's why Christ is coming now. You've thrown the wheel out. You shouldn't have. "How so?" Scientists say the appendix is unnecessary and must be removed, that one must get rid of it when it starts feeling painful. How can you say it's not in place? A time will come when it will start functioning. Doctors say, "the appendix is inflamed, let's cut it out." I'd rather die than rid myself of it, because the disease will appear elsewhere. No organs should be cut out, because it took the Lord millions of years to create this appendix. And now, some stupid doctor finds it unnecessary and "chop!"—it's out, freeing the person from it. Many times the appendix revolts and says, "don't eat meat. Animals shouldn't be slaughtered." Beans, lentils, and string beans won't cause pain. We say, "get out, appendix! We'll still eat meat." But the appendix has companions in the heart and mind. If you cut it out down there, his friend in the heart and up in the mind will die along with it. That's why Christ says, "these three elements in life: conditions, forces, and laws, must be put in place." That's what Christianity implies, and herein lies the deep science of life. I don't want to give you an empty philosophy, but I want you to check and try in life what I'm telling you. How will the world be fixed? It will be fixed when all the screws are set in place, and life starts functioning like a watch. I'll give you an example: A person bought a watch that soon stopped. "I spent so much money. I haven't even worn it a week and it stopped," he said to himself. He goes to a watchmaker and asks him to make it work again. "How much money do you want?" The watchmaker looked at the watch and said, "ten coins."—"Okay." The watchmaker blows into the watch's mechanism, a lodged flea jumps out, and the watch starts functioning. "Will you really charge me ten coins just for one blow?"—"That's the amount." And the Lord will come, He'll blow, and everything will function. How easy! These critters belong elsewhere, they need not sit inside the watch.

Christianity is a philosophy that wants to free the human soul from all kinds of parasites, so the screws in the tongue, in the mind, and heart, may fall into place. Therein lies salvation. And when all the nuts and screws are put in place, when the mind and heart are in place and in order, the conditions of eternal life will follow. Then the resurrection will be feasible and possible. I know that putting these screws in place is a difficult and hard task, but when it's accomplished successfully humanity will celebrate its jubilee on earth. Children—sons and daughters—will sing life's new song, that their parents found and adjusted the screws, and a bright future is coming for them. The nations will heal, praise, and honor the Good Lord that their spiritual leaders, priests, preachers, teachers, kings, and ministers found and adjusted their screws, and that a bright future is coming to their lives on earth. Everyone will sing one song, but it will be life's great song which will touch the bottom of their hearts and souls. This song will reveal the past in its entirety, the whole future will flow, the Spirit of the new life will express itself. But, someone will say, "why the screws? What can they do?" The path that needs to be taken is drawn on these screws. They unite, they tighten the broken parts of life. And the one who examines their spiraling grooves, and the hand that screws them in, will understand the deep meaning of the great laws that move everything toward a definite purpose. These are Divine forces that, according to God's will, will soon appear in life, and will adjust and put into place all diverging elements, direct the Divine juices toward the human soul, place the human soul in it's true environment, will create the most favorable conditions for its development, and will bring forth life's real elements. Then our soul will suck, like a child sucks from his mother's breasts, pure and unadulterated milk. Then the roots of Divine Consciousness will appear in our subconscious, and the stem will rise upon it. Branches will grow, the leaves of our self-consciousness will develop, and in the furrows of the latter, buds and flowers will appear—the flowers of superconsciousness, of the angels.

When this happens, it will be a sign of the *spiritual* spring. The human soul will be in the realm of immortality, beyond the grasp of death, sin, and crime. And with conviction and faith, with certainty and knowledge, we can expect the priceless wealth—the fruit of the tree of eternal life, the leaves of which serve to heal human disabilities, and the very fruit for maintaining the immortality of the human soul and its unity with God. And this great event is on the verge in today's life.

Lecture held on 12 October 1914 in Sofia

FEAR

"Do not be afraid of those who kill the body but cannot kill the soul. Rather, be afraid of the One who can destroy both soul and body in hell."—Matthew 10:28 (NIV)

Fear is an oppressive feeling of the soul that exists not just in people, but also in animals. It's a feeling put into the living organism to carry out a certain mission. Fear implies that the environment in which we live or the conditions in which we exist are adverse or harmful elements [that threaten] our lives. When a child makes a mistake for the first time, immediately the feeling of fear arises in his soul. Whose soul is quiet and peaceful when committing a minor sin? Immediately a sense of fear arises within. So, various elements arise in the soul that feel threatening. Assuming you have a house—let's say the floor is made of pine—fear immediately arises in you, because it can set on fire and burn. There is, then, a certain element in your floor, substances that can burn in flames. They can consume these properties and your whole house will burn. Having worked in the organic world for thousands of years, this feeling made people and animals slaves of fear. But fear also has a good side: thanks to *it*, vigilance has come about. Many animals grew longer legs due to fear. An animal with long legs is always fearful. You can take this as a fact: A rabbit's hind legs are very long, but the ones in the front are short. If the front ones were also long, they would have been even more advantageous in running.

Now, I'm not going to talk about the role of fear in the history of evolution. Modern-day scholars say that religion originated from fear. Christ turns to His disciples because He knows they're in that category, fearing for their houses, their bodies, and says, "do not be afraid of those who can kill the body, but cannot damage the soul." Why? If you have a certain capital invested in the bank and someone lights your house on fire, don't worry, because you'll make a new and better house. So, while you have the capital of your soul put into another place, there's no need to fear.

Now let's take the second part of the verse, who to fear: "Fear the one who can destroy both the body and the soul." There have been many disputes regarding the second part of the verse: who is this second one of whom we should be afraid? Some say that the one we should fear is the devil. I say the one we should fear is God, in the sense of being careful not to distress Him, and that means to be devout. If I interpreted the Divine Law of life, I wouldn't tell you who to fear or not fear, but I would tell you how to fulfill God's Law. This is the negative form of fear. But the positive form comes when we sin: whoever does the will of God has no need to fear. But whoever doesn't do it will always have fear in his heart and will never be calm and free. In the verse I read, Christ wants to assure His disciples that there are some laws in the world that regulate human life: "Even the hairs on your head," He says to His disciples, "are numbered." Not a single strand of hair can fall randomly. If we observe God's Law, I will be under God's protection, like the birds. In modern-day Christians there is a misconception in our relationship to God, to religion, and consequently many sufferings arise in the human soul. Some, for instance, regard religion as just going to church, lighting a candle, and crossing oneself, and they think they're religious by doing these things. But religion is something much deeper. The most profound essence in religion is to love God. Once we have this basic Law within ourselves, we'll be ready to do thousands of other things for the Lord. But how can we show love for the Lord when we don't see Him? Christ says, "your Father is in Heaven." I turn my eyes and see He's not there, and say to myself, "when I get out of the body, I'll go to that place." Christ turns to His disciples and tells them, "do not fear those who are in the earth and kill." Who are the ones who kill? If you read the first verse, you'll see that power is given to the wicked spirits to kill, but this power doesn't extend to good people, but to the evil ones. The modern-day Christian says, "I want to rule over my brothers." You see that Christ didn't give the apostles authority to rule over people, but over bad spirits. Every one of us must rule over them. Whoever doesn't understand this Divine Law will always make mistakes. There will be an ambush by these spirits, from here or there. The people have various methods for challenging the spirits, but the spirits aren't afraid of this. They're neither afraid of sticks, nor words. To have power over an unclean spirit, you must not possess his weaknesses. If you have them—you may be educated, a philosopher, a minister—you'll be their slave. They'll cause intrigue, they'll dethrone kings; they can do everything. If you don't possess their weaknesses, you're their master. That's precisely why Christ commanded the spirits. He was pure, and when He said, "get out!" they replied, "we're listening." Those who bring and treat diseases are also bad spirits. You'll say, "strange," right? That's the law. If you borrow money from someone, don't you have to return it to them? If you injure someone, don't you have to pay for his treatment? The devil harms, and you call the Lord to repair these things for you. The Lord grabs the devil and tells him, "you wrecked that person's house. Now go and fix it!" and the devil struggles to fix it. And afterwards he says again, "please, bring down the house again." Now, why doesn't the Lord answer your prayers? I'll tell you: Because you're sinners. When these workers come, you can't control them, and they run away. When the Lord sends them, you must have the power to order them, to stand over them with a whip, because the moment you let go of them, they will all run away and your house will remain incomplete. Some say, "we can't exist without weaknesses." If you can't, they'll kill you, take your body, your money, they'll lock you up—there's no other way out. Now, Christ comes and says, "I'll tell you who to fear." He says, "don't tread over God's Law." The second part of this interpretation implies the fulfillment of God's Law, so your bodies and souls may be free.

Every one of us has to make a little revision in the heart and mind, to see the weaknesses in them. If you like to tell fibs, all the spirits of deceit are around you; they're in your house. You attract them. If you like gloating, all the spirits that gloat are also around you. And if you were clairvoyant, you would see that there are hordes of them in your houses, who only eat and drink. If you hate, all the spirits of hate eat and drink at your expense. That's why people die. When they come and sit for a day or two at your house, you start complaining, of course: "My head hurts here; my hands hurt; the feet; the stomach; the heart; the lungs." Why wouldn't they hurt? These evil spirits draw juices from you, and your eyes start fogging up, you go blind, you go deaf, your feet and hands also start to hurt, and one day they grab you and take you to the grave. And when you go to the Lord with torn clothes, He'll ask you, "well, son, did you eat everything I gave you?"—"Father, forgive. We ate, drank, and fornicated. We won't do this in the future." And because God is good, He says, "as long as you learn the lesson, I will credit you again." And that's why Christ says, "I will tell you who to fear." This dread, this fear, is *prudence*. When the negative feeling unites with the positive in man, the sense of caution and the ability to reason, then prudence is born in him. Fear is the negative side of prudence. Therefore, Christ wants to say, "don't separate these two elements from each other, because once you separate them," that is, "once you separate your reason from the feeling of fear, without using one to control the other, you will lose your body and soul altogether." What does hell mean? You'll see that it lies in those limited conditions of development where you'll spend a life of suffering, and the only thing that will remain in you is a naked consciousness. And do you know the situation of someone dead? One day you'll experience this feeling more tangibly. When the dead man is just bones, his soul circles around these bones and says, "how beautiful they were!" and cries, "this is the remaining treasure. The plaster is gone." The bricks and tiles are there, and after awhile these bones will restore their original temple, and that's why the Lord asks the prophet, "son of man, can these bones come to life?" The prophet replies, "you know, Lord!" The Lord says, "go then, and prophesy to the Spirit to come and bring them to life."[1] One time, Edison played a little prank on some of his friends: he made two skeletons move automatically, connecting their feet and hands with wire. He put gramophones on the hands and electrical lights in the eyes, and then these two automatons started talking: "We were once like you. We ate and drank. Look at us now!" Everyone became afraid and started running. It took Edison a long time to convince them that this was just a prank devised by him. With the current mode of abnormal living, each person will find himself in a skeleton, unable to work, think, or act. That's why Christ turns to His disciples and tells them, "do not be afraid." In order to regulate that feeling, fear, we must completely rely on the Divine Law, on the consciousness within, that we are connected to God. Sometimes the thought arises in us: "We want to see the Lord. We want to see Jesus Christ." You see Him every day, as long as that feeling of love awakens in you. He's there, and you feel it. You just have to open your spiritual eyes in order to see Him. You currently see the outer appearance of things, but you don't see the essential. Every day, every one of you is in contact with the Lord when you suffer and love. When a person suffers and is in a sickly state, the Lord heals him by binding his wounds, causing some pain, and the patient complains. The Lord explains the reasons for these sufferings: "You suffer because you did not fulfill my commandments, but be patient. I will heal you."—"But this pain is unbearable."—"Yes, but when I told you not to violate the commandment you didn't listen."—"But it'll take a long time."—"You'll learn." From now on you have to make an attempt. This is something the old Christians used to do, to be

---

1 Ezekiel 37:3.

able to go out of your body. Your mind speaks, "it would be glorious to go out." Glorious, but you need to have knowledge. First, you have to get rid of all the weaknesses of those spirits that surround you, and when you go out you need to tell them, "nobody can come near my body, otherwise there's a whip waiting." But if the spirits know you have weaknesses, the moment you leave your body, they'll take it away. That's why modern-day people are strongly connected by the Lord to their physical body, because if they leave the body it'll be even worse for them; their evolution will cease. Christ turns to His disciples, who want to follow Him, to understand those mysteries of the Kingdom of God, and I think the method for longevity lies here. Now, I'll relate a fact to you: Take people who suffer and who get angry, who pass their lives through many storms: their life is short-lived. Those who are calm, as they say, "well-disposed" people, and don't get angry, don't worry—they have a long life. That's why Herbert Spencer says somewhere, "when the external forces of nature balance with the internal processes of the human organism, we will have eternal life in the physical world." What are these external forces? They are the harmful elements. When we are balanced, when we come to understand what we want, what we desire, and know how to react to the harmful elements and subjugate them, we'll be able to live on earth as long as we want—one hundred, five hundred, or a thousand years, and we'll be able to leave again whenever we want. It will depend on us. After living several thousand years, we'll say, "we lived and now we want to go on a long walk to the other world." Then our relatives will accompany us, the way they send us off nowadays when the train starts. That's how we'll leave. We'll be free, we'll take out a ticket and we'll leave, and our friends won't follow us and say, "the poor man died."—"No," we'll say, "I'm going for a walk. I'm going to visit my Father's house. One day I might return again." And they'll wish us safe travels. Christianity is the kind of science that must prepare that journey, in which you have to travel a long way. Don't think the place you're going is very close. It *is* very close, but also very far. "Close" and "far" are relative things. If you are moving at medium speed, it'll take you 250 years to go to the sun. But if you travel at the speed of sunlight, you'll go in 8-9 minutes. In 9 minutes you can't even go from here to the Boris Garden.[2] I need 20 minutes to get from here to the Boris Garden, but the sunlight travels 92 to 93 million miles in 9 minutes. When we talk about space, we refer to it in terms of the speed at which we move. If we were going to the closest star, Alpha Centauri, do you know how many years it will take? Thirty-four million years by train, and with the speed of light, 3 years. But if you say you want to get to the nearest universe connected to our universe, with the speed of light, it takes 90 million years. So it'll depend where you go. If you go to the sun and move with the speed of a train, and your friends ask how many years until you return, say, "250 years to go there, and 250 for the return trip—500 years, and 250 years to live there. So, after 750 years, we'll return back again." If you ask someone who is going to Alpha Centauri, after how many years until he returns, he'll say, "34 million years to go there, 34 million years to return, and the same amount of years sitting there. So, I'll return in 100 million years."

These are abstract philosophical ideas, attainable only by angelic minds. You can't grasp this space of 34 million years. You need an angelic mind to grasp the greatness of God in this thought. And Christ turns to His disciples, saying, "do not be afraid." He looks up and adds, "don't worry about these little houses that you have. Don't worry about these little things, because your Father has great things in store for you." Make sure to keep your soul pure and bright. If you possess it as capital, you can travel through these spaces. One day, when you leave for Heaven, you won't bring your body. You'll leave with your soul. Your body will remain on earth, because it was taken from here. It's a wagon made from the elements of the earth, and while you're in the kingdom of these four elements of the earth,

---

2   A public park in downtown Sofia.

you'll be in the wagon. When you come to a mountainous place where you'll have to go along the narrow path, you'll leave the wagon and go on foot. That's why Christ says, "don't worry. When you reach the mountainous path, don't lose your soul and stop your evolution."

You want to become masters. Don't become masters over your brothers. The biggest crime of modern-day people is that they want to dominate one another. You shouldn't command people. You can, and you should, command the bad spirits. I want you to command a bad spirit, to teach it, but I don't want you to command people. That's what Christ says. You sometimes want to know who is bigger, and who is smaller; who is older, and who is younger. But the fact that you're bigger or smaller, older or younger—so what? The Lord may have sent you sooner or later. Man can be at the tail-end or the head—so what? One day the Lord will put you on the tail, another time on the head; one day on the spine, another time on the feet—it's useless. These things aren't essential. The power lies in this: to feel like a master over bad spirits, to tell them to listen, to do this or that. "I want to scare my wife by beating her." Well, today you beat, tomorrow you beat, but she'll run away, and you'll go begging after her. Man's power is within; that's where he should turn his attention. Every one of you must learn to control these spirits. I know many seek Christ for help. How will He help them? He ties [the evil spirits] up, yet they untie them. You can't help these people. Will Christ deal with you, will He deal with your foxes and wolves? Put them to work. This idea is, perhaps, in somewhat of an allegorical form, but I give it to you as a rule: You can't become masters of your lives until you learn to control these spirits.

There are seven steps you have to take before you can rule over bad spirits. The unclean spirits are afraid of the light. The first thing you have to do is to turn toward God. Why turn? You're now turned toward God with your back to Him. There's darkness in your world. Circle around and turn with your face toward the Lord. Unless you turn to Him you can't. When you want to shake the dust off a garment, how do you turn it over? Consequently, take your heart and your mind to turn them and you'll shake the dust from inside. Turning has a double-meaning: turning toward the sun and turning the garment from the inside to shake the dust off.

The second thing is repentance, reviewing and doing away with the bill. You put a sign over your company: "I stopped paying; I neither give, nor do I take. I'm doing an annual balance-sheet." You balance things out, you calculate: you need to get this much, and you need to give that much. Finally, you have a debt of 10,000 remaining. There's nothing left for you to do other than to go to your creditors and beg—that's repentance. You take out your notebooks: "Friends, I'm an honest man. I don't know how, but I lost 10,000 leva. Forgive me and excuse me. Can you give me a little more credit?" If you don't beg, they'll lock you up. Once they look over your account and are convinced that you're honest, they'll say, "we had dealings with you before. We'll forgive. We'll re-credit you."

Forgiveness and salvation are two interrelated things. What we call salvation in Christianity comes after passing through the two steps: turning and repentance toward Christ. He says, "I'm giving you a new credit line and sending you back to earth to work." You re-open your company: So-and-so is back in business, giving and receiving.

The fourth step is rebirth. I'll explain rebirth using another process from agriculture: A farmer has a garden which he reaps and re-sows. When the new apples begin to sprout, it's rebirth. There's hope there, that the new garden will give him fruit again. And in Christianity, after passing through this process, rebirth happens in us—the new begins to sprout up. Rebirth is a process of blooming and flowering. There's repentance, forgiveness, salvation, rebirth, and new birth, the fifth. In the new birth, man is released from the karmic law of cause and consequence. You are then free citizens, masters. No one can rule over you. Only in this fifth step can you rule over the bad spirits. Only when you're in the place of Christ can you command the spirits. Then you'll be a disciple of Christ. It's a high post. He gave His disciples power over evil spirits and sent them to heal and resurrect people. How can this power be given when man barely turned and still hasn't looked over his bill? They still haven't forgiven him; he has yet to be reborn, and he wants to rule the world! It can't happen. You have to pass through these four steps and then you'll be full masters of your position. Now you're sitting and wondering, but you still have fear within yourselves whether you have this virtue or not. There are two extremes in Christianity: some act more humble than they really are, but some feel more sinful than they are in actuality. One is an extreme, and the other one as well. Honestly say to yourself, "I have 10,000 leva in the bank," and not, when you have 10,000, to say 5,000—you're lying. You have 10,000, but say 15,000—you're lying. If you have 10,000 leva, put them down as 10,000, not higher or lower. We always have to speak the truth, the way we know it in ourselves. We have to speak clearly, definitely, positively—then our external relations to people will be good. Why? Because the spirits that guide you live in Heaven. When you settle your bills with your spirit, he'll arrange them with the other spirits, and they can't hate you. They may say, "I will kill you." You'll answer them calmly, "you can't because you're tied up." Someone says, "I'll do this."—"You can't. Go ahead and try." One day someone said to me, "if I pull out a revolver, you'll see."—Get it out. What if it stays in the air glued to your hand?—"Then I'll pull out a knife."—Get it out. Have you ever pulled out a knife to see what it is? You don't pull it out just like that. There must be permission for this from above. If from above they want to test you to see if you're hard, whether you have patience and self-denial, they may put you in various trials, and you have to endure them. But if there's no permission from above, the whole world may come down, and it'll just wander around you. An Englishman made a bet for £4,000 with another one who had 40 bulldogs, who said, "there are no dogs more dreadful than mine. You can't even get close to them." The first Englishman made the bet and drew a circle around himself, but the other one released the dogs on him. But they just wandered around the circle and couldn't pass through it. Finally, that one Englishman made a strange whistling sound, and the dogs ran past the crowds. How did he scare them? He had some power within himself. He didn't chase them with a rifle or with a stick. He had some power that he used. That's why they ran away. I ask you, "where is your power?" One day some bad spirit may say, "when I release my dogs."—"Release them. I'll draw a circle, and the moment I whistle, they'll disappear like smoke." The power lies in this Divine whistle, and whoever has it, he's always free and in command.

You now have a method for governing the bad spirits, to not have their weaknesses. If you are scared, all the spirits of fear will surround you. So, remove all these weaknesses from you. "But," you say, "I won't do this. I won't smoke tobacco," and again, the next day you smoke again. Do it without saying it. "I decided to plant," but you haven't planted anything yet. Plant it, then call your friends over and tell them, "come friends, to see what I did." They'll be happy. You say, "I decided to be good. Come and see my plan: I'll do this, I'll do that." You won't do anything. I've seen millions of plans. Hell is constantly full of plans. You think of doing something; don't say anything. Just say, "Lord, help me." And when your garden grows and gives fruit, gather all your friends and tell them, "eat, drink, and rejoice." Then the Lord will bless you. This is Christianity. And when Christ tells you, "do not be afraid of those who kill the body, but fear those who kill the soul," He wants to say that whatever they take can be taken, as the proverb says, even on Easter. One day the term will expire, and it will be taken. You're a tenant; your wagon will be taken away and you'll say, "they kicked me out of the house." Why wouldn't they kick you out? Be grateful that they were kind enough to wait for you all these years. The spirits are masters of the elements you have on earth—they belong to them. That's why Scripture says that in this world we are "foreigners," that this earth in which we live isn't ours.

The Lord sent us to take it forcibly. And you want to conquer it, to be masters, but wait— conquer the spirits first, because every element has its master. You can't become masters of water if you don't conquer the spirits of water. You can't be masters of the air until you conquer the spirits of air. Neither can you be masters of fire, and so on. Therefore, Christ gives us a law that we must act upon: the first thing is to be pure and then turn to Him. Now, because Christ is coming to this world, how will He find you? Of course, He'll find some wealthy, and others poor. It is said: "And upon this foundation from above, if I give anyone gold, silver, precious stones, wood, hay, or straw, any work will be made visible. For the day will show it, because with fire it is revealed, and the fire will test every man what is the work: to whom the work which he has built shall stand, he shall take a salary. But to whom the work is burned, he will suffer, but he himself will be saved from the fire."[3] And anyone who doesn't keep the virtue and doesn't fear the Lord: "Let's give such a man to satan for destroying the flesh, that the spirit may be saved in the day of the Lord Jesus." If you acquired experience from so many thousands of years—you suffered, you held the banner of Truth high, you didn't fear those who kill the body, and you sacrificed for the triumph of righteousness, the celebration of the Kingdom of God, the Lord will raise you again. He'll resurrect you. And that's why Christ says, "do not be afraid of those who kill the body." If they kill your body, your soul will remain free, and this is precious in life. Any other path that deviates you from the Truth is detrimental both to your body and to your soul. For the cowardly, the faint of heart, will not inherit the Kingdom of God. In the righteous work of the Lord, in the righteous work of mankind, in the righteous deeds of the nation, in the righteous deeds of society, in the righteous work of the home, in the righteous deeds of the individual soul, there must be neither fear or dread, nor hesitation; no cowardice, no retreat from the great origin

---

3   1 Corinthians 3:10-15.

of life. Righteousness is always right. Love and fear are incompatible things in the human spirit, in the spirit of the real human. Where there is Love, there is no fear. And where there is fear, Love is not there. Love is a sign of completeness, unity in all the forces, feelings, and abilities of the human spirit. And fear is a sign of absence, a division in this inner harmony of the soul's peace.

With these last words, I understand the high, the noble, the good in man. I don't mean that impudence, that rudeness, that cruelness of heart, that insensitivity that often passes off for bravery and fearlessness. The ideal of heroism is in this: when they place you on the pillory for a righteous deed, to accept with generosity all sufferings, all the disgrace, all the blasphemy, and all the gloom and accusation of those surrounding you, even if it's the whole world, and to tell your Mother, "for You, who gave birth to me in God's world, I sacrifice everything. In your Love, I find my last pillar of support for my soul. The fear of the world, of those who kill the body, is antiquated. I'm not afraid, because I know You. Whether you give me death or life, I accept both equally with gratitude. With You, even in death there is meaning. Without You, even life has no purpose. In death or in life, may You always be the bright crown for my spirit."

Lecture held on 19 October 1914

IN THE BEGINNING WAS THE WORD

"In the beginning was the Word, and the Word was with God, and the Word was God."—John 1:1 (KJV)

This is the hardest nut and the most philosophical question in Christianity. Thousands of arguments took place on the basis of this verse and, of course, the various philosophers, preachers, and people of different creeds interpret it as they see fit. And in the Orthodox Church there have been disputes over the Word—they even fought over it! But the question can't be solved with fighting. What ought we understand in the ordinary sense in the words "in the beginning was the Word?" What is that beginning? When they want to discuss a certain philosophical question, modern philosophers make some assumptions: they take something like a principle and use it to explain a specific thing. For example, a negro preacher explained the creation of man in the following way: "God struggled all day and made man with clay. He placed him on a knitted rack and let him dry off three more days." However, one of his listeners asked him, "what's holding up the knitted rack?"—"That's none of your business," the preacher replied. Modern philosophers have a woven rack where they *cure* the Word and man, solve all questions and say, "man is made of clay and cured on a woven rack." And when you ask about the woven rack, they'll say, "it's not your business to know this." But because that woven rack stands in the path where we are going, if we move close to it, we stop and walk around it. That's how an Evangelical preacher spoke about the prophet Jonah and said, "the whale struggled for a whole hour, and really found it difficult before swallowing Jonah." In the same way, now we sit for hours trying to solve the question, but it's still unsolved.

"In the beginning was the Word, and the Word was with God, and the Word was God." Here the main idea is the Word. What should we understand by the "Word?" That wise Divine act, manifested through certain vibrations that we can perceive. So, when things become visible, tangible, accessible to the human mind—something that is formed, understandable to us, we call it the Word. For instance, you say a word—that's the *Word*. The word "любовь [love]" consists of how many elements? How many letters? Six. If you could separate these elements you would understand what Love is composed of, in relation to people. That is, not in its original sense, but in its manifestation. If we come to the very meaning of the Word, what it is, what God is, those who want to resolve the matter will find themselves in opposition. You can never define that which has no form in itself. God is something without form, therefore we cannot define Him. What is God? Tell us! In order to define Him, you have to give Him some boundaries, a certain form, to place Him in a human point of view, in a certain position and place. Those who write about God and the Word believe they solved the question. They explain it, but as the negro or Evangelical preacher—either on the woven rack, or in the whale's mouth. But that's not an explanation.

It is said, "in the beginning." In these words I understand an intelligent act when all beings created by God sensed within themselves that He creates, and they began to work alongside Him. I will use an analogy: assume that a mother gives birth to a child and says, "the beginning of my child starts now." This is *her* beginning of the child, but not the beginning of the child's wisdom. What does this beginning resemble? Whimpering and crying, where nobody understands what the child wants to say. The beginning mentioned in the Gospels is intelligent. When the child reaches 21 years of age and begins to reason, then we can claim that it's the beginning of intelligent life, that is, when there can be a proper exchange of thoughts between the mother and the child. Therefore, "in the beginning was the Word" implies that beginning when we began to understand God, that is, when we stopped whimpering before Him. For many centuries the people wept and wanted this and that. And to clarify my words in scientific form, I will point out that these are all stages of life through which this human child has undergone. So, this *beginning* passed through millions of forms, starting with the smallest. And because the child constantly cried, the Lord had to constantly sew new clothes, that is, to turn him into a bird, then a mammal. When that capricious child reaches the point where he can understand its beginning, it means the Word entered *him*. That's why the Evangelist says, "the beginning is marked in the book of Heaven as an intelligent form of structure and order." Everyone begins with disorganization—everyone begins as clay, which is dried up there on the wire rack. But when you get down from the wire rack and stand on your feet, the Heavens write about you: "In the beginning was the Word, and the Word was with God, and the Word was God," and that beginning is now the head of man.

I will explain with another analogy when this Beginning starts: Imagine you are walking along a river, following it until you reach the spring. You reach it and say that the beginning of the river is such-and-such a spring, and stop. Yes, it's the beginning. No philosopher can say that it's not. This is the *visible* beginning, but there are other beginnings of which we don't know. Perhaps this water was brought from the ocean, wandered through space in the form of vapor, and then fell as rain. Maybe it passed through earth's layers and reached the spring, and so on. Therefore, we say this river starts from such-and-such a spring, but only in a simple sense. "In the beginning was the Word" indicates that intelligent beginning of all mankind, when the Word appeared in the form we see as it exists. Of course, now you're far from that beginning: millions of years passed and everything is muddy.

Now I'll give you another comparison: If you read the Epistle to the Galatians, you'll see that it speaks of the fruits of Love. Take a fruit and assume there is only one seed in it. If you plant it, that will be the beginning of its development. And if you ask the tree about its beginning, when it began, it will answer you: "From such-and-such a time, from the planting of the seed." Therefore, when they ask you what you were in the past, you can say you were a seed, planted by the Lord in the ground so you can sprout, branch out, bloom, and give fruit that can ripen. Our intelligent life is a tree. And that intelligent beginning is now placed in our head. And the body shows how many millions of years man passed from that beginning below, under the forces seen in the aspiration up towards the earth. The head is the symbol of the original beginning, when man was planted.

Now I won't go down that path and start explaining far and wide the profound reasons for this, which would be very complicated for many. To stop and explain the original state of the world and the forces that acted upon it; to stop and explain that original intelligence that acted [upon the earth], and so on. These are abstract things over which even the greatest philosophers kept their silence. When they asked the great Egyptian Master, Hermes, about these things, he just closed his lips shut. What did he mean? It means that man must leave his body and go and investigate these things. And when they say that someone is silent, I interpret this silence like so: "Get out and go investigate." For example, someone asks me where the springs of Maritsa are located. I explain to him, but he can't understand. Finally, I tell him to be silent and he'll understand. That's what Hermes wanted to say. Someone will ask how this is possible. If you ask, you're not in that place. You're still children who build their cottages, busying yourselves with toys and dolls. Many millions of years must pass until you rise to the point where you can think and reason about this profound question. Those who can understand me will shut their lips and I'll tell them, "come with me and we'll go there." I have thus explained the question philosophically. The moment I shut my lips tight, it now becomes a practical solution to the question, not a theoretical one. And when people ask me what the beginning is, what the Word was in the distant past, I go and tell them, "let's go there."—"We can't." Then play with your toys on Earth, whether that means building your houses, or marrying, whether you become merchants, or wage wars…only when you pass through this entire process of development, when you grow up, become wiser, and say, "down with the dolls!" then a Master will be found, who will shut his lips tight and say, "come with me."

Those who want to follow the path of Christ must have a definite view of Truth. Don't think it can be acquired very easily; don't think the path you're on is easy. No, there are difficulties. I'm not saying it's extremely difficult, but there are big obstacles. The one who decides to go this way must be ready. And nature always places great obstacles before us—beams, which we have to constantly use, until we prepare for the long way. And the issue for man isn't just to go, but he must also reach [his destination]. And you, you walk for a day or two, or three, after which you say this stuff isn't for you, and you return back. And when the people inquire what news you're bringing, you say, "forget it! It's useless stuff." Only when you go to that eternal spring, where human life began, where the Word was originally, you'll understand the former appearance of mankind; you'll understand what the sons of man were like. And what we call the "image" of God (regarding the people on Earth) is a caricature. When I look at the people who sit and say now that they're created in God's image and likeness, I laugh in my head, because from my viewpoint I see caricatures of people, whose thoughts, mind, and heart are completely spoiled. The appearance they speak of, that it has God's image and likeness, is spoiled. It's not like it used to be. And when the Word, through which everything came into being, saw that its creation in the image and likeness of God, turned into a caricature, it sent Christ to come down from the *invisible* to the visible world, to tell those [who were] deceived, "stop lying! What you have now is not in God's image. It's *your* image." They will object:

"But in the beginning I was created by God. I'm born of Him." How are you born from God? That beginning was clear and pure, but now there's some impurity in you.

So, in order to understand the profound meaning of the doctrine that Christ preached, we must purify ourselves. And the word "purification," in another sense, means "lightening," which is a process of organization; that is, the intelligent process in our construction. The body derives from the Law, according to which there is some conflict between the forces. There exists a certain force in us, a certain aspiration to get closer to God, but at the same time there is another beginning that draws us to earth. Therefore, our head is connected to Heaven and draws us upward, but the body draws us down toward the earth. In this way we are crucified. And how can someone think [when he is] crucified? After we die, a Nicodemus must come, pull out the nails, take us off the cross, wrap us in linen, and after we feel lighter, we'll rise up. This is the resurrection. Resurrection is an act in which we begin to see things in their place. We start returning to the Word, to God.

Now you want me to tell you about God. What can I tell you when you're still crucified? You're still not light. You say, "talk about love." What should I say about it when you're still crucified and experiencing pain. The only thing I can say to a crucified person is to endure, to suffer and be a hero in the suffering. I can give him only this consolation. That's the freedom of men—they must go through the process of suffering, an example given by Christ himself.

So, Christ set in our brain the beginning of the Word. The Word is the manifestation of God in the Spiritual world. The Word implies the angels. So, initially the angels are impelled to move by God and He is in them. And when the Gospel-writer says, "and the Word became flesh and dwelt among us," he implies that from the angels the Word comes down, takes on another form and comes to man. When we speak of the Word, which in the beginning was with God, and was God, we must take into consideration all those Beings that evolve, apart from that of mankind. They are something grand—sons of thought, of intelligence; that's what they are. This doesn't mean they have the same form that we have, but they are wise beings. And when Christ incarnated on our Earth, He came to preach that Word in articulated speech. Our speech is a translation of the Word. I have spoken on another occasion about the real translation of words. For example, if someone asks us about the translation of the word "river," what the words "spring," "light," and "warmth" mean, we'll say that light is a translation of Truth, and warmth is a translation of Love. There's some correlation between the words: just as light illuminates the outer objects, so Truth illuminates the human mind from within. Just as warmth helps the plants to grow, so also Love, when it enters us, drives those feelings that make man grow and rise higher. And so, whoever wants to know the original form of the Word should make the right translation.

Of course, in Bulgarian the word "Слово" [the *Word*] has one meaning, but in the Greek language, in which this phrase from the Gospels was first written, it has a slightly different meaning. In Greek, this word begins with the letter "λ"—Logos, but in Bulgarian it begins with the letter "С." This fact also shows that the Greek and Bulgarian people are not of the same opinion, in the same field. When the word "Logos" was written in Greek, the Hellenes aspired upwards toward the Angels, and our letter "С" is a crescent symbol, which means we are on the opposite side of the Astral World. We don't have light and that's why we take it, reflected by the moon. Therefore, we can say that by the Word the Slavs are a people who descend downwards, that they reached the deepest place where one may descend, and that they will now begin their new evolution. This is the reason why I can't explain to you, and you can't understand the Word, because in your brains, in your minds, the moon shines. In you, the images, the figures, everything is vague, but when daylight comes, or when Christ comes in a new form, everything will become bright and clear to you.

So, in the "Word" I understand that wise Beginning that creates and forms the thoughts, desires, and actions in us. And now we have to return to that Beginning. All contradiction in individual life and between peoples will disappear only when we return to it. And the way to return is by *lightening*. If a river that travels downwards from the spring, going towards the sea, asks me what to do, how to return to its origin, I would reply that it has to evaporate, to lighten, to rise up in the air so the winds can carry it towards the spring, to the head from which it came. And I tell you that you must apply the same law: This is the law of self-denial. This is why Christ says, "if you don't deny yourself and follow Me, you will not be saved." We have to deny matter—the houses, the children, the things with which we are tied as if with thousands of ropes. You say you want to go to the Lord. You'll never go to Him if you don't cut the ropes that tie you down. Preachers and priests preach about Heaven, but all are connected. Be quiet! You're deceiving the world. You're learning from the moon and seeing things in its light. When the sun rises in your mind, then you'll have another concept of the world and Life. You'll see how wrong your views used to be. And therefore, self-denial means lightening. Some say they don't want to deny themselves. Okay, but they're going down the slope and traveling to the oceans. There's no other way: either going upwards, or rolling downwards. But to rise up, to lighten, the sun must illuminate us within. The moon cannot vaporize us. On the contrary: it is often the cause of turning vapor into density. By the same analogy of the sun and moon, the first chapter of Genesis says that God created these two principles and that the whole truth lies in them: the Moon is the process of descending to Earth, and the Sun is the process of ascending to God. The sunset also implies a descent, and its rising implies a process of new evolution. And that's why the moon tells you every 28 days the story of your downfall. If you ask yourself why you have fallen, why you can't think, why you have no will, the moon will tell you. All its phases will tell you the reason for your fall. And then someone asks how he can rise and go to God. Get up in the morning when the sun rises, watch God and you'll find the way. Some believe they should constantly think of God. No, there may be a thought in you, but you may need certain conditions to get it going. The seeds of your salvation exist, but only when they begin to *act* upon you, then you'll rise.

It is said that Christ came to save the world. Save it? In what sense? When Christ came, all seedlings, which sat for millions of years, so to speak, in a potential, in a frozen state—they unthawed from under the icy crust and came out of the ice age. Now, I'm not going to explain to you how the Earth went through an ice age at some time. And it often occurs in spiritual life as well. If the moon shines in your mind, I'll say that you are in the ice age—your big prehistoric animals are gone, the vegetation stopped, you only have a minimal life—as much as the moon gives you. And if you ask me what you should do, I'll tell you that the sun should illuminate you. Christ must rise in your soul, to appear in your horizon and, with His rays of Truth, to act upon you.

Now, you may tell me that Christ will come. Yes, He'll surely come. But when He comes, where will you be? On the equator or the north pole? In the temperate zone or the south pole? You need to take into account and consider how the rays of Christ will fall into your soul, whether vertically or inclined. We all have to come to the place where God has to meet us, that is, of the Divine Earth. If you are clairvoyant, you'll see that there is another *Earth*. If I were to begin explaining the occultists' understanding of the Earth, the movement of the spheres, you would say that it's better not to know all of this because you'll be in great contradiction. I'll tell you why: When they discovered radium, the scientists were scared and began to argue that all the theories and views that they had so far would have come to an end, and that it was better for science not to deal with this element. So I say, when Christ's radium comes, you need to adjust your views and life from the bottom up and from the very roots.

And so, in the quoted verse, John addresses those who understand. This is the most profound question in the Gospel. The ones for whom it is written have understood. One day you too will begin to understand. If you say your mind is confused, I reassure you: The moon is still shining upon you. When the sun illuminates you, this question will become clear to you. As long as you are sincere and stand in the place where God wants to put you. According to these laws, the conditions for your growth will surely come, but you have to wait. But those, for whom God has risen, must deny themselves, to lighten, not to roll down, or, in philosophical terms, your thoughts must have *content*. In the same way, your thoughts must also have a *goal* to pursue. A Christian who wants to fulfill his task must know why everything happens. For example, children are born. Why? You say the Lord ordained this. The drunkards can also say, "the Lord gave the wine so we can drink." Did He create it, or did we make it? The Lord created the grapes, but the wine is our invention. In the same way, you take flour and knead a loaf; but did God decide for you to do it? No, it's your invention. You put two stones to grind the grain, but did God decide for the grain to be ground into flour? No, it's your will, because you can't digest the grains in your stomach. So when modern-day people say *this* is the truth, that is the truth, you have to ask them, "is this Divine Truth or yours?"—"But I preach Christ." You preach *your* Christ.—"But I preach God." You preach *your* God. Don't lie to me! I say: I can't be deceived, nor can I lie. Every person preaches *his* Christ, *his* God. When a young girl falls in love with a young man, to her he's an angel. She would die for him, but once they marry, she firmly believes that he's a devil and now she's dying *because* of him. Who, then, is right? In life, we too say that we would die for our Christ, but when we marry the Lord and see that He's not as we expected, we don't want Him and claim that He's a liar. Therefore, when we say that "in the beginning was the Word," what *word* do we understand? The Word, according to our conception of the original Word, which is the basis of all people?

That Beginning, upon which we are all held together, connected as one organism, from which we draw the same juice, or some other parasitic beginning?

Every one of you must first resolve the matter and know in which beginning you stand. You'll say, "but I know." I constantly hear the same thing: the husband says, "I," the wife says, "I." Everyone says, "I. There is no-one like me. I'm big," but looking at him, he's just a 5-centimeter branch of the tree. And someone is even just a leaf. Soon autumn will come and you'll fall. You'll go to the root of that tree and then you'll understand that there's another beginning—one is above, the other one is beneath. And so, every one of you must know where that Beginning is—in the root, in the trunk, in the big or small branches, in the leaves, in the unripe or ripe fruit, or in the seed of the latter. If you say it's in the seed of the ripe fruit, I say you are now someone who needs to leave and go check the original *beginning* of which John speaks. If you say you're in the leaves, then you'll have to wait for many millions of years. "But I'm in the unripe fruit." You still have to wait until you ripen well.—"But I already bloomed." Good, but perhaps a storm might come, and you might not be able to endure, and you'll have to pass through the roots again, back through the trunk, to grow again and begin a new life. If you had time, I would stop on the question of the falling of the fruit. Many people tell me, "talk to us about where we were at some time." I know where and what you were. I can tell you, but do you know what you'll tell me? Someone will say, "if that's true, it's a big lie." And when they tell someone outside, he'll say, "this is a big lie." But the lie is a shadow of truth. You can lie while you have truth; that is, in order to fool someone, you have to deceive him with some truth. The lie is a companion of truth—wherever there is truth, there is lying and vice versa.

But let me return to the question: How should we apply this wise principle in us? Someone will say this is a force that acts. What do you understand behind the phrase "force that acts?" This is so vague in the minds of modern scholars. They say it's a force that builds, but how does it build? They'll say that they attract and gather, but how? Two people hold hands and attract; the magnet attracts metal fragments. Okay, but there must be certain ratios in attraction. It is this inner power that must attract our thoughts and feelings to the wise Beginning. And in order to know if we are attracted to this wise Beginning, whether we are from the earth, we need to sense when the contradictions will cease in us. This is a sign that we are moving towards the Beginning. As long as there's a struggle, we stand between two principles and are like a traveler who lost his sense of direction to the four corners of the earth, and instead of traveling East, goes West, and can find his way only when the sun rises. They'll say, "his end has come." The end of what? When finishing high school, does the student die? No, this is the end of his study in school and the beginning of his entry into the world. And do you know what the word "end" originally meant? A courageous, wise, and skillful person who knows how to work and who can carry everything. And now, when the people say, "his end has come," it means the work is done. When you reach the end of the fabric you weave, you'll remove it and cut it; that is, the end of weaving will be the beginning of dressing. And after you dress and the people praise you for the fine garment, don't be proud, because you didn't make it. Don't be proud, but thank the tailor who managed to cut and sew the garment. There are some who, when praised this way, think it's about them. No, the praise belongs to the tailor; they're just advertising his work. Once your garment is poorly sewn, distorted, immediately you'll say you don't want to visit that tailor. For example, they turn to someone with the words, "you have noble thoughts," and he starts imagining he's a big deal and becomes proud. Wait, these aren't your thoughts. Thank the one who gave them to you and didn't deceive you.

If there's a storm in your mind, are you able to know how you're moving? You are unable [to know]. Now there are vague ideas in your mind. You say that Christ is a principle. A principle means a beginning—the source, the wellspring. When you go to that wellspring, you can then taste pure water. And if we draw from the source of Christ, if we drink of this water of Life, our thought and desires will surely become clear. Then another result will ensue: the construction of our bodies will go along the right path, the sufferings and pains will disappear, and we'll have the right conception. We'll be able to speak useful things to people and quench those who are thirsty. Christ told those women, "the water I give will be a spring that flows into the soul." And every morning you come here to drink from this fountain. Good, but I, who love to speak the truth and don't like lying, want you to run a pipe from the abundant spring from which I draw. Pass this pipe into your yard and when the time comes, turn the faucet and drink. I speak to those of you who want to be Christ's disciples: at least pass a little pipe one centimeter long and draw from this water. And when the world falls into scarcity and the people thirst, your pipe will quench you and you won't suffer from thirst. The spring will be in your soul—this is the Beginning; this is also the end. And do you know what the end is? When you connect a faucet from the spring into your home—that's the end of things.

So, we have to look upon the thoughts and desires we have as something given to us. We are only required to *use* them. Every thought comes and goes; you can't hold it. Don't think that you can keep your desires. No, just as food passes through us, by the same law spiritual thoughts come and go. They are forms that carry some of life's juices. Use the juices hidden in them, but disperse the dust in space, which will be replenished. If you keep them in a bottle for a long time, the juices will spoil and the Lord will hold you responsible for this. Some want to become wealthy with thoughts, but [other people] can easily reach in and rob them. Like money, the thoughts don't recognize a master, but they recognize the one who has them. Some person can reach into your heart and steal your desires. For example, a young girl loses her heart and starts languishing, or someone else grabs another's thoughts and [the other person] goes insane. Why? Because they don't understand the essential law that every thought and desire is sent from the *Invisible World*, so we can use them, and then let them go into the world. When there is movement, when there is an exchange of thoughts and desires that we send out, we'll receive the necessary juices for life. And therefore Christ says, "I am life." Life is essential for us. And so, we must harness all our thoughts and desires to get life. And when we acquire it, we'll be free citizens, and we'll be guided toward that Beginning, toward the eternal spring, from which we must quench our thirst.

When someone dies, they say, "he went to the other world." If the seed is ripe, he'll go to that world, but if it's unripe, it will fall near the trunk close to the root and won't go. Someone says he's ripe. If you really are ripe, the Lord will come; He'll take the fruit and carry it to a good place. Therefore, everyone must ask himself whether his seed is ripe. Now you'll say, "I believe in Christ." Good.—"He will save me." That's also good, but you'll fall near the trunk of the tree for a long time until the seed ripens in you. Only after ripening, then you'll have spiritual freedom. The only wealth a man will carry from Earth to Heaven is this little embryo. And when he goes to Heaven, man will yet again plant, for a new life, because over there it's the same school; there's work there as well. And when they preach a higher science to you there, how will you understand it if you don't have abilities, if you didn't learn to guide your thoughts and desires on earth? If you want to understand Christ's doctrine and be in the position of the robber on the right side, to whom Christ said, "today you will be with me in paradise," you have to work. Some will say that they too are crucified. Yes, but on what side? If you are on the left, I feel sorry for you: you won't enter Heaven with your sufferings. If you are crucified to the right, I'm glad because your deliverance has come. All who are crucified on the right—teachers, priests, philosophers, kings—will be saved. But if you are crucified to the left, you will again return to work in this world. This is the Divine Law.

The Beginning: this is the right side; this is Christ. And this means thinking in accord with the Divine Law, applying it in life and not having two minds regarding things. Some of those listening to me say to themselves, "whom should I listen to? What the church says, or the things this man is preaching?" In this case, you, my friend, have two heads. If the church and I preach and teach about the Divine Truth, there can be no contradiction and the results will always be the same. In other words, if we act according to the Divine Law, the apple planted by a priest will grow in the same way as the apple planted by me. We only need to look at the results of our actions. Why do you doubt? You have a candle you can use to see whether we speak the truth. Someone meets me and asks me if I'm black or white. Don't you have a candle? See!—"But I don't see." Then you're in the dark. I know you and see what you are. For example, you're an Evangelist. You say there's no faith like yours. Then how is it that you can't recognize the truth? Friend, you're a person who deceives both himself and others. The Truth only has one image and it is Harmony, self-denial, Virtue, Wisdom, Righteousness. When you acquire this image you'll certainly have Peace, Tranquility and Strength. Then the world may turn, the sea may be stormy, but you'll be quiet, relaxed, and free like the birds that fly with their wings. As soon as your right or left wing cripples, you'll dive down head-first into the ground. The earth says, "whoever has only one wing will remain with me." Sinners are birds with only one wing. The devils say, "we need people with one wing," but Christ says, "I need people with two wings." We have two hands, right and left, and if we possessed the law of the dilution of matter, we would be able to fly with them, to rise. We would be free to leave our body whenever we wish. Now you're afraid of death and say, "the devils are evil spirits; they'll hinder us." What can they do to you, since they too are limited by the same law? If we have control over both wings and Christ is in us, we have nothing to fear. The fear in us shows that we're not with God. And the Scripture says, "perfect love drives out every fear." If you have fear, love is not in you.

Now you are wondering how Christ will save us. You're strange people! Once you sow the grain of wheat your salvation has already come, and there won't be years of hunger. You want to be angels. How can you be when you aren't sown, nor have you emerged from the ground? The angels fly like birds, and you are plants. Then how will you transform so quickly? Do you know how many forms you have to pass through? In the word "forms" I understand the forces you need to master. To be able to change a form, you need to know the laws of the forces that operate in it, because they limit you. You have limitations: for example, you have to eat three times a day, and if you don't eat you lose your disposition; if you don't drink you also lose your disposition. Someone says, "I'm strong." You're strong only for three days.—"I'm a patriot." If I keep you hungry for three days you'll start thinking and asking for bread. We must acquire *living bread*, and we mustn't take it only from the earth. For us, the earth is a lender. Every lender and all bad spirits are put in these positions and say, "we'll give you some bread, but you have to pay us such-and-such amount." But you have to become wise. When ten wise people are found, they'll tie up the devil and say, "this wheat is not sent from our Father above." Therefore, in order to detect what is sent to you from above, you must have a pure mind and a pure heart.

"In the beginning was the Word, and the Word was God." Let's ask ourselves whether this *Beginning* is in us, whether we are *in* God and God is in us. I'm not saying you're not in God. I even argue with assurance that you exist, live, and *move* in God, but God is not in all of you. Because a person may be a dried out root and the juices from the tree may function, but they may not penetrate in him. If you are a dry root, of what use is Christ to you? We need not only be in God, but God must be within our mind and our heart.

Now, what did you understand from today's lecture? Remember the following thing, which from a purely practical viewpoint is important for you: you have to run a small pipe from this spring in your yard and from now on, do not disturb either me or the priests. You say that our priests don't preach. They're not your attendants. Make a faucet and drink. You say the priests are bad because they don't give water. Install a faucet from the spring into your home and stop this *Eastern issue*.[1] When you run a faucet from this spring all disputes will disappear. The English scientist Drummond said there are three elements for which we constantly eat: two of them are air and water, which the Lord gives us, and the third element is the food for which we constantly work. If we have become slaves in acquiring only one of these elements, what would be our state if, in the same way, we acquired the other two elements? Our situation would be three times more burdensome. One day, when we become wiser, the Lord will freely give us the third element, and then we'll be free citizens. Now we're in the third stage of our development.

Christ resolves the matter and says, "I am the living bread." When He enters us as living bread, we'll all be free—men and women, and children, and priests, and teachers—and then we'll deal with more important things as God ordained. But now we're just clarifying politics—who has more, who has less. Now everything, including wars, rest on the *bread*, and when someone has his necessary bread, he wants to take the bread from others to have more. Christ says, "I am the living bread. I will solve the issue. I will be a *Beginning*." The beginning of what?—Of freedom, of intelligent life, of wise deeds, of transformation in the world. This is the Beginning. Therefore, when you want to work with Jesus Christ, unite with this Beginning. And when you unite you'll have all goods. Christ's power will be yours too, and everyone in this world who are on the right side of Christ will be your friends. Then you'll all join; you'll go out with a candle

---

1 The so-called Eastern issue began with the conquest of Constantinople by the Turks in 1453, partly culminating in the victory of the Christian states over Turkey during the Balkan War in 1913, and finally by the ceasefire at the end of the First World War, concluded between the Convention in Turkey in the city of Moudros on 30 October 1918.

to search for your brothers and the Lord will give you advice about what you should do with your brothers on the left. You'll come back to Earth to help them until all, both on the right and the left, return to Heaven to be one with Christ. This is the Beginning, this is the Word, this is God, of whom I preach to you this morning. And this living Word that builds, lifts, and transforms the world is inside you; it is the *living* Christ.

Lecture held on 8 November 1914 in the city of Sofia

THE SPIRIT AND THE FLESH: EBB AND FLOW IN LIFE

"For the flesh desires what is contrary to the Spirit, and the Spirit what is contrary to the flesh. They are in conflict with each other...But the fruit of the Spirit is love, joy, peace, forbearance, kindness, goodness, faithfulness, gentleness and self-control."—Galatians 5:17, 22 (NIV)

Generally, people have very vague notions of the profound laws on which life rests. The world in which we live is governed by laws, rules laid down by God long ago when He arranged the universe. And when He introduced the first man into it (Scripture is silent here) the Lord taught him Heavenly knowledge for a long time. He introduced him to all the basic laws of this great structure where he was placed to live. He showed him the properties of herbs, introduced him to the qualities and processes of the elements, and when He made him master over everything, He said to him, "if you observe the laws I set, you will always be happy, joyful, blessed, and you will succeed in everything you do. But on the day you transgress my commandment, everything will stand against you." The two trees of which is spoken in the Scriptures testifies to this fact: "the tree of life" and "the tree of knowledge of good and evil." If I were to stop and explain to you the type of trees they were, I would deviate too much. I'll leave it for another lecture. These two trees in Heaven were alive, intelligent. They had a certain power, some qualities in them. And the Lord said to the first man: "There is great danger in the tree of knowledge of good and evil, and the day you touch it you will lose everything. The elements hidden in this tree are not for you. You're not strong enough to control them. In the future you may study them, but for now you can use all other trees, every *thing* in life, but not the tree of knowledge of good and evil."

I won't stop to talk about the deep reasons that led Adam to transgress the Divine commandment. Some preach, [saying] we must have faith. Indeed, faith is necessary, whether positive or negative. It's the foundation in life; life can't exist without it. Beings, however small they may be, starting from the microscopic and reaching to the highest—[they] all have faith. But what is their faith? An unbeliever says, "I don't believe in God," but at the same time this statement shows he believes in something: he believes there is no God, which means he still must *believe*. I would like to see how one can exist without faith, not believing even in himself. As long as he believes in himself, it means he has faith, but faith in his own mind. When we say that someone is an unbeliever, it's not right. It's half of the truth; he's left out faith in God, but he has faith in himself. And so, faith can be positive and negative. Adam and Eve, having manifested this principle in unbelief in God, because Lucifer entered the garden of Eden, believed in the latter and left God. As a result, the *fall* happened. And apostle Paul says in the message to the Romans, "whomever you show obedience, you become his servant."

This morning my lecture will be on the two great laws that I formulate like this: "the law of opposites" and "the law of likeness." These are laws that we can check every day. They're not abstract philosophy. They're not like reincarnation or the transmigration of souls; they're things that we can check within ourselves every day. And the dark side of this view of the laws will become somewhat clear. For example, you are at the seashore. You see the sea quiet and calm, but suddenly you notice that it begins to gradually agitate and rises toward the shore, forming a current, what scientists call a "tide." There are places where the sea rises to 60 feet in height; then you must escape as soon as possible. This is the only way to save yourself, otherwise you'll be overtaken and swallowed by the waves.

And this tide, this rising of the waves lasts 12 hours. After 12 hours you'll notice that the waves start receding back toward the sea. You can see this often, sometimes every day: in 24 hours, coming forward once, receding back once from the shore. This ebb and flow happens in you too. Where? Of course, not in the high mountainous places; not in the high peaks of life, but in the low places. This happened to you often: maybe you go down to the shore when it's quiet and you start singing a nice song; the moment you look, a wave comes and lifts you with your nice song, or at the very least completely drenches you. Or you board a boat when the sea is quiet, a storm comes, overturns the boat, and you find yourself in the agitated sea. One might think this is an exaggeration of the facts, but this is true in life. How many times people disappear in this sea of life with their songs, dreams, and ideals! You're looking for the cause without understanding the laws of nature. When the old philosophers said, "know thyself!" they meant for man to understand these two laws of the calculated *ebb and flow* movements. In your mind these two words are vague, but I'll try to explain them to you. This manifestation in modern science is called the law of *rhythmic movement*. In all things there is a flow from the center to the periphery and from the periphery to the center. In all things there is *overflow* and *outflow*, rising and falling, birth and degeneration. In chemistry there is action and reaction. "Action" is overflow; after this comes "reaction," which is outflow. If you observe a timepiece, you'll notice that its sound is loud at first, then starts to gradually weaken, to die down and at one point seems to stop, then becomes louder again, and weakens again. The same happens in your heart. If you put your hand on your heart, you'll notice that sometimes it starts beating faster, and you become frightened. The doctor says, "this man has heart palpitations." It's an overflow of your organism, a tide that affects your heart. This law works everywhere, and when doctors tell someone that he has a "heart defect," I say simply that this person has a certain overflow in the mind, in his heart, in his spirit, and after 12 hours this overflow will die down, and the palpitations will disappear. These 12 hours may be 12 seconds, 12 minutes, 12 hours, 12 days, 12 weeks, 12 months, 12 years, 12 centuries, 12 millennia, 12 million years, and so on. It's all the same. The attitude of these things remains the same. That's how this law works.

In the aforementioned chapter that I read, apostle Paul refers to the law of the *flesh*, which is the law of outflow. The law of the Spirit is the law of overflow. The law of "opposites" includes the law of outflow and the law of "similitude" (the law of overflow). *Miasms* form in some places, whose vapor can spread germs, and diseases form around that place. This law works in our brain, in our heart, and in our spirit. Impurities oftentimes form in the organism, which give way to diseases, and we call them "rheumatism" in the joints, in the feet, and in the head. Then we feel pain and start complaining. If we are wise and understand the law, we can place a strong barrier in the place where there is overflow, a big wall. If we are stupid, however, we stare at the shore of the stormy sea. People are constantly saying, "the world is bad." *Bad* in what?—"Well, in this common war!" It's an overflow of the forces, and in this overflow there's crashing, so everyone runs and says the sea is coming. And this running they call "war." They ask what will happen to the world. I say after 12 hours, or 12 weeks, or 12 years, all this will die down. The blood-soaked areas will dry up again, and people will ask, "what was that? For what reason did this sea rage against us?" The sea didn't rage. It breathes and when it puts some effort into breathing its *cage*, its chest rises to 60 feet. But when the sea breathes and takes its breath, you have to be 60 kilometers away, on some high peak. When it breathes out, you can go to the shore and enjoy yourself, but if you see it start to breathe in, run back again to a high place.

These two laws of opposition and likeness, if we can understand them, are two great things in the world. One of the laws of likeness is a Heavenly law. The other law, of opposition—this is the law of the Earth, of the organic world, of the flesh. You get up in the morning feeling indisposed; your whole world is upside down. You don't want to work, your mind is confused. You say, "the Lord didn't create the world properly." All the devils are in your mind. You're ready to argue with everyone; you've thrown your life preserver and are waiting for someone to step on it. You're ready to explode: this is the law of opposition. On the day the woman, upon seeing the man having thrown his life preserver—if she understands the law, she must run two kilometers away and say, "in my husband today there is an outflow of spirit and an inflow of the flesh." You shouldn't laugh, because tomorrow the woman will let go of her life preserver. It's a law. Not everyone releases their life preservers at the same time. Ten years ago I lived with a family. It comprised of 7 members: father, mother, a son, and four daughters. I made small observations and checked this law; it ran like a clock. All the members from this family alternated every day of the week. On Monday, the father is indisposed, his life preserver thrown. Everyone says, "father is indisposed, [he's] frowning, yelling, and shouting." Everyone hides and just looks for the cause. On Tuesday, the father is cheerful, but they see the mother has let go of her life preserver. The father smirks and says to himself, "today your mother is on duty." It's interesting that on Wednesday the older son throws his life preserver. Everyone laughs because they know him, and in that way they all take turns. I knew who was on duty and when, and the program ran without fail. Good, this is kind of nice. If someone lets down his life preserver, and the other one doesn't, it's easy. But when they're both on duty and have thrown their life preservers, it's said in scientific terms—when they both have "outflow," then it's bad. Here is what apostle Paul says in the above-mentioned chapter, that the flesh counteracts the spirits, and vice versa. We can't reconcile these two laws. It's unthinkable because they have a diametrically opposite movement: one moves forward, but the other [one] backwards. The law of opposites is a law that destroys; it destroys the harmony, happiness. If it comes in you, upon returning, it steals all your household goods. When you find yourself in this law of opposites for a long time, it can have an impact on your mind for 12 minutes, 12 hours, 12 years. There are certain periods in life that influence man's character from the very beginning. If some child is conceived and born in the period of opposites, he will certainly become a criminal, the biggest vagabond. He can't escape the consequences because they gave him those elements that stimulate life in another direction. If the father and mother are under the influence of the law of likeness, they will conceive a very noble son or daughter, with a good and well-developed mind. That's how these great laws work, and the first people, before sinning, understood them. But after sinning they forgot them.

The people want a priest to preach to them after church, but he's in the law of opposition: his vibrations, his mood, his sermon this day can't bring blessings to the people. He can serve out of necessity; he's obligated. If he were free, he would take his cap and go somewhere. But the people want him to preach to them. What will he preach to them? He'll cut them down: "You're this, you're that. You're bad people," and he'll send them to hell. On this day he says a lie; he spoke of himself, for what he spoke was reflected in you. You were a mirror, and he was looking at you. He was living under the influence of the law of opposites. They speak about a famous American preacher in the city of New York, who preached for a long time under the influence of the law of opposition, and uttered such terrible things that he scared all the parishioners as if the world had ended. Because [he's] under the influence of this law of opposites there often remains sediment in the stomach that can't be digested and separate the juices, and harms the whole organism. One day they take the preacher and drive him to the hospital, to cleanse from his stomach these small *papillae*. They stuff an *intestine*[1] into his mouth, drop 4-5 kilograms of hot water, washing the stomach once, twice. They clean the *sludge* from it, and the second week the preacher appears in church and preaches the "Kingdom of God," on "the coming of Christ," on "Love," and so on. The people say to themselves, "look now, our preacher is transformed." So I say, when a preacher or orator goes out to preach in church or in the chamber, he must remove all the sludge from his stomach, from his heart, from his mind, and then speak to the people.

You get up, let's say, in the morning, and are a little indisposed, but you cannot give an account [as to why]. Five to ten minutes pass; your mind starts to clear up and you say, "thank God, it's *illuminating* me." A period of time passes, bad thoughts come to you again and you say, "where did this devil come from?" People can't understand there's a law that acts periodically and systematically in the world. No devil came here with a trap to catch you; it's a Divine law. The Lord says, "I gave you a mind to think about the ordinance of the world. I explained to you one time about this law, but you forgot it, and now this law itself will teach you." When modern-day societies come to understand the profound meaning of these two laws, only then will the world be able to repair at the root; the courts will be repaired, everything [will be repaired]. Some ask how the world can be repaired. It can. When we start acting in accordance with this law, the world will settle as God initially ordained it. The same causes produce the same results: opposing reasons produce opposite actions. The Hindus, who know these laws, clarify them with the word "karma," the law of causes and consequences. But karma can be karma in overflow, and karma in outflow, that is, good karma and bad karma. In business language it means to give or take: if you give, it's an outflow; if you take, this is inflow, and whomever you owe will come to you exactly at the day of payment to invite you to pay. "Date of

---

1 Deunov is most likely referring to a tube.

payment" means a law that regulates things. This law is governed by such debtors and by the person who has to take. Therefore, when God put us in the world, He made certain conditions: we certainly signed, saying we'll do this or that, but now we tell Him, "we don't owe You anything."—"Is that so? I will apply the law on you. I will apply the law of opposites." You beat someone, he'll beat you too; you love him, he too will love you; that is, whatever you do, that's what they'll do to you. These two laws rule and act on earth. *Likeness* is always repelled by *likeness*. A hen climbs atop a heap, another stronger one goes and drives him away. Why don't both of them start crowing? The law says thus: Only one cock may sing on one heap. So, in the world there can only be good or evil. Two evils cannot stand in one place. Two saints can't stand next to each other; a scholar with a scholar, the same. Take two doctors, the same again. Regarding this, a Turkish proverb says, "a cotton-worker can't get anything from a white dog," because here on earth these two laws are at work, the "opposites" and "likeness." Goodness strives for evil, and evil toward goodness. That's precisely why the one who wishes to live on earth must have bad people as friends, and the bad must have good people as friends. The law is different in Heaven, but this is how it is on earth. The one who wishes to get together with good people, with people like himself, will always have misfortune. Why? Because there must be an exchange. Let's say a business man owns fabricated cloths worth millions of leva, and his neighbor also has such cloths: to whom will both of them sell? Their interests don't match. One will say to the other, "get out of here! Go to another place, on the other end of the earth. I'll trade here." It is, therefore, the law of opposites. This is why Christ, who understood this law, says, "we must *deny* ourselves, to let others live in this place." Once man denies himself, he becomes a servant, and as a servant, the Lord says, "I love you." But if anyone says, "I also want to be a master," God says, "there can't be two masters; one should be the master and the other a servant." Evil is born when both want to become masters. And if they want to become masters, and insist on this, God says, "two masters can't be with Me; if you insist on this, go to the other end of the world!" And what is the other end of the world?—The Earth. That's why the Lord sent the people on earth. In all of you who want to understand the law of likeness, the law of contrasts works, and that's why you are unhappy. You have to get out of the law of opposites and enter the law of likeness, and the law of likeness is self-denial. To deny oneself doesn't mean to lose your life, not in the least. You'll just replace one service with another. Let's say two candidates want to be principals of a high school: if one of them acts under the law of likeness, he'll say to the other one, "you become a principal. I'll become a teacher." But if they both want to become principals, there will be intrigues before the minister. Each one of them will say, "I'm more capable." Who controls them here?—The law of contrasts. And the doctrine of Christ falls into the law of likeness. Christ came on earth to establish the law of "likeness." He says, "I don't want to rule over you, but want to teach you how to be happy, and if you love Me and fulfill My law, you'll be happy." You're indisposed, you have hatred, you gossip, you're unhappy—you're in the law of opposites. You have to leave it, or, in scientific terms, get out of the law of "contrasts" and enter the law of "likeness." In other words, to change the conditions and environment. Come to love. "How will I love?" You really can't learn to love until you go to the *place* of Love. You see how wise this is. Get out and go to those places where you can draw the elements necessary for your happiness, for your heart. You can't do this if you are in the law of opposites. Then for a single chair, for a professor's department, many of you will fight. Once in France they organized a competition for a department and 15,000 candidates appeared. Well, how many people can sit in it? One candidate for one chair. In this world, certain desires arise frequently. Why? You're jealous. You want that department. You hate someone and try to get him out of the way. I can clearly answer you: I know why you hate him; either you or he wants this department. The law of contrasts in life is unrelenting; this law acts in our thoughts, in our hearts, and in our bodies. The cells, these billions of cells from which we are assembled in our bones, our nervous system, the stomach, the lungs, the heart, the brain, all the cells of these organs fall under these two laws of opposites and likeness because inflow and outflow occurs in them. A person is angry, he's indisposed, so there's an outflow. An inflow must necessarily come into him. How? He'll concentrate; he'll direct his mind up toward God; he'll climb this mountain where the Lord is; he'll go and talk to Him, and when the outflow passes, he'll come to earth.

I don't understand the inflow only when it's in the sea, but also when the inflow rises in the vegetation too, when there's moisture in the air. Once it ripens, every thing begins to dry up: we have a law of contrast, which prepares the soil for the coming year. And the other law, then, has its place. The law of contrasts must remove the old clothes. You undress: this is the law of contrasts. You dress: this is the law of likeness. Your body is filthy: you have the law of contrasts. You bathe: you're in the law of likeness. Every day we get up and wash the face. Why? By habit. Today you have to go before the Lord because there's an outflow in you. You wash your face and say, "I'll remove the burden from my heart. I'll bring down the sludge from my mind, and then I'll go up before the Lord." The washing of the face by pulling the hands from top to bottom shows this. But you, when you're unable to interpret this, you wash yourself and continue to stir the mud all day. And the work is going nowhere. How will it go? The mud is in you! You have to be on some high mountainous place.

We have to apply this law, as apostle Paul says, in the "fruits of the Spirit." And they are "love, joy, peace, long-suffering, kindness, compassion, faith, gentleness, restraint." Love: this is the father;

joy: this is the mother; peace: this is their child. So they are a triangle that falls into Divine things. Whoever wants to be blessed must possess these things. Then he's in Heaven. After this comes the second category that goes to the angels: long-suffering: this is the father; kindness: the mother; compassion: their child. Acquire them and you'll be among the angels. The third category: faith: this is the father; gentleness: the mother; restraint: their child. And so, I say, according to this law of likeness, you have to first have a father. Who is your father? Faith. "But I have no faith." For you, friend, I have a bad opinion. If you don't have a father, you are born of illegitimate parents. Your mother didn't give birth to you in a divine way. That's what I interpret when someone says, "I have no faith." And when he says, "I have faith," I congratulate you; you have a very noble father, who comes from a great origin, of a royal family. "But I don't believe in this father"—you are the lowest bastard. Let's come to the word "gentleness." We said gentleness is a mother; she's from a royal family. You believe in gentleness, so you have a mother. "But I don't want to be gentle"—then you're without a mother. Therefore, a Christian must have a father and mother—faith and gentleness, and he himself is restraint. When we say "restraint," we must understand this refers to *us*, the child of our father, faith, and our mother, gentleness. Some say, "I want to go among the angels." You can go, but you have to be born from a father, long-suffering, and you must be conceived by your mother, kindness. She must carry you in her womb, and you, when you're born, what will you be? Compassion—an angel, a saint. If you are compassionate, you're an angel; you have a father among the angels above—long-suffering, and a mother—kindness. This is the law that regulates human life. It's the basis of a philosophy that can be discovered every day. This isn't a speculation at all; it can be checked by anyone. I'm not lying, just as I don't like it when others lie to me. If I lie, it means I'm stupid, just as if they lie to me, I would be stupid. I exclude the law of contrasts from myself. If I'm in an outflow, I go to God. If I have an inflow, I come to earth to work. But if I'm with God, who will lie to me? That's why I say in one of my previous lectures: Where the Lord enters, no devil can enter. Where there is no God, the devil is there. When someone says, "the devil is stepping on me," I understand what he wants to say. If the Lord is in your heart, the devil can't step on you. In this law of likeness, we can neither turn evil into good, nor good into evil. A white-bearded old man appeared before a saint who lived 20 years in the desert, saying, "I'm a great sinner. I implore you to pray to the Lord to forgive my sins." When the old man went away, the saint began to pray to God for him. An angel appeared and said, "your prayer is not accepted before God, because this old man is the devil. To test him whether he is telling the truth, tell him thus: 'I will pray for you, but you have to confess your sins and go up to a cliff and say, 'Lord, be merciful to me, who am a great sinner, the abomination of desolation,' and repeat these words for a whole year.'" After some time, the old man came back to the desert, but the latter told him what the angel ordered him to do. "How?" cried the devil. "I can't do it. I, who rule the world and command it. I don't want to pray. You pray!" Then he said, "old malice cannot become new virtue." Those who preach the Gospel must know that we can never turn the law of opposites into a law of likeness, that is, we can't turn to God a man who lives constantly in the law of contrasts. We can't make him happy, just as we can't turn woman into man. A woman wants her husband to make her happy. How can he make her happy when she doesn't love him? He buys her a suit, [she's] dissatisfied; [he] brings meat, it's no good; the house isn't built properly; this and that isn't in place. Well, how will he satisfy her when she's in the region of opposites of her mind, and when all the things the husband can do aren't in the condition to alter her temper? Neither is the woman capable of pleasing her husband if he's of such temper. She may cook for him, clean the house, but he'll still remain unsatisfied, because he lives in the law of opposites. And then some come to me and say, "I don't know what to do. My husband became difficult, like a wasp." I think coolly and answer: He is, unfortunately, under the law of contrasts. He's in an outflow. Put him in your wagon, harness your horse, take him to a high place, to breathe [out]. That's what your husband wants. Take the reins of the horse: "Let's go today, husband, for a little walk." And when a woman wants to take her husband to church, she takes the carriage and says, "we'll go to the Lord. So-and-so will preach at the church and we'll learn something."

Now we sit and say, "repair the world." Well, how can it be repaired? If a swine grunted for millions of years under the tree and after eating all the pears, starts digging at the roots in the ground and asks, "where did these pears go?" how will the tree bear other pears? [The swine] will spoil the whole tree. And you, when you don't find the pears above, start digging down, saying, "the money we are looking for is buried in the earth," and become depressed. I tell you: You're in this region of the law of contrasts; there are no pears, no possessions. You need not dig in one place, but must throw your sack over your shoulder, take your sticks, and go to another place. Because when your Master comes and sees you digging in one spot, he'll give you a good beating. This is what the Lord is doing now on earth. We dig and look for pears, but the Lord says, "hit everyone 25 [times]."

That's why I say to apply this law. The wife shouldn't dig around the root of her husband. When there are no pears, wait. The husband also shouldn't dig around his wife's root. The preachers [shouldn't dig] around the roots of their flock; the students [shouldn't dig] around the roots of their teachers. All of you—apply the law, and you'll come to understand life as the Lord created it. It's a philosophy that we can apply in this world, and it's so simple that everyone can understand it. But if you say, "I can't do this," I'll tell you that you're in the swamp, in the mire of opposites. When you say, "I can," you're in the law of likeness. You'll take a step forward and will enter the path of salvation. Some say, "I can't love." I'm sorry, I can't help you, because you're in the area of opposites, where you collect the sludge, the mud. "I can love." You're in the law of likeness, and the Lord will be with you. You get up in the morning [feeling] indisposed. Say to yourself, "today I have an outflow. Let me harness the wagon, take the yoke off the horse. I will travel." Don't stay there. Don't walk around the tree to pick pears when it's not time [to do so]. You'll find them in another place, farther. Get up, go and pray, if you know how to pray. In the power of prayer you'll become stronger. To pray—this is the highest and most noble occupation that can be done in this world. Only this way can the heart rise [higher] and become more noble. I'm not speaking here about the outer side of prayer, where only the tongue is involved, but that prayer in which the *conscious* pursuit of the soul toward God expresses itself, the higher Love. But not everyone sees it that way. Some people say, "I can't pray," others laugh and say, "it's delusional for us to pray. Me?—an educated [person], who graduated, to pray to the Lord?" But our scholars are inconsistent, and here is why: They want a job and they make a statement: "Because my father was such, my mother such, because I need it, I very politely ask you to appoint me. I promise to perform my position exactly and accurately." Isn't that a prayer? Yes, it's quite characteristic of prayer. Yet when it's a prayer to the Lord it's considered shameful! While we have people who only pray to those like themselves, and not to the Lord, the higher good, the world will remain as it is. They live in the law of contrasts. How can we be good when, with every step, deceit is our companion? We deceive ourselves, our neighbors, and the Lord. We have unknowingly given citizenship to the lie. We act in fear. Let's get rid of the fear. Let's put a slogan [upon ourselves] to speak the truth at least before God. Let's say, "today I will not speak deceptively before the Lord." If we make a mistake, we should say, "I sinned," and not, "so-and-so is the cause. I sit a little higher than him," like the Pharisee: "I have a higher opinion of myself." Then we're in the region of the law of contrasts, in a dungeon. Let's say correctly, "I did this," because when we confess our mistakes we'll rectify ourselves. If you read Tolstoy's confession, you'll find a good example of this: He became great when he confessed his transgressions. There's only one or two such examples in history. Can you make this confession? If you want to become ennobled, an angel, a saint, it's very easy. In a day, you can become an angel 10 times, as well as a devil. Some don't believe in reincarnation, but you can reincarnate 10 times a day. You're an incarnated devil if you want to kill a person; then you find yourself in the region of the opposites, and are in the condition to commit all kinds of evil. If you're in the law of likeness, you're an angel. If you're ready to sacrifice yourself or to do something noble, you're a saint. But you can't hold on to this position for very long. They say that man is made in God's image and likeness. I will interpret what I understand by this. When they say, "they made someone a general or minister," didn't he exist earlier? He existed; he was a simple citizen. And when the Lord says, "let's make man in the image and likeness of God," He wants to produce, to make man a general, to dress him in a general's uniform, to put on him a general's epaulettes. But man didn't fulfill the will of God, and the Lord discharged him, taking away his epaulettes and clothes. This is the fall. "Remove his uniform," He said, "because he doesn't perform the general's duties properly." You turn to the Lord. He says, "today you bear the image and likeness of a general. Put him in paradise." After 5-10 minutes, you don't follow the law, He says, "discharge him." If you're angry, or indisposed, you're out of paradise. A year or two pass, you begin to repent, the Lord says, "bring him. I'll make him a general again." Many times—every day, every hour—the Lord can make you a general or discharge you. If you are well today, you are an angel of Heaven. Tomorrow you are unwell, He sends you on earth. If you don't pray, if you don't obey the law, you'll be a devil. These two laws of opposites and likeness regulate the world. Those spirits who live under the law of opposites have no disposition to return to the law of likeness, and that's why the Lord can't carry them from one region to another. The first thing in Christianity is the border that exists between these two laws. When we come to the border, we have to leave all the luggage, thoughts and desires under the law of contrasts, and to enter the law of likeness in a pure state. Then the Lord will put on us His clothes, and will declare us generals again. Because of the disobedience of the commandment of God—not to reach for the forbidden fruit—man became naked. The Lord stripped him of his general's clothes and man was forced to make them from leaves. The Lord said, "soon, make for him clothes from flesh." That's why you're dressed in that flesh that you have. If you want to throw away your flesh, when will you throw it? When you enter into the law of likeness. This flesh will fall from you, and the Lord will give you a general's garment with epaulettes, which will be very colorful. This is the Christian philosophy. You can apply it in life. This isn't a philosophy of the past; it's a philosophy that is applied in practice. You're reborn every day as angels and devils, and vice versa. This is reincarnation. Now they argue and say, "whoever believes in reincarnation, we will throw him out of church." How will you throw me out when I believe in the laws of contrasts and likeness and live according to them? When I live according to the law, whether you throw me out of church or keep me in, it will hardly affect my soul. When I live with God, when I don't hate anybody on earth, and I try to love everything purely, can someone throw me out? Only one can throw me out: God. This is the teaching I preach to you. And I tell you that only on the day you sin, you are banished by the Divine Church, paradise. What are modern churches? They are just a distant remembrance of the majesty of the past. Do you know the secrets hidden in these churches? If I sit down to interpret what a church means, what these stones mean from which the churches are built, to tell you about the priestly garments, the candles that are lit—in everything there is a profound philosophy. All the laws of God are written on these priestly garments. They dress each day, but forget to read what is written on them. Do you know what the garments of the bishop mean? The crown, the crutch, twisted on top like two snakes, and so on? What about the censer and the incense? We closed the book and say, "ah, it's a very holy book, don't touch it!" But the Lord says, "watch out not to scratch it on the outside. Keep it clean, but open it carefully. Read a little every day and notice these valuable things it contains." These things—the church, the garments, the icons, the candles, the censer, the books: they're all in place. You must carefully guard the contents of the Holy Book; you'll understand the law of opposites and likeness in it. And when you understand them and carry Christ's cross on your shoulders, ready to be nailed, then God will say, "here, this one will be with me in paradise." You'll be saved. It happens instantly: I can be in Heaven now, and I can also be in hell. In an instant, the moment I doubt God and think badly about Him, I'm at the bottom of hell. The moment I love God in my soul and say, "forgive me Lord!" I'm with Him, and He stretches His right hand and brings me back.

Now I'll give you an example and conclude. In the past, somebody died and they took him to hell. He lived there for a long time, for centuries, suffering and praying to the Lord to forgive him. Finally, the Lord said, "open the book of life and see if he did even one good deed in his whole life." When they opened the book, they found that once he gave a carrot to a poor man. Then the Lord said, "this man can be released." He commanded an angel: "You will give him this carrot to grab onto, and that's how you'll pull him out of hell." However, other sinners got ahold of him. Latching themselves onto his feet, and the angel brought them to paradise. But the one who had the carrot said to the others, "this carrot is mine," and the moment he said this, the chain broke, and everyone fell back again to hell. Let your carrot assist in the salvation of others to rise to Heaven, because otherwise if you say, "this is my carrot," you'll fall down again. They may get ahold of your clothes, your legs [but you must] keep quiet. Don't say anything. On the day you say, "this carrot is mine," you're far from the Lord. Selflessness always lives under the law of likeness. Sacrifice and self-denial for others—this is Christianity.

Lecture held on 2 November 1914

THE MILK OF THE WORD

"...as newborn babes, desire the pure milk of the word, that you may grow thereby, if indeed you have tasted that the Lord is gracious. Coming to Him as to a living stone, rejected indeed by men, but chosen by God and precious."—1 Peter 2:2-4 (NKJV)

One commandment of the Mosaic law says, "do not desire," but in this message from Peter it is said to desire. Which one is right? Both are right in their own opinion. However, if Moses is in Peter's place, he will be crooked, and Peter, if he is in the place of Moses, will also be crooked. Moses says not to desire—what?—power, wealth, a woman, and Peter says to desire—what?—the milk of the word. Why? Because it's necessary for spiritual growth. The first thing the child looks for when he comes out of the mother's womb is breast milk, because when he sucks, he grows and develops. And Peter says the same: to find the breast that will feed us spiritually, because if we don't find it, under the same law as the child, we cannot live. After 3-4 years, when the child grows up a little, his teeth grow, which means that his body is already adapting to solid food. The same is true in spiritual life: difficult teachings shouldn't be perceived from the very beginning, which can cause death.

The verse asks whether all those who live on earth sucked this milk of the word. Not all, and that's why they die. The mother mustn't just give birth to the child and have milk, but this milk has to be *unspoiled*. How many mothers poisoned their children with their bad milk! If the mother is angry several times a day, she will poison the child with her milk after a few days. Likewise, the priests, who are in the place of mothers when they preach, and the teachers when they teach, when they are disturbed and anxious, they poison their flocks and followers. Modern people suffer from great ignorance: they know a lot, about geometry, arithmetic, grammar, botany, physics, about the movement of heavenly bodies, how God created man, how the latter developed, but the essential knowledge, the necessary *milk of the word*, they don't have. And do you know what they resemble? There is an anecdote about a Turkish sage who said he knew everything that happens in Heaven, at what time the Lord rises, what He does, what the angels do. One day, as he related this to the Sultan, the latter called another philosopher like him and wanted to expose them, that there are things they don't know. He said to them, "I wish to take an excursion with my ship in private and for us to have a friendly discussion." They left. As they conversed, they were served a tray with bread and milk. The sultan told his companions to dip morsels into the milk. When they crumbled the bread, he mixed the morsels and said, "let everyone eat his own morsels."—"How would we know whose is whose?" the philosophers objected. "Well, if you don't know the morsels which you yourself crumbled, how will you know what happens in Heaven?"

In the cited verses, Peter later directs his listeners to the living stone. We know there are only dead stones, from which they build houses. But as you see, there are also living stones. If you could interpret the word "stone" in a spiritual language, you will find it has another meaning. By the word "stone" in the spiritual sense is meant a complete character in which all forces are balanced, the developmental process is harmonic; the brain, the lungs, the stomach, the nervous system are in order and function well. This is why Christ says, "be a stone that can grow and develop," and elsewhere, "you have to build a Divine home," meaning from *such* a stone.

But let me return back to the words "milk of the word." Some people often say, "we want to be spiritual." What do they understand by that? Whether to shut themselves within, to be calm and think, and contemplate? It doesn't make them spiritual. To be spiritual means to be in touch with the surrounding conditions, the environment, the soil on which [you stand], and at the same time to know how to react properly on this soil, this environment and condition, [upon the] elements that create life. The highest position a person can occupy is when the mind, the heart, the soul—all these forces, because they *are* forces—are at their peak, in their maximum development. The stone, in its natural state, cannot absorb a liquid substance. But, if it is baked in a kiln, it serves as lime-wash. And the Lord, when He wants to white-wash His home, He bakes the stone, adds a little water and when a reaction forms, He smears it with white-wash, referred to in spiritual [terms] as purity and kindness in life. When sufferings come, it means they let you into the furnace, to transform into the necessary spiritual lime. There are some hard stones which, even after putting them in the furnace, don't bake. They are considered completely useless. They take them and throw them out on the road.

Now, when Peter says "desire," he wants to express this inner process of baking, to form in the mind those higher forms that, through the process of dilution, will be able to pass from one world to another. You have two thoughts in your mind that worry you. Take one—don't pity it, but put it in the kiln. Put wood on the bottom and bake it. And when you bake every thought like this out of the thousands that fly over you, it will be the same as baking several thousand kilograms of lime and selling it. With that, not only will you get rid of a large amount of luggage that weighs you down, but you will also have a big profit. What happens in the physical world happens, by analogy, in the spiritual world too: every process on the physical plane is simultaneously a process in Heaven and vice versa. If you understand this correctly, you will know that when you suffer on earth, Heaven rejoices, because when they bake you in the kiln, you, who don't understand the deep reasons, say, "our life is burnt!" but in Heaven they cry, "how glad we are that this stone will turn into lime!" When you think, "these angels above have no compassion for us," they say, "we do, we do. We see that you, like us, are becoming white and pure." We must desire not those things that thicken and harden, but those that expand our souls, minds, powers, and abilities.

But you'll ask, "how can we apply this *practically* in life? I have mischievous students, naughty children. How can we influence them?" Or, "I'm a priest. I have people who are unruly and unbelievers who can't understand the philosophy of life." Or, "I'm a merchant. My associates and clients want to rob me." You're all complaining. Why? Because your rope is thin and weak and you want to lift a load of 100 kilograms. Of course, then the rope will break, and the load will fall. How can one live in the Old Testament, but apply Peter's doctrine? You're friends of Moses, but you also want to be friends of Christ. Moses says, "do not desire," but he doesn't say what to do next. He says in one place, "love the Lord," but how will I love Him when I haven't seen Him? In another place he says "to love your nation," but regarding other nations he speaks differently. I'm speaking of the Mosaic law in a broad sense. Of course, when Moses set his law, conditions were different. His law was a preparation of mankind for the doctrine of Christ. Moses' law is the first hemisphere of the earth; Christ's teaching—the other [hemisphere]. You can live on it when it is illuminated by the sun. But when it is away from the sun's rays, you can't live. And in modern-day social life our wishes come from the application of this Mosaic law. The people want to be wealthy, to be learned, but by adopting this law, not everyone has the opportunity to be rich and learned; therein lies the conflict. On the physical plane, there aren't conditions for all people to be wealthy and learned, but everyone can be kind. Desire virtue, which isn't from the physical world. In India, there are people who understand and apply this law even to animals. An animal, however ferocious it may be, if you can come into contact with it, it will love you and become your dear friend. The predisposition to harm you will disappear; it is ready to fulfill your desire. And when Christ said, "love your enemy," He understood this law.

So, the first thing Christianity recommends for purifying mankind is suffering. The hard stones must pass through the kiln so they can turn white; the raw bread must be baked so it can be eaten. It's the same with man: you can enter Heaven only as baked bread. Only then will they put you on the table and *break* you. Why did the Lord give you a mind, a heart; why did He give you eyes, ears, a tongue? You need to think about why they are designed. I throw these questions and leave you to think about them. You say, "I want to serve God," but you don't understand how to serve. I know people who supposedly understand the laws of the occult, but they can't serve God. Knowing them, they need to be able to apply them at least for their own development. Some want me to tell them many things, philosophical and occult-related. I can tell you, but first I want to lay a firm foundation, and then build on top of it. So, every stone we set, to be well-cut and put in place in the corner. We have a great task, to fix this world. I see that this edifice on which life is now built is breaking down, and that one day the Lord will call us to build a new one. But will we know how to build it when He calls us? That's the question. To be ready, from now on we have to feed on that milk of which I spoke. To be ready like this, because one day, when God gives us a new garment, we shouldn't stain it. Some little ravens asked their mother to move them to another nest. She asked them, "well, will you bring your dirty butts with you?"—"We'll bring them too."—"You can't. You'll sully the other nest too." Some unwise women say, "why did the Lord make me a woman?" Here is why: As a woman, you're studying an art that you wouldn't learn as a man, the art of preparing milk with which you have to feed your children. You are purely and simply *governesses* of the Lord who raise His children. If you don't fulfill your maternal duty, the Lord will ask you, "why did I put you in this esteemed position? You shouldn't have given such milk to your children."—"But we already gave."—"Don't give it again. Otherwise I will fire you."—"But I want to become a man."—"You won't become a man. If you keep wanting things you don't deserve, if you're still stubborn, the second time you'll become an ox."

The philosophy of modern Christians doesn't rest on a sound basis. Every sect believes and preaches, "what we preach is the true Christian doctrine. The other one is not." But no-one can determine exactly what the true Christian doctrine is. We say we are the crown of the world's creation. Let's not deceive ourselves and God. We're not a crown; only those who completed their development are a crown. We, who are still croaking in the swamp, are nothing but frogs. We, who want money and houses, who are willing to sell even the Lord for them, we are not a crown of creation, but a crown of the fall, of hell.

We are facing a dilemma. We have to ask ourselves: Can we walk for a long time along this path? We can't move farther. Modern-day humanity has reached a limit where, if it takes another step, it loses everything. But a step in the other direction, a step forward, a step upward, and its future is great. So we already must think about where we are going and deny the *transient* that leads us to downfall. Christ says, "whoever loves his mother and father must deny them and follow Me." And man must be ready to say, "I no longer want the milk I had until now. It's better to die without milk than with *such* milk, for death without milk is better than spoiled milk." We must give up all the deceptive things that corrupt our thoughts and desires, that poison our lives, and seek to find the Divine Truth. My intention is not to scare you, but to turn you to think of yourselves. Take a look at yourself; see how your face looks, what color it has. If it's very red, it indicates that it's excited, that the body is in an unhealthy state. If it's too pale, it shows apathy toward life. Neither one or the other are *Christian*. But if you use Christ's food, of which apostle Peter speaks, you'll have a good disposition, happiness, joy, an upswing in your spirit, courage and determination in the struggle. If you were saturated with that *living* milk, no germs would be able to live in you. If I had a little more free time now, I would give a description of what a Christian ought to be in the full sense of the word. You have some aspirations, you want to be good, to love, but you can't. Why? Because you don't know how to do it. A doctor was summoned by a wealthy young woman suffering from boredom. The first thing he recommended to her was exercise. "How can I exercise!"—"If you don't exercise, you will perish."—"Then I will exercise. Please, give your instructions." He gives the instructions and she starts exercising, and her boredom went away. You often sit with your arms folded, or you turn your thumbs in one direction, then the other. The twirling of thumbs must stop, and you have to start exercising, to work. Then the Lord will bless you.

In this respect, women must work because the Lord gave them the key from paradise. They hold the key to the Kingdom of God. "Peter" is a feminine name. However, women are a little weaker in character and soon give up their tasks. She loves a man, but when she sees another one she says, "I'll marry this one. If I can't marry him, there is no life for me." But after 2-3 years she gets over him too and is ready to marry another one. The Lord now says to the women, "you who hold the key to the Kingdom of Heaven, if you don't follow My commandments, I will drive you out so you can cry outside, to repent and throw away all your sins." When we don't follow Christ's commandments, we deviate from Him. We constantly hand Him over to Pilate, to suffering, to daily nailing on the cross. And you ask why the world isn't fixed. How can it be fixed when we torment our Lord every day? Let's stop sticking nails in His body. In reflection, they affect us. Do you know the saying about that fisherman who found a precious fish and wanted to give it as a gift to the king? The door-man didn't want to let him through and in order to let him enter, the fisherman promised him half of the profit. He entered, but when the king asked him, "what do you want as a reward?" he replied, "50 blows with the stick."—"But how so?" said the king. "I want this reward." After striking him 25 times, he said, "I have a partner—your door-man. Please, give the rest of the 25 to him." And Christ, when you stick nails in His body, says, "bring my partner and nail the rest in him." What happens nowadays is nothing but the rest of the sticks, half of the reward we asked for—"how I suffer. My soul will burst!" It will burst because of how many nails you stuck in the Lord! You're sick—"let the doctor come." The real doctor who will heal you won't enter the house while you continue hammering the nails. What I preach to you, as you see, is a fully practical teaching that everyone can apply. When a bad thought comes to you, when you desire something that isn't good, put this hard stone in the oven, so it can transform into lime, with which you can lighten your soul, to make it bright. If you practice thusly, you'll see how your soul will shine.

This is the doctrine that apostle Peter preaches. You consider him a simple fisherman, but he's such a fisherman who baked and didn't eat raw fish. In what should you bake it? In the Divine fire, Love. And when you bake it like this, you'll say, "see what an excellent fish [this is]!" If we don't become collaborators of those who live in Heaven, what place will we have in *that* world? And when the Lord says to deny ourselves, to lose our lives, He means not to lose it to the swine, but to those who sit in a higher position than us. Only then can we gain [something]. You'll say that this law is incompatible with the laws of nature. It's compatible. Those who will eat the juices will sow seed, and from it a new tree will grow and bear fruit. Therefore, in order for us to grow, we have to enter the path of development. Then the angels will take part in our work. In order for them to take part, we have to pay them something. In order for them to sow us again one day, in better living conditions, we must prepare the *reward* starting now, while we're still living on earth. If we eat the milk of the word, we'll come closer to them, and finally to Christ.

In this work, I want every fear to disappear from you. Whoever wants to work with Christ shouldn't be afraid of every process. Bake all your consciences in the Divine fire, like the fish you catch. The fish, one of two, must either be baked or salted: it's the same with man. There's no middle way. Otherwise, it will start stinking. When Christ says, "if the salt loses its saltiness," He means if *you're* not salty, you'll be thrown out, when they would otherwise put you in the pot. I would prefer to be baked, and not salted. Salt is for the earth, but the fire is for us. The process of the fire is better because it's a process of growth, of life. Salting is a process of preservation, to save the seed from spoiling. In other words, you may be in two situations: either in the position of growth in the Divine garden, or a seed in the Divine barn. Make an attempt on yourself, but an attempt on this verse that I read to you. It has a profound meaning. It's possible to write volumes on the following: how to construct life, how to educate the children, the men, the women, the students, society, and so on. Everything is in that verse. But it has to be sown well. Where? In the mind. Boil this verse in the Divine water, bake it in the Divine fire, and this seemingly bizarre verse will instantly become a food whose juices you can perceive. If you eat that milk of the word that Peter talks about, your face and your social position will change. I want you to embrace this Divine method and prepare for another life, for Heaven.

This is what I want from you this morning, to *desire*. Up until now, you didn't desire. Now I want you to desire the milk of the word, to enter into the positive side of life, and then whatever you want, the Lord will give you.

Lecture held on 16 November 1914

THE TEACHERS

"But you, do not be called 'Rabbi'; for One is your Teacher, the Christ, and you are all brethren."—Matthew 23:8 (NKJV)

Christ grasps these words somewhat differently than society. From a purely organic point of view, the world has several institutions that are Divine, such as the father and the mother, the home. They are the first institutions on earth; there are no more noble and enlightened institutions than the home, and nothing ranks higher than the father and mother. True, there are many fathers and mothers on earth, but they're actually an arrangement of step-parents. In relationship to the organic world, fathers and mothers play an important role: they give their children the qualities of their souls with their blood. The education of the children is determined by the qualities the mother puts in the child in his fragile age. By the word "blood" I mean not the ordinary blood, but the blood which, in every happenstance in life, remains unchanged; [it remains] one and the same. I won't stop now to explain the difference between that *bipartite* blood. I can only say one thing: that it's not that transient changeable blood, but the other, which like rose oil essence rises above the rose water and which itself has real value. The noble seeds that the mother puts in the child's blood are a valuable fragrant essence that spreads and gets carried into the surroundings of that now-grown child. That which modern people refer to as "upbringing" is just taming. In the maternal education the process is in the root: there it forms and modifies the mind and heart. In taming you have just one outer shine. You can tame a monkey, you can train a dove, but once you put them in their natural state, they'll live according to their first life. In the United States of America, they made attempts: the government granted huge sums [of money] on the education of local Indians. Some of these Indians completed various colleges and universities, but upon returning to their people, they forgot what they learned and went wild again. Only if some of them turned and absorbed Christianity, a change happened.

Such is the condition of the teacher regarding spiritual life. To be a teacher means to give birth to someone. Christ doesn't say, "don't teach," but, "don't use the *title* of teacher," the title of a sickly mother, because what kind of child will such a mother conceive other than a sickly one? If the mother has some organic, mental, and psychological weaknesses, the child will be no exception. Can the modern teacher teach his students, for example, how oxygen and hydrogen combine when he himself doesn't understand the properties of these elements? He can attempt, but these elements don't obey him because he's not their master yet. Another one may learn about the rotation of bodies up in space, but ask him to mathematically define with a meter, and not with hundreds of thousands of meters and kilometers, the rotation of these bodies around the sun. He won't be able to determine it for you exactly. I too can make such calculations, but they won't be exact. If the difference is by a few centimeters or millimeters, I understand, but by a few kilometers or hundreds of thousands of kilometers, I don't understand. Now these are hypotheses, assumptions. You often stop and say, "why didn't some things occur like this or like that?" If you make wrong calculations, who is to blame? Many make mistakes in life. You want to build a house: You call an architect over to make you a plan and the calculations for the amount of stones, trees, iron, nails, sand, lime, and so on. You'll buy these materials, but if you don't make the necessary exact configurations, your building will fall, and you'll suffer under the ruins.

I will explain my thought with an anecdote from Bulgarian

life. This happened around the forties-fifties[1] years. Some Bulgarian from the southern part of the Balkan peninsula, on the other side of Thessaloniki, went with his father to work as a gardener. He turned 20 years old and didn't make anything from it. He had enough and decided to follow some other more fitting occupation for him. At one point, he settles to work with a tailor and says to himself, "here's an easy occupation: I'll just sit and add." After a week, a Turkish *bey*[2] comes to the shop and tells [the apprentice's] Master to take the yardstick and scissors to sew pants from *sukno*,[3] and these kind, *birbutchukliya*.[4] But the Master didn't feel well and sent the apprentice, who only studied for a week, telling him, "go, I'll come after you." The apprentice goes with the bey, waits for an hour, [then] two. The craftsman didn't come. Then the bey turns to the apprentice: "As I see, you're old [enough] to know the craft. Can you make pants for me?" The *journeyman* answers, "I can." The bey pulls out a big roll of *sukno* and says, "I want you to sew for me *birbutchukliya* pants." The apprentice starts cutting from here, from there. The bey sees that what the apprentice is cutting doesn't resemble *birbutchukliya* pants and tells him, "the pants didn't work out. Sew me at least a *saltamarka*."[5] The apprentice grabs from here, from there, measuring, cutting. The Turk sees that the saltamarka is also not working out. "You'll at least cut for me a tobacco-pouch and if you don't cut it, I'll beat you," he said at last. So, many of you have also barely sat for a week with a craftsman, taking the

---

1 Deunov is referring to the 1840s and 1850s.

2 A ruler of a region, like a lord or governor, sometimes from a military background.

3 Also known as broadcloth. A dense, plain woven cloth, typically made of wool.

4 Traditional baggy trousers that are wide at the crotch and gather tightly at the ankle.

5 Similar to a doublet. A snug-fitting jacket that sits above the hips.

scissors and yard-stick, like that Bulgarian, and are ready to cut, to be teachers. Christ says, "don't be *such* teachers." For someone to be a teacher, he must have *positive* knowledge—only one way of understanding, to have no exceptions. To have an instrument with which to heal, and at the same time to kill, this doesn't mean you have positive knowledge. If with one knife you do an operation, cutting from someone the diseased flesh, and with the same instrument you cut his throat, you can't say that you used your knife properly. It's now a criminal act. But some will say, "we didn't do such a thing." Oh, how many teachers I know who cut their students' throats! They cut the legs, hands, ears of many! In a moral sense, I understand. The Lord didn't install these people as teachers; they are *self-made*. In every church there are such teachers who sat, like the above-mentioned Bulgarian, only a week in school and are about to preach.

Now what should you understand by the word "teacher?" This word relates to the purely spiritual world. It's not a teaching to teach people how to build churches, how to plant flowers, cabbage—this is not teaching. Good teaching implies an act of higher self-consciousness. A purely spiritual process must take place: between the teacher and student there must be a complete awareness of the task they have to accomplish, to have an exchange which exists between the mother and the child raised by her; the teacher must convey certain truths and the student [must] use them properly. I will give you another example to clarify. They talk about an Englishman who went to hunt in India. When turning on a trail he felt a heavy blow upon his left hand, a blow dealt by a tigress. She was content only to break his left hand so he wouldn't shoot the rifle that hung on the right [side]. She picks him up and carries him to the lair to her 3-4 little tigers. She sets him down, pushing his head and saying, "you be quiet, because I'm going to teach my little ones." She makes the little tigers try to choke him. They walk around him, but are afraid to approach. The hunter at one point decided to raise his head, to see what's happening, but the tigress pushed his head again and repeated, "I told you to be quiet. I'm teaching my little ones." So, as you see, the tigress is also a teacher. The hunter saved himself somehow, but said the hardest part was when they pushed his head, so the little ones could choke him. Anyone can knock down. Teaching, however, implies a person who can learn to build in the mind and the heart, who understands the deep meaning of the elements that can renew, to build a new spiritual home, a spiritual body that, as Scripture says, will one day resurrect. The Lord is waiting to build this body.

How are children born? In order to live, they have to be born in the ninth month. In some cases, on the seventh month, but it's not at all random (whatever month the parent wants). This is the law: the nine-month period required to form the body must be fulfilled. And how does its formation begin? First, the extremities are formed: the legs, the hands, then the brain, the stomach, and finally the lungs; and once the latter form, the breath begins, and then if not born, the child can die. So nature doesn't create lungs in the very beginning, but the outermost arrangements [first], the legs and arms. In the same way, the *higher* things are formed in you. The human soul in the mother's womb also teaches: it doesn't sit in a sleep-like state, but takes part with the spirit of the mother; they both work to create the body. By the same law, the student and teacher must work together with the help of the Spirit. That's why Christ says, "One is your teacher." And why do people love Christ? Because He gave something to the world: "I gave life to those who do not have it, so they may have this life in abundance." You want to become teachers. I'll ask you: What are you willing to give to the one you want to teach? If you taught someone and afterwards he became worse, I understand that you haven't taught him anything. Modern-day Christians and churches have a great weakness for teaching. It's not a bad aspiration in itself, but one must know the laws of teaching. Ordinary laws require teachers to have a certain degree, a certain examination before a commission, and then an order for appointment is issued, that is, for official entry into office. It's the same in the Spiritual world: one has to wait until the Divine Spirit illuminates and guides him. The one who isn't illuminated by the Spirit of God has no right to teach, because he'll transgress the Divine Law. When we grasp the deep meaning of these words of Christ, which have an internal and external expression (now I'm talking about inner Christianity, about that which can connect us with all the regions of the invisible world), then we'll understand the meaning of teaching. You want to be a teacher. I ask you: Where did you study? From what school did you graduate?—"But I read the Bible. I know the Gospel."—It's not enough.—"But I know the Christian faith."—It's not enough.—"But I'm from such-and-such a church."—Did you study in Heaven, in that higher establishment where the angels study? Do you understand the inner laws of nature, how man is arranged, his mind and his heart; what is the relationship of his soul to his spirit?—"I read about these things."—What?—"The soul here is an abstract concept, an idea of a combination."—From *what* is it combined? The human mind is a combination of abilities. Well, how are these things combined? He thinks he knows something. It's not that kind of combination, my friend. It's an *actual* combination, but not in separate parts. And due to that darkness that we have, we speak so incomprehensibly about the mind and heart, without knowing how to say where the heart is. It has three locations: one, the physical—you know where it is. But where is the heart of your feelings and your mind? You meet a person and say he's bad. Why is he bad? Years ago, a buffalo in America went completely mad and scared everyone around. They thought about killing it, but a boy was found who read animals' thoughts. He put his hand on the buffalo's head and asked it, "what is it?"—"A thorn is lodged in the hind part of my leg. It's tormenting me." They removed the thorn from the leg and the bull calmed down. One day, you also go crazy. The people sit to pour water on you. I say: On the hind part of your leg there's a thorn. Remove it and it'll subside; no need for hoses. Learned people, professors, doctors are so funny when they explain how the mind of a person became damaged, and they determine the diagnosis: "There's such-and-such an infection, an operation needs to take place." I see nothing but a little warming of the brain. Four or five months ago they came to tell me that the son of a doctor was first sick of a runny nose, which then became more complicated, and at last the doctor determined there was pus in the brain and that surgery had to take place. I said, "there's no need for surgery at all. There's a 99% chance that the child will die if you operate on him. Otherwise he'll get better." They go, perform surgery, and the son dies. To the doctors, the surgery was, of course, a "success." I say that people also perform surgeries in the spiritual sense as well: they cut some parts in order to heal, but that's not healing. Modern-day people say that in order for somebody to get better, he needs to [feel] berated: "You're a vagabond, a robber, such-and-such." There's no need to *beat* like before. Do you think that with these sounds of yours, which will enter his ear, you'll change him? Not in the least. The law is different: in order to teach others, you must first teach yourself. You're bad; everyone around you is bad. A mother that conceives and starts acting nervous and slandering: I can predict her consequences and to fully describe the character and fate of the youngster, what will happen in the future with him. The irritable mother shouldn't think that the child she'll bear will be a saint, who will look after her in her old age. One day he'll take revenge and say to her, "it would have been better if you hadn't given birth to me." In the same way, the disciple will tell the teacher, "it would have been better if you didn't teach me." A teacher in the full sense of the word must be pure like crystal water, a good example in everything. In him there mustn't even be a shadow of hesitation, doubt, and unbelief. When Christ gives this instruction, He wants to point to us the great danger to which we expose ourselves, and the great responsibility we bear before Him for the mutilation of some souls. Every mother, every teacher, who don't know how to educate, will be punished.

Now, the views modern people hold regarding God's laws, Heaven, angels, are vague and erroneous: They have no idea about these laws and about Heaven. Heaven, first of all, is organized too intelligently and knows what it does. And between angels and humans there are some proportions, as there exist between us and the plants and animals. Since we don't know how to educate, we unload with our goad and our staff 40-50 blows on the beast, with which we plow the field, and we think we're doing our duty. The Lord says, "one day I'll teach you how to manage the oxen and how to plow a field." Some think the Lord can't degrade, can't turn people back. If He turned some angels into snakes and animals with horns, He can also make you grow hooves. He can turn you into angels or devils; He can even alter your shape. And because shapes are important in the world (they regulate our lives), we must pay close attention to them. If I build for you an unhygienic house, leaving no window on the south side, but leave these only on the north side, and I also build it deep in the ground, do you know how you'll feel after living in it 6-7 years? Several doctors will start entering and going out of your house. Also, those teachers who tell you that you need not have windows to the spiritual world are first-class liars. Over there is the sun of life. I would even say that your roofs should be [made of] glass, so the sun can shine on you from above. If you make such illuminated houses, your shapes will transform and you'll become very beautiful. Regarding what I preach to you, I can make, and you too can make, an experiment, and in 4-5 years you'll see what the results will yield. I don't teach that you have to run [away] from life. This world, according to my belief, is very good, and people are very good; only I find that in the heel of the foot they have a thorn. That this is so, the apostle Paul says it and implores God to remove the thorn. This thorn may be in another place, but in most cases it's in the heel of the foot, because we are attached to this world with our feet. We need to learn to remove this thorn *scientifically*, because Christianity, in my view, is a deep science. A girl wants to marry a young man: she sees he's a handsome, well-behaved man. She asks, "can he feed me?" He receives 4-500 leva per month.—"Ah, he can. What did he study?"—"Such-and-such."—"Good." But these things aren't really essential: this man may be fired tomorrow, and this income of 4-500 leva may disappear. If the woman understands, she must ask and watch his heart and mind; she must be a clairvoyant, go into his house, walk around his rooms, his library, see how his books are arranged, see his kitchen, his garden, to visit the garden of his love, his compassion, his justice, the kind of flowers he planted; to go around and see how it's organized, and if everything is in order, she can say, "look, I'm marrying this man." This is the real marriage. The man must do the same. Many want to exchange their position: they discuss the question who should be a man and who should be a woman, why God created the man the way he is, and the woman another way. What's so bad about this? One time, both the men and women gave birth, but recently the man lost the ability to give birth and left the woman to do this. The Bible says, "Abram begat Isaac," and it doesn't say that Sarah gave birth. When man gave birth, the world was in perfect condition, and when he ceased to give birth, the world broke down. The man must give birth in order to be a good teacher. The mother can give birth to a child, putting all her noble qualities in his soul, but if the teacher is unable to cultivate these noble qualities, nothing good will come of it. So, the teacher needs to give birth. The teacher shouldn't resemble that priest who, when he wasn't in a normal state, during christening of the children, held a child in the bowl a little longer and it died, but he said, "give [me] another one. This one couldn't be baptized." When you baptize as teachers, your mind must be in place. This baptism implies bringing into the child, whom you are teaching, the Holy Spirit. The priest, as a teacher, must know the Divine laws.—"That's what the church wrote." To bathe the child in water is not a baptism. Modern-day priests, teachers, and judges are professionals, working for money—for 300-500 or 1,000 leva, which they are paid. In America they get more: $3,000, that is, 15,000 leva. According to the perception of the true doctrine of Christ, they are not God's servants, but ordinary workers. The first thing a spiritual teacher has to do is to reveal to the disciple the *invisible* world, like the mother when she conceives, saying to the child, "wait 9 months. I will bring you into a world new to you, and I'll show you its wonders. Now you shouldn't move and jump." After 9 months, when she gives birth, she becomes his first teacher, and other teachers will elevate the child's education from where the mother left off. She leaves her job because the child comes into a new region where he must have a new teacher, that, which the Gospel says, "for a man to be born a second time."

My lecture should prompt you to think more about yourself; the desire to be teachers shouldn't arise in you, because man suffers from great ignorance. But sit down like the merchants, see what you have to work with in your inner *safe*, whether you have someone you know in Heaven: have you sent someone a letter there? "We believe in Christ." But do you know Him? Do you know Paul? Do you know Peter?—"But the church says we can't communicate with that world, that it's wrong." This is great ignorance. Communicating with the spirits of hell is acceptable, but with Heaven it's wrong! To send a message to the devil is in the order of things, but communicating with the saints, to talk to them—don't disturb them! Then why do you disturb the devil? What kind of logic is that? This is a teaching that isn't supported by any laws. The way I know, the old Christians had direct contact with Heaven. They spoke to God, with the saints, and that's why they died with such readiness and self-sacrifice. They weren't like the present ones: "Wait for me to die, so then I can see." You won't see anything. When your house falls over you, what will you see? You'll wait until they dig you up.

Christ describes to his disciples the false teachers, who, dressed in mantles with long robes, preached, but actually deceived the converted ones, and he reproached them for this. The same thing is true for our time. If Christ comes now, he would say the same thing. He hasn't changed His mind. Christ is silent, but when He speaks and tells the truth, it'll hurt us very deeply. He'll lift up, and we'll see all the mistakes.

I'll give you two examples from Greek history. Two artists, sculptors, competed [to see] who understood the art better. So they got each other to prove who is the better sculptor. One made a cluster [of grapes] so skillfully, so life-like and natural, that he deceived the birds who swooped down to peck at it. The other one carved out a beautiful woman and draped the veil [made of] stone so skillfully that when the other artist came, he said, "lift the veil so I can see the statue." So the first artist deceived the birds, and the second one [deceived] the bird-master. I now ask you too: Who do you want to emulate? The birds or the craftsman? I would prefer the second one. You want to dominate the whole world, but how will you dominate it without the necessary knowledge? This knowledge must rest on a spiritual basis. Knowledge in the spiritual world is like a cauldron full of steam; it has power. In the spiritual world, knowledge has such a relationship as the physical forces. You travel along the streets of Sofia, the trams are moving here and there, but on top of their roofs there's a rod, which, when it slips out of the wire (an electric conductor), the tram stops immediately. So there must be some contact, through which the electricity must pass and put the car in motion. Have your teachers put the rod on this wire? Did they connect you with the electric current? The mechanism of the human car may be excellent and in good working order, but once the rod slips out and doesn't connect the car with the current, there's no movement forward. People look for the reason for the stoppage of movement elsewhere, when it can be put aside by grabbing the wire and adjusting the rod. Then the tram-driver will turn the apparatus, the electricity will flow, and the car will take off. In order for your thoughts to become active (since they are a driving force), you need to unite with the spiritual world. By the word "ability" I understand the form in which a certain force is limited, that is active in the spiritual world. When the form is dismantled or broken, the force cannot manifest. There are areas in our central brain where certain abilities sit, and these abilities are united with the forces in the spiritual world and work. If your rod isn't in place, these forces don't work. Other than that, other conditions are required: there must be railroad tracks, the tram-driver must understand his art; many conjunctions are required. And you, like a master, must often walk through your country, to see whether all the workers are in place, how they do their jobs. You often judge those who govern, that they don't manage things well. Well, how are *you* governed? You say this one or that one isn't very smart, but how are you within? Your judgments will be as accurate as you are upright within yourself. We say about a person that he's good, but in what does his goodness consist of?—"Because he treats us politely." This doesn't mean goodness, not in the least. Tomorrow, when he greets us impolitely, we'll say [he's] "bad." A good person is always good; a bad one—always bad. He can't be a saint one day, and a complete vagabond tomorrow. It's unthinkable. You say the bad person can repent? Do you know how many thousands of years are required for this? When a child is born, does he suddenly become a professor? He'll study at least 12 years and his consciousness will gradually develop. When the inner spiritual world is studied, the laws of Christianity will be understood. It has a goal to fix the world, to fix families, to set harmony between man and woman, brother and sister, master and servant. The modern world suffers, not because it's bad for someone to be a servant, but because he doesn't know how to be a good master. Doctor Mirkovic[6] used to say, "I don't want to be wealthy a second time. I want to be a servant to a master." You want to be masters, to have millions of leva.

---

6   One of Peter Deunov's first disciples.

Oh, then you'll be the most miserable people. You'll be prisoners surrounded with your money. One million leva on your back—it's a heavy load. You envy such people and want to take from their load, to put it on your back. This is a misunderstood doctrine. Will you compare yourself to that mule, loaded with icons: when everyone started bowing to the icons, it started kicking, thinking they were bowing to him. If the people honor and envy you, it's because of the crosses and icons that you carry. And what are those crosses? Virtues. Thank God that he put them on your back.

Christ turns to his disciples and tells them, "do not call yourselves teachers." But someone will say, "I turned it over to the Lord." Good, if you learned it, the Lord will bless you. But if you gave birth to him crippled; if you broke his mind and his heart, what will the Lord say? There will be consequences in Heaven; you'll have to answer. All of you here—how many people you crippled in this world! In the other world they'll appear, whoever has a lame leg, whoever has a dislocated hand: they'll all get together (your pupils) and will tell the Lord what kind of teachers you were. This will be so, for a fact. And then the Lord will say, "I fine this teacher 10,000 talents. Shut him in the dungeon until he pays the fine." The Lord never jokes. He's good, kind, just, but very strict. He'll take such uninvited teachers and impose a fine of 10,000 talents and He'll add, "shut him in the dungeon, to learn the art of teaching." And when you pay off your fine, when you bear all the suffering, in time you'll become very wise and good teachers. But do you know how many thousands of years will pass until this happens? This is how the fallen angels and people learn nowadays.

We now say, just as the church isn't doing well—let's show it a good example. I want you to have the power to modify things. Look at Moses: he grabbed the staff and it turned into a snake. He became frightened and the Lord said to him, "hold the tail," and when he caught the snake by the tail, it turned back into a staff. "But," you'll say, "he was Moses."—So what. He also studied, but he studied with the greatest teachers in Egypt. He wasn't stupid, because the Lord never chooses stupid people as leaders of humanity or of a nation. He studied for a long time and graduated from an eminent school. And you see how many miracles he performed before the Pharaoh. Moses wished for two things: to become a teacher and at the same time a rescuer of the Jews. First he said to himself, "this is not for me," and went into solitude, grazing sheep for 40 years, to redeem the sins of murder. And do you know what he did? He gave himself to deep reflections, because he was a devotee of all of Egypt's secrets. For murder, he studied 40 years. And in that time he devoted himself a second time. I ask: How many years did you graze sheep? To be shepherds—it's a great thing; it means being teachers. Have you recognized your teacher? Your father, your mother, your grandfather have been Christians for 2,000 years, but have they recognized Christ? If you recognized him, say the password He gave you, like in the military (in order to let you in, they want you to tell them the password). What is your password, your key word? Learned people must have some motto; and what must *our* motto be?—To serve Christ. How will we serve Him? By learning. How should we learn? Are you friends with the school? Walking around outside the school is one thing, but being inside is another thing. Where are your school books, your school certificates? You don't have a certificate, but you want to become teachers! It's the same with some priests and bishops: they also don't have it. And when we live in such deception, we want the Kingdom of God to come! The Kingdom of God is coming now and is revealing all of humanity's dirty things. The nations have now taken up war to defend their cause. Defend the Kingdom of God of justice! Every nation must have as much as it deserves; it's the same with every person. Seriously ask yourself the question: Do you know Christ? I don't want an answer now. If you can give the answer within a year, it'll be a blessing for you. You may say, "we saw Christ." Paul saw Him: "Saul, Saul, why are you persecuting me?" And he said, "who are you, Lord?" The Lord heard. Have you heard your teacher? When you raise a scandal in some religious society or God's temple, are you not persecuting Christ, like Paul? Then He'll say to you as He did to him: "Saul, Saul, why are you persecuting me?" and, "it's not easy for you to kick against the goad."[7] Paul realized his error and the Lord said to him, "because what you did, you did out of ignorance, I will send you to the Gentiles, so you can learn the lesson," and they beat him 3 times with 39 strokes. The Lord only beats the mature ones like this; He never beats the children. Thirty-three years, the years of Christ. When they hit you 39 times, you'll rise. These blows must be endured. The iron-smith, when he wants to make some knife or other instrument out of iron, also applies these blows. You're on the anvil; the Lord is striking you from above. He's not actually beating you, but says, "out of this material I want to make a knife, a rake, or a quill." If you're one of the bad people, he'll make a knife out of you, to slaughter bad people. If you're one of the better ones, he'll make a quill, to be held in hand by some writer. The quill, which the writer uses to write, has greater intelligence than the rake they use to plow the earth. You'll say that there's no intelligence in the iron. It too gets tired. Take a razor: when it's sharpened, after some work it too gets tired, gets used up. Every thing gets tired. An Englishman made an attempt, seeing that machines did too; everything gets tired. When the machine gets tired it starts making some new sound and the machinist says, "now the machine must rest." And in man, by the same law, the same reaction occurs: he gets tired and wants to rest. The great Teacher says, "in these cases, leave your brain to rest for a week, and after that it will start working again." Every thing requires its own time to work and to rest. Examine how plants develop and how caterpillars hatch and you'll understand the law. Your thought may take the form of a caterpillar or a butterfly. In order for man to succeed in the world, he must have only *one idea*. This is [both] true and false. He must have

---

7   Acts 9:5 (KJV).

more thoughts, but they must all be noble. They put covers on horses' eyes, so they can look only straight ahead, so they're not afraid of tangential influences. And it's better for man to have such covers, aiming at one idea, a noble one. If you can't have a lot of noble ideas, have at least one. Keep it as a target point that can raise you and deliver you. We say, "Christ delivered us." Moreover, "He redeemed us." But redemption has its bad side too, because when a bad man wants to use the benefits given to him, [he] can always make the wrong conclusion about things. Knowledge shouldn't be entrusted in ignorant hands. I'm talking about reincarnation, the dangers it poses to those who misinterpret it. The caterpillar, for instance, which has a hundred legs and crawls on the trees, may say, "I don't need any philosophy. A leaf is enough. When I find it, I'll eat it and it's finished." But one day it wraps itself in a cocoon and hatches as a butterfly, and now says, "now a leaf is not enough for me. I need flowers, to stick my trunk in and suck out the juices, their aroma." To enter the spiritual world, you must remove that skin you're wrapped in, like the caterpillar. If you don't remove it, in the spiritual world you'll occupy the space of a leaf, and you'll understand the spiritual world as much as the caterpillar. I want you to enter the spiritual world, but I ask: have you hatched? When you enter the spiritual world, you'll understand the meaning of an ox, an ass, a wolf, a dove, a fox, and so on. In every form that exists in the physical world, a great idea is embedded, and he who understands this idea will understand the meaning of things in the world.—"But the wolf has teeth."—It doesn't mean anything. If the hedgehog has spines, they're created for nothing else but strategic reasons, to be able to protect itself from the serpent or some other creature that wants to hurt it. It catches the serpent by the tail, starts eating it carefully, and when it swallows it, it watches out for itself with these spines. In time, this hedgehog will also change.—"How can it change?" you'll ask. Do you know what form *you* have in the spiritual world? There is a verse in the Bible where the Lord calls Jacob a worm. But, you'll say this is in a figurative sense. Christ too refers to his followers as sheep. Do you know what that means? Sheep: these are all the souls in whom the spirits live, and just as sheep in this world give us milk and wool, by the same law the souls give man the necessary milk and wool. Try this teaching. Why are you in this world? Put the mind into action. The very first thing you have to learn is to remove all doubt, to come into contact with the spiritual world and if you can *project* it, your friends will immediately come to your aid. How is you hearth? If you make it very hot, that is, if it has the same power as the upper part, you can *bake* whatever thought you want. If your heart doesn't have the necessary heat, it will fall. It depends on the heart how far you can send your request. "I prayed," but I see that your prayer stands only two hand-breadths over your head. You'll pray 5-10-100 times from the bottom of your heart, until you succeed in sending your request to the Lord. And when it reaches His ears, He will answer you. What will you answer to the request that hasn't reached Him? When you pray, you must concentrate, forget everything that is around you. You have to bring yourself to that state where nothing, other than the prayer, passes through your mind. I ask now: Is the hearth of your heart, your mind, hot enough to send your prayers upwards? But there's mischievous children around you. The Lord sent them to earth to learn, because in Heaven they didn't live peacefully. He *degraded* them. The Lord doesn't want people who make a ruckus in Heaven. They'll learn to plow, to dig, to make shoes, and in time, when they learn the lesson, they may even become royal sons. Before getting into Heaven, you'll go to an inspection committee that will ask you questions: what are your thoughts and feelings; what is your compassion, your love for your neighbor and to God, and many more questions. Because now Christ is coming and the books of life will open, as they say, and the people will be judged whether they deserve or not to go one class above or to enter Heaven. Everyone will be given what he deserves.

That's why Christ turns to you and says, "One is your teacher—

Christ." I want all of you to remember this Teacher, who came 2,000 years ago to redeem you from sin. And you're still looking for Him! Did Christ write His name in your soul, in your heart, even once? If He wrote it, I congratulate you. If He hasn't written it, try to meet Him and ask Him to write it. And when He writes His name, don't go out blowing the trumpet and bragging: "Christ wrote His name in our book." No! It's not necessary for you here, but in Heaven. When you go there, the angels will stop and ask you: "Take out your notebook," and if the Lord signed it, they'll say to you, "you're free to enter." Then Christ too, and the saints, and your great and small brethren, will meet you with branches, and there will be great joy that you came. There was once a rule in the Pythagorean school, when accepting some disciple, the first year to put him through the greatest ridicule, and if he could endure the mockery, they accepted him. And Christ is now sending someone on earth to mock you—"He wants to become a saint. He should have his head examined. He's a crackpot; he's a little crazy; he's a blockhead."—This is the Pythagorean system for accepting disciples. If you can endure these mockeries, know that you've passed the exam. And then you'll be accepted. However, if you get heated by the attacks and say, "Me? [You] wait [and see]!" you're lost. "My husband is bad." How do you know he's not purposely put there by the commission to test you? Endure for a year, pass the test, and then the Lord will say to the husband, "you will no longer mock and harm your wife," and you'll see how he'll become gentle as a lamb. But only then, when you endure and when Christ says so. Remember this teaching; I speak of its outer side. They're ideas thrown together, as long as you can distinguish the deceptive from the noble. When Christ's teaching enters you, it will raise you. You will recognize people; you'll see their souls. Often two [people] meet and ask each other: "I'm a Christian. Do you believe in Christ?" If you're Christians you need not ask; the question itself shows that there's no Christianity in him. I will never ask what flower is given; when I smell it, I'll know whether it's a rose or carnation. My nose is in place. If my sense of smell is dumbed down, paralyzed, or I'm blind and can't see, then I may ask. But if all my senses are healthy, just by seeing or smelling the flower I can, by its outer covering or its aroma, recognize what it is. In the same way, every soul manifests through its outer sides, through the actions. I see you from the inside as carnations, but some still haven't bloomed. You have buds, a promise to develop in the future. I don't want you to only bloom, but also to flower out and ripen. The angels come like the bees: they will *fertilize* the flowers in the souls. If you blossom, you're already in communion with them. What a deep science this is, and how many more things you still have to learn! I need to give you 10 lectures. But if I were to explain these things, which are very tiring, you'll say that it's not interesting, and you'll fall asleep. And you're right, because you're still not ready for this. A time will come when you'll be ready. For instance, if you start eating honey and over-eat, you'll start shaking. Why? Because you over-consumed. You associate with some good person, constantly drawing from him, but at one point you say, "get away from me! I can't look at him." You should have been given as much honey, and to associate with the person as much, without shaking. In the same way, you too shouldn't give too much of your honey. One teaspoon is enough, and not an entire bowl, so the guest doesn't start shaking, because even the Bulgarian proverb says, "an overly exalted saint is also not dear to God." You read and read and you shrivel away. Read just one verse, stop on it and think: "God is Love." Think about what kind of attitude Love is and feel this Love in yourself. It shouldn't be as when we eat an apple or the cat [eats] some mouse. To love you—it means for me to come into you. To love me—it means to be inside me. When you have the image of a friend, you put him in a prominent place. Our heart represents the astral world; the mind: the pure spiritual world. If your mind can ascend to a certain height—there is your spiritual world. What happens in the brain is a reflection of the spiritual world. Every thought is a form in the spiritual world; I understand [it as] every noble thought. And the thoughts differ in form and content. When a noble thought comes, it produces joy and happiness. And when you raise your mind and heart toward Christ, He will grab you by the hand and will bring you to the Divine garden. He will take you to the wellspring of Love, to taste it. You will experiment with tasting things. There won't be a happier moment for you than this one. And when you enter, you won't say, "let my husband enter." No, everyone must enter by himself. There shouldn't be vouching for someone else. In everyone there must be a deep desire to enter by himself. If he's capable, you will help him enter too, but the incapable, the crippled, must stay out until they heal. This world is for the crippled. Those who need to enter the school must be pure; purity in thoughts and desires is necessary. It's also necessary to have total selflessness, [and] later on, self-denial. It's the higher degree: It [means] to pass the exam. Now, the first thing required of you is purity in thoughts and desires, and unwavering faith that whatever the Lord says will come to be. When you put the Lord in front of some thing, there's no need to ask yourself whether you'll succeed. You may be a teacher, a judge, a priest, a farmer; if you do your job, there's no power on earth that can hinder you. You'll have many obstacles, hardships, and trials, but they're necessary for your growth. The sufferings that are sent are a blessing.

Now I leave you with this thought: to recognize your teacher, Christ. When you recognize your true Father, then the angels, and the world, will be your brethren, and not just one or two but by the thousands. For thousands of years they will walk you around their abode in Heaven. There's many nice things there, long walks, exemplary schools, new suns, new beings, and so many more things! And then you'll say, "we now understand the deep meaning of life, why one must live." It will happen when you have only one teacher. If you say you have two, I'll say, "you're lying to me, and God." There's one mother on the physical plane. In the spiritual world—one Teacher; in the Divine—one Father, who is the Lord. Altogether they are three: one on the earth, among the angels is the Teacher, and among the gods is God. When you pass through these three, then every one of you will understand the deep meaning, the inner side of the present life, and with happiness and songs you will bear all the sufferings. There will be no anguish for you in life, and the issues between men and women, between parents and children, and between all nations will be ameliorated. Then there will be no question: "What will happen to the Bulgarian people?" Let all Bulgarians turn to God. I guarantee them that everything will be in order. But if they carry on the same way, they'll receive 39 blows with the stick. This is how it's written in the Divine Book.—"But Russia is such-and-such." [Russia] too: if it follows the Lord, it will be blessed. If it doesn't follow Him, it will take 39 blows with the stick. It's the same with Germany, with France, with England, with all: the Lord beats them one after the other, on the same basis. Everyone here on earth must fulfill the will of our Teacher, our Father. I believe that you have all the desire in you to fulfill it. I see that you've turned a new page now, and like the prodigal son, you say, "Father, forgive. We sinned. We ate and drank what you gave us. From now on we will no longer do this. Take us as servants in your home." Be sure that your Father will forgive everything. He will dress you, He will slaughter the fattened calf, and will make a feast for you, and there will be joy in his house because his prodigal son has returned. He will put on his finger a new ring. He will bless him and say, "let's go to school, son. Go learn again!"

Lecture held on 7 December 1914

IF YOU LOVE ME

"If you love me, keep my commandments."—John 14:15 (NKJV)

Christ's teaching is for this world, and not for the other one, as most people claim. There is a correlation between the invisible and the visible world, just as it exists between the roots and the branches of plants.

When we walk along the paths of Christ, the saints and enlightened beings rejoice because we unite with them, and they feed us. The tree nourishes itself from the roots and branches—above and below. If we keep Christ's commandments, He'll give us everything we ask for in His name. If they don't give us what we want, it is because we transgressed. The earth is not a place of sufferings—it's a school. Without her, we can't rise. We brought the earth to tears more than once, and when she gets upset because of us, she shows her attitude with her earthquakes—her fur bristles up from our evil deeds.

When we listen to His commandments, He'll reveal Himself in us through enlightened thoughts [and] desires.

Divine Love is a necessity that expresses itself through grace. What is grace?

Example: In the River Thames there are little ships, 20-30 thousand that catch fish, and sustain all of London. During an out-flow these ships remain on dry land, in the marshland. An in-flow comes. This is grace; they rise and start floating toward the sea, going out to fish.

In grace there is an in-flow: we must search for these moments of Divine Spirit during in-flow. If we lose this moment, we'll lose the grace, and we must wait 12 hours, which are 12 weeks, 12 months, 12 years, 12 centuries, etc.

First of all, we must apply Divine Love; it works in the heart, [which] is the most important organ. The heart calculates the pulse, and when the Divine heart pulsates, we come back to life. We gather in-flow.

On the day we disregard the Divine commandments, disharmony appears in us and we're no longer Christians. We'll search for Christianity within ourselves, yet we're not Christians. We often ask ourselves whether we lost [His] grace or [whether] we gained [something] more in this world. We can make mistakes, but Christ will judge us if we don't correct them. We shouldn't repeat the mistakes again, but we should correct them. We need to learn from our mistakes, that is, we need to free ourselves from our bad thoughts, which means not speaking to the devil, otherwise he'll gradually invite himself entirely within us, and he'll tell us, "if you're not well-disposed go outside; I like it here." The example with the camel and the miller, in whose water-mill she wanted, and was allowed, to just warm her snout, her head, and gradually she invited herself in completely, and said to the miller to go outside if he felt cramped in her presence. She liked it there. The people come out of themselves every day, because they gave way to the devil within.

First and foremost, we must cleanse our heart; secondly, our mind. When we don't muddy the river, it'll cleanse our hearts by itself. "I will give you a spring of living water." That's why we counteract every evil thought with a good thought, and with the course of time we'll cleanse ourselves.

Love consists of the commandments of Christ, and in keeping them. That's why we must gradually study them. The master will show us the method, the order of studying. Love isn't just a feeling, but an intelligent act implying sacrifice. It's a backpack that gets carried all over the world. Everyone must carry that backpack, even if it's heavy. We'll rise with it and learn Christ's commandments. When we experience sufferings, it's because the Lord is testing our love. And if we take the sufferings without complaining, it shows that we have Divine Love. An example: a wealthy [man] in Paris tested his relatives [by] seeing whether they would support him while he pretended to be very poor. Whoever took care of him became an heir to his wealth; the others were excluded, even if they were upset at him. Such was their award.

Christ says that if you love Him, you will keep His commandments, and they refer to our brothers, sisters, teachers, societies, and others. And we must maintain these relationships toward everyone. We must avoid the *skirmishes* in life, which exist in all Christian denominations. They preach Christianity but do not fulfill it. A Christian will show his strength in his fight with the devil, who is a great coward; once he shows him his net, [the devil] runs away. He's the father of deception, and that's why he runs from the truth, from the light.

They built a bathhouse in a city. For 8 years the citizens argued whether the floor-planks should be sanded down or unsanded, and the bathhouse remained unfinished, because they couldn't agree. Both sides gave their motives regarding the comforts and discomforts, and the practicality or lack of practicality, of the smooth and coarse floor-planks, and vice versa. They took their dispute before a great architect for a solution, and he advised them like this: one floor-plank sanded down and the [one next to it] unsanded, to satisfy both sides. One should act the same way with Christians, who are dogmatists, who hold on to the outward appearance.

Every morning we should read one chapter from the Gospels, to search for a commandment in the chapter, and to apply it throughout the day in our life, and then Christ will come into us. He'll make a dwelling in us, and in that way we'll understand the profound, Divine things. Life is eternal and Christ will reveal many great things to us, but gradually—we're currently unprepared for these great mysteries. For instance, someone wanted the Lord to reveal to him at least one of His great mysteries, and the Lord sent an angel who took him up, leaving his body but taking his spirit along with the human heart. After seeing numerous wonders, he started praying for them to return him, because he couldn't withstand it when they carried him to all the high places in the Heavens. That's why, when we keep the commandments, we'll prepare [for] this journey, and we will not want to come back. First of all, it's required to have a healthy mind, a healthy heart. Every morning we must make attempts: do we have fear? This is a spiritual *fever*. That's why we should breathe deeply, and with this we'll come into contact with the angels, with the Heavenly forces. People easily turn bitter every day, but this isn't a principle in life. People must turn from bitter to sweet, like the fruit—out of a flower it first turns into green fruit, and then ripens and becomes sweet. The Lord says, "everything will turn into [something] good." The bigger we are, the greater the sufferings we'll have. This is how it is with the children, the men, the saints, etc. Christ says, "how much longer will I have to put up with you?" We search for Him, we find Him, and when He comes into us we crucify Him. He'll rise and leave, but when will He return again? After 10-100-1,000 years or more? Christianity isn't difficult; it's easy. Those who die for Christ die with joy, and their names are written above. It's better for us to die like Christians who suffer than as criminals. Moses will come for such; Elijah will come; the prophet John will come, and with a whip they'll fix everyone. That's why Christ says, "my burden is light." The Lord who speaks to us will guide and steer us. The greater the sufferings, the closer Christ is to us. If we have no sufferings, the Lord is far from us, and that's bad. That's why everyone must fulfill Christ's teaching in his own place—as a headmaster, and a teacher, and a professor, etc. This is Christ's commandment. Through fulfillment the Lord will also help us, and the Lord will lift us, [He] will turn us from small into great people.

From the moment he promised and dedicated his life to the

Lord, Ivan of Kronstadt[1] became *John of Kronstadt*, but earlier he was dull-minded. To dedicate our lives doesn't mean going into the forest, but to fulfill His commandments in our lives, and to dedicate our minds, to warm our hearts, for our souls to be reborn, for our spirit to live and rejuvenate itself.

24 January, in the year 1915, Burgas,
in the home of brother K.P. Stoychev

---

1 A Russian saint and member of the Russian Orthodox Church, who died in 1909.

EIGHT THOUSAND YEARS

8,000 years X 365 days = 2,920,000 days

8,000 years X 12 months = 96,000 months

96,000 months X 4 weeks = 384,000 weeks

384,000 weeks X 7 days = 2,688,000 days

2,920,000 days X 24 hours = 70,080,000 hours

70,080,000 hours X 60 minutes = 42,048,000 minutes

42,048,000 minutes X 60 seconds = 252,288,000 seconds

The longest period from the creation of the earth is the first period—the descent of man from Heaven to earth, and it's after the mammals.

The plants were the first to descend. The first period is 75,000 years.

By "Adam" we understand the white man, the spiritual man; and the spiritual Adam is from the time after Christ. Every race before that knew about the white race, and they waited for it like a Messiah. The oldest race is the white [one] in the physical world; all others are older in the spiritual world, but younger in the physical world. After the white race comes the sixth race—the *illuminated* race, called the Sons of God. Nature will change for that race, as well as the climatic conditions. Currently, people's evil thoughts and desires have given form to a dark band around the earth.

The Lord submerged man (Genesis 6) in the astral world.

Jacob, a robber, a liar...and the Lord said to him, "you will not be called Jacob."

The physical body was formed for millions of years, and now it's complete. The astral body is currently being formed.

A calculation: 8,000 X 12 X 4 X 7 X 52 X 365 X 24 X 60 X 60 = the number of years since the formation, the creation of the world.

The length of each era is marked on the earth's layers.

To descend into hell—you'll feel tens of thousands of kilograms heavier. Only heroes descend into hell—that's how it's described in Greek mythology. And there, in hell, are valuable things; a population lives there, and is aware that this place is theirs. They live—whoever goes there must take their form. Hell is like trash gathered for more than 20 years, and it's now deteriorating and rotting, and whoever values the trash will make use of it, and whoever doesn't will say that it's useless trash.

The center of the earth is the biggest hell; one hundred kilometers from it and around it there's a solid band where a different population lives; there's another band that's 100 kilometers from that one, and so on. Our earth has a bright, solid band around it [at a distance of] 100 kilometers, through which sunlight and other light [penetrates it]. There's a population on that band—the astral world; around it is another band 100 kilometers away, and so on.

There are 7 outer bands around the earth—7 Heavens, and 7 bands inside it. At the center of the earth is the fire—hell.

(This was spoken to me by Master P. K. Deunov, in the home of D. Tsaneva, in the evening during dinner at their house).

The deceased may be in the astral world, but they live in the physical world and appear during seances; they talk about their worldly affairs, where is their money, documents, disputes, and other things. This is the state of their consciousness and enlightenment in a spiritual sense.

We, who work on the spiritual plane and form our astral body, will *consciously* enter the astral world.

He who awakens people's hearts to do something good—He is called the Lord. And this Lord, through his Son Jesus Christ, constantly teaches every person many good and ideal things. And whoever listens to Him will be blessed.

(On Sunday, January 1915, the Master—Mr. P. K. Deunov—left by railway to Yambol on the afternoon train at 1:50 P.M., accompanied by the friends from our circle by the train station).

7 February, in the year 1915

A conversation with the Master P. K. Deunov in the home of the Stoychevs in Burgas.

EASTER

"Go therefore and make disciples of all the nations, baptizing them in the name of the Father and of the Son and of the Holy Spirit, teaching them to observe all things that I have commanded you; and lo, I am with you always, even to the end of the age."—Matthew 28:19 (NKJV)

In the sermons of the entire Christian world, the text of the resurrection of Christ is chosen for today. In America alone there are 80-90-100,000 preachers, and in Bulgaria, 3,300 priests who preach about the resurrection today; it's being talked about everywhere. Since so many people speak of the resurrection, I want to make a small deviation.

Of course, many examine the issue historically and philosophically: is resurrection possible? The argument is from a purely physiological point of view: is it possible for a person to rise? Ideologists and theologians write and struggle to prove that resurrection is possible, but they too can't prove it. I stop on these words: "Go therefore and make disciples of all the nations, baptizing them in the name of the Father and the Son and the Holy Spirit." The teaching on the Father and the Son and the Holy Spirit is a profound teaching. What is this science? Frequently you say these words, "'Father,' 'Son,' and 'Holy Spirit,'" but what is the meaning of these words to you? They will have meaning for you only when they can produce some effect. When you hold a matchbox, you can never know its power if you can't ignite it. Only when you light it can you feel its power. And resurrection will be a subject unknown to you if you don't ignite this word like a match, to produce light in your mind and your heart, or if you plant it like a seed, to grow and see its fruit. It's enough in a person's life to have two, or even just one of these words that can be understood properly, and he'll become a genius. When he understands two such words, one becomes a saint, and if he understands three, he'll become one with Jesus Christ. So, in every spoken language are words, which, when understood, acquire a magical meaning for us. When Moses lifted his staff before the Red Sea, he said one word and it parted. And Christ, when He was in front of Lazarus' tomb and lifted His eyes up, He said just one word: "Lazarus, get out of the tomb!" And in the beginning the Lord said just one word, and the world came to be. We know how to speak and write properly, grammatically, with commas and periods, with question marks and exclamation marks. We debate many philosophical questions, but we don't know how to organize our lives. We resemble that philosopher who went out to go boating on the sea and in conversation he asked the boatman, "are you a man of science? Do you know anything about astronomy?" And when he answered, "I don't know," he replied, "you lost one fourth of your life." After this he asked, "do you know something about geology?"—"I don't know."—"You lost two fourths of your life. Well, don't you know mathematics?"—"I don't know."—"Three fourths of your life you lost." At one point, a terrible storm arose, and the boat was in danger of capsizing. Then the boatman in his turn asked the philosopher, "do you know how to sail?" The latter answered, "I don't know." The boatman in his turn said, "you lost four fourths of your life." Now we sit like that philosopher and ask how Christ was born and how He came to earth, but if a storm rises in our lives, some hardships and sufferings come, we don't know how to sail and start sinking. Then where is your philosophy, mathematics? How do they help you? But mathematics is a science [of] how to build our lives wisely; biology, how we should put the cells in order and organization; geology, what our relationship to the earth is, and so on.

There are three periods in the life of Christ which are important—they are in every life: birth, death, and resurrection. Notice that when Christ was born, the angels appeared in Heaven and announced, "peace among men." So, Christ was born triumphantly, but we see that this triumphant Christ had to die the most disgraceful death. And it is asked, "why did He have to die like that?" Modern-day people die, and they frequently ask me why they die. Christ died disgracefully and finally resurrected. Now I'll make a little comparison: How did death appear in the world? We know that when Adam was in paradise, God expressed life and death in the form of two fruit trees, one of which He called the tree of life, and the other one, the tree of the knowledge of good and evil. In a pure occult and mystical sense, in tree of life is understood all the aspirations of nature toward the Divine, the aspiration that runs from the bottom to the top; it's the inflow that grows. The tree of the knowledge of good and evil, however, goes from top to bottom. Now, how did death come about? In the most natural way. If we let two trains from two opposite sides move toward the same point, what will happen? A crash. Adam found himself among two such trains and when he didn't know how to escape the crash, he died. And every one of you will end the same way if he touches the forbidden tree. On the day he touches, the same thing will happen to him, because when he touches he will enter that great current from top to bottom, toward earth, only the Divine power can help him escape this current. This is precisely why Christ came to earth, so He can bring people back to the original stream of life, in the opposite direction, which we call resurrection. In order to understand this teaching, we have to understand the teaching of the Father and the Son and the Holy Spirit. What should be understood by Father?—The teaching of Divine Wisdom. By Son?—The teaching of Divine Love. In Spirit?—The teaching of ascension, the evolution of man. And it is said in Scripture, "whoever believes in this teaching will be saved." We have to understand the laws of this teaching. What is required of us? Every one of you is a father, but do you understand your *calling* as a father? Everyone has been in the position of a son, but do you know what a son's relationship to a father should be? You're not like the Spirit, but you will be. Precisely now you're in the process of the Spirit, namely this Spirit that lifts the people and which now must raise the Christ in us.

In order to properly understand Christ's teaching, we have to free ourselves from many entanglements in this world—not to deny the world, because that would be a misunderstanding. The world has two faces: a purely Divine face and an outward face of things, and when it's said we have to deny the world, it must be understood—to deny all those elements that have a transient, deceitful character that don't carry anything essential in our lives. But everything that serves to raise us on earth, we must keep it, because in another place the Scripture says, "God so loved the world that He gave His only begotten Son, to help it." That the world has two sides is understood by another verse from apostle Paul who says, "the image of this world is transient, but there is an image that does not change." A man is born, grows, and thinks he'll fix the world, but he reaches 45-50 years of age and notices some weight loss. He feels his strength leaving him, and he gets smart and starts telling the young people to work for him. He becomes softer, more polite, because he's weak and because in him arises the thought that he's aging and that he may die tomorrow. He doesn't give credence to such thoughts that he can resurrect. Modern-day people are *infected* by the view that one can't resurrect to live again. This is precisely the biggest deception in present life. One can resurrect just as one can die; they're two interrelated things. If you come into conflict with the forces that act in nature, your form will be destroyed. If you don't understand the laws, you'll be crushed. We have to free ourselves from certain obstacles that our souls inherited.

I'll give an example and explain a great law that regulates life. Several English sailors left a ship to visit a European city. They traveled around the city, went to various pubs and drank. Upon returning, they got on the boats, but forgot to untie them from the posts where they were tied. And they started rowing with the oars. They rowed and rowed all night, thinking they were approaching the ship. In the morning however they saw that they were still by the shore. Why didn't they reach the ship? This little rope that was tied around the posts—it kept them attached. People can't rise precisely for that reason; they're tied to a post. I have often seen little children catching a bird and letting it fly with a string. The bird flies up, but drops to the ground again. All people are tied like this. People should have an ideal. What kind? The kind that can pull them toward the sky.—"They flew but fell. I don't know why." They're tied. You have doubts in your mind, you have important issues you haven't solved. Untie your boat, row with your oars, and move toward the goal. We can't avoid the consequences of the causes. We think that our thoughts and desires exercise no influence, but actually every thought, however weak, exerts an influence. Moses, I think, says in Deuteronomy that God takes the crimes into account up to the fourth generation. A crime must be dissolved in 100 years. Those who studied the law noticed the following thing: if a black woman has relations with a white man, a white child may be born in the first generation, and if not in the second or third, a black child will surely be born in the fourth. If it's born in the beginning, good—the karma will end. The law works the other way too: if a white woman has relations with a black man, the black child may be born in the beginning, and if it's not born then, it will surely be born after 100 years. And the people wonder: "From where did the Lord give us this black child?" Some great-grandmother of yours had relations with a black man 100 years ago. This law also works in our feelings and thoughts. You sit during the day and a bad thought comes to you. Why? A hundred years ago, your spirit had relations with a black man. We call this black man the devil. One of your bad desires is also your child. This karmic law is strict. We have to protect ourselves well, because we can't avoid the consequences. We should never give way to a bad thought in our minds, because it will create its own form, and in the future, whenever it may be, it will stumble us. It's not a matter here about someone being born from a black or white man. The point is that there are vibrations of black and white people that differ. Black people aspire toward the earth, and not toward Heaven. They are people of that tree, from which your first mother ate. White people, who are now coming, are people of the tree of life. Therefore, from whichever tree we eat, we will become. And the tree of life is Christ. When this great thought of Christ penetrates you—not an abstract thought, that Christ stands on the right side of the Father, but Christ, the force that penetrates our whole earth, and when that stream penetrates into all beings from small to great, then there is salvation. When Christ died, it became dark. The people felt that darkness, and Scripture says that Christ entered hell and preached that doctrine there, and all who listened to him came out of hell and came to earth. Weren't *you* also there when Christ preached? You were, but you forgot. And what did Christ tell you when he came down there to pull you out of the darkness?—"Go, and sin no more," because you will give birth, as I just told you, to black children. Suffering after suffering will come. And because Christ is on earth, He resolved to redeem mankind, and He will do it. There's no force on earth, however powerful it may be, that can counteract the power of Christ. He says, "the sheep My Father has given, no one can take them out of My hands, because there is no-one greater than My Father." And if any doubt comes into your soul, it's your black father. Break your ties with him! The pure soul must never intertwine itself with the impure. When a mother's child gets very dirty, does the mother immediately hug him? No. She first pats him well, then washes him, cleans him, dresses him with clean clothes, and then kisses him. This is the simple philosophy of life. Someone will come and tell you, "but you don't love me."—"Your clothes are muddy, my friend. You're muddy, sister. Come, I'll pay for your bath. Clean yourself. Wash yourself—just as you should wash the body, [do] the same with your heart. And after you do this, only then will you rise." Now, do you know why Christ suffers? The cross represents the *house* of mankind: the unfolded cube makes a cross. But Christ was crucified on this cross, and God says now, "wash your house, open your windows, cleanse everything." Some say, "kiss this cross," but this cross needs to be cleansed. The cross is in the mind, in the heart. The people can't kiss this cross until you cleanse it. We are all crosses, *living* crosses. We need to raise up these Divine crosses in our hearts, and when we do this, we'll draw a circle (which means eternity), and we'll make from the cross a wheel or propeller so it can move.

Therefore, with His doctrine, Christ wants to show the basic laws through which we can change the order of things. And we *can* change it. We first have to have an idea about this, and secondly, to strive to achieve it. Modern-day people can't achieve it due to one simple reason: there exists in them an unrelenting egoism; everyone wants to be first. An artist represented this really well with one of his paintings: he painted a mountain peak on which an idol is erected, and the millions of people look up toward that peak, and if someone tries to climb up and reach the idol, the others grab him and don't let him go. And so the people constantly battle, and nobody can go up. In the races at the Olympic games in ancient Greece, the one who reached the target first, he got the wreath. In the pursuit for Christ, however, everyone can take this wreath as long as he tries to fulfill Christ's doctrine.

So, we have these three things in the doctrine of the Father and the Son and the Holy Spirit. If we can enunciate these three words in their full sense—when we say "Father," to feel the pulse of that being that moves the world; to feel it like that, the way a mother can feel the pulse of her child. And to feel the Divine Thought means to understand it and recognize it. Then, as the Lord says, "before you ask for anything, I will answer your wishes." We must have excellent filial attitudes to God, to perform the duties we have toward our Father. He didn't come to earth, but He sent His Son. Many are afraid of sacrifice and say that there's no life in sacrifice. And many, out of thoughtlessness, stop at the words of Christ, who says, "if you do not eat of My flesh and of My blood, you will have no eternal life." We eat every day to live. Don't you think this grain of wheat, these grasses, whose juices we swallow, don't die and don't sacrifice themselves for us? But they say, "we die so you can become people." How many billions of creatures serve us! And what do we do now on earth? We deal with scholastic issues, like those old theologians in the Middle Ages who philosophized how many devils could dance on the tip of a knife. We constantly deal with this.

I say that Christ's teaching contains within itself the meaning of life. There's always a lowland in two great eras. If we look at our brain, we'll see that it also has dents and protrusions. Human thought can circulate thanks to these grooves. And the earth has such dents that create some currents—thanks to them we can live. Someone says, "I don't want to live in the lowland." Well, where do you want to live? How many devils can live on a mountain peak? Not everyone can live there. Everyone [is] in the grooves of his own life: once in the lowland, next time on a peak, a third time back to the lowland, a fourth time on the peak. There will be a descent and a climb, until the law is understood that evolution is movement along a broken line. However, when someone learns Christ's teaching about the circular movement in eternity, he'll enter another evolution that won't go up and down, but will go in a circle.

On the other hand, the teaching of the Spirit is a real doctrine that modern-day people refuse. When the Holy Spirit works in us, it implies both unity and multitude. The Father created things, the Spirit is the multitude from both poles, and Christ represents the juices that constantly flow into the tree of life. The Spirit represents the conditions in which we live. Modern-day astrologers say that man is in communion with the entire universe, that is, that all beings find themselves in some interrelation: the heart, the mind, the ears, the eyes correspond to certain beings in space, and when they have conflict amongst themselves, then the person experiences something active in the respective part, in the legs or head. Sometimes your hand hurts, or any other part; this is an influence that comes from outside, an influence, as they say, from Jupiter, from Saturn, from Mars. Someone might object: "How can Mars affect people?" We say

[that] England exercises some influence: the land of England, or the peoples that live there, the English peoples with their thoughts exercise this influence. Consequently, those beings who live on Mars also influence us with their thoughts through space. When they form a current, and we, when we feel that current, become war-like. Now everyone is under the influence of Mars: they will fight until this influence achieves its goal, for which it exists in the world. Don't think that the teaching of Christ is a doctrine of peace; it is for peace, but if that equilibrium is broken, there will be war. And only through war can the broken equilibrium be restored after time. And we know that law from practical life: when the woman wants to draw out the butter from the milk, she beats it in the bottle. And war in the world will cease only when the butter is extracted. Now why do the people fight? Christ says, "I want butter. When you smear it on yourselves, you'll become softer, because now you're hard and rough." Now the butter is getting beaten, and when Christ rubs you, you'll become gentler. This is so; it's shown in the parable about those foolish maidens who forgot to take oil for their lamps and remained outside. In order to enter the Kingdom of God, you must have oil.

This is the teaching of the Spirit. I speak in an allegorical sense; but if you too think about it, you'll understand the relationship of those forces that soften. And do you know why the Lord created the modern world? Those spirits, which were the first ones created, became crystals. After that, our world had to be created, so new cells could form, not as a crystalline, broken, geometrical form, but in circular form. A crystal, a diamond, must become a living cell so it can develop, like a plant. If you examine this idea well enough, you'll see that even the most noble plant must overturn its wooden, immobile cells into meat and nerves, so it can feel and move, just as animals feel and move. In the same manner, we too must pay everything so we can form that cell that creates saints. We are dead now; in Heaven, we are planted with our heads upside down. We have to sacrifice ourselves so we can become intelligent cells, to become one with Christ and when we pass through His body, through His mind, through His heart, only then will we be able to become strong, to understand the profound meaning of things. Of course, these things are very abstract and if I were to let myself explain them, I'll stray from my subject, and this will be of no use to you.

The first thing in life is obedience. A Greek disciple in ancient times wanted to study the secret sciences and he therefore went to Egypt at the school of the so-called White Brotherhood. As he was showing him around, the chief priest of the temple of Isis led him to a statue and told him, "this is the Truth."—"Why didn't you bring me to the Truth first, but showed me around everywhere else? You should have brought me here in the very beginning," said the student. "You can't," said the priest, and added, "don't lift the veil of this statue; don't touch the curtain. Study it from the outside." A strong desire formed in the disciple to see what was underneath, under the veil. He said to himself, "when I lift the veil I will find the Truth, and when I return to Greece I will possess great power." One evening, he went out quietly; he got into the temple, lifted the veil, but in the morning they found him dead in front of the statue. What did he learn? Someone says, "lift the veil. I want to see the Truth." It's dangerous if the veil is lifted. One must be prepared for the moment. Christ came to prepare us to meet this moment without fear. First of all, we have to understand the kind of life that leads us to salvation. Afterwards we have to pass through another process, of which He says, "if you are not born from on high, you will not see the Kingdom of God." And He told Nicodemus that if he is not born of water and spirit he can't get into the Kingdom of God. So there are two births, but not reincarnations, because reincarnation implies a process of stoppage. Reincarnation is a law of the disharmony on earth: to be reborn means to begin the work again which you left off. They catch you, jail you, and when you lay there for 20 years, 15 more remain, you run away. They retrieve you and throw you in for another 10 years, so they become 25 again. After 5 years, you run away again, they catch you again, lock you up for the third time and impose on you an even greater punishment. This is reincarnation—a person who doesn't want to lay in prison. Or, in another sense, when you are sent to the earth and don't want to live as God ordained, but want to run away easily. Then they'll catch you and throw you in prison, and if you're constantly running away, your prison sentence will not expire for centuries. The law of the new birth implies for man to fulfill the will of God. And it's not difficult to fulfill it. Truth always lies in the profound reasons for misunderstanding life. Modern people have the tendency to criticize; everyone sees the mistakes of others: "So-and-so doesn't live as he should." Well, do you live like this?—"He doesn't think right." Well, do you think correctly?—"He's not good." Well, are you good? Above all else, one must know himself. He has to study his construction. Did you find out why the Lord gave you a nose; why he gave you two eyes, and why some eyes are black, others are blue or green, and why you have these little eyebrows on top? A figure-eight forms. What does this number mean? It reveals the number for *work*. And the nose—it's a rake. When you put a person horizontally, it shows that he must plow, and then Divine grace will descend and whatever he sowed will emerge. What does thinking consist of?—To concentrate your thoughts. And what does this concentration consist of? I once met a Bulgarian in Varna, un unbeliever, with free-thinking views, who complained to me: "I won 8,000 leva. I gave them to a businessman who went bankrupt, and that's how I lost [them]. But, good Lord, I will win again." I said this person understands the law. He's not an occultist, but admits a law that will teach him to win again; the Lord gives, the Lord takes. These things are transient in life. The Lord tries us with them, just as a mother tries her kids. You can try what your child will be. The mothers often say, "my angel," but try and see if he will become an angel. Give him an apple, and ask for it again. If he returns it to you, he will become and angel. If he doesn't return it, he will become a devil. The Lord gives you a blessing and says, "give it to others too."—"I can't give it." Here's an *unknown* that you didn't solve.—"I don't believe in life." You have another unknown, another x, that you didn't solve. You run from life; you have a third x. We say x is equal to so-and-so, and we can't find out mathematically what it's equal to. This x has content; we'll find its value when we work. In order to solve this x, we must harness our thoughts and feelings. Oftentimes, when someone can't solve the x's in his life, he cries and is unhappy. The world is a school. Who told you to enter this school when you don't want to learn, to concentrate? Then it's better for you to enter the plant, the mineral. By persistent concentration you will learn the doctrine of the Father and Son and the Holy Spirit, and you will love the Lord. They say, "love is foolish." It's an x yet again, which has some value, and I can solve, according to this doctrine, the mystery of Love.

Now, the Teacher of this doctrine comes every morning and throws a single idea in our souls, but despite this fact, we are still impoverished. Why do we become impoverished? Because we can't appreciate the idea that Christ gives us—"I want glory. I want this and that." The goods given by Christ are much more essential. The glory of God in this instance costs a lot more than the glory of men. Christ wants to put all of you in power, to become a master over life and death. And do you know who creates death? Those billions of spirits that constantly destroy. Every day you are filled with doubts, envy, yet in spite of this you want to be progressive people! People even meet who talk about occultism, but their thought is not free, and they don't understand life. Christ has risen: He showed the way we have to go, through the process of birth. Do you know what birth is? Tolstoy talks about one of his sons, how he dreamt one night, that he's having difficulty and he's struggling to give birth, and felt such pains that when he awoke in the morning he asked if women felt such pains when giving birth. And when they answered him affirmatively, he said, "it's hard for someone to be a woman." An idea arises in your mind, which, until you give birth, will cause you much suffering. But don't think that sufferings are a bad sign. Like the mother, you too must give something of yourself to your child. You must give life and power to some noble thought, and finally you must have the courage to remove the stone. Don't sit like modern-day philosophers and ask and reason whether Christ can rise or not. There are people who were there when Christ rose. Someone will say, "prove it!" I can prove it, but you'll still have the same attitude. There's a certain law that needs to be observed. And what is proof for? Take the person on some path, point to the way; he'll try and check the truth.

The last hour has now set in, and we all have to rise, and we will rise. And in this resurrection we have to ask ourselves not whether Christ rose, but whether our time for resurrection is at hand. This is the question. They ask whether Christ lay for three days in the tomb. For 8,000 years now you're still constantly laying in that tomb, and isn't that enough time? It's enough. And this angel from above is Christ calling, that the second coming is at hand. How will Christ find you? If the stone of your tomb is closed, how will Christ say, "Lazarus, get out?" Your loved ones and friends need to do this favor for you, to roll away the stone from your tomb, and then Christ will say, "get up!" and you'll rise.

To all who listen to me this morning, I roll away your tombstones. Christ is coming…He will stand in front of your open tombs and will say, "come out!"

Lecture held on 22 March 1915

THE VALUABLE PEARL

"...who, when he had found one pearl of great price, went and sold all that he had and bought it."—Matthew 13:46 (NKJV)

This morning I will speak to you on the most insignificant verse in the aforementioned chapter from the Gospel of Matthew, in relation with another law, the seventh and greatest law of nature: the law of origin.

There is an origin in everything, male and female. Who doesn't know what a man is and what a woman is? There is only a debate which of the two genders stands higher. They say, "in the beginning, when God created the human, he made man," and the men, when defending this question from their point of view, conclude that they, because of this, stand higher. The women, however, when defending their cause, say that they in fact stand higher than men. There is a debate on this topic even in the sciences, between scholarly people. For a long time, scientists weighed the brains of men and women, to see how many grams they weigh, and by the weight they determined their qualities and said that because the man's brain is heavier, the man stands higher. But there's an axiom in hermetic philosophy that every truth is a half-truth, and the opposite, that every lie is a half-lie; that is, that every statement is half true, and every negation, again, half true. Therefore, when a person claims something, if he wants to be right, we have to remove 50% of his claims. Don't you know that Bulgarian saying about the man who became frightened and said, "woman, I saw 100 bears and ran away!"—"Reduce a little," said the woman.—"Yes, there wasn't 100, but there was 80 for sure."—"Reduce, reduce."—"There was at least 60."—"They're too many. Where will 60 bears get together to chase you?" and the man reduced, reduced, until he got down to one and finally said, "hey, well, some noise came from the bush. It looked like a bear, but whether it was a bear, I don't know." And in modern-day philosophy there are many over-exaggerated things. This stems partly from the fact that people don't view things *objectively*, meaning from a masculine side, but *subjectively*, from a feminine side. The conscious: this is the masculine side; the subconscious: the feminine side. In philosophy there are terms; they say that a person has an objective mind, and another, a subjective mind. Every object must be seen from the viewpoint of these two minds, and then we'll have a proper concept.

Now you'll say, "how does the aforementioned verse relate to the man and woman?" There is [a relationship]. Consider how pearls form. They say that sometimes a little sand falls into the clam, and the clam starts releasing a liquid from itself, which surrounds this little sand so as not to bother it. It moulds it like a sculptor. Not only does it make it smooth, but it also makes it a *valuable* pearl. That little sand, if it doesn't fall into the clam, wouldn't have any value. Because it has some roughness, it starts disturbing the clam and makes it think: To throw it out? It can't. To kick it out? It has no legs. To say, "get out!" It doesn't have a tongue. The idea comes to mind to make it valuable: "You're my enemy, but I will love you and will make you valuable." Here is the teaching of Christ, who says, "love your enemies." You would throw this sand out, but the clam creates a pearl out of it, for which you pay dearly. Not only that, but Christ praises this clam for having done a wonderful job. If Christ comes, will He find your works crafted as well as the work of this clam? Will He find pearls? You say, "we don't have the [proper] conditions." Women say, "when we have to work, the men cause us to stumble. We don't have the conditions, we have no house, we don't have this and that, we can't work." And the men, from their side, say, "we can't work because the women bother us. We don't have this, we don't have that, society hinders us," and they stop. But that clam doesn't say that it lacks the proper conditions. Without legs, without arms, without a tongue, and without a human brain it creates a pearl out of sand, and Christ praises it. I ask you: Can't you also do as much as this clam? You can do even more.

But let's discuss the basic law: The outward forms are a result of the inward differences that exist between the man and the woman. Every indication, every trait of the human face is due to an inner deep cause in the soul of man. As you observe this concept, you may see that there's not much difference between the man and the woman. Sometimes the woman wants to become a man, but the man scoffs at [the idea of] becoming a woman. If I ask you what [gender] you want to be born, you'll all want to be born as men. What progress, then, would there be in the world if everyone born were men? Didn't God create man in the very beginning? The latter, however, said, "I can't do this. I can't do it alone. How will I cultivate such a large garden all by myself? Paradise, the trees in it, even the animals in it—they can't understand me." Then God said, "very well. I will make you a companion, like you, to help you." And so, this great law appeared on the scene, this process that moves the world. There wouldn't be any progress, or development, or enrichment, if this law didn't exist. The only thing you know in nature is just the female gender; the male gender is *invisible*. This sun that you see, is a *female* sun. The masculine sun can't be seen. This [feminine] sun draws energy from the masculine sun. And modern-day science confirms it: energy always occurs in the negative pole of the electrical currents. The word "negative" or "passive" is regarded by some people in a bad sense; by "passive" they understand weak, without character, no will, but it's a misunderstanding. And that's why they replaced the word "negative" with the expression *cathode rays*—the pole in which all energy appears. Based on this principle, I will clarify many things. One has a brain, but sometimes you say to yourselves, "there's nothing in my mind." Why is there nothing? Because you're a barren woman who doesn't give birth. "I can't love."—You're infertile. Whoever can't think and feel, whether he is a man or a woman, can't give birth. And every thing that doesn't give birth, as is said in Scripture, is close to hell. I would like every one of you to know how to give birth; it's the greatest blessing, when one knows how to create and nurture. How can one not give birth, and be unable to create a good thought, a good desire within himself? It's a creative principle that is worthy of *thinking* beings. Of course, I'm not talking about that creative principle, which can create something out of nothing (the Creator), but about that being from a male and female gender; that, which in Christian philosophy we refer to as Christ, *the man of God*. That principle, about which Christ says, "the Father dwells in Me," nobody has seen. No-one has seen God. No-one has seen the Father of the world. We know the mother. God appears in us as a mother that creates, nourishes, and teaches. Him—we don't know. And it's said in Scripture, "Christ came on earth to reveal the Father." By the same law, the man that came down from Heaven originally resembled that little sand, without form, meaningless, and the Holy Spirit, after working for a long time, made a pearl. And that's why whatever is in you, you must thank that Divine consciousness that labored a long time over you.

And according to this concept, sometimes the value of things lies in their content, sometimes on their surface. Take a marble stone, crafted, chiseled by a great sculptor who put into the stone a wonderful idea. Where is this idea? In those thin lines where this artist passed over the stone. If some fool comes and destroys those lines, a simple stone will remain which has no value. Everything that gives you value—they are your noble thoughts, desires and deeds, which a Divine Spirit has drawn upon you. Only those features that God can put in your brain, your heart, and your soul can give you value. And in scientific form, the same thing is said: modern scientists argue that the more thoughts your brain can produce, the more *creases* it has. And what are the creases? These are the nested traits which can be seen on it. These creases, these brooks, channel your thoughts. Some people want their faces to be smooth, like a ball. They think a person is beautiful when [his face is] smooth. No, then the face is a *mask*. There must be certain lines on it to show, first, that he's good; second, that he's just; third, that there is love in him, that he's wise, that he's a truth-lover. All these things must manifest themselves outwardly. Therefore all people are a written book where their qualities can be read. Some people ask me, "have you listened to the Lord? Have you heard Him?" I answer: Not only do I listen to Him, but I also see Him. I see Him when He speaks to me, and I listen and hear His words. Human words can only be heard, but the Lord's can be *seen*. God, who is glory, incarnated in Christ and became visible. And every one of you is Divine glory, spoken, embodied, visible, and they ask me if I heard or spoke to the Lord. For 2,000 years I've been hearing Him. Christ's teaching is an excellent philosophy—not a philosophy with which to touch in the darkness, but a philosophy with which we can see, touch, smell, and taste. There's an anecdote that a European scholar, who was involved in the occult sciences and wanted to trace the deep mysteries of nature, ended up once in a society where everyone was blind, with eyes indented inward. When they conversed with him, they said, "well, how does this person differ from us?" And when they touched him, they understood that his eyes protruded outwards; that was the only difference. They said to themselves, "wait, let's move this protrusion inward, so he can look like us." And modern-day philosophers are of this caliber: when they find a person with protruding eyes, they look them over and say, "you, now, will think like us. You'll have the same concept of the world as us, about man and woman, the way we think." Okay, but this philosophy relates to life, to a great reality, which we have to check every day, every hour, every minute, every second, because we have to work, to build. And we ask ourselves, "why these misfortunes?" Don't you have a positive philosophy? You're wise people; you measure heaven; you know how to make various compounds;

you know what oxygen is, hydrogen, nitrogen, but you don't know how to organize your own home. So there are things you don't know. Some say, "there are unachievable things there." But if we talk about these things, everything is relative—it's not absolutely unattainable. Everything is attainable, but it requires time to understand it. A child first begins to understand a little, then more and more, and when he matures, his view of the world changes. And now I ask you this question: When you come back to earth after 1,000 years, what will your views be? Of course, they'll be like the present, *plus* something—one plus something else.

Let me return. Why this difference? People shouldn't be the same. The law is such that people are essentially the same, but [they] differ in degree; there must always be a difference between people. This is a Divine Law. And if you want someone to love you, there must be a difference between him and you, but it must be *harmonious*, like the tones in music where there is a difference, and precisely in that harmonious combination of the difference lies the harmony that we admire. Let's come to an explanation of this harmony that must exist in man and woman, applying this Divine principle: The woman is an emblem of Love. Love cannot appear in man (not in the mustachioed man, because a woman can have a mustache too, like some animals do), but she has some qualities that distinguish her, and these qualities will always abide in her. But in man is found that other Divine power, which is called Wisdom. When Love and Wisdom marry, Truth is born. If you want to know the Truth, you have to find your father, Wisdom, and your mother, Love. And they, when they give birth to you, will tell you what is Truth; that Truth will manifest. Truth is along the paternal line. It's also a *male* gender; it's the son of these two. The father and mother, that is, Wisdom and Love, when they conceive again, will give birth to Virtue: this is your sister. And Virtue and Truth combine [to give] Justice. That's how this question stands.

If you want to create this pearl, your soul must certainly cultivate it. And with what do people busy themselves? They often ask me, "well, do you preach things consistent with the church?" I answer: I preach things that are consistent with the great Divine Law: I don't lie before the Lord. Whether my teaching is in accordance with your views is indifferent to me. For me, it's important for my views to be in accordance with the great law, not to be a liar before God, before Heaven, before the angels, before the saints. That's the important question for me. If everyone understands the teaching in such a way, and thinks that way, there's nothing to fear. Some say, "but you have a goal to form some sect." Those who form sects are, according to me, very petty people. Anyone can form a sect: take an axe, chop the wood, and you'll create a sect. Or take a hammer and crush a rock, and you'll create a sect. Go among the people, get in an argument, and you'll form a sect. Sects are easily created. In an American church they argued regarding a question: when the sacrament is sanctified, whether to raise the cup. But those who cried that it should be raised, forgot to raise it. Oftentimes we too forget what we preach, [along with] that principle that unites us. Our task is in bringing the Kingdom of God on earth. I want us to form a sect, but what kind? To become transmitters of the Divine Law, which will conquer all minds and hearts, so everyone will become—men and women, and children—sons of the Kingdom of God, to live a life on earth as it should [be lived]. And now, when the people complain to me, "great misfortunes came about," I say to them: I'm glad that your prisons are being destroyed. Your old beliefs are falling away because if you don't pour out the old water from a bottle, new water cannot be poured in. When Christ came, the Jews had to cleanse themselves in the same way, and to live a new life. But they said, "we recognize Moses. We don't recognize you. You want to create a sect." But He, as you see, didn't form a sect, even though He was a heretic from the Hebrew point of view. Some ask me, "are you orthodox?" I may be orthodox before God, but from the viewpoint of the church I might not be. They also said to Christ, "He wants to destroy our nation."

But after 2,000 years we shouldn't think like the Jews anymore. I ask: What did the Jews gain by crucifying Christ? Nothing. They scattered throughout the world. To crucify a man—there's nothing easier than that; four nails is enough.

Let me return back to our subject. I want you to think, to think deeply about things. And I will tell you another thing in relation to this principle about man and woman. First, you must love the Lord with all your heart, with all your soul, with all your mind, with all your strength. Second, to love your neighbor as yourself. Third, to love your enemies. I just spoke to you about your enemies, about that little sand. And when Christ came on earth, He didn't come to save the good, the righteous, but those sharp little [grains of] sand. For them He descended into hell, to bring them out. And [in order] to remove these pearls from the clam, this clam needs to be taken and opened. By the same law, people are taken to Heaven and when they are opened, and this pearl is found in their soul, it's taken out. When someone dies, they say, "the clam died." And they go after the clam saying, "the poor clam had to go!" I say that it went to Heaven, to bring the pearl that it formed and cultivated, because if it hadn't made it, it wouldn't have gone to Heaven. It would be of no value.

Let me return back to some basic features of man and woman. Those who studied human structure for a long time say the outer traits of the person are due to his inner nature, that is, whatever a person is inside, he's the same outside. Regarding this, there are no two convictions. They say that the feet of the well-constructed man or woman must comprise one sixth of his height. The face must comprise a tenth of the height. The chest, a fourth. The length of the hand from the wrist, again, a tenth. The measurement twice around the wrist of the hand must be the measurement of the neck. Of course, when you come to the individual, there are some minor differences: some men and women are more elongated, pear-shaped, others with round faces. What is the cause for this? The people with round faces aren't so active; they are people who reconcile, [are] diplomatic, [regardless] whether [they are] men or women. Round faces are more inherent in women. They fall into the category of their mother. As I describe these things to you, I want to give a new direction, for you to perceive Christianity in its profound meaning as a science of life. Christianity is a positive science, which must teach us how to live. Only in application do people differ. There's an application in the physical life, another in the spiritual life. Men and women cannot be the same. There must be a difference between them. If the man is active and agile, rejoice and don't say, "I want to be a man." There must be activity in every manifestation. If not in the physical realm, then in the mental one; if not in the mental one, then it must be in the heart. But a person must always be active. Activity means work, production in a three-fold direction—physical, mental, and spiritual. Not all people can work simultaneously in the same place, in the same direction, but in different fields. This difference which is between you, can also give birth to disharmony; it depends on you. When they're both short-tempered, when one of them says something, the other one must listen. When one of them plays [music], the other one must listen. This is the law that operates in the physical world. If one is silent, the other one values this sense of patience and will pay off in another respect. However, if the woman doesn't uphold this behavior, the man will say, "there's no wife worse than mine. She has a very long tongue. May the Lord free us, either me from her, or her from me." Don't think that you'll be liberated. In the other world you'll pursue each other again, if you pursued each other here. What can change your life is the understanding of the Divine Law and its application in life. You'll make a lot of mistakes; you might make them by the thousands, for which the Lord will not judge you. He will forgive you. I can assure you that He will forgive you if you just learn the Divine Law and work.

But if, after 100 mistakes, you didn't learn any lesson, the Lord will not forgive you. All things in the world must be used. If the pear has thorns, if the rose has thorns, it is in the order of things—they're not haphazardly placed. "But," you'll say, "there are thorns." Whoever goes up the pear tree shouldn't wear soft clothes, so they don't tear. I've seen a lot of children remain on the tree, then afterwards they have to use a ladder to get them down. Whoever doesn't know the law says, "this pear [tree] is thorny. It needs to be cut down." It's thorny, but it gives nice pears.

I'll give you another example that equally affects the man and the woman, but the example is for the latter. A woman, who was very feisty, stubborn, didn't fulfill her husband's will at all—whatever he said to her, she always did the opposite. One time she wanted to sit on the well. He said to her, "don't sit, wife, because you'll fall and I will remain without a woman." She didn't listen to him. "I'll sit." She sat, but fell in the well and sank in the water. He started crying and shouting, "didn't I tell you not to sit. If you listened to me you wouldn't have fallen!" After one hour he looked, and from the well a devil with white hair jumped out. "What is it?" asked the man. "Ah," he said, "my hair turned white on top in one hour from a woman." He said that and ran away. The man began to ponder how he could use this case, and he finally came up with something. When he started visiting homes where there were evil spirits, after dispensing with all means—spells, prayers—to get them to come out of these homes, and they still wouldn't come out, he thought to say, "run, because my wife is coming!" and then they all fled. In that way, the woman who fell in the well did a great deed for the world, because when she went in the well and the husband saw that she scared the devil, he understood that the devil is only afraid of a woman, and not from a man. And just by shouting, "run, because my wife is coming!" he expelled all devils. When one suffered, thousands were freed.

This is why women have the keys to the Kingdom of Heaven. And when Christ said to Peter, "I give you the keys to the Kingdom of Heaven," He implied this profound inner law, that between the man and the woman there must always be a significant distinction. In that distinction lies the basis of love, which the man has for the woman. On the day the woman changes the position in which God placed her, the man will not love her. Whatever diamonds, rings, necklaces, and silk skirts she puts on, no outside force is in the condition to make her man love her. The man is the Lord to the woman. She has to see that the Lord lives in him, and in order for the Lord to love her, she must deserve His love, by doing something for Him. Since He himself cannot come down to work, He gives us a mind, a heart, and strength—everything to conquer the world, to lay down order and organization, in return for which He will send us all good things.

Some say, "the Lord will come to fix the world." Even now He's fixing it, but not alone, but through others—the Germans on one side; the Russians, the French, the English, on the other side, are fixing it with their cannons. Some ask, "when will they stop fighting?" Naturally, when that *wall* is broken, which they're breaking. It can be calculated mathematically how many hits a certain stone can withstand. Some stone breaks from 100 hits, another from 200, a third from 500. In the same way, a guess can be made when the war will be over. Naturally, when the necessary amount of projectiles and bullets are fired—when a new consciousness enters the people about their purpose on earth. And then the people will say, "we did a wonderful job!"

And when Christ turns to His disciples, He tells them that this person, who looked for the pearl (the meaning of his soul) and upon finding it, he went and sold everything he had in order to buy it. If you're not ready in this world to sacrifice everything (you have to sacrifice something), but to gain some pearl, something wise, because there are people who sacrifice their whole state but gain no pearl: they sacrifice it for drunkenness, for billiards, for cards. If I found the pearl spoken about by Christ in the poor, I would sell everything I have. It's not enough for someone to give away everything to the poor in order to do some good, because when Christ says that some good must be done, He means to say that that good must be done *wisely*. It wouldn't be wise to give to the wolf a lamb every day. They do it in the zoo, because they keep the wolves there as a curiosity, but we can't apply this law in society. We can't sacrifice the lambs to the wolves; we can sacrifice them to the people. It makes sense.

Another example: In the past, in prehistoric times, there were two kingdoms, surrounded by an impassable mountain range. In both kingdoms there appeared wise people, saying that whoever could dig through that mountain to make a path between the two kingdoms, he would bring the greatest benefit to these two nations. And this can happen provided that whoever begins working can't turn back at all until he digs through the mountain. Many showed up and started digging, but when they reached somewhere, some passer-by would come tap him: "What are you working, chap?" He turns to explain, and in that time everything that was dug up covers it [back] up. Finally, a royal son appeared and got to work. People passed by, asking him what he's doing, but he just kept quiet. Good, but a philosopher came who wanted to show him an easier way to dig through the mountain. Then he too was deceived, turning to listen to him, but when he looked ahead he saw the hole he dug, buried again with dirt. He told himself for the last time that whoever wants to talk about whatever, he wouldn't turn, and when he started digging, they came again to ask him, but he truly remained deaf to them, until he dug through the mountain, uniting these two kingdoms. And then he married the royal daughter of the other kingdom, and these two nations lived happily ever after. This isn't just an allegory. It's a great truth. The big mountain that separates these two kingdoms is man's sin, which separates earth from Heaven. And if you are a clairvoyant, you would see between earth and Heaven that black wall with strongholds, cannons, and guards. Christ dug through that mountain, making a hole. That's why He came. And when He says, "there's only one way that leads to the Kingdom of Heaven," He implies that hole, that narrow path. It's been 2,000 years since that narrow pathway was dug, but few walk along it. There are many wide paths, but they don't lead there, where the narrow one leads. Many people don't believe and say, "prove this thing to me." Of course, it can be proven, as long as a person is willing to get out of his house. But he says, "I'm not coming out." But he'll go to that wall and return back again. That's why, when you know that you'll pass through that hole only through the law of *gender*, between man and woman, you have to become one kin. And when we speak of being born again, of repentance, we imply that harmony must form between us and God. If the Lord doesn't love you, who could love you? Someone says, "I don't have friends; so-and-so doesn't like me; such-and-such doesn't love me. The Lord doesn't love me." It's not true; the Lord loves you. Learn to love Him too. He's not invisible. You can see Him everywhere. This Lord, of whom I speak—every day, at least ten times a day, speaks to you. He meets you, gives you advice and such. When you're thinking about doing something and meet some friend on the street who tells you, "don't do it," the Lord speaks to you through the one who met you. And now, when I speak to you, again, the Lord speaks to you. The words are mine, the outer-wrapping is mine, but the *content* is from the Lord. You're receiving a gift: You'll remove the package, the outer-wrapper, and you'll find the content. Therefore, you men and women on earth, must understand each other. You have some wrapping around [you]: you want to become great in the world, wealthy, to have houses, to have knowledge, strength, for everyone to love you; whatever you desire—to do it in one swoop. Well, okay, but this doesn't happen via lottery. You have to learn this Divine Law and begin inside, within. And if, for instance, you take this verse about the pearl, and during the year or month, you spend only 10 days in long reflections on it, do you know what secrets you would learn from it? Like a scientist, when taking several prisms and putting them in some combination, he can see under them the smallest microscopic animals, which cannot be seen with the naked eye. In the same way, if you put the prisms in some combination, which exist in your mind, you'll see many things that cannot be seen with the naked eye. Like the scientist, when he looks at a drop of water under a microscope, he sees an entire movement inside, an entire life, an entire world, but the ordinary person will see nothing. And so, the one who benefits from Divine Wisdom can see everything the others cannot. You get up some morning [feeling] indisposed [and] you don't know the reason. You can't succeed in something; there's a reason. You're ailing; there's a reason. You're not beautiful; there's a reason. Beauty must be an ideal both for the man and for the woman, because all angels, saints, Jesus Christ, are beautiful. When the woman says, "my husband doesn't love me," I understand that she's ugly. The soul in which Virtue, Righteousness, Love, Wisdom, and Truth are written—that soul is great, beautiful—everyone can love it. And if someone doesn't love you, it means that you don't have these traits. Go to the Lord and say, "Lord, put more of your hammer over me and write these virtues." If the Lord doesn't work with His hammer on someone, he will be an ordinary stone without value.

Let's now come to the application, how the man and woman should work. They want to have children. The children are *truth-bearers*. You, who want to understand the truth—only your children can tell you about it. You, who want to learn humility—only your children will tell you what humility is. A woman who never gave birth can neither be good nor humble; she will constantly be proud. The same applies to the man: Every one of his thoughts, every one of his desires—when they are born, they are alive. A great *being* is hidden in them, an angel, who will one day be your friend. The children you have now were once just a dream in your mind, to whom you gave a garment. You have this pearl of which Christ speaks, but some of you want, instead of enlightening it, like the clam—the little sand—to throw it out of yourselves. You say, "the Lord didn't create it well," and you knock it around. But it loses its meaning. Don't knock around the lines the Lord put on the human soul. I'm against those philosophers who say the world isn't created as it should be—"Wait for us to carve it." The woman, for instance, in order to be a little thinner, tightens herself with a corset. To not become obese, fast. You now eat three times a day. Try eating once or twice, to see what noble features will develop in you. You say, "it's not possible without food." Do you know how much you need to eat in a day? In life there are certain laws that regulate eating. Some days you don't want to eat, so don't eat! Wait until your desire to eat comes back. But the man says, "my wife must eat, otherwise she'll break down." Well, she's broken now: if she doesn't eat, she'll get better. There are even animals who don't eat when they are unwell.

So I say, the pearl, which Christ speaks of—you have [it]— but some of you want to throw it out, but it's abortion. And the greatest evil of modern woman is abortion. The statistics state that the city of New York, in the year 1905, had 100,000 abortions. It's not permissible for a person to abort a child, neither from his mind, nor from the womb, or from his heart, if he wants to be a Christian. If a good thought comes to you, you say, "I'll abort it." You'll abort it, but then you'll be sick. Someone says, "I had a bad thought." It's not a sin that you thought, but the sin consists in aborting. Everyone aborts and wonders why the world isn't fixed. You already have idiots in the world. The bad thoughts that torture you, the devils—they are the children—those thoughts, those desires, which you aborted at some time, because they say, "you're an unworthy mother." They hinder you in every undertaking and you become an unhappy person. That's why it's best for you, if you want to be happy, to have the honor of entering the Kingdom of Heaven, from now on, not to abort and pray to the Lord to forgive the misuse of all those good wishes and desires, of all your children you aborted, whom you killed and robbed of their wealth.

This is why in the future we have to nurture every noble thought, every single noble desire, because they will leave a mark on our noses, eyebrows, eyes, and we will acquire Apollo-like types. Now, for the time being, people look scary, ugly. Now if they go to Heaven, when they see the nice angels, they'll run away from there.

That's why we have to pray to the Lord to help us turn *white*. And that's not too hard. If a clam can make a pearl, which Christ praises, when you enter Heaven, for what will Christ praise you? Someone will say, "I was first minister of Bulgaria," but Christ will ask him, "well, what good did you do for the Bulgarian people?"—"None."—"Do you have a pearl?"—"I don't."—"Get out! [Get] back down to earth until you make a pearl, because without that pearl, I won't accept you in the Kingdom of God." A bishop comes along: "What did you do?" Christ will ask.—"Well, I taught the people goodness. I believed in You."—"Did you make some pearl?"—"I didn't."—"Out!" But [regarding] the one who made a pearl, He will say, "I'm happy, son, that you didn't embarrass Me. Come, you're a worthy son." You too, men and women, when you go to Heaven, you'll meet a son—your pearl—who will say to you, "thank you, mother, that when I was a great sinner, you took me inside your womb and made me a man. Now in this world I will be a servant to you with all my soul." This will be your joy.

This is what Christ wants to say with these verses, from which I chose the least important. But see how much it contains within itself. The others contain much more profound things, which you'll learn one day, not here on earth, but when you go to Heaven, because then there will be in you a new understanding, new feelings, and new abilities. Then you may see other images, which you'll understand. For now, this is how much can be given to you. If you are given more, you would be unable to bear it. It would mean for a soap bubble to swell more than it should—it'll burst. This is why when Christ says, "you women are a symbol of Divine Love. God lives in you," the women need to listen quietly, modestly, and must appear worthy of carrying Him. You say, "you must know, Lord, that the world today isn't the way You created it." There's no need to *lecture* the Lord. When He speaks, we must remain silent. And when He is silent, we'll begin our lesson. We'll say, "I did this in such a way; that, the other way," and then He will say, "you're right in such-and-such. You're *wrong* in such-and-such." Therefore, His teachings are to listen to Him and apply this teaching in life. And when Christ tells the woman, "love your neighbor as yourself," He means to love the husband as herself. Also, when He tells the man to love his neighbor, He means to love his wife as himself. And if you [model yourselves on the basis of] these examples, then your sons and your daughters will follow them. This is the creation of the pearl—the alchemical law, applied on the physical plane.

Lecture held on 19 April 1915

THE NEW FOUNDATION

"For no-one can lay any foundation other than the one already laid, which is Jesus Christ."—1 Corinthians 3:11 (NIV)

"I am the way, the truth, and the life."—John 14:6 (NIV)

These two verses are interrelated. What should we understand in the words, "no-one can lay another foundation?" I'll take the verse in its ordinary, broad sense. Foundation: this is a prosaic word. Who doesn't talk about foundation? You're building a house, you say, "I'm laying the foundation." You make some chemical compound, again you're looking for the foundation. In geometry, the foundation is called the *supporting point*. Consequently, the existence of life itself requires such a foundation, such a supporting point. What is the precise basis of this foundation? It is said that no other foundation can be laid, i.e, we can't change the foundation of life. We can't change human thought, human desires, human will power, that is, we can't change them in their essence. You can't make a thought to not be a thought. You can make it good, bad, or neutral, but you can't alter it any more than this. So, you can change its outer form, but never its essence. Therefore, I speak to you about a basic law: "No-one can alter this foundation which Christ laid." This foundation is such that we are under the authority of one law, under the foundation of good and evil. We stand over a foundation that also produces at the same time both joy and suffering, rising and falling, enrichment and impoverishment, and health and sickness. This foundation laid down by Christ—and for that reason He descended from Heaven to earth—has two supporting points; this is a principle. When you make a bridge over some river, you can build this bridge only over the two supporting points, the two end-points, and all the weight will fall either over one, or the other side. Well, Heaven and earth are the two supporting points on which human life is built. The most profound idea that we can penetrate is the first foundation, the first supporting point. Desires: these are the second foundation, the second supporting point. And what we call will is the process of building. When someone talks about the human will, we understand that two supporting points are always required. When we start building on them, our will-power will manifest. Consequently, according to this principle, human will-power can never manifest unless there are two supporting points; it can only manifest during the building process. We must understand the deep meaning of the doctrine of Christ. We shouldn't just *think* we understand it, but actually not comprehend it. A lady told me the following anecdote about a young woman from Sofia, who studied everything before marrying but didn't complete the culinary arts. And when she married, she wanted to cook beans for her husband, but didn't know how. She goes to one of her neighbors and asks her, "how do you cook beans?" but doesn't say she doesn't know.—"Well," the neighbor replied, "we put it out to boil, then cut the onion, then put in the butter."—"Well," the other one says, "we also cook it like this." After a week, she asks the neighbor again: "Well, how do you cook the meat?"—"In such-and-such [a way]."—"We also cook it like this." But the neighbor, wanting to test her, whether she really knows how to cook, thought of deceiving her. And one day, when the husband of the inexperienced young bride brought snails, and the latter went to ask the neighbor again how to cook snails, then the neighbor told her, "we crush them in the mortar, put on rice and water and boil them."—"We too," the other one says, "cook them like that." She returns home and cooks the snails in the same way. Her husband comes for lunch and upon seeing the cooked snails, he realizes whether his wife knows how to cook. Contemporary religious beliefs also include such cooked snails. However, these snails shouldn't be cooked like this. You need a fundamental understanding of things. What is the basis of human thought, one of the great basic laws that creates? Above all, we are *thinking* beings. Secondly, [we are] beings who feel; and thirdly, [we are beings] who act and build. Outside of this, you can't lay down another foundation. You can't act in any other way. If you act in another way, you can degrade. You can only go in two directions, either up or down. There is no middle road in this world. Since everything moves, you can't stand over one supporting point. The two supporting points are always fixed, but everything around these points is moveable.

To clarify, I will relate an example from modern science so you can see our illusions about life. If we run an electric current under a pile of iron sawdust, some shavings that are closest to the current will be magnetized and will attract each other. This sawdust turns to the others with the words, "do you see how I attracted you with my power? If I'm not here, you too wouldn't be around me." But if we move the current, another piece of sawdust will magnetize and will become the center around which all others will come together. And when you say, "I can do this," or, "the people gather around me. I'm influential," this means the current works near you. The moment the current changes, you'll go to the periphery. Therefore, you must know that the foundation is not within you, in what you think and feel at a certain moment. In order to know if you have a foundation, whether you found it, the moment you find your supporting points you should feel deep peace within yourselves. Many philosophers teach the world, but they themselves haven't found *their own* supporting points; they're not calm.

When Christ said, "I am the way and the truth," and with that He indicated the two supporting points. And life is a process that derives from this path and from the truth. On this basis, we can't build another way. For example, what is aspiration? The aspiration of a spirit in space is to incarnate; the aspiration of a child who incarnates is *growth*. In that growth, he climbs from one point, reaches a certain height, then starts descending, forms a curved line that ends at the other point: Youth and old age are the two supporting points in life. When you pass from childhood to old age, you'll find the two pillars of your life. After that, when you return a second time, you'll build on these points, if you haven't forgotten them. But if you forgot them, you'll start again. There are people who only cross over but never build. A curved line must be drawn over the two supporting points. This is the law of movement. This movement is expressed in human thought. What is the thought of man? It's the law of laying, of gathering material on these two foundations. We have to build again using some plan. Let's come to the human body. Let me give you another clarification: When man comes into being in the world, he first forms the limbs of the body. Out of all the organs, the last one to form are the lungs. When the respiratory system forms, the child must be born immediately. Hands are the product of human will. The face, nose, mouth, lungs, stomach—these are human *desires*. That's where we experience what we want to taste. Man's brain is the organ of human thought; there we can experience thought. When we speak of thought, we mean the brain. But when we come to the human brain, we'll see that the productivity of human thought is in accordance with the thickness of *gray matter*. The larger the wrinkles in the gray matter, the stronger the thought is. Some say that the brain itself produces thought. This is not right. The human brain is similar to a land that doesn't give birth itself, but the creative power comes from space: it's the sun that acts upon the surface of the earth, and because it has a foundation, upon that foundation the sun builds, produces, creates. The human soul is the human sun, which shines on the human brain, generating these thoughts. Every creature thinks. You think the ox doesn't think? It also thinks, but in an ox-like way, with limitation. The snake too, and the lizard, and the fly. Every creature thinks, and according to its thought, creates its house for living for its body, its organism. Our current organism is the fruit of thought that we have; according to that thought that is within us, man is built. You can make your lungs very wide—one meter, for example. If the human spirit makes an effort, it can make the head very big, but the size of the head is not the only important thing; the important thing is whether he can cultivate it. For the earth is also large, but when the Lord sent man to earth, He said to him, "go and conquer the earth, the elements." And because we couldn't conquer the earth, the Lord gave us a small earth, which is inside our head—our brain. When we know how to conquer our brain, we'll find the laws through which we will conquer the earth too. If you can't master your brain centers, your feelings, if you can't direct your will, how will you direct something outside of yourself? So we can't lay down another foundation. There's some law that limits our activity; only in a certain direction and within it we can do everything to be omnipotent. And our happiness or misfortune will rest on this great idea, the extent to which we are going in the right direction.

With this lecture, I want you to think about how to start building your life. An example for clarification: Along the path of a traveler who went to study in the east, a wild bull started chasing him. In order to escape, this traveler found an empty well. He went inside and grabbed hold of a tree which grew in this well. The bull came above, started looking, but at the same time the traveler noticed that a snake was waiting for him at the bottom of the well, and he thought about what to do. He couldn't go up and get out, nor could he let himself down. He's holding tightly on a branch. At one point he notices that on top of this tree there's a little honey, and when he forgot the bull above, he started licking the honey and feeling joyful. But after a little while he noticed a mouse from the walls of the well, which started gnawing the tree. The traveler then said to himself, "even this honey will not save me. One day, the tree will be gnawed, and I'll fall next to the snake." This bull is the fate that pushes man, and the snake is death that man expects. But, in fact, the bull is birth, the serpent—this is old age. They're not dangerous things. Why is the bull chasing you? So you can work. You're lazy. It wants to make you run. Why all the sufferings in the world? They're the bull, who chases the world today: kings, generals, officers, and judges—all flee and preach liberty to the people. When you meet them, they're all wise philosophers; they think the world was arranged badly. But how can you reason when you have no foundation? Can a person who is running [use] reason? It's no evil if this bull chases us because if we are strong we can go back and catch him by the horns, and he will stop. There is a hero in Jewish history, Samson, against whom a lion came out, but he caught him by the mouth and rent him. This fear of the bull is due to the fact that we haven't found the two supporting points.

"Nobody can lay a foundation other than that which Christ laid." Well, what foundation did Christ lay? How did He live on earth? When you take the nine blessings, He gave nine rules to live by. He also gave two great laws: love for God and love for the neighbor. These are the two pillars on which to build your life. The contemporary social life and family must also be built upon them. A woman who doesn't love God, who doesn't love her husband, can't run a house. A man who doesn't love his neighbor, his wife, can't run a house. Of course, when I speak of man and woman, I don't mean your bodies, just as you are in your houses, because the way I see them, they're quite modest. I mean the human soul in its esteemed manifestation, that soul which in the future can create a much better house than it has right now. The soul that appears ignorant may one day have much greater knowledge, can be much more scholarly. In order to find the two supporting points upon which to build your life you need to make a curved line and start building. You need not wander like modern philosophers. Among those who study the sun scientifically, some say that it holds five million degrees of heat, others say two million; a third kind, 100,000. A gentleman allows himself to say it's just 32 degrees; another one, that the heat is below zero; a third—that the sun is melted, so it sends heat. But now there are other scientists who object to it and say, "if this were true, then all of space would be warm, but the fact is that as long as one goes up, it gets cold enough to freeze." That's why these scientists say that the sun sends just energy, and the latter just transforms here on earth: namely that the earth produces warmth and light, for indeed when you climb up you will see that over there in the sky it's dark, gloomy. These people argue; however, the facts show that both are right, but there is a misunderstanding. I say: If you're sensitive to heat, the sun is warm, but if you're not sensitive, the sun will not have any heat for you. Heat is something *relative*: Some people put five cubes of sugar in their tea, others [put] one, and even this is sweet for them. This is why first and foremost we must get rid of the illusion of thinking we know everything, like that woman who thought she knew how to cook crushed snails. Nor should we cook the truths in such a manner. Europe is cooking the snails the same way right now. The second time, the European nations will cook another way.

But let us return to the essential idea: We must *create*. Some of you who are listening to me this morning are unhappy: some are unhappy with life, some have great ambitions (a very esteemed opinion of themselves). A few days ago a friend of mine told me, "before I began studying the science of the hand, I had a very high opinion of myself. When I started looking at the lines, I found that on my hand is only a little pride and vanity. I was ashamed of myself." You think the same way, that you know a lot, but when you enter life, you can't deal with it. Some young lady, before marrying, dreams: "When I marry, I will arrange my house in *such* a way. I will dress like so. I will live with my husband in such-and-such a way." She drafts a project for herself, the way projects get drafted for laws. But when she marries, after one month both of them look disheveled, which means the project hasn't been implemented, just like the laws adopted in the Chamber are often left unattended because they haven't been adapted to our conditions. And when one of our ideas doesn't get put into action, we say, "we're unfortunate, fate is chasing us [away]." No fate is chasing you, but your foolishness pursues you at every step. We must learn to think properly. When a person comes to you, you have to form the right concept of him and act with him just as you would want others to act towards you in the given situation. And we must act well, because whatever we do will follow us. Forty-five years ago, in Varna, some gentleman who graduated in Europe in music became a teacher and started teaching the children of the wealthy townspeople to play [music], to dance, and so on. But one day this gentleman argued with the citizens and they fired him. Being a very touchy, prideful man, he spent all his money and sat around hungry for three days. A priest met him, who was acquainted with him, and invited him as a guest. The gentleman thanked him and after telling him his story, the priest pulled out and gave him two white *medjidiy*:[1] "When you spend them, come back to my home, until you find a job." One or two months passed, and because the gentleman had a very good grasp of the Turkish language, he was appointed as secretary of the Turkish governor of the time. After one year, they convicted the priest of being a rebel; he had suspicious letters and books. They took them and handed them over to the scholarly Bulgarian secretary to look them over. He examined them, separated all the suspicious papers, hid them, and that way the priest was justified, but he was astonished at the secretary's behavior, who said to him, "the two white medjidiy you gave me when I hadn't eaten for three days—they saved your head." If that gentleman knew how to act, the citizens wouldn't have driven him out, but also if the priest hadn't invited the man who hungered for three days, and fed him and given him the two medjidiy, the latter, as secretary, would have hung him on the noose. We must deal with every thought and action in our lives in the same way, by asking ourselves what the causes are for our misfortune, if we are unhappy; what the causes are for our

---

1   Turkish silver coins.

pride, cruelty, greed for wealth, and so on.

So we have to start thinking: "You're cruel"—This is not yours. It's faulty revenue, left over perhaps for you as an inheritance by someone. An example for clarification: Years ago in Sofia, an Armenian approached a Jew with a sample of diamonds, of which he had an entire bagful, but he wanted to sell them for very cheap, for 20,000 leva, because he managed to import them without tax. The Jew rejoiced and asked the Armenian to bring his diamonds to a place where he counted the 20,000 leva and took the bag with the thought that he was now the owner of great wealth. When he went home, the Jew opened the bag, and what did he see? Only the sample was a real diamond, and the rest—ordinary glass. In the same way, you too may carry this bag home with you, thinking that you're rich, but when you open it, you'll see that it's full of junk. According to the law of inheritance our ancestors leave us some wealth, and it's virtue, but the rest is junk—it's the evil in us. And so, we have a faulty conception about life: we think we're good when we aren't. That is, we think we possess some capital, when we actually don't have it. So we have a faulty foundation for life. Apostle Paul, when turning to the Christians of his day, says, "nobody can lay another foundation other than the one laid down by Christ." And Christ says, "I didn't come to do My will, but the will of God," the first supporting point, and then, "I didn't come to take the lives of men, but I came to *give* My life to them," the second supporting point. And truly, that's why Christ came, to give us life. He preached and fulfilled the love for the neighbor, because Christianity is love for the neighbor; it's a science of love, and whoever learns this science can build. But this science doesn't rest on sweet words, kisses, and gifts, because I doubt when someone starts giving gifts to another, that he's thinking well of him. An example for clarification: A fly stopped in front of a spider, who started praising her: "How beautiful you are, what nice eyes you have. And how colorful your wings are. I have never seen such beauty."—"Can this be true?" asked the fly.—"Ah," said the spider, "there aren't any creatures as beautiful as you. I have a mirror. Come in so I can give it to you, so you can see yourself." And the fly entered to look at it, but she never escaped. When someone tells you, "you're very beautiful. Come, I'll do this and that for you," you'll enter, but you won't escape, like the fly. Those are the gifts. It's corruption. I'm not saying not to give or accept, but in gifting, the mouth, the thought, and the heart must act as well. In [the gift] must be included human wisdom, knowledge, love. I know many women who have turned corrupt over gifts given by men. The woman acquires a watch, a ring, hats, but she has forever lost her honesty; she is disgraced. I know many who have come to power, but they come down, defiled, tainted, having lost their purity. Society praises them: "This is a famous person." Yes, he's famous, but once he was a diamond, and now he's mud. So we cannot lay another foundation. If we can fulfill our duties in the world in a way required by the laws by which we abide, move, and develop—good. If we can't, then we don't fulfill them at all. Don't rise to power to control people by disgracing yourself, by selling yourself. Do every act selflessly, like Christ. Someone says, "I can't." Why not? But you can slander, you can hate. A person capable of praising must also love; just as one is possible, the other one is also possible. Whoever cannot hate also cannot love. But whoever hates can love too. It's the same law. You have just one supporting point. Find the other one too, and when they unite, hate and love, they'll give what is necessary in life, they'll give you *direction* in life. I don't recommend you become saints in the ordinary sense of the word. A true saint means to be able to master the two principles in life in such a way that you can use them for your *ascension*. Just like you can tame a lion, a snake, in the same way you can tame a devil too. You can't make him good, but you can make him harmless. Start with your thoughts. A thought that torments you—this is a lion, a snake. Don't try to chase them out or kill them, but tame them, conquer them. Have the bravery of the negroes, who have understood the psychology of lions, so when a negro encounters a lion, he doesn't step away from his path, because in the slightest deviation or turning back the lion will pounce on him and will tear him. On the contrary, he starts heading toward the lion and starts saying to him, "you're a disgrace," and starts spitting on him, walking directly toward him. When the lion is 3-4 steps from the negro, he makes way for him. That's what you have to do too. If you encounter a lion on your path, don't turn back or to the left or to the right, but look him directly in the eyes and tell him, "get out of my sight you disgrace," and he'll get out. But you'll say, "is this possible?" Whoever is swift can do it. Whoever is cowardly cannot. When a house is collapsing, even if we run, we can still get crushed. If one day the earth is to be destroyed, if we are people of faith, we will rise and go to Heaven, to the other supporting point, on the other end of the bridge. If there is danger on one end, we'll pass to the other one and we'll defend our position. That's why, when you have that bridge, your enemy can never do you any harm, because you'll be strong enough to raise that bridge, and between you and the enemy there will always be a pit, which the enemy will be unable to pass. This enemy must know the laws very well to be able to attack you in that position. That's why good people cannot be conquered, because they have two supporting points, and when they find themselves in great danger on one end, they go to the other end and defend their position there. This is the foundation we must apply. Jesus and Christ: the two words mean the two supporting points. Jesus: this is the man who suffers on earth; the human soul that suffers, which produces its salvation. Christ is the man who conquered, who serves God, who is ready to sacrifice himself. Therefore, you must also be Jesus and Christ. Someone says, "but *He* is Jesus." Yes, anyone can be Jesus when he suffers and carries his sufferings like a hero. If you give him a cross, he'll carry it. He will never object. He'll be like Socrates, who married the worst woman in Greece, and when they asked him why he married such a woman, he replied, "if I can conquer this woman, if I can deal with her, then the other hardships are nothing to me." Therefore, if you, men and women, can deal with one another, you will solve one of the greatest tasks. But if you are unable to handle this, then you cannot handle anything in the world. Some ask why people marry. That's why—to deal with one another. Man and woman: these are the two supporting points upon which life is built. They say, "why did Adam need a woman to get him in trouble?" God didn't make trouble for him, but made him work. In Eve there was *initiative* and a *mind*. She was a very wise woman, much wiser than you who think you're smart. Modern culture and knowledge is owed to her. She sinned, but then appeared and corrected [her sin], as she said to her husband, "I put you down, I will lift you up. I will save you now, so you can learn to think, because you had no mind. If you were wise, you wouldn't have wanted me to come to earth." If you, women, understood this law like your old mother, you would be very wise. But you don't understand it, and are constantly upset. I don't like you. You're bad daughters. Your mother is much wiser than you. Look how skillfully she's been working for 8,000 years. Don't think that Eve doesn't work. Today's civilization is owed to her. Adam just fulfills her commands. He only knows how to fight, to pull out a knife, and when he returns to his wife, she asks him, "did you finish it?"—"I finished it."—"You did it well." We must lay a foundation *here*. Let go of the illusions in thinking that they'll teach you in Heaven when you go there. In order to teach you in Heaven, you have to carry *raw* material within yourselves. What do you carry within yourselves? Tell me. I would hire a train to take you to Heaven. How many days would you stay there? Would some of you even have enough money to stay one or two days? Others would spend all their money after ten days and say, "let's return back on earth to earn." So we have to lay down a foundation when we understand what Christian life consists of. I won't talk to you about salvation and such, like others have already told you—they're elementary things. What is required now is a wise build-up upon this social system. We have to ask ourselves: How should our future generations be educated? How should our future judges, teachers, priests, fathers, mothers, sisters, friends, businessmen, machinists be? "Time," they say, "will create them." But time asks us, "what do you want me to create for you?" Just as the snake appeared before Eve and said, "why don't you eat from the fruit of the tree of the knowledge of good and evil?" In the same way Christ now appears before her and says, "why haven't you eaten of the fruit from the tree of life for thousands of years?"—"Because we are forbidden," says Eve. "Why are you forbidden?" Eve *wants* to lie, but then decides to say the truth: "Because we sinned."—"Ha!" says Christ, "if you correct your sin, if you throw it out of you, you'll be allowed to eat from this tree of life. And like you ate of the forbidden fruit of the tree of the knowledge of good and evil, you experienced its contamination. In the same way now, when you taste of the fruit of the tree of life, another science will come, another social order, diametrically opposed to the modern one." To you, these things may be allegorical, but for me they are a reality. These trees are in our brain: one of the trees, of the knowledge of good and evil, is in the back; and the other one, of life, is in the front. The Russians say, "the Russian man lives in the back of the mind." Now the Russians are starting to live with the front of the mind: they renounced drunkenness. In Russia, nobody until now thought the people could live soberly. Now, with a royal decree, drinking is forbidden. So the same law that produced one evil until now, produces something good.

Now Christ says, "are you now ready to think? Not to live with your hindbrain, not to *try* but to think, to build, the way I will tell you." But we say as the modern-day neutral countries, "what guarantees do you give?" Everyone wants a guarantee: Italy, Serbia, Greece, Romania, and Bulgaria; without guarantees we cannot leave the neutrality. We say the same to Christ: We tasted of the tree of the knowledge of good and evil and saw the evil that befell us. Let us think a little whether the same evil might befall us again if we taste of the tree of life. "We maintain neutrality," tells us Grandpa Radoslavov, but nothing will happen with neutrality. Neutrality: that's one supporting point. We have to find the next one to start passing [to the other side]. In the same way, in Christian life, neutrality is kept until a certain time. After that, we have to start war. You have a bad thought—it's war. You're born, you die: this is war. You become wealthy, impoverished: this is war. Life, from one end to the other, is war. But this war must be justified on the principle of gaining, rather than losing. In Italy, the tripartite agreement or union gives guarantees, but are they able to fully fulfill their promises? When a wolf ate a sheep, a large bone got lodged in his throat and he started to growl. A stork came to his aid, dropping its beak into the wolf's mouth, and pulled out the bone. And after that, it asked him to repay for the service: "You should be thankful," the wolf said, "that I didn't bite off your neck."—That's a guarantee. We, who build according to the same law, we too are solving a great issue in life. Bulgaria isn't the only one contemplating whether to fight or not, but we also decide with Heaven. Christ is asking all of us a question: with us or against us? And we must decide: with Christ, or against Christ? Neutrality is now gone. There's a big race in the world. Everyone is fighting and everyone has to go on one side or the other side, and a great question will get solved. What happens in the world happens at the same time within us. Now, I just want to rescue you from the illusion, not to think that we can win without suffering. No! Gains are always preceded by a great loss; joy is always preceded by great suffering. If the mother doesn't lose her beauty, she would never have children. If the young girl doesn't leave her virginity, she would never become a mother. This is the great law in nature. We have to know how to digest our thoughts, how to think. A bad thought arises in you to commit a crime, to steal. To get rid of it, focus your mind in another direction. Turn your gaze to the soul of the man, give him love, tell yourself, "if I were in his place, would I like it if they robbed me like this?" If the thought of doing evil to someone comes to you, stop immediately and think to yourself, "if I were in his place, would I want him to act like this toward me?" You, men and women, how do you solve these questions? Sometimes you're angry at your husbands and bad thoughts come to your mind: to get rid of these men and to find others to live with. Or the husband says, "away with this woman! It would be better for me to find another one." Like all women, they're made from the same mud. That's why we, men, shouldn't be fooled by the outer appearance of women. Let the man and the woman in such cases, when they get angry, ask themselves this question, "if I were in my wife's place, how would I like my husband to act toward me?" And vice versa, and whatever answer they get, that's how they should resolve the matter. If the wife says, "my husband is bad, I can't stand him," she's not a woman. She doesn't think correctly. I know cases when son and daughter want to kill their father because he's bad. How do they know he's bad? What is *bad*? Whoever is bad today may become very good tomorrow. Today the wife hates the husband, but not even one or two days pass and she says, "I love him." How so? Can you love somebody who isn't good? You can't. So there's some false imagination. We have to think correctly.

This concept must be applied in life. This isn't difficult. If a thought to do something bad comes to you, tell yourself, "I'm a servant/son of the Lord who sent me from Heaven to earth, and in this moment my Master/Father is watching me," and right away your thought will change, because you'll think that He won't approve. What will the Father think when he sees his daughter tormenting her husband? There's a saying that there are three types of women and three types of men in this world, but I'll relate it only in regards to the women, because whatever they are, so are the men. An anecdote says that the Noah of olden times had only one daughter, for whom three candidates appeared, and loved her so much that no-one wanted to relinquish her to another. Noah found himself in a quandary. To satisfy all three, he turned his donkey and cat into beautiful girls like his daughter, and married off all three to the three candidates. After one year he went to see them. He asks one of his sons-in-law, "do you like my daughter?"—"She's nice, but sometimes she scratches."—"Well," said Noah, "that's her nature." He went to the second son-in-law: "Have you taken a liking to my daughter?"—"She's nice, but sometimes she kicks."—"That's her nature." He goes to the third son-in-law: "Have you taken a liking to my daughter?"—"Ah," he said, "she's an angel." Noah said to himself, "that's the real daughter." So, in order to be the *real* daughter, you should neither kick nor bite. This is the new foundational teaching of Christ—to neither bite nor kick, but like a human, to think deeply and perform your duties on earth; wherever you enter, to bring joy and happiness. When you see a sad person, to comfort him, to enlighten his mind. But we need knowledge for this. Study your heads, your hands. This is science. When you start studying them, you'll form a proper conception of your development; you'll see how numerous generations lived before you and the level of development you reached. You'll grasp things properly and you'll know how to orient yourself in the right direction. The hand never lies. By *touching* you can have the most accurate understanding of the person: when you shake hands with him, you can come to know his heart, his character, and disposition. They say that someone is stupid. He's stupid because he doesn't have a lot of *knots* related to sensation, to impressions on the hand, because it's noted that on the hands of the stupid, bad people, these knots are few. Why? Because they don't need this, they don't need that, but just food and drink. Man needs culture, and in this culture Christ established the foundation: "I am the way, the truth, and the life," and, "love toward God and love for the neighbor." If you can apply these two laws, love toward God and love for the neighbor, there won't be a force on earth that can oppose you. There won't be a thought that will not obey you and doesn't come to serve your ideal. The one law of love stands behind. If you apply it, you'll love people, but if you lack the Divine Law of thought, the first law will lead you to many bad things. Only the Divine Law can ennoble human love, because from great love someone can exhaust the one he loves, can suck out all his feelings, steal his heart, and exhaust him. This isn't love, it's ignorance, it's parasitism. That's what octopuses do, who, when capturing their prey, out of love they suck out its blood with their tentacles, and it weakens, becomes tame. Some men tame their wives the same way. It's not taming if you take her strength and say, "my wife has now become smarter, more intelligent." This is not smart. Today you will exhaust a woman, tomorrow another woman will exhaust you. Christ says, "I came to give life, not to take the lives of others." Can you give life to your husband, that is, to make him think, not to tell him, "I want to make you think." You can make your husband become exactly what you want, but you mustn't put him on the anvil, but between these two forces, between these two laws, which will heat him up, and he will change. Man's beauty depends on this heat; the further you are from the center of these two laws, the uglier you'll be. Iron is black, but when you heat it up, it becomes red—we have a red race; after this it'll become yellow, and finally it will turn bright, and you'll say, "the iron became beautiful." Yes, it's beautiful, but if you remove the heat, it'll become ugly again. Therefore, you can be beautiful, wise, bright, insomuch as these two laws act upon you. This isn't just a hypothesis. Make your hind and front brain work more proportionally, so you can have a single point of reference, and you can immediately acquire what you want—the best children, friends, and everything in the world. But you have to start working inside yourselves, and when you apply the law of Jesus Christ, "love toward God and love for your neighbor," to make attempts. When it's for a good cause, the word "I can't" must be deleted from you and replaced with the word "I can." When you come to wrongdoing, say "I can't." As long as it's for good, say "I can." Should a good thought come to you, say "I can." Should a bad thought come to you, say "I can't." Just as the woman weaves her cloth, moving the shuttle from one hand to the other, and then again to the first one, in the same way, she must weave her thoughts, her desires, her character, by moving from the negative pole when a bad thought comes to her, and then to the positive pole when a good thought comes to her. And when she weaves her character like this, Christ will send her a craftsman to cut a suit for her, in which everything will be in place, and then everyone will love her. The same applies to men.

This is the new foundation that Christ wants to lay—knowing how to work. Don't doubt the Lord. Some say, "is there a God?" Leave this stupid thought on the side. The only powerful proof of God is, "I exist, therefore God too exists." There's no stronger proof than this. I think, therefore God too thinks: my thought implies the thought of God. My action suggests the action of God. Anyone who thinks otherwise has no logic; he doesn't understand the basic laws of logic. I love, therefore God loves. God is a perfect, great being, who moves and guides all people. And when a person begins to doubt God, he has already doubted himself and his neighbor. Don't think that we'll embarrass Him with this. It's very pleasant for Him when He sees that we don't listen to Him. When the devil sinned, the Lord put him in a fire to burn him until he confessed that He was the Lord. It's the same for the one who philosophizes a lot on earth. The Lord says, "you bring this man to me and put him on the fire." And when he starts heating him up, He'll ask them, "what forces are working in you?"—"I'm suffering."—"No, think what the reason is. Where is your mind?"—"Well, this is hell."—"Why is it hell? What are the reasons for this?" Hell is a place where the Lord teaches people to think. Some ask, "well, where is hell?" We're all in hell. Earth is the 13th sphere. The Lord will put us into this fire, and if we're good we'll get out of this hell without getting burned by the fire, just as the three Hebrew servants were thrown into the fiery furnace, who walked and sang praising the Lord in the midst of the flames. Yes, if I go into the fire, in hell, I will sing there. Some tremble [with fear] from [hearing of] hell. If I go there, I will sing the same song you sing. There's no bad place; it's something relative. If God is with you, there's no trouble, everywhere is good. If He's not, if you don't understand His laws, everywhere is bad. So the first groundwork, the first point of reference is you; the second is Christ. Join together, the way man and woman join, the way brother and sister join, because unity is power. In unity there's work, build-up, thoughts, feelings, aspirations, civilization.

This is the thought I leave for you: "No-one can lay another foundation." And the foundation is that this life, which you now live, is the best life that the Lord can give us on earth. The Lord cannot, in any way, give us a better one than this. It's excellent, full of such goods that we can do miracles. You still don't suspect what great wealth is vested in it. You don't suspect what powers the future holds for you, what you can be, what you can achieve. The little child in the mother's womb is microscopic, but in the ninth month he becomes an independent organism and the mother gives birth to him, gives him conditions to rise and grow. After 20 more years he becomes a man and starts thinking. By the same law, man is now a microscopic being to God, but one day, when he develops and is born again, when he rises higher, he'll understand greater things. But in order to rise we must change the shape of our head, our mind, our heart, our character. We must feel the great harmony of life in our spirit, and then we'll enter the realm of the angels, we'll come closer to Heaven. This is the new foundation of man.

Lecture held on 10 May 1915

DIVINE PROVIDENCE

"Indeed, the very hairs of your head are all numbered. Don't be afraid; you are worth more than many sparrows."—Luke 12:7 (NIV)

Modern-day people require many arguments, facts, and logical conclusions to be convinced of Divine Providence, which, through certain laws, guides human life. All thoughts, desires, and actions are governed by known laws. Sometimes what happens to us, which is strange to us, we assign a faulty interpretation and as a result, over time, and for many generations, we form a strange philosophy that everything in the world is arbitrary; that is, that there's no order or structure; that the law favors the strong, the wise, the clever, and so on. Do I need to prove that this is a great misconception?

When observing the life of Christ, we see that Christ always paid attention to little things. He tells His disciples directly, "don't be afraid, your life is secure," and gives them an example that none of the five sparrows fall on the ground without the Father's will. Why didn't Christ take one sparrow, but used the number five? There's a law here, and everyone who finds himself under this law of the number five doesn't fall without the will of the Father. With the second comparison, Christ tells us, "rest assured, the hairs on your heads are all numbered," and stops there. We can say to ourselves, "what is the importance of the hairs on our heads being numbered?" That's precisely the importance. In order for these hairs to be numbered by the Lord, for Him to keep an account of them, they must have some meaning in themselves. Do you know how many hairs are on your head? Many have numbered them. Some people have 250,000, others 320,000 hairs. And all these hairs are taken into account by the Lord, as a gardener keeps an account of his fruit trees, putting a number on each tree. We can pull out a hair from our head and throw it away, but that hair performs some duty, a great function on our head. If I now begin to tell you about the significance of the hairs, I'll stray from the [main] issue, but I'll return to the comparison with the sparrows, which underlies, on one side, that our *physical* life is also under the protection from the same Divine Providence. It's necessary for us to establish faith in this Providence, because only when we believe in *it* can we develop properly. Every doubt that creeps into our minds and hearts, that the world is devoid of providence, distances us from the proper understanding of the order of things and forces us to strive in creating *another* order and other rules according to our views. When man and woman marry they think the Lord gives them authority. The husband says, "you lived with your mother like this, but now you're entering my home under a new jurisdiction. I'm a little touchy, prideful, easily angered. Beware, because if you insult me, I will apply this strict law." The wife, however, tells her husband, "I'm very sensitive, delicate. I haven't learned to work, so don't try to make me do some difficult task. If you break this law, things will immediately change." As you see, all people prepare their own laws. But what happens in the end? Both get into an argument. Why? Because the position they assume is faulty at the very foundation. The real, fruitful marriage is not something created on earth. There are three kinds of marriage: some which are carried out in Heaven, others on earth, and the third kind, in hell. Some are carried out by God, others by people, and the third kind, by the devil. When you enter a marriage established by God, it will bring love, peace, and joy to your home. There will always be agreement between the man and woman; no bad word will be heard. They'll live a happy life. When *people* bring you together, it will be solely to perfect yourselves: there will be rubbing between you, so you can iron [yourselves] out, because two sharp stones cannot grind flour. This marriage is not a Divine creation, but man-made; your work will be according to your mind. When the Lord makes something, being all-wise, He always arranges things well. When people arrange something, they don't arrange it well enough, so there's always grinding, which is necessary for cultivating oneself, for ironing out one's character. However, when the devil marries you, then there will surely be discord in the home, depravity—everything bad. In every home where such a life exists, the marriage was established by the devil. Therefore, give everything the exact attribution and don't mix the actions of God with that of the human, nor with the ones from the devil.

In order to think properly and logically, we have to understand the *origin* of things. If there is something wise in today's science, it's that they find some laws in the world that regulate the relationships of things, of the elements, of bodies. We have established laws of physics, of chemistry, of the human soul, which regulate the relation of things, and no-one can transgress these laws without bearing the consequences in one sense or another. So there are three types of people: some who grasp things in their Divine manner; others in a human manner, and the third kind in their devilish manner. The first situation is when we grasp things the way they were ordained in the beginning by the Lord; the second is when one thinks the Lord doesn't interfere in all things and that we must intervene to make things smoother. When the Lord does something, we say, "the Lord was unable to do it. Let's correct it." The third condition is when everybody wants to become the Lord. Thousands of years ago people perceived things in their Divine manner, but in their decline they lost that conception. You too, when you're in good spirits, in your spirit you believe in God. If things go well for you, you say, "thank God. The Lord takes care of us." But when misfortune comes, you say, "the Lord forgot us." On what grounds do you claim the Lord forgot you, that He is the cause of your sufferings? The Lord says, "because *you* forgot me, I too will forget you." If you distance yourself from Him, He too will distance Himself from you. Some think that God, Who is unchanging, constant in His love, when they start distancing themselves from Him, He ought to then run after them, like a mother after her child, crying out, "wait, son. Don't distance yourself from me." No! The Lord sits in His place and when you say, "the Lord distanced Himself from me," I understand that you distanced yourselves from Him, not Him from you. The way of movement of some people around the Lord is correct, with minor changes: some distance themselves a little from Him, but then come close again, like the path of the earth around the sun. The path of others, however, is like some wandering comet: sometimes it comes far too close to the sun, and then for centuries it doesn't come near. You're the same, when you distance yourselves from the Lord you say, "the Lord forgot us." I tell you: After 75 years, when you come closer to Him, like Haley's comet, the Lord will remember you again; it depends on the orbit in which you move around the Lord. When your path brings you closer to Him, He will remember you again. And now all of you move along a certain path, but you cannot understand me equally. Why? Because not all of you move along the same orbit. And I don't judge you. I look at things very objectively, philosophically. But you'll object: "This is our way." It's a question whether the path is such, or whether you made it such. I tell you this is not your path. There is a railroad between Sofia and Varna that constantly breaks down and consumes large expenses. Did the Lord do it this time? If the Lord had built it, it would have been built very wisely. But people made it, and that's why they made it in such a clever way! If in the construction of a railroad you act according to the laws of Divine Providence, no misfortune will happen to you. Still, the technicians have a better grasp of building needs than Christian believers. Regarding life they say, "we have to mathematically calculate what turns and what slope the railway must make along its path, in order to regulate the speed of movement, because if this isn't performed, there will be a crash," and the Christians say, "the Lord is good. He thinks of us. Whatever slope we take, it's all the same." But when the car turns over they say, "things aren't going well for us." They won't go well, of course, because you act stupidly. Your train turned over because you haven't taken into account the laws of Divine Providence when establishing the turns of the railway.

This is why you, in some cases, will have to gather experience from worldly people, becoming *their* disciples. It's no shame to be a disciple. And when it comes to spiritual things unknown to worldly people, the latter must be *your* disciples. You can't be teachers everywhere: some places you'll be teachers, some places [as] students.

Divine Providence strictly defined all things and phenomena; nothing is accidental. All events, whatever character they may be—physical, psychological, or social—are guided and directed by a higher Being, who cares about their course. Just as they put the machinist to care for the train's machine, because the life of the passengers depends on the machinist, it's the same with our earth, which moves in space. It has its own machinist who sometimes puts into the machine more fire, and sometimes less. The path of the earth has some curvatures, turns. The earth sometimes comes closer to some larger planet that affects it. These are distant things, which you will study and understand in the future. But now, regarding Divine Providence, which is necessary for you, I'll give you an example, a story you can take as prehistoric legend, because the events that are talked about are inconceivable, allegorical. Some assign this story to the time of Solomon, but these things mentioned in the narrative refer to a much earlier age. They say there was once a very learned and wise king, who understood the language of all animals. When he gathered the animals every year at a gathering, teaching them, mentoring them, and finally concluding his speech with the words, "what the Lord has done, no-one can destroy." In one of his gatherings there were two large eagles, called "roka." One of them said, "I can destroy what the Lord made." The king said, "very well. Prove it with facts," and he dismissed the council. In the same year, the daughter of a [different] king was betrothed to another king's son. When they married them, upon returning from the temple, rejoicing with one another, one of the eagles descended, lifting the bride, taking her to a distant island, and dropped her into his nest on a large tree. The bridegroom remained alone without a companion. Disheartened, he started traveling. Boarding a ship, after a few months of floating the ship crashed and the waves threw the dispirited traveler onto the same island where his companion was carried off. He started complaining to the Lord: "Isn't it enough, my God, the misfortune of having lost my wife, but now, to be thrown onto this barren island? It would have been better if I hadn't been born." His wife, who was in the nest of the same tree where the bridegroom mourned his fate, heard someone crying. She came down, and when she saw it was her own husband, she hid him in the nest. When the time approached for the next gathering of animals, the two eagles came, lifting the nest with the bride and bringing it to the meeting. The king began his lecture anew, and again concluded with the words, "what God created, no-one can destroy." Then the eagle interrupted again: "I destroyed one of the Lord's deeds."—"Prove it," the king said to him. The eagle, after telling the story of the wedding, the king wished to see the bride. The eagle called the bride out of the nest. But when she came out, the bridegroom came out with her. The eagle, upon seeing that what the Lord had done couldn't be destroyed, burst in anger. By *eagle*, it must be understood as the human *mind*. We sometimes say we can destroy what God created, to change the form of things, but in the end the things remain the way God ordained them, and we, like the proud eagle, burst in anger.

Contemporary teachers say, at every turn, "master your mind. The world doesn't run on stupidity." I say: Thank the stupid ones. The Lord holds the world because of them. There are no wiser spirits than the devils. Have you entered their kingdom, to see how they live? You speak of human intelligence, but if you descend to these fallen spirits, you'll find knowledge of physics, of chemistry, and spiritual manifestations—a lot of knowledge for lying, deceiving, to be able to do everything. But their knowledge can't bring order and harmony to things, because they don't rest on those elements that can *cement* life. Knowledge must be cemented via Divine Love. Therefore, when someone speaks of knowledge and facts, I ask: Do you have cement to solidify these things? If you have that cement, you actually have Divine knowledge, but if you have naked facts, without cement, they can't serve a purpose. I ask you: If you gather 200,000 or a million sheep fibers and don't know how to combine them, of what use will they be? Only when you spin them and weave them in a specific way can you sew together clothes and dress yourself. By the same law, when we can solidify our thoughts within, our desires by this Divine cement, Divine Providence, we can create a garment with which to dress our inner nakedness. Also, that Providence is necessary so we can live and develop. And that's why Christ says, "do not worry," and asks why the five sparrows don't fall. You have the number five in other places too: 5 senses, 5 fingers; it's an emblem of man on earth. The number five represents man—the smart, wise person—and says this wise person doesn't fall as long as he doesn't transgress. While you're wise and fulfill the will of God, you won't fall. In the day, however, in which you transgress, the Lord will allow one of these sparrows to fall on earth, and if it falls, then the hairs on your head will also start falling, meaning that your life will be destroyed.

So, always keep in mind that Divine Providence keeps watch over you while you walk, without wavering, keeping its laws. Should you distance yourself from it, your life starts deteriorating. Turn back to the sun of this Providence so growth may begin again.

Lecture held on 24 May 1915

TEMPTATION

"The tempter came to him and said, 'if you are the Son of God, tell these stones to become bread,'... Then the devil left him, and angels came and attended to him."—Matthew 4:3-11 (NIV)

I'll take the verses from 3-11, where it talks about temptation. Many of you read this chapter and pondered over the three temptations. At first glance it seems like the temptations offered by the devil are very simple. But in these three temptations is a three-fold understanding; that is, the Gospels don't show the *fall*. The great truth hidden in the three temptations is an enigma. Why exactly did the devil have to tell Christ to turn the stones into bread? These are three *psychological* moments in the life of each person. Everything Christ experienced in the temptations must pass through each one of you too. Some might not be at that stage yet, but a day will come when they must pass through it. That's why you must be clear about the sufferings you'll encounter.

Don't think that immortality can be acquired easily; whoever preaches such a doctrine isn't preaching the truth. When we speak of immortality, of fulfilling God's Will, we understand something different. Consequently, we must recognize these three setbacks in every man.

The devil says to Christ, "if you are the Son of God, tell these stones to become bread." The word "if" assumes a different condition: "if you are the Son of God..." But would it have been wrong if Christ was able to turn the stones into flour? There was something tempting for the devil, to be able to witness the process of Christ turning a stone into a plant. But Christ, who understood God's commandments very well, knew that every thing has its own purpose;

that is, even stones have their own purpose. Now, I'm not going to stop [and discuss] the esoteric side; one day, when you come into the condition of purity in mind and heart, only then will this truth be revealed to you. Every one of your *examinations* proves your purity.

Do you know what would have happened with Christ if he were to give in to this temptation? The devil appears at a moment when Christ is inactive, and says, "here's an opportunity—if you are the Son of God, you can apply this knowledge and these laws." But Christ answered him, "man must not live by bread alone, but by every word that comes by the mouth of God." These stones are sinful spirits, fallen people; the devil hides in them. If Christ were to try and turn the stones into bread—do you know what it means to turn a sinful spirit into bread? Christ says, "if a man accepts the word of God…" this has a practical meaning; every one of you is trying to turn the stones into bread. Some say, "why doesn't the bread grow, so we don't need to knead it?" In Germany and England they're trying to think of a way to turn inorganic matter into organic, but if contemporary science were to deviate down this path, the greatest debauchery would develop. What saves modern-day people is work and labor, and if stones were able to turn into bread, all of you would binge out. I know that people often want to turn stones into bread; for instance, you meet a bad person with a corrupt mind and heart and say, "why can't you turn this stone into bread?" But if you turn him—this is not the way to correct someone. Some say, "let's marry off this spoiled person, so we can fix him." This is not allowed. Christ says, "you're living stones," but there's also dead stones. Therefore, a young woman who understands the laws should never marry a sinner, or, a debauched woman shouldn't find herself a good man. What will come of this? Criminals will be born in the world. This is the first teaching that the devil preached to Christ—to turn these stones into bread, that is, to pleasure himself. Christ says that people rectify themselves only when their hearts accept the Word of God.

Now, some tell me, "you came to fix the world; you'll have followers." Yes, there will be such debauched followers, but the world will not be rectified like this. The world will be rectified with every word that comes from God's mouth. And when the human soul receives it, it'll be alive.

Of course, this principle touches on another one—eating, for instance, which is now one of the lowest principles in the world. Eating is an important process in Life. And do you know how many secret forces are hidden in the stones? Do you know what's concealed inside these little bottles? Christ says, "whoever can come out of God's mouth has the authority to unseal these little bottles." I often hear people say, "why didn't God give me the power to fix the world?" This resembles that queen who said to her husband, "let me rule for three days, so I can fix the world." She ruled for three days, and do you know the first thing she did? She first hanged her husband. Those who interpret Scripture say the devil tested Christ with the first temptation, to see whether hunger would frighten Him. But Christ says, "it's indifferent to me whether the stones turn to bread or not. I have food which I constantly receive from above."

Later on, the devil takes Him to the battlement of the temple and tells Him, "if you are the Son of God, throw yourself down." At first glance, this is a very flagrant temptation, but something else is hidden in it—this temple [represents] *man*, who stands on the highest point in his head and ponders over the structure of Divine things. And the devil tells Him, "Go down among your fellow citizens and live like them; go down and drink as they drink. Since you have knowledge and power, don't worry about falling; do it, and know that your virtue won't be tainted by this." Christ answers him, "do not tempt the Lord your God, because I have no need to acquaint myself with these citizens." Doesn't a father of ten children have an obligation to educate them? The father may know his son, and the mother may know her daughter, when they always walk along the same path. This temptation refers to contemporary Christians; for someone to run into the desert and rest there—it means to experience life less, and not to stand [strong] like a guard.

And so, you're constantly on the battlement of the temple—the second temptation implies that we tempt God within ourselves. This is the passing from one condition into another one; from one church to another one; from one doctrine to another one. If you come down, you'll rely on your abilities. In the principle of the second temptation, the evil one encroaches on man, but in a different way. You're not allowed to do as David did; before making him king, the Lord gave him power, and what did David do? One day he stood on top of the temple, saw a beautiful woman and came down; but afterwards, a prophet appeared and told him, "you became the reason for this doctrine to become defiled, and from now on there will be no order." And so it happened—his son fornicated with his wife, with his sisters. Yes, David came down from the top of the temple to show he's the Son of God, but then he had to run away. Now many of you will come down, but will be like David: if you're a wife, your husband will fornicate; if you're a husband, your wife will fornicate. This will be the result if you come down from the roof of this temple. That's why Christ says, "do not tempt the Lord your God, because I have everything and don't need to come down."

Finally, the strongest temptation came, which is very closely related to this evil spirit. The devil took Christ to a very tall mountain, showing Him all the kingdoms in the world and their glory, and said to Him, "if you fall down and worship me, I'll give you everything." Then Christ answers him, "get behind me, Satan. Go to your kingdoms. I cannot come and don't need to go to your kingdoms."

How does the third temptation relate to societal life? After a woman or a man pass through the first or second temptation, a prince will come who will declare them to be pure and innocent, and will say to them, "if you love me, I'll give you all my wealth." Then all the relatives conclude, "he's a wealthy prince in a high position. Quickly, go get the priest!" and they worship [him]. How many American women married such princes, but then divorced afterwards. The devil *promises*, but doesn't *give;* he's a pimp. Christ says, "get away. Go to your kingdom, to your wealth. I don't need your teachings. I have enough within me, which was given to me by the Lord." There are modern-day young men who give into the third temptation—for instance, the young man marries, but actually does it for the dowry that the young woman has in the bank. I recently read a book titled *For Love*, written by a colonel, which describes how you can deceive a rich young woman. But Christ says, "get away! You must bow down only to the Lord!" Do you know what it means to bow down? To bow down means to accept something within, to go back, to impose limits on yourself, to become a slave, to lose your freedom. And when you bow down to such a spirit, you lose your freedom. Christ says, "get away!"

It's now written in the newspapers, that such-and-such young woman has whatever amount of money, and you ask if these marriages are successful. This is corruption in modern society—corruption everywhere! The entire world has fallen into this third temptation; there's no-one among us who hasn't bowed down. It's good that you're bowing down, but do you know what the result will be? When a woman bows down to such a man, she becomes a whore with him; as a result, she'll dishonor herself, and then all the rest of her life she'll mourn her days away. Nowadays mothers and fathers sell their daughters for money, to these corrupt young men—and on top of everything they even give them money! I say: It's better for your daughter to remain unmarried than for you to give her away, and to bow down to such a spirit. You say, "two thousand years ago the devil tempted a lot." I want to know what the devil is doing today in your homes, in your hearts, in your souls. Yes, you became his friends; you purchase each other, you mask yourselves, but you must say once and for all, "get away! Leave my spirit in peace!"

And afterwards it is said that the angels of God came and ministered to Christ. After passing through these three temptations, the angels will come to rescue you from the fourth [temptation]. When a young man offers a young woman wealth, glory, and honor, and she rejects him, he decides to kill her; and the devil decided to kill Christ in the same way. You say about the young woman, "but he'll kill her!" Let him kill her; it's better for her to die than to fornicate. In this case, death is an advantage—to die for an idea, for a Divine thought, is a privilege. Of course, I don't want you to get discouraged.

And so, when someone doesn't want to break these ties, then we'll say, "go away! Go to your kingdom!" This is a Divine law. Only those who can lead a pure and holy life must remain with God. Modern-day people say, "if we live this way, what will we turn to?" Well, what have you turned to? Do you think those people who are currently dying in the war are dying for Christ's teaching? Therein lies the false philosophy of modern society. If we accept Christ's teaching, we'll have families and society that will stand thousands of times higher, and we'll create music—much better than the current one. We'll create a social order thousands of times better than the current one. Someone will say, "then we'll live in the forests." Animals live in the forests, because there was a time when they bowed down to the devil; and if you also decide to bow down to him, you'll also become *four-legged*. This is Darwin's theory: if an ox repents for his sins and doesn't listen to the devil's teachings, he can become a man. There was a time when man was a beautiful being in Paradise, but when he didn't listen to God, He gave him a bear-hide.

Now contemporary people carry some guilt. When we become Christians, we think we understand Christianity; we start going to church, we listen to great preachers—but whether these things make us Christians is still a question. There's something more essential. One of Socrates' disciples, after listening for a long time that man must humble himself, started wearing torn pants, and Socrates told him, "your pride shows even through your torn pants." I'm much more embarrassed by people with torn pants than people with top-hats. Dress nicely, but once you dress, thank the

Lord and live the way He wants [you to live]. See how that bird is clothed—for them God gave 200,000 leva. If God dresses the bird this way, how much better will He dress you?

The devil said to Christ, "if you are the Son of God, turn these stones into bread! Throw yourself down from the temple!" Years ago, in Sliven, a devout woman, who wanted to prove to the people that the Lord exists, climbed on top of a roof, said, "in the name of the Father and Son, and Holy Spirit," and threw herself down. Nothing actually happened to her, but did she convince the people that the Lord exists? They insulted her, saying she's crazy. The devil shows up and tells you, "I'll give you all of this," but years later, like the prodigal son, you return with torn pants. Even now, at these times, you're all wearing torn pants in a moral sense. Leave this state, so you can return back to the life you had. And you'll say, "we're not worthy to be called your sons or daughters." This is a deed that every one of you must do.

There's a danger along the path of Christianity: the second temptation gets driven like a plow into the people and they start thinking they can fix the world, that they'll give new ideas. With the third temptation, however, man becomes a businessman—he becomes "smart." The father tells his son, "son, you have to be a smart man. Look, someone stole and made himself a house; you too should be like him." This is the third temptation that you worship.

Earth isn't the only place of judgment, but the Lord too will judge you. And the one who preaches a different doctrine is from the evil one. Modern-day people must break away from the doctrine that ruined their minds and hearts. We must destroy it. And if someone dies, let him die for the Lord and to become a force for raising the world.

And so, these are three great temptations that will come into your heads. Some of you are in the first temptation, some are in the second, and others are in the third. [You must] withstand them, so you can withstand the fourth one as well, after which will come the resurrection—then God will give you power. And when you sacrifice your life for the glory of God, then God will raise you in return. That's why we must love God and no-one else.

Do not unite your hearts with corrupt people. I knew a wealthy American lady who married a corrupt man in order to change him, but she was unable to do it. Don't try; such a man will beat and torment you.

May God bless you with good husbands and wives! May the Lord bless you with good sons and daughters! May the Lord protect you from bad sons and daughters! Down with bad husbands and wives; down with bad sons and daughters! May the good sons and daughters be praised! This is the Word of God that we must keep.

Lecture held on 20 June 1915 in Sofia

THE PRODIGAL SON

"Jesus continued: 'There was a man who had two sons.'"—Luke 15:11 (NIV)

Christ is incomparable in his examples. The prodigal son is a magnificent subject, upon which great preachers in the world have held fine sermons, drawing lessons on how [future] generations ought to live. As far as I know, all preachers from the time of Christ until our time have limited themselves [on the topic] of the prodigal son only to the point of his sinning and return, but in this example Christ imparted a much deeper meaning. The sin of the prodigal son is a *result*, yet we must know the reason why the younger son left his father. Everyone says the younger one was a sinner; a person may suffer in the world without knowing the causes. I'll give you an analogy between these two brothers: a gentleman went to confess to a well-known preacher in Russia. This gentleman was a criminal who committed a murder. He confessed his crime and the confessor advised him how to absolve himself from his sins. As you know, there are certain laws that require the confessors not to tell the things they hear in secret, but the murderer went out and told a guard who committed the crime. According to the laws of today they'll ask, "since he committed a crime, does he deserve a pardon?" This is how people who grasp the world superficially reason. But those who understand will say who is actually guilty.

Then what are the reasons? I see in the young son the spirit of a gentleman, because he had the courage to tell his father, "father, I want to study and will let my older brother inherit your estate. And because I'm not needed in your home, give me the portion of the property allotted to me." I see in that son an act, much better than your sons' actions; after sending them abroad, they spend 40-50 thousand leva. This young man was noble, because he put this question before his father, and we see that the father didn't object in any way—he gave him the inheritance allotted to him, which he, in the course of time, spent in a debauched life with women, in eating and drinking. Can anyone commit a crime in the world; can anyone commit some evil, some intrigue, without some woman's presence?

It's said that after consuming everything, the son went to some townsman and wished to work for him: "I'm accustomed to labor. I worked when I was with my father." The man sent him to look after the swine. This young man preferred to look after swine rather than commit suicide; he preferred to look after swine rather than to go and steal from people. I ask: how many people in modern society would follow the example of the prodigal son? How many would follow the example of the prodigal son in church? It's said that after tending to the swine, the son came to his senses and returned to his father. The father found a good trait in his son and slaughtered a calf in his honor. Christ knows that in Jewish history Isaac had two sons, Jacob and Esau; in contrast to his brother, Jacob liked to deceive—for a [bowl of] lentils he too went abroad and served fourteen years for that [bowl of] lentils and two wives. When they gave him his first wife, they deceived him. Consequently, you might also try to deceive, but you'll serve fourteen years; that is, you'll redeem your crime in whatever way.

In the parable, Christ says the older brother became angry, because his father slaughtered a calf for a man who fornicated. He goes to his father and says, "you never even gave me a goat to eat and drink with my friends."

And so, all the people who transgress in the world are the younger brother. All tax collectors are the younger brother, but the older brother[s] are ministers, head priests, bosses, judges, and teachers, who teach the people and say, "we always govern wisely." Actually, the younger son left his father's house because of his older brother, because he was very jealous and irritable. The young son says, "I fear you might deceive me, the way Jacob deceived his brother." The law says that debauchery always proceeds from *older* people: if the woman sins, the man is to blame; if the man sins, the woman is to blame. Because the one who sins is the younger one—children always sin, but the wiser and older ones, even if they sin, don't get caught by the law. They might steal, but they do it in such a way that they don't get caught; but the fool who steals will certainly be caught, because he doesn't understand the "supreme" law, on which the entire modern society rests.

It is said in the parable that when the son returned, the father rejoiced. Why? Because this young man brought to his father's house a noble feeling. He returned with humility and said, "father, I sinned before Heaven and you, and I'm not worthy of your house." He expressed real love. And when Christ says we have to become servants, He means to say that we must become humble.

Now, you never fornicated, but you know how to get upset. Yes, I know a lot of preachers and bishops who are saints, but hatred will certainly manifest from their hearts. They will want the calf to be slaughtered because of them, and they will say, "only us saintly people can teach the world." Oftentimes the wife tells her husband, "you will serve me!" The husband, however, tells his wife, "*you* will serve me!" In another situation the husband says, "I order you and you will serve me," but the wife won't serve as a sinner. The characteristic that Christ points out is that deep humility that every human soul must possess. This has an even deeper meaning, but I don't want to touch on it, because it is a controversial topic.

Now, we know how to smoke people out with tobacco. Do you know what tobacco is for? The devil gets smoked out with tobacco, and everyone who smokes is smoking out the devil, and he calms down. That's why, when your wife is upset, you should cover her with tobacco [smoke]. One night, a preacher remained without tobacco and he became very upset. Everyone started asking, "what happened to the preacher?" But when they covered him with tobacco [smoke] he calmed down. In the same way, the young son too, who knew his brother's greed, gave him a little "tobacco." Let's say someone is upset with you. Give him a little smoke. For instance, some preacher is upset with you; give him some smoke—give him something. If you put in his pocket 5, 10, 20, 100 leva, he'll chuckle. Preachers and bishops—smoke all of them out with tobacco. Some say they don't want to give money. Give so you can free yourself! It's the same with the older son: the father calms him and tells him, "son, whatever I have is yours," that is, he's giving him smoke. And when someone asks me how the world will get better, I tell him that it will happen the following way: become a servant and tell your father to give everything to your other brothers, and the more sinful you are in their eyes, the better it is for you.

Modern-day people preach culture. I don't fear the word "culture," but I notice that spirituality is not satisfied with it, because it claims that culture corrupts the people. Culture means to cultivate something—a field, fruits, strawberries, cherries. But modern-day spiritualists think that if people become a little smarter, the world will decay, and they say, "let's keep them in ignorance, so they may know that they have no rights." And when Christ came on earth, He went to His older brother and said, "the Son of Man didn't come to be served, but to serve in the world." But they still didn't believe Him. Again they frowned and said to the father, "get him out! If he enters, he'll destroy everything in sight."

And so, what is the application in all of this? We all love such Christians like the sons and daughters of today, who are gentlemen and tell their fathers to give them whatever is owed to them, and when they finish their studies they'll feed [their fathers] in their old age. But when the son finishes university, do you know what he does to his father? He's embarrassed to call himself his son, and keeps him afar. The false understanding in Christianity stands precisely in this: all people who hold property are righteous, without exception in this. Give a vagabond ten or twenty thousand leva and he'll begin to love order. And therefore the anarchists in the world, who want to destroy the current order, are the older brothers, but Christ prefers the younger brother. Because no matter how we restructure contemporary society, if we don't transform our own thoughts and desires, the order will always protect those who have money, and they will always be strong.

Now the servant wants to become a master. The woman seeks a man who is rich, who is educated, has mastery over some craft—she's an aristocratic lady who wants to live luxuriously, [and] doesn't want to be a servant. The man is the older brother; he too seeks a young girl who is rich, and says it's indecent for a man to work in the world. The man leaves his wife so another one can come in her place, but Christ shows us an example of how to act: to invite the younger brother in our family. Therefore we can accept another woman in our home when she says like that son, "father, I sinned." Christ says the man has no right to leave his wife, except through grace, but if the wife reaches that humility, so as to become his servant, he must accept her. If he accepts her, it will be the will of God. This is the teaching of Christ. And now what do you do? A man falters, the wife searches for another one more righteous; she finds another, he too falters, then she looks for a third, and so on. But the married woman is not permitted two husbands, nor two wives for a man. If modern-day people give themselves permission to do this...

In the two sons from the parable, Christ shows what kind of relationships must exist. He shows the deep love that the younger son had for his father. In the same way, the younger son knew that his father understood him.

They often ask me how someone can be saved. I listened to preachers who say that through the blood of Christ the people will be saved. In contemporary medicine this physiological fact exists, in which an anemic person can have his vein opened and have blood taken in, and his sickly organism recovers. Well, good. If Christ's blood saves, then is that blood in *your* veins? Are you ready to accept this blood? If someone is ready to accept it, he can be helped. If you never gave your own blood, you never saved anyone. For two thousand years Christ has been saving. He sends that blood through the mother to every child about to be born. That is why Christ says that if man is not born again, he cannot enter the Kingdom of God. Therefore man must accept this blood. I would like all preachers from all churches to be tried in order to see how much they like the world. If we hang them on four nails, they'll curse. Yes, Christianity is preached very well when one has two thousand, ten thousand, twenty thousand leva! That's how it is in America: there are preachers there who get paid one-hundred thousand leva. Christ says, "one cannot serve both God and the mammon at the same time." One cannot preach the Word of God with money. The preachers have no right to preach with money. Those of them who are carriers of the Truth—let them preach without money. Let every one of them have a trade and earn his living through labor. But today, when the prodigal sons start returning, the preachers become indignant. If we take Christ's blood from modern-day preachers and try it, we'll see that it carries unclean thoughts, unclean desires. I will kiss those who have clean blood. And when we praise ourselves, they will give us a little blood to try. Like a touchstone for every preacher or priest before becoming a bishop, he must have a little blood removed and must be told, "you carry the blood of Christ." And that blood of Christ must be in all our tendons. Only that blood will save us; only that blood will usher in the love that Christ preaches.

I don't think evil of anyone. Whatever I have, I will give. My rule is to serve. I don't want to rule over people, but you cannot escape this law. Your blood will create *internal* fruits; when you acquire it, this blood of yours will create all those fruits that your soul will eat. And that blood circulates in Heaven, in all heavenly fruit trees. We therefore send juices to those fruits, and when we enter the Kingdom of God, we will eat from them. And those who preach otherwise don't understand Christ's teaching. We speak that which we ourselves have tried.

Now, the example of the younger son who returns to his father—does he live in us? Some will say, "how can a fornicator live in us?" Yes, I wish for ten such sons to live in us. I would like to have that great quality, humility. Humility gives birth to culture. The humble person gives birth to culture. Show me a prideful person who did some great deed. The older brothers created war. They ruled, but all those younger brothers will inherit the Kingdom of God. They say, "we will give everything." I tell you that something will come from the son who says, "father, give me my inheritance." You'll say that such a person will give himself to vices. Let him give himself [to vices], but he'll return to you, while the other son who remains with you will suffer, will get upset that you didn't pay him a goat. There are Christians who sit on two chairs.

Now, there are people in churches who don't agree with me. Let some of them prove otherwise and I'll give them a blessing. No, he must have the courage to go to the priests and say, "give me this!" Give this man the freedom to try this Divine world. The wife doesn't want to live with her husband—give her her inheritance; the husband doesn't want to live with his wife—give him his inheritance, release him, let him go. You'll say this isn't a Christian doctrine. Your wife wants to—let her have it; your son want to—give the inheritance allotted to him. The doctrine I preach to you isn't for weak-minded people. Those of you who are weak-minded, who can't think, should forget what I said. But you, who are able to think, should ponder on this subject. But those who are spineless—throwing this backpack over their backs is a difficult teaching. The woman rejects you and wants freedom. Give it to her. But then you'll say, "if we act this way, what will happen?" As if your current actions lead to a more favorable social order!

Lord, this is no order; it's not a teaching! We must be born only from one father and one mother. Eve gave birth from two [men] and sinned, and every woman who gives birth from two men sins. This is what the prodigal son means. When he returned he said, "I sinned, because there were profound reasons in life. I'll sin no more, so make me a servant and to me it'll be the greatest pleasure to serve."

Now, let's return to our Father. He's in the world. Some say that God is in Heaven. From my understanding, God is on earth, in your homes. Some preach that the one who dies will see God. This is a square lie. Whoever *lives* will see God. I say that people don't die. I want them to rise. Now people say, "we will all die, but at least wait for us to save some money, to prepare shirts for ourselves." You, in the way you prepare shirts like this, will not see God; this is not how the prodigal son returned. What do you do?—"Let's fix ourselves up, like we're going to a ball, and go to God this way." You won't go to Him this way. How did Christ return to God? The Father put him on the cross, to be baptized with a pledge—such is the Divine law of Love. And you, who are Christians, you now say, "which priest should bury me?" When these priests start—not to bury you, but to resurrect you—then they'll take you to the Kingdom of God; otherwise which priest wouldn't sing to you for money? It's burdensome for such a sinner, to have songs sung to him. Therefore we, who are preparing, must live. Don't put in your mind [the idea] of being buried, and for the priests to sing you songs for comfort. You'll just leave the body, because it's a possession, and you'll say, "I leave you my body for an inheritance. Put it in a grave and I, who am going to my Father, He will give me." I would like God's angels to sing to me, and for the Lord to comfort me, only when I go to my Father and say, "Father, I sinned." In that way I will give a wonderful example to all society; then Christ will say, "today this man humbled himself. This son was dead but [now] he lives." I would like to slaughter a calf for such a son, and I will call all my friends so we can eat with him.

Of course, I wouldn't hold a feast like that American for whom one of his relatives died and left an inheritance of thirty million dollars. He was a herdsman and when he received the inheritance he held a feast for the citizens of San Francisco, and they ate and drank for three whole days. And what came of this? They started rolling down the streets, and when he spent everything, he became a herdsman again and said to himself, "it's better for me to be a servant." Now you'll say, "if I have thirty million leva, I'll buy an automobile, I'll buy a house, a piano, I'll hire a teacher;" you will even give one-hundred thousand leva for them to speak of you. I would like the true Bulgarian to return like that son and to tell his father, "father, I sinned and want to be your servant." I would like to see more of these priests and my heart will be joyful for them. I will be joyful like never before! And now everyone cries, "how? We can't stand this son!" Christ is still not with you. To not give way to any hatred—this is a great Divine law; this is the prodigal son.

Now I ask you, are you ready to let go of your husband if he wants to leave you? If I were to start explaining the law of inheritance, you would understand why Christ preached like so. Christ preached about the present-day and his parable about the prodigal son was given because of *us*. And in the next culture, when we create this prodigal son, we must put up his bust (this is our opinion). I ask: who is worthy enough to check the Divine books? When a person dies, he doesn't become a saint. He's a saint when he *lives*. I don't believe that people who died became saints. Whoever lives, whoever doesn't die—he's a saint, but whoever dies is not a saint. I love Christ because He lived, and all those who are like Christ are saints. When we begin to understand things this way, we will become saints. You need to start living and then you will be saints. If you can deny yourselves, you are saints. When the saint enters a society, he spreads joy everywhere—that's a saint! If it's a question regarding the dead, then there are a lot of saints in Bulgaria: Stambolov is a saint for the Stombolovists; Karavelov is a saint for the democrats, along with others. Of course, these people also have their own right...

And so, don't think that when you die you will become a saint. No, you will die and you will suffer. We struggle against the process of death with the process of resurrection: "Father, I sinned." And that son resurrected! His father put his ring on [him], dressed him, and he resurrected. That's why the slaughter of the calf is an emblem: the calf is a child. When a child gets sent to the Invisible World, they slaughter a calf; when the child returns, it's the prodigal son. This is true, just as in the physical, in the Spiritual World as well. And when a man is born, he becomes a sacrifice.

Now I want to leave two things in your mind: first, to put in you the conviction not to sit on two chairs. If you are Christian believers, say that you are. What kind of Christian are you? "I'm orthodox." What do you believe in? "I believe the blood of Christ is in you, that the Spirit of Christ is in you." Second, we must have humility. Every one of us is tormented due to a lack of humility. For example, someone looks at you the wrong way and you get offended. Know that you're a servant, and desire to receive God's grace. We should have the courage of that gentleman to whom his friend said, "you're a vagabond and a robber," and he passed and thanked him for not disclosing everything. This is the prodigal son. But what do modern-day people do? When the devil bribes us, we file a lawsuit against the people, but we ought to sue the devil. This is Christ's teaching: we must return back to our fathers, and Love must reign in our minds. We should be warm-hearted and sincere. What is good before God is good for humanity. I believe only in the blood of Christ that gives birth to good fruits. I believe in a church that has such fruits. I believe in a church that gives birth to fruits of Christ—Love, humility, forbearance. And whoever lacks such fruits, I don't believe [him]. Let's say you're rich, you have a thousand leva: we must return like the prodigal son and know that we have nothing within ourselves. Everyone who preaches the Truth is poor. And whoever speaks of Christ, that he doesn't know Him, will be a liar. Christ established a church of Love. We are obliged to love the saints because of God, because they are our brothers. I know they have some weaknesses (I take all these things into consideration). I would like for there to be heroes in every church, and then we will be a Christian nation that lives Christian-like. And if the world says something because of you…in this world they won't greet you any other way.

I would like to be in the prodigal son's place. I play the role of the younger brother: I'm among the wrong-doers in the world, and I'm not any more righteous. Yes, I may be righteous before you, but before God I'm not. How much more bread must I eat in order to become such as God wants me to be. I don't want you to think of me as being greater; I want you all to *try*, and then you will say, "we tried him." If something is not right, tell me, but don't speak behind my back that it's not right. We need to preach a doctrine of *trying*. Like the younger son, I want to take on the role of humility. It's not easy. To have your wife torment you is tough. There's no greater struggle than the one in which man humbles himself and receives internal self-consciousness. This is very tough, it's heroic. Only the great souls can perform this role; only the younger brothers can perform this role. And Christ was one of the younger brothers. He was the first to serve the people for all their sins, but God raised Him, because Divine blood flowed in Him. He said, "the Father lives in me."

I, along with all of us, must have the blood of Christ. Only then will that blood give birth to saints, and teachers, and men, and women; only then will you have such children as you desire. Try to give to the younger ones only when you have *the blood* that Christ has. If you don't have such pure blood, open up your arteries so it can flow in. And then you will sense a joy that nobody is in the condition to take away from your soul. Then you will be connected to the Invisible World and you will speak to the people through sight, and not through touch.

I ask you, what role do you want to play? Some will say that it's very tough. Try yourselves and God will bless you.

Lecture held on 27 June 1915, in Sofia

PRAYER

The Gospel of Matthew, Chapter 6

My lecture this morning will be on prayer. From a purely philosophical and scientific side, there is much dispute on prayer. There is also a dispute in church on how one should pray. Religious people argue over the form and method, whether we should pray standing or kneeling. People of science examine whether there's a need for prayer, that is, whether prayer is something normal in human life, or if it's something abnormal. I need to explain this matter to you from a religious viewpoint: prayer is an act of the soul. It is a spiritual state (I express myself this way because we don't have a better word), an aspiration that determines human speech. In order to express [oneself] through prayer, a certain *form* is required. Consequently, speech is created so one can pray.

Now, I will take the word "prayer" in a broad sense, so we can understand what [kind of] thing it is. There are four kinds of prayer: first, prayer can be purely *physical*; second, prayer can come from the *heart*; third, prayer can simply be a form of the *mind*; fourth, prayer can be an aspiration of the soul, an act of the Spirit. It therefore depends on what you pray with. For instance, when you have a need, the prayer flows from the aspiration of your body, that is, the body prays in relation to the body. Such a relationship exists when the body of the person is sick. At first glance it's an awakening and an aspiration for communication.

From the viewpoint of embryology, when a child is conceived in the womb of the mother, his organs begin to form. Initially, the child doesn't move. First and foremost, his extremities form—first the hands, then the feet; the intestines take form later on, then the brain, and finally the lungs take form. Then the child starts moving and shows that he requires a higher act. Such a state is experienced by the human soul as well. It too awakens; it too is born. Some person might be very learned, very strong, but when the time comes to be born, he feels a weakness and a need; he feels the need for God. Therefore prayer is a sign that the soul needs to enter the Spiritual World; it needs to be in the arms of the deity. This is prayer. And so, prayer flows from self-consciousness, and with the Spirit it holds the consciousness of the person. The human soul must pray for a long time before it reaches that Divine source. So, in order for the soul to become clean, one must pray. You will ask why. Just as the respiratory system is required for man, so he can breathe and create the necessary energy, prayer is necessary in the same way, so we can nourish our spiritual body.

There are many erroneous views regarding prayer, stemming from our crooked understandings, and that is why we often bother God about petty things. Just as children kick and roll when they want something from their mother, we also act the same way with God. When the soul is born, and while it lives on earth, God does not take account of our transgressions, but upon entering the Spirit, one must pray. The soul cannot ask for whatever [it wants]. When blessings come, one must only have a pure heart and a strong mind. Therefore, it's not a matter whether God will give us food and knowledge; once we know how to pray, God is ready to give us everything we want. He won't deny us any good thing.

Now, those who begin to pray are often tormented by the question whether God will hear them. In order to hear you, you must be a child of nine months. If you are an older child, God will pay no attention to you. And that's why prayer isn't for everyone. There are people who awaken prematurely and become damaged. Some say, "let's awaken this person." Good, but we will damage him. Why? Because he enters the atmosphere of communication with certain elements which he will be unable to withstand. Scientists know this from experience and they never ask the children to solve problems beyond their abilities. The desire to become winged beings shouldn't arise in you, but you must have a relationship with God. You must have a relationship with your mother so she can give you food. Then you'll gradually vacate your mother's vicinity, and when you grow up she will lead you in the world. Everyone who becomes a Christian asks whether they are late. You are late if your mother gave birth to you, but if you are still unborn, wait. You don't have to chase the people, do you? Everyone [belongs] in his place.

In the Bible we have a lot of examples of prayers. There are various prayers when you read the psalms: prayer for sins, prayer for assistance, glorifications. Psalm 51 provides such a model; another model can be found in the 6th chapter from Daniel, when he prays and confesses his sins; Abram is also a model, along with all the prophets who prayed.

But now let's come to the *understanding* of prayer, because the prophets and David understood really well how to pray. Before anything, the prayer requires complete confidence and trust in God. The mind must not be scattered. God, who foresees our difficulties in the world, created sufferings for us, in order to concentrate our thoughts within ourselves. Because, when it comes into the world, the soul is in danger of being swallowed by various impressions. Hence sufferings arise in various ways, so we can return to God. Prayer is power in life. Man cannot develop without prayer. Christ recommends silent prayer: "When you pray, you need to be alone." Some say, "let's have several of us get together." Its use for two or three souls is something else, but the prayer that serves the development of the soul must always be singular, to connect with God, with the image of every Love, virtue, purity, intelligence. He's the only being who recognizes the needs of your soul, and will act so delicately, so tenderly, like no-one else. And that is precisely why everyone who awakens too early gets damaged. Turn to God; turn to Christ. Christ is God; His attitude toward us is fatherly. And when you grasp Christ like this within yourselves, you will sense a peace, a joy, which will refresh your hardships. Because, when you enter the Spiritual World, you'll find such difficulties as the child finds when it is born in this world. When all your enemies gather together in order to stall your development, this is the experience of the saints, of good people, of all who begin to pray, and that's why everyone who enters the Spiritual World must begin with God. And when one doesn't take this path, there is a Divine *tension*. Keep God, believe in yourself, have affection for Him, love Him with all your heart; whatever stumbling blocks you may have, hold on to Him! Just as the child says, "mom!" we too, when we turn to God with the name with which we know Him, He always replies. This is a law for every development. People may appear and tell you this is such-and-so, to point out various teachings to you. Those of you who have a lot of time can try all the teachings, but those who don't have a lot of time, let them turn to God. Deep down inside, let your soul hold onto God. Believe He's before you; believe that He surrounds you with His powers, with His arms.

Now, the philosophers have certain views on God and, of course, in a mental sense they're right. When we speak of God, it depends on how we look at the question: when we look at God in relation to prayer, we have in mind the words in Scripture: "Call to Him in the day of sorrow." In another place it is said to throw off your sins. If you go to God with hidden sins, you are unborn. Before anything, you must confess before God, and if He tells you to confess before your brothers, only then should you do this before the one whom you offended. This is a confession before people—it's the way for anyone who wants to become a Christian. Now, the question of how to find the proper confessor arises in you. First and foremost, you will find the souls who live in Heaven; that is, when you find God, you will go to the spirits and there you will confess your sins, and then their angels will let you confess, if necessary, before the physical world as well. Only in this process does the development go in a normal and correct [way]. When we unite with God in this way, and we are in agreement with all righteous souls, there will be no hinderance in our actions. If you loved some soul, this thought is transferred to the spirits. No-one can acquire wealth, perfect knowledge and perfect virtue, if he didn't confess his sins through prayer. You will say, "when we strengthen a little we will *coerce* God." You cannot coerce Him; God will not listen to you. I speak to you from the experience of all the past and all the present generations. Prayer is something that is *consistent* with our life, and the more highly developed someone is, the more he will enter into greater communication with God. Prayer is a conversation with God, in which we begin to have influence in the world. In a prayer-like condition, there shouldn't be any irritation, nor offense; you must throw off all this. And when you enter that secret room, you must sense that you are in communication with the angels. That is why Christ says, "God will iron out your communication with the peoples." And if He blesses you, the material blessing will follow.

When breathing happens correctly, the body is strong, but once the respiratory system is not properly developed, the breathing is incorrect and the children are unhealthy. The same law applies to your soul as well: there are many sick souls, because the development didn't occur correctly in them. And just as we need to improve the breathing through artificial methods in this world, it's the same in the Spiritual World where there's a need to perform prayer—this law is true. And so, in relationship to our heart, the feelings must go without hinderance according to the same law, but once we begin to make an effort to love and to think, this shows that in our soul there is a certain abnormality.

Now I'll speak to you about the power of prayer. In one place, Christ hints at and says that the bad spirits don't come out, except through fasting and prayer. And notice that when the representatives of the Jewish peoples prayed, they always conquered. This is true even among the Egyptian peoples: while the Egyptians prayed, they had an excellent culture that lived for thousands of years, but when that crude materialism ensued, immediately all the misfortunes came over Egypt. This is true even in relation to contemporary peoples. Examine and you'll see that the downfall of a country takes effect when the people stop praying. Even in our time there began to appear quarrels in the family, in society, but I say the only cause is that we either stopped having communication with God, or we stopped doing the will of God. They say that the English won the battle in Waterloo because of rainfall and Napoleon's artillery couldn't work. Whether it's like that or not—whoever wants to can check the history.

There are many examples of the power of prayer. In the year 1899, during the great famine in Russia, of which Tolstoy wrote, a family lived in a remote part of the city. [They] remained without food for three-four days. Then one of the children began to pray and said to his parents, "soon we will have food, but when we receive it, I will pass away." It happened that a citizen of St. Petersburg got lost in the area, [and he] looked where to take shelter and [went] to that little house where he found the family that hungered for four days. He gave them food and money, so it could serve them in the future as well, but a little afterwards, just as he predicted, the child passed away from this world.

I will also relate to you an instance from Dr. Tyler, a preacher in China. Thirty-forty years ago, when he decided to go to China to preach, he calculated that he needed twenty-thirty thousand leva. When his friends heard this, they said that he was off his rocker.[1] However, Dr. Tyler began to pray and acquired twenty thousand leva. He's the only missionary who sustained himself through prayers, and around 1870 he sustained 600,000 preachers. But immediately his faith was put out, the power of his prayer decreased, and it happened

---

1 The literal words used by Deunov are, "one of his planks is off," which is also the Bulgarian way of saying someone is "off his rocker."

that even his followers had to pray to God. And what came of this? Some wealthy American businessman, who had moved to Australia, made a promise to himself that if he gained this-and-that amount, he would give such-and-such amount of money for Godly deeds. His affairs prospered, he met Dr. Tyler and gave him the money to use as he saw fit.

But you must always have a *need* of that for which you pray. If you pray to God for excess, He will never give it to you. You can pray and the Lord may hear you, but if you want something excessive for yourself, He will not give it. Pray for the Bulgarian nation. When it goes well for all Bulgarians, your affairs will also go well. We must pray for all in the right context, and when God blesses everyone, then He gives. Now we pray, "God, give me a penny!"— No! Ask for 200,000 pennies and then take one. Or, you can pray like this: "God, give me a little!" Then the Lord says, "Go to some person so he can give it to you." You think of praying for a loaf of bread, don't you? From God we must always ask for that which the people cannot give us. And so, don't be content with pennies, but desire from God *great* things.

Now many ask themselves why our priests don't pray. Prayer cannot be forced. *You* go and pray; turn to God for them. We say that they are such-and-such. No, pray for them in secret. In collective prayer is salvation. Why, namely, in collective prayer? Imagine you are a military leader and have an army of 100,000 people. Let's say that you're exposed to extreme cold and your soldiers are afraid of dying. I ask you: what meaning is there in the large quantity of your soldiers when every one of them is freezing? By the same law, one by one we're dead, but when they pray together, the people become a powerful force. Therefore, in order to be accepted by all hearts, the path of salvation is through prayer. And so, in today's conditions, prayer is necessary. You would be able to repair your homes through its power, [and] your children; you would be able to do great things.

Christ says, "whatever you ask for in My name, it will be given to you, and if two or three ask, it will be given to you." What should we do in this important moment in our life, in our development? How will we be able to fulfill our tasks given the confusion that came into the world? We must all come into communion with God and to call on Him—therein is the only salvation. And the prophets say, "when you search for Me, you will find Me." When we search for God through prayer, so He can manifest in us and we can manifest in Him, our salvation will come. Some say they have debts. Debts are a society of bad spirits who corrupt our hearts, corrupt our soul. And so, communion with God must be personal. If you don't enter this way, a lot of misfortunes will come after you. Whoever enters this way develops correctly, but whoever doesn't grasp this life will have many sudden changes. Because the development of the individual is reflected in society and in the church; that is, whatever the aspiration and direction of this individual, such is the aspiration of all people.

I will relate an example of prayer from Bulgarian life, taken from the current war between Greeks and Bulgarians. A Bulgarian soldier, a teacher by profession, after his retreat from Thessalonica in enemy territory, hid for a long time in a cave. (This instance was related to me by General Dr. Dukov). When he was hungry, the soldier began to pray and noticed a turtle carrying a piece of bread. It walked to him, left it, and turned back. He took this piece and satisfied his hunger. And when he returned to his home, he said, "children, there is a God." In that war, many Bulgarians believed, because from experience they saw that there is a God.

And to you, who are here this morning, if you know how to ask, God will help you. Someone says, "*you* pray for me!" I tell you: go to God, pray to Him; don't look for anyone. In the event that God doesn't hear you, then you can look for other people. And therein is a great stumbling block. When that Bulgarian prayed, God helped him, and you are that turtle. If you just turn to God,

He deeply understands the need of your soul, and will reply. And when we reach such a life, we must forget our relationships on earth, and [must] consider ourselves as sons of God. When we accept God's blessing, then we will serve on earth, regardless whether we're among the Bulgarians, among the Greeks, or among whatever tribe; that is, we will enter a given nation when we serve God. Every nation has its own calling. Every nation must fulfill some mission. One time it was the Egyptians, Romans, Greeks, English, Germans, Americans, but now the Slavs are coming. All nations must serve God, and before Him they all stand as *individuals*. And whenever we acquire that prayer, then the new philosophy will come, and the new science will clarify the meaning of things. Then nature will understand our language.

Originally, before the fall, when man passed by some fruit-bearing tree, it just bowed to him. Now the trees not only don't bow to the people, but raise their branches up. When we reach that condition, we will see that these animals, whom we assume understand nothing, are intelligent. Make an attempt with your dog: for instance, sometimes you enter well-disposed and the dog comes to you, but sometimes you return upset and the dog puts his tail between his legs, because he understands your condition. That's why Christ says, "always seek your God and His righteousness." Then we will have that knowledge. I know that many of you have hardships; many of your faces show that you're restless, that you have some need, that every one of you has some thorn—individuals, and families, and society have a thorn and we wonder what to do with these thorns. We need to go to God; He will remove them. We must return to our Father, who can love us, can cherish us. And then our faces will shine, our minds will awaken, our hearts will become joyful. And so, turn to God. Make an attempt, when you pray, to sense God's presence in your soul. And when God is present, He will give you external *proof*, because when He comes to us, He will bring a blessing.

In the beginning, Ivan Kronstadt wasn't so smart, but one time he prayed so sincerely that his life altered and then he became John of Kronstadt. When did Tolstoy become *Tolstoy*? When he thought about committing suicide and made his confession; then he prayed, "God, save me from this evil." This happens with you too.

Turn to God, unite with Him, devote yourselves to Him and He will teach you. You'll know that all people who carry goodness pray in secret. And Gladstone was a man of prayer. All great people from antiquity prayed in secret, yet we modern people stand in a waterless place and complain that we're poor. Return to your God, because He's calling you. He wants to bless you. He is now saying to everyone, "return my children." And that's why this raucous is now being raised in the world; the children started coming together. Our souls are beginning to come together, and we will understand each other. Then the language of the Father will speak, and when He speaks, we will notice that nature outside will begin to speak. Now when we meet some person, we think what he thinks of us and are afraid. Let's turn to God.

Now, I'll tell you something: in much talking the Truth cannot be told. If in ten words I could tell you everything, it would be very well for me, but now I had to use thousands of extra words. The extra words are a massage—you know, when a person gets sick, they massage him.

And Christ says, "when you pray, enter your secret room and God will reveal himself to you." What perfect words He has! And so, whoever is united with God is a blessing to the nation. In that sense, I would like the Bulgarians to pray this way, and only this way can these people rise. A time will come when the people will understand each other. And now, you must turn to God like that Bulgarian in the cave, with a request to bring you *living* bread from above. One time, when Elijah prayed, God sent him a raven, but to that Bulgarian he sent a turtle. This shows that God takes care of us. Have faith, pray for an end to all quarrels, [and] every crooked understanding.

Pray for God to enlighten us, for us to become servants of this nation, for its goodness, so all individuals may find that goodness.

This is my lecture this morning, and I think you won't misunderstand me, because I relate a law: to always pray. Pray individually and God will bless you.

Lecture held on 4 July 1915, Sofia

THE GOOD SAMARITAN

"Then he turned to his disciples and said privately, "Blessed are the eyes that see what you see. For I tell you that many prophets and kings wanted to see what you see but did not see it, and to hear what you hear but did not hear it […] "Which of these three do you think was a neighbor to the man who fell into the hands of robbers?" The expert in the law replied, "The one who had mercy on him." Jesus told him, "Go and do likewise."—Luke 10:23-37 (NIV)

My lecture this morning will be on the good samaritan. I will take the verses from the 23rd to the 37th. This good samaritan has become very ordinary, that is, we think we understand him. We may say in a certain practical sense we understand his significance, but I will look at this question from a slightly different perspective.

And so, a conversation begins between a law-maker, a rather educated man, a philosopher of his time, who is deeply rooted in the teaching of Moses. He is interested in a very important question: he approaches Christ and asks Him, "Teacher, what should I do in order to attain eternal life?" Christ answers him, "what is written in the law? How do you read?" and he answers Him, "to love the Lord your God with all your heart, and all your soul, and with all your strength, and with all your mind, and your neighbor as yourself." But, you see, later on Christ wanted to explain to him who is our neighbor. This story is a drama; that gentleman who comes from Jerusalem and goes to Jericho is a character. You read the story. Those who write dramas want to create characters. The Samaritan is another hero in this drama. Before him, a priest appears, but because he's busy, he passes by and says, "this is none of my business." The priest walks on the right side of the road and when he notices the fallen man, he goes to the left side. After this, a Levite passes from the left side, but he too doesn't stop. Finally, a Samaritan passes and stops.

Now, we have the following characters: the priest, the Levite, and the Samaritan with his mule (you can call it an ass, because Palestine is full of these animals). The Samaritan stops, dresses the wounds of the robbed person with wine and oil, puts him on his beast, takes him to the city of Jericho, provides him with lodging at an inn, and on the next day gives two denarii. You'll say this is a simple task, and so what if some priest passed, some Levite, and after that some Samaritan who bandaged him. Yes, but when you read the story of some writer, you study the characters (because every writer wants the characters to stand out). Christ presents four types [of characters] to us: the first is a traveler, who is going to Jericho to gain, but he's unlucky; the second is a priest; the third is a Levite, and finally the fourth is the Samaritan. Christ says, "from these three, who appears to you to be the neighbor of the one who fell [victim] to robbers?" The Samaritan, of course.

Keep these characters in your consciousness, because you may play the role of either the priest, or the Levite, or the Samaritan—you can play four roles in the world. Everyone plays them, because the world is a scene in which the people play these roles. When you read some novel, you always stop on the hero of the story, and in that story the hero is the Samaritan. He didn't even think that his actions would spread, and he would become an emblem to the whole world. Various interpreters say that this is a parable, but we know that Christ took example only from *real* life. The drama that Christ presents happens in Heaven and on earth. The traveler came from Jericho—this is Heaven, the higher world from which people come. Jerusalem however is the earth, which means people descend from above, from Heaven toward earth. But there are robbers in Heaven; even apostle Paul says that above us there are bad spirits. But let us leave this more profound meaning and return to societal life.

Who is that Samaritan? The priest and the Levite are man and woman: the man is the Levite, and the priest is the woman; the Samaritan, however, is an *outer child* who performed a good [deed]. But you'll retort and ask if it's possible for a father and mother to be so cruel to their children. I know mothers and fathers who throw their children out. I know a lady from Varna whose father left her; she became a fornicator and married a "Samaritan," who now lives in Sofia. When your daughters sense a heaviness within they say, "I want to leave [this] home," because the parents are priests and cannot surmise their condition. Every soul that came from the Invisible World has a certain pain, a certain wound; for instance, in order for a given person to be nervous, there's a deep reason. They say someone is nervous; nervousness isn't an illness, but the nerves [represent] the *mental life*, and when they don't harmonize correctly they form diseases.

These four types from the parable represent man's four bodies. Man is wrapped in four bodies, through which he passes in his development: physical, vital, astral, and spiritual body. There are three other bodies, but they're *unchangeable* forms. We'll speak of the forms that can change. The word "body" is understood to be an *organized* world. Consequently, in that sense the mind is organized, the human heart is organized, life is organized.

Now, Christ converses with the scholarly law-maker and says, "you go and do the same," that is, take on the role of the Samaritan. The Samaritan always expresses the progress in the world. This is the knowledge, but the priest and Levite are just actors who go to gain and do nothing in the world. And when the people have extra money, they say, "let's perform a play, so we can laugh. We have extra time and can now do theater." Life is a theater, a performance. The children can play it, but I say that this is just *rest*, and when we have to develop, it's not the right time for a performance.

Here in this parable there is a drama and a performance. I ask why those two didn't stop to help that man. Because between them and the one who fell in the hands of the robbers there was no semblance. The law is such that you cannot help someone whom you do not love, and this is the reason why they passed by and continued. But the Samaritan, whose heart carried this Love, took out his wine and his oil. The oil is the soul, and the wine is power, which must be handed over. One must grasp the Samaritan in a broad sense. Don't you think that many of you are in the condition similar to the one who fell victim to the robbers? Your wounds require oil and wine, and they don't need words, philosophies and craftiness. In order to bind up the wound of the sick one, a new stream must be poured into the human mind and the human heart. And when the oil and wine are poured, this is the Samaritan. I would like for all Bulgarians to be Samaritans. We want all priests and teachers to become Samaritans. We want all lawyers and judges to become Samaritans, because these are honorable positions.

In America the honorable rank of D.D is given. With us, D.D means "dee," but the doctors in America have to have this D.D. Then, even the rank L.L.D.D is given—doctor in law, doctor of divinity. The priest and the Levite from the parable were doctors of divinity, that is, L.L.D.D, but they didn't do anything. Then a Samaritan passed by who didn't have the rank of D.D, but he only had a mule, oil, and wine. He said, "I don't understand this D.D," got off the mule and asked, "how did you fall here?"

Now Christ gives this example for our time, that is, for you and for me. And in Bulgaria there are Samaritans. I'm happy that there are women who are Samaritans in Bulgaria. In that sense, the Samaritan is Christ, who came from above, but the one who fell to robbers is the human race, which fell into the hands of robbers—men, women, and children. And Christ came from above.

The parable has [both] narrow and wide significance. Christ says, "you do the same." Have the disposition of your Spirit; have the disposition of your mind. Your will must have this disposition like that Samaritan. If we don't have the disposition in the Spirit, but only in the mind, this is not a disposition. The priest had a disposition in the mind and said, "I have very important tasks and don't have time to deal with these things." The Levite said the same. But we're presented to serve God. Christ says, "to love the Lord your God." The "neighbor" is a by-word that we recognize in this world. You cry for a neighbor, but when your neighbor is found, you look upon him like the priest or the Levite and say, "there's no time." I know a lot of young women who, when their neighbor comes, say, "he's not for me; he only makes 300 leva." Everyone philosophizes like this. And the age in which we live, and in the future, we must apply the law of the Samaritan.

Now, some want to make acquaintance with ministers. It's not bad for a person to have acquaintance with ministers, but the reason is out of self-interest, to have a patron. Friendship [should] never change; it's a great law that unites people. If you have a friend, he's always ready to serve God, and when he finds you fallen in the street, he'll sacrifice himself for you. By this parable, Christ shows how the world will be fixed. Some say, "we should choose deputies, to appoint priests." Now, there are official and unofficial priests; some only say they don't want to wear a kamelaukion,[1] but Christ presents precisely those whom God predetermined. I'm not referring to the *official* priests. Whoever the father is, such is the priest; whoever the mother is, such is the teacher: teacher and priest are synonyms to me. When the father fulfills his duty, then the priests will fulfill theirs as well, because the fathers gave birth to all of them. We say, "the priests are bad; the Levites are bad." Why are they bad? Because their mothers and fathers are bad. Therefore all present-day people will die, remaining only as fertilizer on the earth. And when God comes with a new rake, He will establish a new culture and will plant new saplings, which will give splendid fruits. That's why

---

1   A cylindrical hat with a flat top, worn only by priests of the Eastern Orthodoxy.

we must not judge the *consequences*, but the *causes*.

And so, the Samaritan is the father, but the one who fell [into the hands of the] robbers is the mother: the man found his wife and bound up her wound. He found his lost Dulcinea,[2] put her on his mule, took her to Jericho and gave two denarii. These two denarii are synonyms for two Divine Laws. Some say, "to give you two leva." If in these two leva you imply Divine Love and love for one's neighbor, you can give them to me. But if you want to fool me with these two leva, thanks! Now, how many men are there who carry their wives like this?

A statistic in London shows that out of 26 million families, only 300 are happy. There are only 200 such families in Bulgaria. These are the men and women of Bulgaria; they're only 200 people, and the remaining 3,000—let God come to their aid. The remaining ones are those who are masters of "emptying out sacks." They're not to blame; this is their nature.

A lot of mice bred in a granary. The master found himself in a dilemma and that's why he let a cat inside. The mice became frightened and said to themselves, "now we'll pay with our skin. What should we do?" Then a mouse came out and said she had an enlightened idea—to put a bell on the cat, so when she approaches, they'll be able to hear it and hide. Everyone started clapping, but an old mouse asked, "but who will put the bell on?" This is contemporary life, an "enlightened idea." Christ also put a bell on the cat, but the world didn't get better. Oil and wine are needed, and the asses must perform their duties. When the mother gives birth to a child who is weak in the beginning, does she perform the role of the Samaritan? She's embarrassed from the opinion of the world and says, "they'll laugh at me." The philosophy of the modern woman is to give birth to a 90-year-old person. All women who give birth to children are young, and while young, a person can do foolish things. Christ says

---

2 From *Don Quixote*, the name of the girl with whom he falls in love.

that in that matter the Samaritan is older than the priest and Levite. This is the existing working nation, and is in the heart of things. Christ therefore wants to show us that we must all have that love in our mind and in our will.

Some ask me how to do good [deeds]. I say: buy yourself a mule and go find a good spring. Every day I meet people [who are] sick in the mind and in the heart. Christ says, "go and do likewise, because if you want to inherit eternal life, you must do the same. But if you don't do this, you will not inherit eternal life." Christ would make that Samaritan a priest. I too would make him a priest, because he did well. The future world will therefore be inherited only by such priests, and God does not want people like us. You will say that Mr. Deunov preaches against the priests. I'm not talking about them; I'm talking about the mothers and fathers. These mothers and fathers must know the Samaritan. And when a mother gives birth, she must give birth with joy. Always, whenever the mother gives birth, she's blessed, and this shouldn't be counted as disgrace. The mother gave birth, and will give birth in the future as well. In old times, the men always gave birth, but nowadays the women give birth. But these men must give birth again; the women have given enough birth. The men of today abort. I see men who carry their offspring for twenty years, but these people must learn to give birth. The Lord says, "since they don't fulfill my law, I will give them the soul of civilized people and they will suffer." And that's why we are sent on earth to eat and drink. When we fulfill our desire for eating and drinking, a blessing will come.

Now, you'll ask who you're from—from the priests, from the Levites, or from the Samaritans. Ask yourselves if you have oil, wine, and a beast, because that ass is snorting. Upon it, you'll put the one who fell to robbers, and when you go in this world, you must have the two coins. Consequently, you need a mule and wine. And when he went to Jerusalem, do you know what happened? Jerusalem was surrounded by a huge wall, but Moses razed it. Christ did the same with His coming—He broke that wall.

Now, I present the question clearly: in this drama, what role do you want to play? The actors in the theater frequently argue who will play the lead role. Christ magnified the name of that Samaritan. Many kings did great things, but no memory is left of their actions, but that Samaritan performed a seemingly simple task on the outside, but his name remained written in Heaven. You may perform the role of the priest and the Levite, but you'll remain ordinary people. The man who fell into the hands of the robbers prayed for a long time, stretching his hands toward the priest and Levite, but they said, "I can't." Only that Samaritan helped him.

Now, let's say you have a daughter and you're taking care of her upbringing. One day, she wishes to enter the world a little, so she can earn. You present her at some ball, until one day they find her on the street wounded, dishonored, thrown out, and she's crying: "Help me." She's fallen into the hands of robbers. There are women who are terrible robbers. The nicest people are men and women, but men and women are also the most terrible. The first kind we call the people of Love, and the others, the people of egoism. I would like for all of you to be people of Divine Love and to see God. The entire world is for you; as long as you have a heart and mind, everyone will praise you and will say to you, "we saw what you did." Anyone can do a good deed and God sees these good brothers. I would like, therefore, the name of everyone to be written up in Heaven, for you to be carriers of that new humanity, to be cheerful and joyous. Leave it to others to worry about your food—there is wealth for everyone. God prepared a lot of food. Some say that they have enemies, but you also have friends. The devil also has enemies. Apostle Paul says, "wherever goodness increases, virtue also increases." Where hatred increases, Love also increases. Our actors should have gone to the devil; he can play all roles. When you study all these philosophies, don't get fooled by the philosophical drama; don't put such a mask on your face; don't present yourselves as being holier; present yourselves as more sinful rather than more righteous, because there's a danger in putting on a mask. I know people dressed in silk, who eat nettles at home, and when someone enters, they hide the bowl [of nettles]. I ask you, do you have that spiritual garment?

And so, bind up the wound of whoever and you will inherit eternal life.

Lecture held on 11 July 1915, Sofia

OLD AND NEW WINESKINS

"And no-one puts new wine into old wineskins...But new wine must be put into new wineskins, and both are preserved."—Luke 5:37-38 (NKJV)

This little parable is classic in its expression and content. Christ makes a great summary of the ideas: He says no-one should pour new wine into old wineskins because the latter will break apart. Do we have to take what is said in direct terms?—No. It's *figuratively* true. An analogy is made of the new teaching with new wine and the old people with old bottles. The old wine, having ceased fermentation, can stay in an old wineskin, but the new, since it's still fermenting, if it gets poured into an old wineskin, will burst it. This parable contains a hidden thought, a great law: Regarding Divine ideas that are being put into this world, new wineskins are needed—more elastic, to withstand the pressure of the fermentation; that is, people who have a mind and heart receptive to the *new* truth. When the mind busies itself with old ideas, thoughts, feelings, the new cannot enter in. In other words, one cannot expect to express energy for achievement in old forms. Young people in this respect are generous. From 90-year-olds you have to ask 90 times until they give one fifth, because they have a natural fear; they feel they are weak and infirm to wield their own powers and resources like the young. And that's why Christ says that new wine must be poured into new wineskins.

When the new teaching flows into the world, it creates a reaction in the elderly—they think it's no good and that it will ruin the world. However, there's no father who wants his son to be born with old ideas. Everyone dreams of a son who is contemporary, to perceive the thoughts and ideas of the age.

Wine in itself represents *power*. Power is required in order to give an impetus to human evolution. This power is nothing but the human spirit, taken in a broad sense—an intelligent force that works and builds according to Divine laws. God's purpose is for everything to grow and develop. God doesn't like the old wineskins. He puts them in the lower cellars, as the vinedressers do. There will come a time when people will be able to drink from the old wine. When you accept the new teaching you fool yourselves if you think that it won't ferment in you, that you'll remain the same people—that's impossible. It's the same as when the sculptor works with a hammer on marble, without breaking off some piece. Many pieces will fly off left and right, and old people must stand at a distance if they're afraid of getting hit by some piece on the head. The sculptor is not to blame, but the old people are, if they don't step back. "I'm sculpting a statue for future generations," he says, "and everyone must watch out." The painter might work with a brush, [or he] might work with a bow, [or he] might work with a hammer—it depends on the manner in which he works. It's not important. What's important is whether he works according to the Divine order of things. When, during work, the grinding begins, we shouldn't say, "our head is going to burst." There's eternal peace in the cemetery. Whoever wants to go forward, whoever strives toward God, whoever wants to grow in Divine life, needs work and struggle. In this quest lies the good of the individual, the good of society, the good of all mankind. Those who want to rest, to remain with the old perceptions of life, don't grasp the active life of the new ideas expressed in the parable of the new wine. Do you know how long it took the vine to collect this wine? And do you still know its power? At first it's sweet, then it starts to cut and finally it becomes so strong that if you over drink from it, you lose your normal condition.

Whoever wants to adopt the new teaching must free himself

from the old wineskins. If you don't have new wineskins, stay away. There will come others, new people, and the new teaching will flow into them. It can be poured into you too, but first you have to sell the old wineskins, to free yourselves from all desires and vices that hinder you in perceiving the new teaching. In India there are famous snake-catchers, who domesticate and send many specimens of snakes to Europe. For this [purpose] they use casks, where they collect the snakes from the smallest to the largest, harmless to very dangerous, and they domesticate them there. One night, however, through negligence, when closing the cask, they couldn't shut it well. During the night all the snakes slipped out of the cask and wrapped around their catcher. He woke up in the morning and upon seeing what happened he didn't budge, because a single move will cost him his life. He had the presence of calmness in his spirit. At one point the servant comes, wondering why his master still hasn't come out. Opening the door, he sees all kinds of snakes wrapped around him. The servant, however, was very tactful: he immediately goes and takes a large cauldron of boiled milk and leaves it in the room. When the snakes smelled the milk, they unravelled themselves from the master and went to the milk. The Indian stood up and gently closed them again in the box, saying, "I need to shut this cask well." You too sometimes will find yourselves in the position of that snake-catcher, and then you'll need the presence of [calmness in your] spirit and milk, and that milk is *intelligent* life.

Christ says, "you shouldn't put new wine into old wineskins," because it will upset you. If some religious person gets upset, he's an old wineskin that was unable to withstand the new wine, the new teaching. You cannot reconcile two opposing ideas. The law of Moses states, "tooth for tooth, an eye for an eye," but according to Christ's teaching the law is just the opposite, to love our enemies. If they hit us on one side, to turn the other one too. How will you reconcile this new teaching with the old one if you keep it? The law of Moses is for an old wineskin, Christ's teaching requires a new wineskin.

According to the law of Moses, because old people are incapable of struggling with the new, they want to capture the culprit and gouge his eyes out, so he can't see or find them, but Christ's teaching says, "you can turn your enemies into your friends. You can disarm them and make them serve you."

Now, let's come to the inner psychological meaning of Christ's words. We should never think in life that we have fully understood the truth, and that there's nothing more to learn, [otherwise] we'll become old wineskins that cease their development on earth. "We're scholars."—But where does your scholarliness stand?—"We read many authors."—So what? We have to look into that philosophy that can straighten out our lives and give us the happiness we're searching for. I also explained the word "ШТАСТИЕ [happiness]" another time: What letters make up this word? The letter "Ш"—three lines turned up, represents the human hand which is working. [The letter] "Т": It shows the directive or power that impels the work. After these two letters comes "А": It's the human nose: You need not only work, but the mind too, so it can know how to work. When you take the letter "С," it represents the human heart, but when you turn it upwards it'll become a boat—that, which can be gained, will be saved. In the letter "И" there is a descent and a rise, from top to bottom and back. These two angles, when you put them side by side, form the diameters of the circle—the wheel that moves the car forward. The "Е" shows the *center* onto which you must hold. And, therefore, you need a hand, power, a mind, a heart, and a high aim.

I will relate an anecdote from Bulgarian life: In our country they believe when fever comes that it's *alive*. A shepherd stopped on a bridge and overheard two fevers speaking. One of them said that she would go and catch the shepherd there in the mountain. The second one asked how she would catch him, and the other one answered, "I'll enter into the first spoonful of milk he swallows in the spring." When the shepherd heard that it was about him, he decided to take precautions. On that day, one of his sheep died. He skinned it and made a wineskin out of the leather. When the appointed time came for him to catch the fever, he put it into the wineskin and tied it. Then the fever inflated the wineskin and always shook it every day at noon. In the autumn, the shepherd untied the wineskin and let the fever go. Then the two sisters gathered together under the bridge again, and one asked the other, "I had the misfortune of going into the empty sheepskin!" And if you want to use the old wineskins, you'll resemble that fever, and when they let you go you'll say, "we learned how to shake the wineskins." I constantly see these people, and when they re-enter life they say, "we learned how to shake the wineskins." These are the modern-day dogmatists, who only shake wineskins. "It's tight for us," they say. No, it's spacious for them, but they don't have food next to them. In the folk belief, of which I just spoke, there's an entire philosophy. The judgment must be understood, because it falsely decides fate, waiting for a new fate on earth. The new wine must be put into our children because it's powerful. The mothers who want to have good children, must be infused with new ideas. If you're with the old [ideas], I don't recommend giving brith. To what will you give birth? Life's scoundrels, of which there are thousands. Holy Scripture says, "be fruitful and multiply." It doesn't say to give birth to ill-conceived [ones], but people in God's image and likeness. It's the new teaching that Christ preaches and which, if understood, will correct the world. Both the vine and the juices are in us. One day, when our vineyard gives grapes, the juices of the grapes will start fermenting. It's an unavoidable law in the world and the one who thinks of living without fermenting doesn't understand life. In another place, Christ says, "whoever wants to follow Me should take up his cross." The new wine—it's the cross. The cross is power for the one who understands. There are various crosses in the world, and the people complain about them. But this is what Paul says about the cross: "I will boast in the cross of Christ." You complain about your sufferings and say they're unusual, unbearable, but you resemble the one who complained about the weight of his cross, and this is what happened to him: The Lord said, "take it away from him," and He took him into a large hall and said to him, "in this hall are large and small, gold, silver, iron, and stone crosses. Choose one." As the man sought [one], he found a little cross and said, "I want this cross."—"Well, this is the cross you carried until now. I gave you *this* cross," said the Lord. We frequently exaggerate our sufferings and want to change our fate. We can't change it, throwing away the weight which we must carry. You say, "when I arrange my things, me and my wife, and even my children, we'll head onto the new path, and then the new wine will ferment." If you think of arranging your worldly things and then following the Lord, you're mistaken. The upbringing is a process that must work simultaneously for all—the father, the mother, and the children: when the mother and father are brought up, the children will also be educated.

I'll relate another example: They speak of the American preacher, Moody, who, when preaching, a child who was listening to him asked his father, "father, why don't you sing?"—"I'm confirmed in the faith; *you* have to sing. These things are for you. We old [people] have heard and listened," he answered. And the child said to himself, "it's very good that I have a *confirmed* father." One day the father draws out a small cabriolet with a horse and heads out, but at one point, the horse stops on the hill, then the child says, "father, the horse is confirmed." If we stop, we're *confirmed*, we're an old wineskin in which the new wine cannot ferment. Yet we're preparing for Heaven, thinking we'll get into paradise to start living an angelic life, to comprehend the Divine truths! How will we understand them if we live in these cellars? That's why Christ turns and says, "new wineskins are needed." Old people are old wineskins, and new people are new wineskins. Nothing hinders old people, but the young tell the old, "wait for us to pour some of the new wine into you." Old people shouldn't be given new wine: the old have completed their evolution. The new wine must pass through the arteries and veins of the new people. There's a struggle in us; there are complaints, because the old wine is struggling with the new. Christ wants to say, "don't put the new wine into yourselves if you're not ready." That's why He says, "first cleanse yourselves." Every teaching and every philosophy can serve us when we're clean. *Plasticity* in progress, underscored by spiritual progress—that's the understanding of the new teaching. If we can look, from an occult point of view, into the mind of the old man, we'll see a candle glimmering faintly. If we see the new man, we'll see his candle shining brightly. We can compare the old man to a land illuminated by the moon, and the young one to a land illuminated by the sun. Mental progress requires new wine. We must ask ourselves if we have it. The one who drinks old wine and hasn't tasted the sweet kind says, "the old is better," but the moment the wine ferments and ages, becomes old, it cannot ferment anymore afterwards. It can only intoxicate people, cheer them up a little bit, but to make them work, to progress—never. If we're unhappy, it's because our life is fermenting. The wine is becoming sour or bitter; it's no longer sweet. I observed Bulgarians: when they come from church and go to the pub to drink, they first gather two by two: "Give a pint of the old wine—cheers!" They drink 1-2 glasses, then 3-4 gather together, continuing to drink, and the conversation becomes more lively, the entire pub starts talking. Then there's a loud ruckus at one point and what do you see? They start beating someone. Why are they beating him? He hasn't built a fence in the field; they have to beat him in the pub so he can make himself a fence! This isn't just in the pub; visit the stock exchange, where business trades take place; you'll say everyone there is crazy. Even a woman, upon visiting the stock exchange, said to her husband, "why did you bring me to this madhouse? I want you to take me to noble people, [not the] stock exchange." When there's arguing and division in the home, the wine has begun to ferment; when they can't create new wine, they want to dominate someone else's. It's the same with the mother who can't give birth—she takes someone else's. So, for the new wine that will give us new life, which will teach us how to live and work, how to create strong relationships between us, new wineskins are required. This is Christ's teaching. They say it's not applicable. It *is* applicable! Why don't you stop for five minutes a day and meditate on it? Take this parable, read it, and stop for five minutes a day to think about the new wine. You'll see the results it gives. Stop for five minutes and meditate on God, on the good people on earth who are constantly working, on the good mothers who patiently care for their children, on the good fathers who care for their families—you'll see the kind of process this new wine will produce. The wife says, "I married, but my husband is worthless." Well, who told you to take an old wineskin? Do you know that by this you resemble the one who stole a donkey and said to the judge, "I was on the pear tree and fell on the donkey, and it carried me away." Tell yourself, "I need new wine," both in ideas, in the heart, and in the world. Someone turns 60-80 years old and plans on marrying and having children! I understand. There are exceptions, like Abram who begot children in old age, but he had new ideas. He wasn't old. Now 40-year-olds are old—"Let our children live on. We're done for!" Then you're an old wineskin; they have to throw you into the cellar. You're a sluggard who doesn't want to understand the will of God. You have to say, "Lord, I understand You. Now I want to work for You," the way a youth works. Down with your old age! Throw away your old wineskins! Get them away from you. People with old wineskins and old wine aren't made for the Kingdom of God. I don't want them to pour out their old wine, but I want them to put the new wine into new wineskins. When they grasp this new Divine thought, it will lift them up with its power. They wonder how to educate people. The method is very simple: When a boat in the sea gets punctured, they put a plug into the hole. If they don't plug it up, the boat sinks. Examine your boat, see whether it's punctured. Plug it up, then you'll be safe. Some day you're dissatisfied, you have a hole in your boat. Your wineskin is punctured. Nothing good can come of it if you don't plug up the hole. There are moments when a person must be strictly obedient, like the child of the machinist, whose house was next to the railroad: the child was playing and when the Express approached, they cried out to him from afar, "lay down!" The child obeyed, laid down, and that's how he saved himself. Sometimes they tell you, "lay down!"—"But why?"—"Lay down. Don't ask why. When the Express passes you'll understand why." There are dangerous moments when we must kneel, and when the danger passes, we must thank God.

But someone is saying, "I don't want to adapt to the conditions. I don't want to be elastic." You'll adapt. The rain won't take into account whether you're dressed or not. It's the same same with the sun, whether you can withstand its heat, but you must adapt to all changes, to be ready to bear them. The rain and sun are doing their work very well. Let the sun shine; let the sea get agitated; let the old wineskins burst. Don't let that disturb you, because the Lord decided to burst the old wineskins and to pour in the new wine into new wineskins. If the people with old ideas and thoughts want to live in accord with the new conditions, they're woefully deceiving themselves. This is fate. Such is the Divine law. The Lord wants you to become youthful, to be reborn. A new form will be created where you will put your life; a real form, not a dream. If you could understand the law in which you now live, you would rejuvenate yourselves. How can this be? When you learn the law, you will rejuvenate internally in your soul. When we speak of resurrection, I understand those forms with which the Lord works in us. We must prepare the new wineskins. Then the Lord will say, "bring them so we can put new wine in them." Some ask, "what is the Lord doing with the world now?" He's preparing new wineskins, creating new wine. And that's why Christ says, "My Father works, and I work for you." And we must be ready so we don't spoil these wineskins, because it's a very easy thing for the mind and heart of man to spoil, but it's very difficult to fix it. Let the Lord see that you're working. You ask why this life is like this. I see in the eyes of many that they're drunk off the old wine; they're hungover, they drank too much. They need to sober up. Joy must fill your hearts, because this world is created for you with all the conditions for your development. "But war, misfortune."—"*Nichego!*" [It's nothing] as the Russians say. "But we'll lose everything."—"*Nichego!*" Nothing is lost. Perhaps thousands of houses will be destroyed, old wineskins, but new ones will be created. Now the Lord is pouring the new wine into new wineskins. Only the drunkards are fighting. If men and women fight, they're drunk. Where there's new wine, there's music, singing, reconciliation. This is Christ's teaching. Read the Gospel and apply this teaching in yourselves. For five minutes a day, think about eternal life, about God, about the good people, about the good mothers and fathers, about good friends. Think about something noble and it will uplift you. Then you'll understand the more profound things. Oh, what things there are for you to learn! But you have to prepare for this understanding beforehand. "What will be the future life?" Excellent! Something you haven't seen, heard, or dreamed [of]. How will man see the beauty of the world if he sleeps? Your sleeping souls must awaken; you have to put on the boiler with the milk in order to do away with the evils. Be bearers of the new wine, the new teaching; preach joy, happiness in the world, and when you suffer, say that you suffer because you haven't fulfilled God's law.

We often say that conditions create life, but man also creates conditions. I already told you about an English lord who went with his daughter and servant on a voyage, and how there was a shipwreck. So in the world you can be a master and a servant. You have knowledge of how to apply the Divine laws—you're a master. You don't know how to apply them—you're a servant. Whoever wants to be a master must come from the new teaching: it carries the mystery of life. If this lord hadn't come upon this empty island, he wouldn't have learned how to cultivate life; that's where he learned this art. In life, we may fall into misfortune; someone may become our master. We should learn how to serve and the Lord will bring us out of the empty island. Thank Providence that you came upon the island to learn how to cultivate the grain of wheat, that is, life. Until now, you didn't learn how to cultivate your mind and heart and, as a result of this, there's hunger and discontent in you. You eat 4-5 times, growing obese, and you complain. Such obesity exists in your mind too. But this fat must transform into energy. You notice that people who work hard mentally, who glean spiritual insight, are never obese. When you gather mass, put it into the automobile of spiritual life and move toward the realization of your noble dreams. Therein lies your prosperity.

Lecture held on 12 July 1915

FREEDOM OF THE SPIRIT

"*...where the spirit of the Lord is, there is freedom.*"—2 Corinthians 3:17 (NIV)

So, the condition of freedom is the Spirit. By the word "freedom" we mean a free life; we understand the inner meaning of things, their relationships—the relationship of thoughts, desires, and willful nudges that express themselves in the world. Where there's a living soul, there's also movement there, which is the result of the will. But this movement can go in a certain direction, or it can go in various directions. In the New Testament is written, "where the Spirit of the Lord is, there is freedom," and elsewhere, "the Son of God will deliver you." The Son and the Spirit are the same thing. The Son is the manifestation of the Father and Mother. The intelligence of the Son is an expression of the intelligence of the Father and the Mother, as sunlight is an expression of the inner state of the sun; we become familiar with the sun through it. How can we come to know man? Through the light of his thoughts, desires, and actions.

I speak of the freedom of the Spirit, because in religious people there is a danger: when someone becomes religious, he becomes twice as bad as worldly people. Sometimes I'm not happy that people are religious. By the word "religious" I mean a person connected to something, as a cow, horse, and other animals are connected to a rope; connected to the house—that too is religion; connected to some political party or some philosophical doctrine—that too is a religion—yes, a religious doctrine, but what kind? The kind that connects the freedom of the person or society. If you're connected to a teaching that debases you, that takes away your freedom, it's an outmoded religion, an old wineskin. And everyone who seeks that freedom—the meaning of life, as modern-day philosophers call this higher consciousness, or citizenship, as political people call it (you can call it whatever you like)—has that intelligence in itself. How will they know that you have the Spirit? If you're wise people, and if, with your thoughts, desires, and actions, you distinguish yourselves with the power of your freedom, and everywhere you enter you carry this grace.

By the word "freedom" in modern-day life is understood *light*. When you travel during night-time, you're not free as when you travel by day, for the simple reason that your path is not clear. In the same way, all religious people, when deceived, have something vague in their conception. You don't know who God and the Lord are, but you know the kings and rulers here; as they punish, the Lord punishes too. From this conception arise the results we see in the world. And from that inner bondage we must emancipate ourselves. How will we free ourselves? A radical change must take place in the structure of our brain. You still haven't studied this structure yet. Every morning you pray and search for the Lord, shouting and saying that sometimes He doesn't hear you. The Lord hears only those people whose ears are open; He doesn't listen to the deaf, and He doesn't speak to them. You have to have a very delicate ear, perceptive, to comprehend from something small what the Lord is saying to you. He likes to see and hear people who labor, who don't occupy themselves with empty things, because He doesn't occupy Himself with stupid things.

Study modern-day religions and you'll notice their level of development. There are some delusions in every religion. I'll tell you what they are. When we want to understand a religion, we often leave a society and enter another one. A young man wanted to hop in the *horro*,¹ and he borrowed someone else's boots. The other one, however, who lent them, told him in the middle of the dance, "listen, hop less. I didn't lend them to you so you could thump hard." Another one came up and said to him, "because the other one embarrassed you, I will give you my boots." And when he started dancing, he started saying, "hop on, friend! Even if you tear them, I'll give you other ones." Whether he says "hop on," or "don't hop," it's all the same: the other man is no longer free. Whether you hop a little or a lot, it doesn't matter; if they embarrass you, your freedom is taken away. So our mind must be illuminated by *true* freedom.

Christ gave a definition of freedom: "What you don't want others to do to you, don't do it to them either." This rule should be our inner law. We should speak and do that which gives freedom to others. A few days ago a lady came to me and said, "I'm astonished at modern-day people: they stand to pray; their prayers are excellent, but when the prayers stop they start gossiping—she saw something, the other one didn't see it well enough; one of them who saw wasn't from God but from the devil; 'You're lying,' 'No, *you're* lying.' We see that no-one has nor gives freedom to others. I want to be free, for us to serve the Lord; not, of course, *their* Lord." I told this lady, when she finds herself again in their company, to tell them what she told me. If you don't have tolerance for people, you don't give them freedom, you don't understand the teachings of Christ. You have a caricature-like understanding of Him. Throw away these caricatures from yourselves. Don't imagine God in this way.

Now, what is religion? It's both a science of forms and a science of Divine Love. If you study one of the external forms, but not its inner content, you'll deceive yourselves and you'll change it, like the lady who changes her dress every day. When she lives 50-60 years, she can make 10-20 dresses from various colors, to put

---

1   A traditional Bulgarian folk dance where people gather together, usually in a crescent-shape, while holding hands.

on some nice ribbons and buttons, but these dresses are *not* the lady: the *form* is not yet a religion. These forms are actually necessary for religion, like suits for the body, but they don't comprise the lady's body. Some relative dies, the people start saying, "I have to wear black. I shouldn't wear a white garment." Wear whatever clothes you want: black, or white, red, green, blue, colorful [ones], anything. It's not a sin. But when you visit someone dead, don't wear white clothes, just as when the street is muddy, you wouldn't wear white shoes, but the kind that the season requires. Worldly people are very smart: they stand in my eyes 10 times higher than many religious people. Through worldly people the Lord decided to fix the world. Politicians and socialists—they'll fix the world, because they want freedom. But someone will say, "how so? They destroy." When building a new house, don't you destroy the old one? If you don't throw away one of your old views, a new thought will not arise in your mind. Some want to teach others how to think, only "seven layers up, seven layers down"—a science of "silence, no talking"—whatever is written apart from this is from the evil one. Others say *theirs* is from God, but the other one from the evil one. That's what it means to be "strong in the hind-brain." Regarding a given doctrine, we must judge according to its results: if it can be applied in societal life and give good results, it's good. If it can't, it's not good. We must apply the freedom of the Spirit. Ask yourselves this question: are you free? Do you have that Spirit in yourselves? When the Spirit comes, it will produce light in your mind and in your heart. That's the sign. Once you start restraining the spirit of a person, how he should think, feel, and act, he'll immediately leave you, like when the teacher comes to class and wants to teach the lesson: if the students are rowdy, he leaves. Then their fathers and guardians will come, of course, and beat them, because they don't listen to the teacher. And so, Moses was the guardian of the Jews. He came to beat them and ask them, "are you listening to your teacher?" And now, when you say, "why did we suffer this punishment," I reply to you: Because you didn't listen to the Spirit. You should have listened to it.

Let's explain the word "freedom." If you find a person whose hands and feet are tied up, and you sit down to comfort him: "The Lord is good. He'll untie you," when you yourselves can untie him, I ask: Are you preaching a doctrine of freedom?—No! Get your knife out, cut the string and free him. And what do you do? You tie him even harder, so he won't escape. The people need to be untied. And when Christ says, "go and preach," He means precisely this loosening. And that freedom must be purely internal. All irritation and misunderstandings between people are due to lack of freedom. If it's about irritation, how much more would the Lord have to get irritated, [the One] who created this world and sees what the world is doing? If the Lord is angry, it's good, but if I'm angry, what's the benefit?—None. But does the Lord get angry? The Lord doesn't get angry. Indeed, in the Old Testament it says, "God's anger," but that is to be understood in an internal sense. That the Lord doesn't get angry is seen in the phrase by Christ: "Why do you call me 'Good Teacher?' Good is only one—God." Whoever is good cannot get angry. Prophetic people wrote that the Lord gets angry. I challenge this: Let someone tell me where the Lord Himself says He gets angry. In one place Jeremiah says, "Lord, You lied to me. I was deceived." How would you agree with this contradiction? That's a delusion. We shouldn't put such delusions about the Lord in our minds. We can admit that they're *our* perceptions. But it's right to say, "where the Spirit of the Lord is, there is freedom," which God *really* said. Love cannot awaken without freedom. While a person is blind, they cannot love him. Nobody loves someone who torments. That which brings destruction cannot bring freedom. We pray to the Lord and during the prayer one of us makes a mistake, someone else taps him. This isn't freedom. This is *acting*. Down with these masks! To stab each other when standing before the Lord. This isn't prayer. When a person prays, he must forget his surroundings, isolate himself, enter his secret room, in his soul; no external thing should disturb him. All of you who listen to me here are not free: I see how you're tied to one pole, others to two, three, ten poles. And I can even prove it 10 times now, not just theoretically, but also practically.

Because you're preparing for a world of freedom—the Kingdom of Christ and the Kingdom of God is a kingdom of freedom—with these old forms, with old wineskins you cannot enter it. You'll barely get to the door. I don't judge you because you're deceived, but I show you the way because you seek freedom. The reason for your slavery is neither woman nor man. We know the reason: slavery followed when the two of them ate from the spoiled apple.

If we want to understand Christ, our spirit must be free. There are two words in the Hebrew language: one of them, "ru-kha," which shows the higher manifestation of God, and the other, "nephesh," which shows the *lower* state of the soul. Take a child who is not yet developed: he starts crying and making faces, and with his weeping, imposes his will on his mother. Finally his mother gives him a nipple and he says to her, "that's how you have to listen to me," and the mother constantly fulfills the will of the child. Why was this child sent to you? For *you* to obey, or for *him* [to obey]? If you're a free spirit, you have to learn the relationship of things.

How can we acquire this inner freedom? Oftentimes there is a good and bad side to prayers and gatherings. When two get together, they must abide by the same standard, so an exchange of magnetic forces can take place; otherwise disputes arise, because the spirit of freedom prevails in all people, and they don't have the same viewpoint. That's why in Christianity the process of cleansing was given before going to the Lord. The first thing is to settle into yourself. How does this settling happen? Before praying with people, pray by yourself, because when you enter the company of people you have to be somewhat ready. First and foremost, you have to pray alone, then with two, three, and so on. And everyone has to contemplate. The spirit will come only to give you certain lessons. And when the

Divine Spirit comes and enters into two souls, it will immediately establish peace and understanding between them. When someone speaks, the other one will listen carefully and find pleasure in the speech of his interlocutor. And when he doesn't find this pleasure, he's saying, "I'll listen to your nonsense, you'll teach me!" The Spirit is no longer there; the devil is there. Gathering and praying—it too doesn't happen by command, but through the disposition of the spirit. If the spirit wants, it'll pray; if not, it'll remain silent. And the first thing is to give this freedom and to have the patience to listen when someone speaks as if the Lord is speaking. If you enter a religious society and become more nervous, you gain nothing. On the contrary, you lose. Many doctors and people know how a person is made up; they have excellent knowledge of physiology; they know which foods are useful and which are harmful to humans, yet they lead lives according to their old ways. They say that smoking tobacco is bad, but they themselves smoke; that drinking wine is harmful, yet they drink; that the consumption of meat is harmful, yet they eat it. They have knowledge, but when it comes to applying, to build, they don't do what they speak and preach. Where, then, is the freedom of their spirit? But Christ wants that freedom. Some want freedom only for themselves, and for others to obey them. Others may obey out of fear, but there's no love there. I will relate an anecdote regarding this: A Bulgarian tailor was once called by a family to cut and sew breeches and a doublet for the bridegroom. He picked up his shears and thimble, bringing his servant along. It was about noon. They roasted a chicken for him, but the tailor, in order to eat the entire chicken, said his servant doesn't eat chicken, but eats beans. The tailor said this in the servant's presence, and the latter decided he would take revenge. And around noon he said to the hosts in private, "my master is sometimes crazy: If he starts turning here and there, you should know that he's gone mad." He hid his thimble before his master started working. At one point, his master started turning, looking for his thimble. When the hosts saw this, they jumped on top of him and tied him up. Upon returning, the servant turned to his master: "Your servant doesn't eat chicken, but eats beans, eh?" Don't say your servant doesn't eat chicken, because one day, when you start looking for your thimble, he'll make it so they tie you up.

The first thing in our relationship with others is mutual respect. I noticed in my observations that some want to study and come at first with fear and respect, but then start to say, "we know more than him," and they become lax, like those young brides who first stand humbly and feel shy, but after a month passes, they open that mouth of theirs and destroy the house. In church, while they're brides, they stand quietly, but the moment they marry it's as if they acquire citizen's rights and reveal their true faces. They'll marry again a second time, but whoever married them once will not marry a second time. We shouldn't distress God by violating His Spirit for freedom even when someone challenges us. I see what thoughts get reflected in me and you—an entire notebook of curves has formed, like the dashes on telegrams. How many of your telegrams are written? A whole bundle. It's shown there how free you are. One day, these telegrams will be brought before the Lord when you go to that world. Everything in the world is obvious. Nothing can be hidden from the eye of the Lord. And I'm not telling you this to scare you. No! God in His being is a Spirit who always wants to teach and correct, and not to punish and revenge. What we see in the world as suffering and punishment is only in terms of form. And if, in that respect, God frequently punishes us, it's to free us from bondage. If you decide to release a sheep from the mouth of the wolf, wouldn't it suffer until you pull it out? Freedom, inner peace, will bring tranquility and joy and will lift up our spirit.

Now back to religion: This religion, with which we want to serve God, where does it sit? Christ says in one place: "I was hungry, and you gave me nothing to eat; I was thirsty and you gave me nothing to drink; I was a stranger and you did not invite me in; I needed clothes and you did not clothe me; I was sick and in prison and you did not look after me."[2] This is why the Lord will judge the earth. You can pray 10 times a day, like the old Pharisees in the streets. You may be like that mother who started praying while her food burned. Do you know what *psychic drunkenness* is? It's not religion. A young lady who often likes to meet with some young man, not that she gains anything, but feels some kind of pleasantness, but this pleasantness, this *tickling*, doesn't show that she's Divinely-attuned. She expends energy in vain. When God comes near us, we'll feel that His action isn't just for a moment, but for a long time. And we'll feel this disposition in the soul, secretly. When some people argue, I go to them, but I don't tell them to be quiet, because I must first be quiet. When a couple argues, if I go, I won't help them. I don't preach morality to them, but stop and pray for them to the Lord. In Varna, 30-40 years ago there was priest, Gancho, "orman-papaz," they called him, who often reproached those who got him drunk. He sees a gagauzin beating his wife, takes a whip and starts beating the man, in order to free the woman, but both of them, the man and the woman, immediately hurled themselves at him, and the wife said, "what right do you have to beat my husband? We'll take care of ourselves and settle our things." And then the priest said, "why did I have to free the woman from the man?" And you, like priest Gancho, enter in order to settle human affairs. Do not enter. You may enter only when the two of them, the man and the woman, call you to talk to them. Show them the law of freedom and how to settle their relationship.

And so, religion must bring people freedom, peace, and joy. If the old persecutions arise, the world will not improve. Many doubts will arise in regards to the outer forms of religion. They'll start saying, "your teaching is from satan."—"Isn't *yours* from the devil?" Whoever isn't from satan must serve mankind unselfishly, out of love for it, and to even sacrifice for it. If you want a prize, or first place, or to

---

[2] Matthew 25:42-43.

fix the world, you're not fulfilling the law of freedom; the Spirit is not in you. You must be *last* in the world, in order to be first before God. If you're first in the world, you're last before God. This is what I know. I don't want human glory. I prefer God to think well of me. When I preach this, some of you don't accept it and say, "I'm not like this. So-and-so is like this." This is from the evil one. Everyone within himself must forget how others are, and to think that he's more sinful than others. This is right. That you're in this position—I don't judge you, but because I want you to get out of it, I show you a way by which you can get out. Follow the Spirit that is in you: you want freedom, give it to others; you want love and justice, give it to others. Like attracts like; this is a law. If you love people sincerely and genuinely, they too will love you. The way you look at yourself in the mirror, if you're beautiful, it too will show a beautiful face on the other side. And when we meet someone, don't tell him, "I love you." Don't speak of love, because it gets lost. Then you actually don't love him. The one who speaks of love the most has the least of it. The one who speaks most about the freedom of the Spirit has the least of it and gives the least amount to others. If my relationship to you is not what it should be, it's not the sweet preaching that sounds like sweet music which will make them such. Music that creates noble aspirations is beneficial. The kind that leaves in man only some *tickling* carries no benefit.

And now, end these frictions between you, this rubbing of "narrow" and "wide," "the Spirit is there," "the Spirit is not there." Whoever among you has the Spirit of freedom, I will give him a white stone where I'll write my name, and when the Lord comes, He will see what is written. When I see your eyes, I know your spirit: when the Spirit enters, the eyes aren't very dark, but they're also not very bright. Sometimes the eyes can lie, like a snake, but it's "nephesh," the desire to swallow, to eat somebody. You've seen how the cat's eyes sparkle in the night-time. She's looking for mice. There's a difference from light to light. There's light that raids, that kills, and there's light that gives life. The Spirit is sensitive to people's weaknesses, and has the ability to enter into those who are on the path.

When you gather again, you will tell by the telegrams whether there will be stabbing. The Lord doesn't want such prayer meetings. In order for all the prayers to be accepted by the Lord, I will give you a method. If you encounter an inconsolable, irked soul, pray to God for him and with him. If you meet a poor man, help him. The Lord doesn't want the rich to gather with the rich, but the rich with the poor, the scholarly with the ignorant. It's not necessary for you to just gather and to sing in concert. Go to some worldly concert; you'll do better. That lady, of whom I spoke earlier, also told me that when she was in that prayer meeting, after half an hour the women started examining and to whisper, "she saw us," and when she noticed she was making them tighten up, she left. I'm not saying it's in Sofia. We're saying that in church the other people don't pray right, but we also pray like this. Cast out the old devil, give freedom and respect to others, pray secretly in your soul, let none of you speak and gossip about others. If 2-3 women gather, they start talking about somebody. One who gossips about others cannot develop mentally. Whoever has this weakness must leave it. If the thought of speaking about others ever comes to you, stop. Don't let the devil in. Don't become his herald. Close your telephone and don't spread his ideas. The devil never says nice words. He speaks of people: "You're a vagabond, a robber, a fornicator." He tricks you into helping him and does his work, but when sufferings come, through them the Lord is telling you, "next time, don't listen to the devil." Anger, jealousy, hate, suspicion, lying, all negative things in the world belong to the devil. Throw this old father out and you'll be free. You'll be with the Lord, who is wise, good, just, compassionate, and loving, who forgives and helps those who suffer, and the poor. If you sin 100 times and turn to Him, He will forgive you! He only punishes the devils. He cursed them and created a great inferno for them. So, whoever doesn't want to be connected with the devils must be merciful and compassionate.

From now on let's start applying Christ's teaching, not to show the world that we're religious people. Let our piety be hidden in us, but in the world let us be like the beautiful ladies who go out with their faces covered, so the sun doesn't burn them, or so they don't blacken from the dust. Hide your beauty inside; don't show it off outside. Don't talk about how you're good, generous, and ready for charitable works, and that you pray three times a day, so you don't become the laughingstock in the world. And Christ says, "in the world, be wise like serpents and kind like doves." Worldly people aren't stupid, but wise. In terms of the *exalted* life they're worse, but in regards to the *mind* they're wiser, [and] we're stupid. Give them an example of some good deed, so they too can give you of their mind. Now they say we have to be straightforward, that we shouldn't be generous. How, then, will we fix the world? When someone looks at us the wrong way, we become angry. How many times do we look at people the wrong way? We don't take that into account. The Lord didn't create us with crossed eyes, but with straight ones. Religious life is precisely this: to have and to give freedom to people, to excuse their mistakes and to seek every opportunity to unite spiritually.

Now let's apply the teaching and preach it to others. No gossiping from now on. Let's say this: no gossiping for a whole year. Make a notebook and say, "today, thank God, I didn't speak of anyone," jot down "7." If you speak, put a "1," and keep an account for the whole year, how many 7's and how many 1's you'll jot down. How well did you withhold yourself? I often see someone's mouth shaking: "I too want to say something," "I too have the word," "I too know something." He starts talking, and the others also start, and now you see someone who becomes an object of gossip. Tomorrow they'll begin the same thing again. When a young man is to be wed, many young women fall in love with him, and everyone praises him and they compete against each other, seeing which one of them will attribute more qualities to him: "His father and mother are kind-hearted. Their family is very kind." When he chooses one of them for a wife, all of them who praised him until that point start: "He's wild, a fool, a simpleton," when they too should say, "he did very well in choosing a wife among us. We're happy." Do you know what this resembles? I recounted some other time an occasion about a prince who entered a big European city: from the 12 most beautiful women selected, who were invited to vote who should offer a bouquet to the prince, each put the ballot for herself. Now you too in this movement are seeking (still not fully prepared), who should give a bouquet to Christ; everyone says "I." Don't vote for yourself. Even without voting, Christ knows who deserves. This is Christ's doctrine: to be courteous, not to speak of others that which we might know about them. The occultists say, "if you want to be strong, don't speak about the people, because the moment you start speaking, you come into contact with his spirit and get infected with bad thoughts." It's better to think well of people, rather than bad, because otherwise you harm yourself. Whomever you gossip about benefits [him] on a psychological level. Doesn't the Lord say, "when you're rich, give some of what you have. How much did you gain?"—"Ten thousand."—"Give half." When we speak good things about someone, the Lord takes him and tells him, "how much did you gain?"—"Twenty."—"Give half to the one who thinks well of you." When we speak well of others, we gain, but when we speak badly about people, they gain. This is the law. If you consciously do it so they gain, I'll be happy with that self-denial. But then don't complain. Aren't you great souls? If one of your sisters has some defect, pray 10 times for her to get rid of it, then go and say kindly, "in you, sister, there is a vice, but don't be angry with what I say to you." Then you'll be blessed.

So drive out of yourselves this devil now—gossiping. The Lord decided to bind the devil this year. And nobody should be upset when he's bound. They'll put him to work. Just as the farmer needs oxen in order to plow, in the same way the devils are useful for work. Either we'll be put to work, or they'll be [put to work]. In order to put them to work, the Spirit must be in you; you must be strong and powerful. I will still talk about this question of freedom of spirit. Now I'll make a small attempt, to see how much you used today's lecture. Religious freedom must be absolute: God is God of love, of freedom. Then every one of us will find his place. And when he plows, and when he digs, and when he does any work, he'll do it with gratitude. This is how life on earth should be, according to the freedom of the Spirit, according to the freedom with which Socrates distinguished himself. He was the lowliest man, yet many kings were forgotten, but his name remained. One can occupy very high positions and still lack kindness. The Spirit requires us to be both like kings and as lowly men, yet equally free. This is the teaching of Christ, which I preach—to have and to give freedom, to have and to give freedom, and again to have and to give freedom, both mental and from the heart, and religious, and civic, and in the home—freedom everywhere.

Lecture held on 23 August 1915

www.ingramcontent.com/pod-product-compliance
Lightning Source LLC
Chambersburg PA
CBHW030145100526
44592CB00009B/123